University
for the
Creative Arts

Fort Pitt
Rochester
Kent   Tel: 01634 888734
ME1 1DZ   E-mail:
                gatewayrochester@uca.ac.uk

glass in architecture

Phaidon Press Ltd
Regent's Wharf
All Saints Street
London N1 9PA

First published 1996

© 1996 Phaidon Press Limited

ISBN 0 7148 2922 6

A CIP catalogue record for this book is
available from the British Library

Library of Congress Cataloging in
Publication Data available

Printed in Hong Kong

introduction

opposite The glass
wall of the Bauhaus
Building, Dessau,
1926, by Walter
Gropius. The use of
glass was built into
the theoretical basis
of the Modern
Movement at its
outset.

Glass is arguably the most remarkable material ever discovered by man. Made from the melting and cooling of the earth's most abundant mineral, it provides a substance that is transparent and rock hard, and so chemically inert that almost anything can be kept in a container made from it. It has given us the lens, the bottle, the fibre optic cable, fabrics and the window. In the 4,000 years of its known history, it has been drawn into use across the whole world of human endeavour.[1]

Its multi-faceted character and usefulness is spread throughout our lives and language, and the abundance and cheapness of its principal raw ingredient, silica, give glass a unique place in the history of artefacts and technology, and make it a very special material for the contemporary designer, from optics and telecommunications to electrical engineering.

This book celebrates and explores the use of glass in architecture, the development of which it has revolutionized since the designers of buildings first fully realized its potential a little over a thousand years ago.

It took 2,000 years after its discovery for the idea to emerge that glass was a material which could be used for windows rather than simply for trinkets or pots. This may have been because the climate of the place of its invention did not require man to create sealed transparent enclosures, and also perhaps because making flat glass was not easy. However, once this imaginative leap had been made, new conceptual languages in architecture

became possible, which are still being developed and explored.

Without glass we would have spent much of this millennium living in dimly-lit enclosures, struggling to reconcile the conflicting demands of weather protection, view, privacy and lighting. Glass has not only protected and served us, it has also given us the glories of the Gothic cathedral and the beauty of the nineteenth century conservatory, and has been used to underpin the revolution in architecture that came with the twentieth century.[2]

While the literary bibliography on glass in architecture is comparatively small (most of the significant books on the subject can easily be held in a personal library), the 'literature' produced every year is vast. The catalogue of technical information produced by one of the glass manufacturers alone is far larger than this book, and a recently published book on electrochromic oxides by a Swedish colleague comprises 630 pages of science, of which the last 100 are references to source books and papers. Glass and transparency are now irrevocably located in the world of high science.

With this amount of information to hand, and considering the speed with which it is growing, it would be foolish of any author to attempt to be encyclopaedic. This book was conceived and written not so much with the aim of covering every aspect of glass in architecture (although it endeavours to cover most), but to help all those who

wish to work with the material to understand what it is and what potential it has, as well as enabling them to understand each other.

Architecture and design today rely on the developing understanding of technology. There is a general conviction in cultural philosophy that if we do not control technology, it will control us. This is complemented by a centuries-old view that architecture is, to a large extent, derived from technology. From Vitruvius to Viollet-le-Duc, we read that architecture flows from purpose and materials, and that the twentieth century obsession with technology (often misplaced) is the inheritor of a long tradition.

Love of technology for its own sake, however, is dangerous, and never more so than when it is based on ignorance. With this in mind, I have tried to produce a book which will enable the architect, the glass technologist and the manufacturer to talk to one another in a meaningful way.

The book is divided into two parts, which comprise two complementary ways of addressing the subject. The first is a narrative telling the story of glass in architecture which avoids detailed discussion of science and technology; the second is a systematic technical review. Although cross referencing between the two parts is included, it has been decided that constant cross reference, with a multitude of reference indicators, would be too disruptive. The index thus acts as an important route between the two parts, as well as being a key to the subject matter itself.

contents

transparent material known to us, I have included a review of the transparent plastics in this part of the book, not least because of the way in which glass and these plastics work with each other in composite systems.

Chapter Three, *Glass in Architecture*, is in many ways the inspirational core of the book, in that it demonstrates how our contemporaries, particularly those who have worked to understand the material, have exploited it, enjoyed it and produced wonderful architecture with it. In this sense, it is a celebration of manifestation rather than method. An introductory essay which describes the development of glass architecture from 1945 to the present day is followed by a set of exemplars. Each of these is a building in which glass has been central to the concept of the structure, and in which it has been beautifully used. Significantly, in most of them either a special glass has been designed, or a new technique developed to serve the concept. The message here is that with technical understanding and prowess comes the potential of virtuosity, and great beauty. These twenty buildings are not intended to be some sort of notional 'top twenty'. Wonderful new glass buildings are being designed even as this introduction is being written – such is the emerging power of the material. They simply represent how skill and knowledge create great architecture.

Chapter Four, *The Future*, describes the exciting world that is opening up in front of us. The last ten years or so have completely changed the way we think about glass in architecture, and have placed a new vocabulary in the hands of the architect and designer, as well as a new and onerous requirement to understand the technology involved. The world of chromogenics, aerogels and high performance chemistries, and the introduction of nanometric technology, is presenting us with a new palette of materials which will produce yet another revolution in architecture, as we grapple with the imperatives of performance, energy use, resources and ecology.

A new generation of buildings is on the horizon, and glass will prove to be the central material as they are developed. This chapter describes the palette and some of the relevant technologies (particularly microtechnology), and also sets out an agenda for the future of glass architecture.

Following these four chapters are five appendices which review the current technical world of glass as an extended glossary. Central technical aspects of the material are dealt with in a way designed for easy access. Manufacturing techniques are described, together with the chemistry, physics and performance of glasses. Other non-architectural glasses are discussed, as are the transparent plastics. The structure of the manufacturing industry is also described, since an understanding of this is essential to any designer intent on addressing a particular issue in glass technology.

Even as this book was being completed, and despite its length and period of gestation, selection and exclusion of material had to play a more important part than a wish to be all-inclusive. This is particularly so in the case of the description of the buildings of the early 1990s.

The last few years have seen a gratifying burgeoning of fine glass architecture, as is evident from the reading of international magazines. It has been a painful, but carefully taken decision by author and publisher not to try to keep up with this celebration of glass architecture at the end of the century by producing a catalogue of buildings: such an enterprise would simply involve the reiteration of the most recently published material. It is more important that this book be seen as demonstrating the immense historic, architectonic and technological foundations for what is truly becoming a new age of glass architecture as we approach the twenty-first century.

01   **history and the architectural context**

1. Kathmandu. In a culture without glass, vision, privacy and protection from wind and rain must be provided by other means.

2. The Crystal Palace, The Great Exhibition Building, London, 1851, Joseph Paxton with Fox and Henderson. The great glass building that launched the Modern Movement.

beginnings

The history of glass in architecture is wound in a unique way into the history of architecture itself. At its highest level of significance, architecture is the fusion of culture and the need for enclosure made material in physical form; it is the meeting point of the need to build and the innate urge to communicate. Both the building process and its inherent means of expression rely on the intelligent and sensitive use of materials which in terms of their availability, suitability, cost and the technology necessary to produce them, vary according to time and place.

In the thousands of years since he learnt to build, man has had to try to meet two particular, and often conflicting needs: on the one hand, the need to create enclosure for shelter, protection and privacy; on the other, the need to transmit light to provide illumination and view. When the search for a material to reconcile the need for strength, stability, enclosure and view has been unsuccessful, man has had to invent complex techniques of screening, or simply accept life in the dark.

Glass appeared as the preordained technical answer to an apparently impossible question: how to produce a material which is perfectly transparent, hard-wearing and strong, at a price that society can easily afford?

As we now know, the physical and chemical requirements for transparency are precise, and are provided by particular molecular arrangements and atomic structures in the material concerned.

These are generally only found in liquids, which do not form good building materials. Glass, however, the super-cooled liquid, retains its transparency as the unique cocktail of atoms and molecules in silica are heated to melting point, and then cooled carefully so that they do not crystallize, to become translucent or opaque. By this accident of nature, man has always had available to him to a material ideally suited to form sheets of transparent rock, made from a substance which is both the most plentiful on the planet, and very easily obtained: common sand.

However, to convert sand granules into a usable transparent product demanded high temperatures and skills in forming which were difficult to learn. Kilns were needed which could achieve temperatures high enough to melt the rocky grains (which were at least small enough to take in heat easily). Even more taxing, perhaps, were the techniques which had to be developed to control the shape of the molten mass as it slowly cooled from a fluid, through its treacly, viscous state, to become a clear vitrified solid.

This background of the extraordinary technique and high skill applied to glass-making is the basis for thousands of years of a carefully guarded and secret trade; a trade based on an expertise restricted to a privileged few, who made it known only with the promise of great reward, and who travelled across continents to satisfy the demands of a continually increasing clientele.

The discovery of glass took place about 4,000 years ago in the eastern Mediterranean, probably beneath an ancient pottery kiln, as the fused silica of the pots mixed with the alkaline ash of the hearth below. By 1,500 BC, pressed and moulded glass vessels were common in Egypt, and skills to make them had spread to the area of modern Venice, and Hall in Austria. It was Alexander the Great who founded the famous glass works in Alexandria shortly after he founded the city itself in 332 BC.

Two thousand years passed between this first discovery, to a time when blown glass appeared, thus making possible the creation of thin transparent sheets strong enough for windows. With this development, new conceptual languages in architecture became possible, which are still being developed and explored; from the simple provision of light and view without a loss of warmth, to the creation of conceptual and technical master-pieces which derived their essential quality from this wonderful material.

It seems most likely that the imaginative leap which led to the invention of blown glass originated in the Syria/Palestine area in the first century BC. The blowing of glass was the first

2

Each of the four chapters in the first part can be seen as an independent and freestanding essay, covering history, current technology, glass architecture in the last decades of the twentieth century, and the exciting promise of the future.

Chapter One, *History and the Architectural Context*, explains how we have got to where we are, and how slowly emerging manufacturing techniques gradually influenced architectural morphology. This chapter concentrates on the five great historical ages of glass in architecture, and how glass-making developed as a technique to support their evolution. There is no attempt here to produce an exhaustive review of all aspects of glass in architectural history. The section is not written as an ultimately comprehensive source text: such a text would be a massive undertaking, much greater than the whole of this book, and beyond the intended scope of its author. An annotated bibliography points the reader to several seminal texts in which different aspects of glass history can be discovered.

This book looks at history as a contextual landscape in which sunlit peaks (and a few dark valleys) illustrate the development of the long relationship between glass and architecture. As the continuous ascent of technical improvement has progressed, a distinct series of 'Glass Ages' in architecture can be discerned, in turn characterized both by a certain stage in technical development and by great buildings, examples of which are described and celebrated in their integration of glass and architectural morphology.

In the first section, the beginnings of glass-making are described and the interdependent relationships between chemistry, making and performance are explained. The nature of glass is as much to do with how it is made as it is a result of what it is made of, and the glass pane, the basis of most of glass architecture, took 2,000 years to evolve after the discovery of the substance from which it is made.

After this introductory section, the next two sections describe the first two ages of glass architecture: Gothic and the secular inheritance which followed it. The fourth section covers the consolidation of technique which took place in the seventeenth and eighteenth centuries, to underpin the development and spread of Renaissance architecture through Europe. The fifth section takes us into the early nineteenth century, with its flowering of the conservatory as an archetype, and this leads on to the sixth section, subtitled 'Cathedrals of Commerce', which describes the development of the conservatory during the technical revolution in the second half of the nineteenth century.

A short seventh section sets out the critical part glass had to play in the development of the 'frame and skin' architecture which evolved in Chicago and elsewhere at the end of the nineteenth century. This leads naturally to the eighth and final section, which covers the subsequent technological revolution in our own century.

The gradually developing methods of manufacture, and the equally slow understanding of what materials should go into glass, are described, through all these sections, century by century. In the review of architecture which this, the longest chapter of the book, comprises, it must be said that focus is placed on the development of architectural forms which derive their significance from the use of glass, rather than on the slow absorption of glass into the evolution of architecture as a whole. For example, the incorporation of glass into the evolving fenestration of vernacular architecture, itself an important sub-plot in the development of domestic architecture from the Middle Ages onwards, is not dealt with in any great depth. The story of the window in architecture, itself a significant one, deserves a book of its own, which this particular text does not pretend to be.

Chapter Two, *Glass Technology*, has the simple aim to provide an overview of what is being made, how it works, how it is made and how it can be used. At the beginning, techniques of glass-making are described, together with the physical properties these create. Then, given the essential and central characteristic of glass, that it is transparent, the nature of transparency is described. An understanding of transparency informs so much of what we, as designers, must consider as we work with glass. This has become much more complex in the last twenty years, given the innumerable coatings which can now be applied to glass, and the way it can be put into complex assemblies. Since glass is not the only

important step in the development of glass in architecture. It demanded techniques for raising temperatures to around 1,500°C, and a certain amount of courageous skill. The technique spread from Syria to Egypt, and was used both for vessels and large flat dishes (the precursors of window glasses); Egyptian glass was so greatly valued by the Roman conquerors that it was used as tribute.

The nature of the climate, however, did not provide the functional imperative for the invention of the glazed window. Architecture, as developed by the time of Alexander and into the first century BC, is well documented by Vitruvius in his *Ten Books on Architecture*. In this lengthy description of Greek and Roman architecture, Vitruvius gives a detailed account of materials and techniques in use. Books II and VII read like modern books on building construction: brick, sand, lime, pozzolana, stone and timber are all dealt with, together with wall building, vaulting and pigments; but glass is completely absent. For all his careful analysis of the relationship between the function of buildings and their design, Vitruvius restricts his comments on comfort and climate to recommendations for room placement and orientation. Winter rooms are designed for fires, with a resulting need for easy cleaning of smoke stains.

A study of Vitruvius, or of Greek and Roman buildings still standing, shows how the nature of the architecture was comparatively independent of the concept of the glazed window. There is so much light and heat outside for most of

3 . The Stoa of Attalos, Athens, c 159–138 BC (reconstructed 1953–6). Glass was hardly necessary in the buildings located in the birthplace of glass, the eastern Mediterranean. The Stoa is a well designed response to the problems of environmental control in a sunny climate. At the lower level shade is graduated from the public street to a transitional space and back to an enclosed space behind.

the year that the building interior is seen as a retreat. Window openings formed part of the architectural syntax, of course, but light is often designed to penetrate construction through columns or holes in a roof (whether this roof be a house atrium or the roof of the Pantheon). The architecture of a building such as the reconstructed Stoa in Athens shows how light, shade, structure and security are modulated without a need for glazed openings. The traditional architecture of the Middle East today reveals the same conceptual basis.

Despite this, windows were part of the architectural vocabulary, with glass as one of a group of translucent materials. Roman window glass was made, certainly up to about one square metre, and

was probably cast. Panes measuring 500 mm by 700 mm have been found at Pompeii, and the Bath House there was glazed with pieces 1 m by 700 mm, 12 mm thick. Typical window glass was always over 3 mm thick and greenish blue in colour. Flat glass was also used for the purpose of primitive conservatories, and Columella refers to forcing frames for cucumbers: growing vegetables out of season was a great advantage to patrician Romans.

The development of the glass-maker's art was concerned both with mixing and forming. The chemistry of glasses is the basis of the performance and appearance, but it is also what makes them easy or difficult to form. Among early discoveries was evidently the fact that the mixture of certain additives to glass reduced the temperature at which it could be melted, whereas others in some way improved it or created a type which satisfied a particular need. Pure silica melts at just over 1,700°C, but even at this temperature it is very viscous (flowing about 1,000 times less easily than syrup), and cannot easily be worked. Soda fluxes reduce the melting temperature to below 800°C, but the resulting composition can be attacked by water. Lime added to this soda-silica mix helps resist attack and promotes durability, but such a three-fold mix is prone to crystallization. Achieving a good balance was a matter for selection and evolution born of experience, eased by the presence of soda and lime as impurities in most of the silicate raw materials available to the ancient glass-makers. Even with an effective mix,

making glass is complicated by the fact that a temperature of 900°C may make a 'frit', but founding it requires sixteen hours or more at 1,100°C (the term frit is applied to the mix from which much glass is made). The evolution of the chemistry of flat glass was gradually refined over the centuries to reach the Roman content, similar to our own soda lime, with its pale green colouration: 69% silica, 17% soda, 11% lime and magnesia, and three per cent alumina, iron oxide and manganese oxide.

The mixing of materials for glass, which remained a matter of imprecise chemistry until the end of the eighteenth century, has partly been related to the content of the naturally occurring or man-made materials, and partly by the evolution of the crucial understanding of fluxes, stabilizers, decolourizers and other performing constituents. The chemistry of the Syrian Belus River sand was no doubt part of the story of the early development of glass in the region where it was born. With its natural calcium carbonate content of about fifteen per cent, its alumina content of three-and-a-half percent to five per cent, and its magnesium carbonate content of one-and-a-half per cent, it provides an almost perfect naturally-occurring base for a glass melt, needing only the sodium carbonate flux to create a 'modern' material. An Assyrian tablet of about 650 BC confirms the ancient recipe: sixty parts sand, 180 parts 'salicornia' alkali, five parts saltpetre (what we know as potassium nitrate) and two parts lime. The salicornia was a plant containing soda. Pliny's recipe of AD first century has similarities, with its one part sand and three parts 'nitre'. Whatever the recipe, the raw materials themselves provided a good basic mix, with lime from sea shells and soda from the ash of sea plants.

The centuries after Vitruvius saw the gradual development of the idea of glass being an important material in windows, and not merely to act as a transparent weather shield. Brilliantly coloured glass was to be found in Constantine's Church of St Paul's near Rome built around AD 337, and such a use of glass as an illuminated, painted surface was potentially much more important in the Mediterranean climate than the provision of clear glazed openings used as protection.

The northward spread of the Romans led to the creation of glazing as we know it today. The glass industry was developed in the Saône and Rhine provinces, manned essentially by Syrian, Jewish and Alexandrian craftsmen, with famous factories in Cologne and Trier. It was in Trier that the Latin term *glesum* (a Germanic word meaning transparent/lustrous) was in use, giving us the name we now use. Middle Eastern craftsmen dominated the craft until German invaders broke their monopoly around AD 600. As the Roman Empire broke up from AD 400 onwards, the centres of glass-making in the Rhine and Rhône valleys remained, and many makers fled to the Po Valley and Liguria.

The importance of the ancient influence of Syrians on glass development cannot be underestimated. The technique of spinning discs, which was to

4. An Italian blown glass bowl dating from AD 50–100. Developing the skill required to blow glass provided the product which was to give us the window, with a technique destined to produce flat glass for nearly 2,000 years.

5. An amber coloured glass bowl, made by the slumping process in a Syro-Palestinian workshop between 200 and 150 BC. This perfectly formed and beautifully coloured vessel, made in the birthplace of glass, demonstrates perfect control over the material, half way between the time of its discovery and the present day.

prove an essential craft to the development of northern glazing, was in use in Syria in the eighth century. It was at about this time that the Venetian glass industry was beginning. Venice, one of the most important city states in the world, was ideally placed, between the Middle East and northern Europe, to act as a centre of excellence as the Syrian craftsmen plied their trade. By the tenth century, the Venetian glass industry was established, and an erstwhile mainly nomadic activity had a new base.

The Venetians were originally renowned for decorative glassware and glass vessels, but they soon expanded their expertise into window glass and lenses for spectacles. Significantly, Venice was to see the perfection of the skill of making mirrors in the fourteenth century, using a reflective backing of tin and mercury, and flat glass made in Venice and in northern Europe was produced both by the cylinder method and by spinning.

At the turn of the first millennium, while the Venetians were establishing their techniques, particularly for the *bullions* produced by spinning, the northern European makers had consolidated and perfected the two techniques necessary to permit the glories of the Gothic Age. By AD 1000, they had established a

4

widespread glass industry, and were using both spinning and the cylinder method to satisfy the increasing demands of the church and their own climate with its long winters and often overcast skies.

The cylinder method was described in the early twelfth century by the German monk Theophilus in his *Diversarium Artium Schedula*. In this early description, a technique for flat glass-making is set out which was to be used for 800 years. A hollow iron tube was used to pick up a ball of molten glass. It was then blown into a bubble that became a sphere which, as it was swung from side to side, became a cylinder with a hemispherical end. This end was cut and pinched in the centre. The centre was gripped by a 'punty', and the other end, still soft, opened up to create a full cylinder. The cylinder could then be reheated, cut down in length, flattened out, and smoothed. Theophilus also gave a recipe for glass which characterized the northern European manufacturing process, proposing one part sand to two parts beech ash; the itinerant nature of glass-making activity contributed significantly to the depletion and re-sourcing of the beech used for furnaces and to make ash. The use of timber ash as the source of soda also distinguished central European 'potash' glass from its Mediterranean cousin, where the source was from sea plants.

The spinning method, inherited from the early Syrians, was still used in northern Europe in the Middle Ages, as is known from a description of its manufacture by Philippe de Cacqueray in

5

1330 at La Haye near Rouen. This Norman 'crown' glass was made by blowing a sphere, the crown of which (opposite the blow hole) was then stuck on to the punty and spun. The blowhole enlarged with spin and became a disc: typical diameters were about 600–700 mm.

The two different methods of making glass in these early days of sheet produced intrinsically different products. The cylinder method made larger, comparatively even sheets in terms of thickness, but the necessary reheating and physical flattening damaged the surface of the glass. Marvering, the process of shaping blown glass by rolling it over a stone, characteristically marked and slightly defaced it, leaving it without the finish of glass emerging untouched from the fire. Spun glass was more brilliant, with this untouched finish, but the spinning produced its characteristic concentric rings and uneven lens form in the centre. Both these forms of glass were intrinsically thin and weak. However, as they were made in gradually increasing sizes, and as the techniques to fix them into buildings were developed, they formed a natural and essential constituent of the architecture of the great churches of northern Europe which followed the end of the first Christian millennium.

gothic

Northern European Gothic architecture may truly be called the First Age of glass architecture and was created by the Christian Church, the greatest agency for construction in northern Europe following the Dark Ages. The change in architectural morphology from the Romanesque to Gothic was fundamental and dramatic. Early medieval architecture had depended on the creation of masonry walls punctured by holes, sized in accordance with the exigencies of the need for light, the frequent concern for defence, and the problems of structural support. The Gothic builders were driven to create a different sort of architecture.

The development of the structure of the great Gothic church is one of the most important stories in architectural history, not least because of the way in which empirical design, carried out without the benefit of sophisticated structural analysis, created some of the greatest structures ever built by man. If the Pont du Gard and the Pantheon are examples of Roman virtuosity with compression structures, the vaults and buttresses of the Gothic cathedral move

6, 7. Romanesque church at St Nectaire, near Clermont Ferrand c 1146–78 (6) and Notre Dame, Paris (7). The Choir at Notre Dame was started in c 1160, and the west front built between c 1200 and 1245. Gothic architecture is archetypally one of frames and membranes, a powerful contrast with the preceding Romanesque architecture of massive walls and openings.

on to demonstrate the unprecedented expression of enclosed volume using a material which could only be used in compression. There were several compelling causes for this development: first, the need to create large spaces to accommodate – and inspire awe in – large numbers of people. The pilgrims who travelled the route through France to Santiago di Compostella created a typical congregation. To such occupant-related criteria were added the acoustic criteria of patrons such as Hugh of Cluny, whose love of Gregorian chant contributed to a wish for a reverberation time which enhanced the beauty of the rolling and overlapping sounds. Above these two functional objectives was the unified desire to glorify God and beat the opposition: rarely has competition in

architecture had such wonderful results.

The need to produce these volumes and spans in rectangular, rather than square bays led to the necessary geometry of the pointed arch; and the stresses set up by the new vaults on the supporting walls and piers below led just as inevitably to the drama of the flying buttress to resist the outward thrust. The result of this evolving technique was the Gothic stone frame, relying on compression, essentially free of bending moments.

If Gothic architecture is a rational response to considerations of structure, the creation of the glass wall that came with it is partly a result of climate. The large openings suggested by the idea of 'frame' implicit in Gothic architecture would have been impossible without the

creation of a membrane to keep the weather out. The role of glass therefore became apparent. In southern Europe, with its hot summers and generally mild winters, glazed openings were not essential for much of the year. In northern Europe, protection from the sun was replaced by a thirst for light, and by the need for protection from the cold and rain. In the huge openings of the Gothic stone frame, glass found its natural place in the architectonic order.

Concomitant with this delivery of architecture from the constraints of the load-bearing wall was an increasing appreciation and love of light. The instincts for mystery and darkness were gradually replaced by a wish to illuminate. This was manifested architecturally by a drive to create ever greater luminosity which, over a period of a hundred years, developed from an architecture of wall into an architecture of glass.

Glass was chosen as the natural infill material, held in a filigree of metal, illuminating the vast new spaces. Without glass these buildings would have been impractical open tents; the existence of glass, and of the skills of the window-maker, were essential ingredients to the new structures.

Transparency (or the frequent lack of it), as opposed to translucency, was unimportant. The openings in the stone frame were of greatest significance at high level, where the potential benefits of transparency were least important; and the window became the illuminator and, perhaps more significantly, the book for a generally illiterate population. In the stained-glass masterpieces of the age, the Bible was illustrated in brilliant colours, and local stories were recorded for the benefit of those for whom the written word was a mystery of unintelligible cyphers. From the outside, these great glazed areas present a wonderful screen, now often gun-metal-dull from corrosion in consonance with the stone, only occasionally revealing their true character with a gleam of reflected light. Seen from the inside, however, they are revealed for what they really are: shining membranes of light, and the glories of their age.

The small pane sizes available to the designers, far from being an impediment in the making of the new glass architecture, drove them to create a characteristic constructional system to span across the huge areas given to them. The glass window became an assembled and very heavy 'quilt' of pieces held together with lead, offered up and held in place to the stonework on a secondary network of metal.

There are two stories which run together in the progress of Gothic architecture which are similar, but essentially different, like plots interwoven in a novel. The conventional story tells of features: stone frames, flying buttresses, vaults and stained glass. Another story, which has a more underlying morphological imperative, relates to the search for light, luminosity and weightlessness, served by the creation of the first great exoskeletal architecture. This other story is in fact the engine generating the development of Gothic architecture, and should be related first.

8. The Five Sisters at York Minster, York, c 1260.

the gothic programme and the search for light

The story of Gothic architecture in general, and the Gothic cathedral in particular, is a difficult one to unravel and demands the forensic skills of the professional historian. The leap-frog progression of the major enormous structures was prompted by their highly competitive patrons seeking to outdo each other in their evolving cultural enlightenment over a period of 400 years, occasionally enforced by fire and structural collapse.

The Gothic style was born and developed as an international force within a hundred-mile radius of Paris. It was in this area that Abbot Suger built St Denis, and later High Gothic produced Chartres. The twelfth and early thirteenth centuries also saw the founding of the universities of Paris, Oxford and Cambridge, the first known composers of polyphony, Leotin and Perotin (both of whom worked in Paris), and the philosophy of St Thomas Aquinas. Panofsky tells us how Suger synthesized and gave architectural effect to the culture of early scholasticism. A significant technical result of this 'rationalism' in the twelfth century was the reinterpretation of the wall in church architecture, as the non-structural part of the enclosure became a membrane.

The Gothic architect's attitude to structure is well known. While perhaps not as strictly rationalist as Choisy and Viollet-le-Duc would have us believe, he seemed to be clear in his attempt to understand structure, and to express it: we can see the evidence of the desire to

8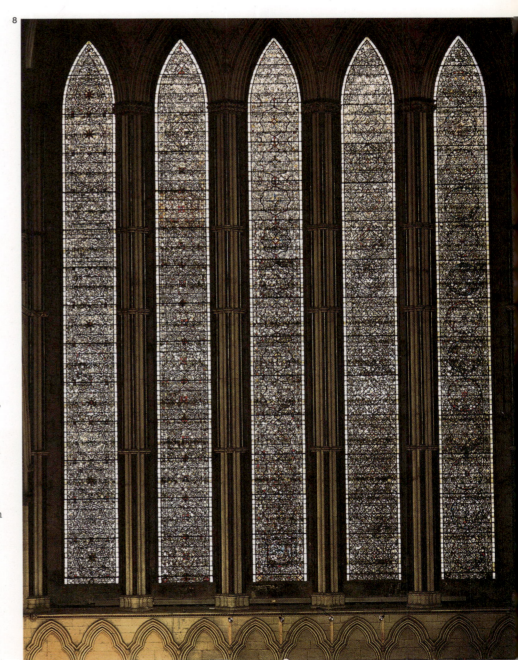

differentiate, categorize and 'logically' express hierarchy, both in the philosophical manifestations of scholasticism, and in the structural clarity of the vault rib, the column and the flying buttress.

The architectural morphology starts with the idea of the frame, and this itself derives from the necessary evolution of the rib and web construction of the vaults. The idea of differentiating and marking the geometry and force lines of structure which was developed in the early Gothic vaults, combined with the progressive thinning of the walls seen in the area of the Ile de France at the end of the eleventh century, provided a structural synergy which produced St Pierre de Montmartre in 1133, and seven years later was developed into Abbot Suger's masterpiece at St Denis. Here we see, in one move, the realization of the principle of frame and infill transformed into the glass wall and column. Within the next twenty years, the potential of this new glass wall was introduced into the work carried out at Sens and at Laon, where brilliant lighting was achieved by glazing behind the triforium as well as the clerestory above.

By 1170, in the new Choir at St Remi in Rheims, the idea of the glass wall is clearly stated in the three-storey elevation, stepped in section, where the clerestory itself not only illuminated the vault, but also provided the potential for maximized sky lighting, so useful in the medieval street patterns that often provided the urban context of such buildings. Five years later, and less than

9. St Denis, Paris, 1140 onwards. The Choir here was the earliest full manifestation of Gothic.

10. Chartres Cathedral, 1194–1120.

11. The Sainte-Chapelle in Paris, 1243–8. This rich and highly decorated royal reliquary built for St Louis of France, containing a fragment of the True Cross, is a powerful exploitation of the architecture of glass, with stone framing refined to the slenderness of metal.

50 km north, Laon received another component of the new Gothic glass vocabulary; the first great west end rose window.

Then, on 10 June 1194, a great conflagration destroyed much of Chartres Cathedral. Fulbert's church was badly damaged, but the saving of its most precious relic (the garment supposed to have been worn by Mary at the birth of Jesus) led to an enormous and enthusiastic subscription programme to build a new cathedral. Funds came not only from the local population, but from both Philip Augustus, King of France, and (indirectly) from Richard the Lionheart of England who was at war with him, but still allowed English priests to raise money. By 1223, most of the Cathedral was complete and it was reconsecrated in 1260. Chartres is one of the masterpieces of Gothic architecture, and one which takes the pursuit of light further forward. Its clerestory windows were the highest constructed

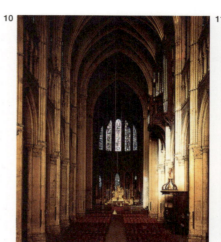

to that date, and the small triforium and high arcade below contribute to the building's lightness and verticality. Moreover, the great glass expression here is in the nave, not removed to the more private confines of the Choir. The structural lightness inside and the huge windows are both made possible by the structural virtuosity of the flying buttresses outside.

In 1210, ten years before the nave at Chartres was finished, Jean d'Orbais, the architect working at Rheims Cathedral, had embodied a detailed development which further enhanced the glass area; bar tracery increased the area of glass, when compared to the earlier plate tracery, by eliminating yet more wall surface. Ten years later, Robert de Luzarches took this development of tracery further at Amiens. Another ten years saw this decennial development process flower into the first work in the French Rayonnant style; the new nave at St Denis. Thus, in 1231, only ninety years

after Abbot Suger's work there, the great age of Gothic architecture matured into a complete and perfectly coherent syntax of structure and glass. The stone responds soared from the ground up and over into the ribs of the vault. The glazed triforium and the enormous clerestory windows produced a luminosity not previously seen, helped by the roll moulding of the mullions which reduced the effective mass of the stone.

By 1243, the ability to produce glass walls with minimal structure was fully realized at the Sainte Chapelle in Paris. This is a reliquary, not a cathedral, and the glass extended from the floor to the vault in one sweep. This aesthetic was transferred into the majesty of a cathedral at Cologne between 1248 and 1300, where the new Choir, 46 m high, was the glassy masterpiece of Rayonnant architecture. Although the French and the English, tied by conquest and overlapping nationhood, were the earliest to adopt the Gothic style, they were by no means alone, and some of the greatest examples of the stone frame and glass architecture were built in Germany and central Europe. Cologne Cathedral was based on Amiens but, by the time it was consecrated in 1322, the building had developed a soaring magnificence matching the later Beauvais. By the middle of the fourteenth century, Emperor Charles IV was instrumental in spreading a grandiloquent version of Gothic from Germany down to Prague, and it was he who commissioned one of the greatest glass walls of the Gothic period, at Aachen. Aachen Cathedral was where German emperors were crowned, and between 1355 and 1414 a Choir was built of amazing boldness and luminosity. Watkin has rightly described this as a 'giant aspiring glass cage', and it is a wonderful precursor to the glass cage of King's College Chapel started thirty years later.

The search for an architecture made of light was fully realized at Cologne and Aachen. The contemporaneous Choir at Clermont Ferrand makes very clear the aesthetic intention of this architecture, for Rayonnant is essentially an architecture not of coloured, but of white glass, with stone framing which derives its finely drawn detailing from metalwork.

In the seventy years from 1230 to 1300, which saw the flowering of Rayonnant, English patrons and their architects developed a parallel stream of glass architecture. The process was initiated by Henry III's decision to

12. The Choir at Aachen Cathedral, 1355–1414. A supreme expression of the Gothic use of glass.

13. Gloucester Cathedral, the great East Window, erected c 1350. The apotheosis of late northern European Gothic glass architecture.

rebuild Westminster Abbey, perhaps inspired by the patronage of his royal rival in France at St Denis and the Sainte Chapelle. The Chapter-house begun in 1246 is Westminster's own glass cage. Ten years later, the Angel Choir at Lincoln was begun, incorporating one of the earliest of a series of great English set piece east windows; a flat closing of the section 17 m high, quite different from the French apse terminations.

It was not until 1291 that England saw the start of a complete Rayonnant

work in the nave at York Minster, an event perhaps to be expected given the new bishop's provenance as a theology professor from Paris University. Its height at 31 m was six metres less than that of Chartres completed seventy years earlier, and 15 m less than the Choir at Cologne being completed at the time, but it is still a fine English version of the new architecture of light and glass.

The ultimate development of

Rayonnant as an architectural ordering system had to await the evolution of the English Perpendicular style, of which a marvellous example is the great east window at Gloucester Cathedral constructed between 1350 and 1360 at the end of the programme to build the new Choir. This was the largest window in medieval Europe to date. Gloucester is full of quirks and apparent irrationalities flowing from the additions and modifications extending over three centuries and beyond. The diagonal bracing in the south transept has been

celebrated by architect Robert Venturi as a 'superadjacency', the overlaying or superimposition of elements operating at different scales, but is actually a magnificent shoring exercise to prevent collapse. The flat arches flying across space at the entrances to the transepts, and the strangely articulated plumbing of some of the responds are the work of great independent spirits.

The east window is a corresponding exercise in glass. In plan, it is part of the

large radius apsidal end of the previous choir, the line of the crypt of which it follows. It is slid between the Choir and the Lady Chapel, and the lower half borrows light from the space between the two: the Lady Chapel is a shadowy presence behind it. The reconciliation of geometries produces a slightly bowed window, and also sets out the radial connections between it and the main arcade. This makes the east window slightly wider than the central space which it closes, and fills the end with light. Light is the imperative in this window, and the whole enormous enterprise is an exercise in white glass, the only use of colour being to fill the spaces between the figures and the drawn niches in which they stand. It is part of the spatial ordering of Gloucester that the window is not very visible from the Cathedral nave. However, this only serves to heighten the impact of the great glass wall when it is first seen from beneath the entry to the Choir.

The architectonic successor to the Gloucester east window, the great east window at York Minster constructed in 1405, is even larger and its luminosity is not compromised by a chapel beyond it. The master glazier, John Thornton of Coventry, finished the window in three years. Measuring 23.17 m high by 9.75 m wide, it is the greatest achievement of fifteenth century glass-painting as well as representing an extraordinary achievement in glazing.

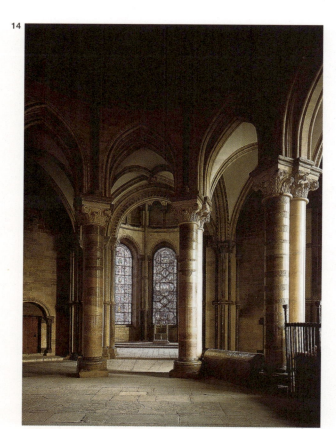

14

14. The Trinity
Chapel, Canterbury
Cathedral, 1184. The
glass of the Trinity
Chapel, and of the
Corona beyond it of
a slightly later date,
constitute a beautiful
chromatic climax to
the Cathedral, with
some of the finest
medieval stained
glass in England.

the development of colour

The dual nature of the story of the Gothic architects' love and exploitation of glass has already been described. The search for, and expression of light and luminosity, and the development of structure and morphology to serve this end, is clearly demonstrated. This incentive recurs throughout the subsequent history of glass in architecture: the Palm House at Kew of 1844, Dutert's and Contamin's Palais des Machines of 1889, and Philip Johnson's Crystal Cathedral of 1977 are all manifestations of the same obsession. The exploitation of colour and glass-painting, on the other hand, is a parallel story which the Gothic designers made very much their own, in a way never to be repeated.

The structural imperatives of the Gothic builders, and the climate in which they worked, made the glass wall both possible and inevitable; but this wall would not have reached its high pinnacles of expression without the manufacturing skills already referred to or of course, the developments in stained glass which provided the palette for the artists and iconographers who produced these paintings in light.

The use of coloured glass at the time of the Roman Emperor Constantine, in AD fourth century, has already been mentioned, and it seems likely that the two inventions necessary for the creation of the coloured glass window were both Byzantine. These were the making of the coloured glass itself, and the method of holding small pieces in place using lead strips. By a little after AD 1100, when

writing his *Schedula*, Theophilus was able to describe the making of coloured glass, a technology known only in Normandy, the Rhineland and Burgundy; the English in medieval times were only able to make clear glass.

Colour was added to the naturally clear (or lightly green-tinted) glass by adding metallic oxides to the glass melt; the coloured glasses were actually called 'metal'. For blue, cobalt was added; for red, iron; for green, copper. The cylinder process was then used to make the sheets. When the tinted glass was too dark to let much light through, 'flashing' was used, where a very thin layer of coloured glass was fired on to the clear glass.

To make a stained-glass window, the sheets of coloured glass were nibbled into shape with a 'grozing iron', and laid into patterns over a drawing of the window design set out on a large white table. Black pigment was painted on to the coloured glass to give the detail: the faces, and the folds and creases in drapery. After painting, the glass was re-baked in a small kiln to fuse the painting into the glass. The glass was then put back over the drawing on the table and joined with H-section lead strips, or 'calms', soldered where necessary. The resulting heavy assemblies were transported as panels to the site and mounted on the iron saddle bars already set into the stone surround. Lead wire was used to tie the assemblies into the saddle bars and was then soldered.

Abbot Suger's St Denis was not only the first great Gothic church but also provides us with some of the earliest

surviving stained-glass panels, and the twelfth century glass work which followed it was the glory of its time. The greatest extant repository is in Chartres Cathedral, the architectonic importance of which has already been described, and which contains some of the most brilliant as well as some of the oldest surviving stained glass. Its windows record the effort to rebuild it after the great fire which destroyed its predecessor, and portray the activities of the merchants and citizens who paid for the reconstruction of their church.

The three windows in the west front at Chartres date from about 1150, before the construction of the new cathedral. Over the north portal is the Jesse window. Next to it is the Incarnation window comprising twenty-four narrative scenes in alternating red squares and blue circles. The third window in the west front shows the Passion and Resurrection of Christ in fourteen panels. The rest of the Cathedral maintains the tradition of the north, dark side carrying Old Testament narratives, and the sunlit south side carrying stories from the New Testament. In its three great rose windows, and the over 150 lancets and oculi all installed before 1230, it contains the most complete iconographic programme left to us.

Gothic architecture was a French creation, but it was also an international style, promulgated powerfully by the French architects and masons who originated it. If we seek English counterparts to Chartres, we need look no further than Canterbury Cathedral in the south, and Lincoln Cathedral and York Minster in the north. These three churches house the greatest Gothic stained glass in England.

William of Sens's work at Canterbury started in 1175 following the terrible fire of the year before. Canterbury was an obvious place for a great project, following Thomas à Becket's murder in 1170 and canonization in 1173. William brought the new architecture with him from Sens, the city which had been the home-in-exile of Thomas à Becket prior to his return to Canterbury and death. After William's accident in 1179, his successor, William the Englishman, crowned the first English work in French Gothic with the beautiful glass wall of the Trinity Chapel, finished in 1184, which formed the climax and final destination of the thirty-nine step climb up the rich internal volumes of Canterbury Cathedral.

The earliest Canterbury windows date from about 1180; they are high in the clerestory and the imagery is large enough to be seen from the floor far below. The lower windows in the Cathedral are smaller than their later-Gothic successors, but the absence of tracery left large openings. As at St Denis, they are divided into panels, each of which contains a scene which is part of a story. The iconography followed a programme later systematized in the *Biblia Pauperum* of the early thirteenth century, and the *Speculum Humanae Salvationis*. After the martyrdom of St Thomas à Becket, his story was told in the brilliant series of windows around the Trinity Chapel.

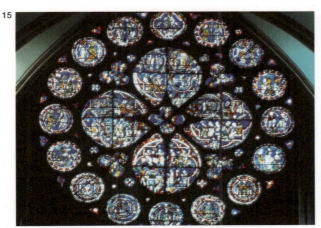

15. The Dean's Eye, Lincoln Cathedral, *c* 1210 onwards. This is a powerful composition of plate tracery circles, characterized by deep reds and blues.

16. The great West Window, fourteenth century, York Minster.

Canterbury is generally considered to be a 'French' cathedral; indeed, not only did its design have its origins in French thinking, but both its glass and its stone came from France. This French influence was also evident in the rather later work at Westminster Abbey where the Frenchman, Laurence Vitrearius, secured the contract to supply glass in 1240. The French and 'continental' dominance of coloured and high quality glass-making from this time and for the next 300 years is part of the history of medieval architecture. The Jerusalem Chamber at Westminster Abbey contains fine examples of this early glass.

Two hundred miles north of Westminster and Canterbury, Lincoln Cathedral houses one of the great early medieval rose windows, the Dean's Eye. Although now only a small country town perched on a hill overlooking the Lincolnshire plain, surmounted by its great Cathedral, Lincoln in the twelfth century was the biggest diocese in England, whose Norman cathedral was

destroyed by an earthquake in 1185, nine years before the destruction of Chartres by fire. Hugh of Avalon, who had been brought to England in 1179 by Henry II to run a Somerset priory, was entrusted with the reconstruction of the new Lincoln Cathedral. It is Hugh who gave us the legacy of Lincoln, its architecture and its glass, and who named the rose windows of the north and south transepts the two 'eyes' of the Cathedral. To the north is the Dean's Eye, protecting the Cathedral against the devils of cold and darkness; to the south is the Bishop's Eye, set to 'receive the Holy Spirit' and the midday sun (and also overlooking the Bishop's Palace).

The Dean's Eye is the only rose window in England surviving from this date, around 1210. In its centre is Christ in Majesty at the Last Judgment, in gold and red, with surrounding topical scenes including Hugh's funeral in 1200. Below this ancient window are five 'grisaille' lancets, prefiguring the great Five Sisters of York to the north. The change in techniques used by the medieval architects, masons and glass artists can be seen by looking south, at the Bishop's Eye in the south transept. The strict and simple geometry of circles of the Dean's Eye is replaced by flowing tracery. The glass here is an early fourteenth century replacement of the earlier window, and contains even earlier fragments.

These windows, with their bright colours, are fine examples of the work deriving from continental Europe and the Seine-Rhine basin, which was the origin of the tradition of brilliantly coloured glass at this time. In England,

the puritanical rigours of the Cistercian order provided the background to another, equally important, glazing aesthetic, that of 'grisaille', using uncoloured or 'white' glass painted with black foliage patterns.

In 1134, the Cistercians had banned coloured or figured glass in their churches. This released the potential in white glass, which the English found easier to make, and which provided a great deal more light. It also released an aesthetic that was quite different from the pictorial representation of previous painted and stained glass, which was not always a greater transmitter of light. To someone who thinks of Gothic stained glass as being the blaze of colour at Chartres or innumerable other great medieval churches, the Five Sisters at

York Minster of about 1260 will come as a strange, almost mysterious experience. On proceeding to the crossing of the Minster and looking right, to the south, a conventional rose window surmounting eight lancets is displayed, bright in the south light. The experience to the north, in the far wall of the north transept, is quite different. Five huge grisaille windows, each 16.3 m high and 1.5 m wide, rise to the roof. Far from giving the light which could be gained from using uncoloured glass, the overriding impression here is of darkness. A silvery, gun-metal hue is enriched by touches of gold and other colours, made extraordinarily rich by the over 100,000 pieces of glass which comprise the piece. The only coherent and recognizable form seen from the Cathedral floor is the blue medallion at the bottom of the central light, an element taken from the twelfth century glass in the earlier Norman cathedral. Tests have shown this earlier glass to have a soda flux, rather than the potash more usually found in England. Soda glass has been found in nearly a half per cent of the pieces tested in York; the source remains

17. King's College Chapel, Cambridge, 1446–1547. Sporadic funding and the Wars of the Roses made the construction of the Chapel very slow. The founder of the College, King Henry VI, wrote that he wanted the building to 'proceed in large form, clean and substantial, setting apart superfluity of too great curious works of detail and busy moulding'. The result is the greatest stone framed building ever built, from its buttressed exterior to its perfect fan-vaulted roof.

18. All Saints, Eaton Bishop, Herefordshire, early fourteenth century. Fine stained glass was not the preserve of the great cathedrals. In this small church, delicately drawn gestures are complemented by the use of the newly discovered colours.

17

unknown. Although the graphic texture of the Five Sisters is based on the drawing of foliage, and as such is strictly representational, the design of the group of windows is one of the world's great pieces of abstract art. Its texture, constructed painstakingly out of very small pieces of leaded glass (the average size is about 35 mm square), and its muted but deeply rich colouration have the power of a Monet painting and share an aesthetic technique – the use of natural forms to create pictorial abstraction, in which the prime experience is one of colour. At York, however, the effective 'canvas' is about 16 m by 8 m.

The development of this first great 'glass architecture' in the subsequent thirteenth and fourteenth centuries saw increasing challenges with the larger size of the 'canvasses'. As windows became bigger, in response to ever-bolder structures and attenuated form, and to increase the amount of daylight, so the glass artists had to rationalize their images, and the glaziers had to improve and vary their technique. The development of tall, narrow windows in the English Decorated style made the creation of large images very difficult, and bands of colour were therefore designed between large plain areas of grisaille. The west window at York Minster, installed in 1338 (and seen on page 19), is a wonderful example of this.

Fortunately for the glass painter, technical progress was also being made in glass colouring. Around 1300, it was found that firing a silver sulphide on to a clear glass stained it yellow, from a pale colour to deep orange; this gave us the

18

delicate colouring at All Saints, Eaton Bishop. Browns, violets and deep greens also appear.

From 1350 onwards in England, after the flowering of French Rayonnant and with the development of the Perpendicular style, grisaille came even more into its own, as can be seen in the east window at Gloucester Cathedral of 1350–60 referred to earlier. Patterns gave way to drawing, and narrative became the essential basis for glass art, not with the brilliant intensity of colour of the French, but with the bright light of the clear glass base. York Minster contains a masterpiece of this period in John Thornton's east window of 1405–08.

The fourteenth century saw more than changes in style and technique, however; it also saw the development of a much more organized profession. By the early fourteenth century, crown glass was being made in large quantities in Rouen, and between 1300 and 1400,

England saw the establishment of glass production across the country: from Bath and Exeter in the west to Canterbury in the east, from Chester, York and Lincoln in the north to Chichester and Lewes in the south, and in London, too, at Westminster and Southwark. By the end of the century, the position of King's Glazier had been created.

The sixteenth century saw the climax, and the end, of the great age of Gothic. The Gothic style, rooted in the Christian church, dominated the architecture of northern Europe for over 300 years, but the essentially secular Italian Renaissance was eventually too powerful a force to be resisted.

Before we move to the developments in architecture, and of glass, in the Renaissance, it is worth looking in some detail at one of the last great monuments of Gothic architecture and its achievements in glass and stone; King's College Chapel in Cambridge, where the glazing was completed by successive King's Glaziers, Barnard Flower and Galyon Hone, both Flemish. King's College Chapel was a great church commissioned by a King for a college, not by a bishop for a cathedral, and it is the ultimate distillation of the stone frame architecture initiated by Abbot Suger some 300 years earlier.

The foundation stone of the Chapel was laid in 1446 by Henry VII, the beginning of a prolonged construction period extending well into the next century, with structural completion in 1515, after the Wars of the Roses and in the reign of Henry VIII. It took three years

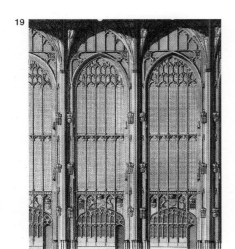

19

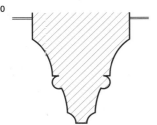

20

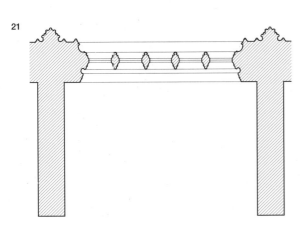

21

19. King's College Chapel, Cambridge, 1446–1547, elevation.

20. King's College Chapel, section through mullion at 1:5. The mullions are carved from rectangular sections of stone to produce a width of 250 mm, with a depth to the glazing of 285 mm, reduced at the extremity to a front face of 30 mm. This fine vertical edge gives the building a remarkable appearance of delicacy.

21. King's College Chapel, plan through a typical bay.

longer to build than Chartres, with the glazing not completed until 1547. The size of the windows in the Chapel demonstrate both the challenge which the architects gave to the glaziers and stained-glass artists, and the tremendous architectonic language which, in a sense, replaced the programmatic significance of the stained-glass iconography in an increasingly secular and educated age. These windows, coming at the end of the first age of glass architecture, represent a glorious climax.

The structural frame comprises piers at about 7.2 m centres supporting a vault with a span of about 13 m, and a height to the top of the vault of 24.4 m. The simplicity of the spatial (and functional) programme gave a plan and section without the complexity of a cathedral, and provided an opportunity for great elemental clarity. The twelve structural bays comprising the north and south elevations are each divided into five panels by thin stone mullions. Below these, the twelve side chapels are each divided into two parts, each of which is, in turn, divided into four panels. The height from the ground to the top of the window arches is about 20.6 m.

The ends of the building are expressed not in rose windows or demonstrative portals, but in windows which simply state the section – a large one to the east, an even larger one to the west – filling the whole width of the elevation.

The east window is divided in half horizontally, and the subjects are taken straight across the stone mullions –

pictorial panellization has gone. Traditional iconography persists in the side windows, but the great west window was originally in plain glass. One cannot see out of the building, other than by looking up, because of the side chapels; and yet the building is flooded with light, both white and coloured.

King's College Chapel is even more remarkable when seen in the context of the glass industry which served it. While English architecture up to this time was amongst the most glorious of the Gothic Age of glass, it was produced without the benefit of a genuinely indigenous coloured-glass industry of any significance. From Vitrearius onwards, French and Flemish craftsmen provided the skills required. The quality of continental glass was so high that what little English manufacturing there was, withered. A typical specification for a building of any importance required 'Glasse beyond the seas and with no Glasse of England'.

In 1547, the first influx of Venetian glass-makers arrived in England, and it is thought that these London-based Venetians created the first lead glass in 1557. The Venetians did not make permanent homes in England, however, and it was not until 1567 that a licence was granted to enable English glass to be made by settlers from Lorraine. They gave us the terminology that is still used in glass manufacturing technology, and created an industry which was to be wonderfully exploited by the new architecture to come.

We sometimes tend to think of Gothic culture, art and architecture as a 400 to 500-year phenomenon, stretching from the time of the early abbey churches and cathedrals to the early sixteenth century and the King's College Chapel. In fact, of course, seen in the total European historical context, and as stated at the beginning of this brief review, it held centre-stage for a much shorter time. Only 200 years separates Abbot Suger's pulling together of the strands of European medieval art and architecture to produce early Gothic in northern France, and the beginnings of the Renaissance in Italy. After these 200 years, a sort of 'two-speed' Europe developed, as Gothic moved from its Early to High to Late phases (eventually to Perpendicular in England), and as the Renaissance metamorphosed from the early classicism of Brunelleschi and Alberti to the exuberance of the Baroque. Michelangelo was painting the ceiling of the Sistine Chapel at the same time King's College Chapel was being completed. This uncoupling of the architectural development of the Mediterranean and northern Europe was accompanied by technical resonances in terms of structure and enclosure, and the whole conceptual basis for buildings, which in time led to the differences between Robert Smythson and Palladio at the end of the sixteenth century. Only when the writings of Serlio and Palladio reached England, to be picked up by architects such as Inigo Jones, did European architecture begin to recohere.

the secular inheritance

In England, a shift in the balance of patronage began to take place with the age of the Tudors, in which glass became as important an inspiration to secular clients as it had been to abbots and bishops. As the new Elizabethan age dawned, and as time and secularization progressed, so did the use of glass by all who could afford it, as well as the reputation and social standing of the highly exclusive, secretive glass-makers. A new, indigenous industry began to develop to serve the new clients, founded by immigrant Flemish settlers.

England in the sixteenth century was one of the foremost powers in a Europe complicated by the struggles of the time between the great nations, their wealth and the navies that promoted the expanding exploration and colonization of the globe. In England, with its comparatively developed democracy and its wealthy aristocracy, the already operating breadth of patronage provided an ideal basis for architectural expansion. Combined with its northern climate, and its remoteness from the Renaissance developments further south, it was a natural place for the evolution of an independent strand of architecture. It was here, the country of Perpendicular Gothic, that a new glass architecture emerged.

While the spread of window glass throughout Europe was extensive for all those who could afford it, in England it generated a new architectural morph-ology. A prime example, Hardwick Hall, near Mansfield on the Derbyshire-

23

Nottinghamshire border, comes down to us both as a building which is an apogee of Elizabethan architecture, and as an aphorism: 'Hardwick Hall, more glass than wall' is a perfect example of the way in which architecture was used at the end of the sixteenth century in England to represent success and wealth in the most flamboyant possible way – it was the Lloyd's Building of its time. It demonstrates also the importance of architecture and, quite distinctly, of building to an Elizabethan aristocrat such as Elizabeth, Countess of Shrewsbury, 'Bess of Hardwick', its famous patron.

Hardwick's architect, Robert Smythson, was a stonemason turned surveyor who had already worked extensively on Longleat between 1572 and 1580, and on major buildings in the Midlands. In 1580, he had moved to Wollaton just outside Nottingham, and created Wollaton Hall for the Willoughby family, and five years later he produced a brilliant remodelling of Worksop Manor for the Earl of Shrewsbury.

22. Hardwick Hall,
Derbyshire, 1590–7,
Robert Smythson.

23. Wollaton Hall,
Nottingham, 1580,
Robert Smythson.

24. Worksop Manor,
Nottinghamshire,
completed 1586, Robert
Smythson.

25. Town Hall, Antwerp,
1561–6, Cornelis Floris.

24

Both Wollaton and Worksop (the latter was sadly destroyed by fire) exemplify the glass and stone architecture in which Smythson grew to excel. Hardwick Hall may have been 'more glass than wall', but much of Worksop Manor was effectively a glasshouse. The fenestration in a significant proportion of its elevations was designed effectively to remove any semblance of masonry wall. Most of the main elevation consisted of enormous windows separated by the thinnest possible mullions. Both flat and curved configurations of glazing were used, much of which had no visible means of support. The idea of the window as a hole in the wall is mostly absent, as were the Renaissance principles of composition which went with such an idea. There is no sign of classical orders, or of the serenity of contemporary Italians.

This glass architecture was an unashamed celebration of wealth and technique. Glass, still a precious commodity, was readily available to the Earl of Shrewsbury, the owner of the Wingfield glassworks, and Robert Smythson exploited it – and the prestige given by its use – with the skill of a virtuoso. Even with the constraints of the small pane size which resulted from the production method, the glassiness of Worksop Manor was its prime visual characteristic.

Compared with Worksop, the new Hardwick Hall was a calm and composed building. However, 400 years after its construction it still creates a tremendous impression. Although less than forty per cent of its elevation is glazed, the glazing still constitutes the principal element in the building's expression, making it almost appear to be stone framed. The dominance of the glazing is not simply the result of a desire for spatial continuity, view and light, but of a wish to maximize the glass area, almost at any cost, with external symmetry as the main ordering principle. One window spans vertically across two floors; some of the chimney structures are removed to the interior of the building to avoid their appearance on an outside wall, but others are concealed behind false windows.

In thermal terms, the occupants paid an environmental price for this obsession with glass. Francis Bacon wrote about the poor winter and summer conditions in houses such as Hardwick, and winter particularly must have been appalling in the New Hall, as it sat on top of its hill, taking the full force of the cold wind. The occupants' answer was usually to decamp from

one part of the house to another in accordance with the season. For the owners, this matter of comfort was worth it, for the sake of the splendour of the extravagant use of glass and, no doubt, for the light the huge windows pulled from the often grey English skies.

The glassy ostentation of private buildings such as Hardwick was matched by public architecture being created at the same time in the Low Countries. The Town Hall in Antwerp was designed by Cornelis Floris (who was twenty years older than Robert

25

Smythson), and was built between 1561 and 1566. Reduced to its architectonic essentials, its front elevation comprises a simple stone frame with huge windows. Its form and detail demonstrate the knowledge the architect had of Italian Renaissance morphology, with its arched rusticated ground floor, and its ornate centrepiece. The predominance of its glazed area over the stone structure, however, proclaims its northern location and hunger for light, and its affinity with the English architecture of the same period.

26

26. The Villa Rotonda, near Vicenza, c 1566–70, Andrea Palladio. It is not part of conventional analysis of historical architectural morphology to refer to climate and environmental design, but the form and configuration of the Villa Rotonda, built at the same time as Antwerp Town Hall, and a little before Smythson's work, demonstrates the different pre-occupations of their architects. The Villa Rotonda is characterized by shaded colonnaded porticos and small windows.

27. The Queen's House, Greenwich, London 1616 onwards, Inigo Jones. Buildings such as this, with its true Italian Renaissance composure, effectively terminated the English exuberance of the previous century, with its love of rich detail and glass.

27

Floris visited Italy, and the reciprocal visits the Italians made to Antwerp to buy cloth for the Sistine Chapel were symptomatic of the forthcoming reunion of southern and northern architecture in Europe.

The story of the origins of Hardwick Hall demonstrates how, in sixteenth century England, great projects were generated, and how the stylistic attitudes in this part of northern Europe were so different from those in Renaissance Italy, for example, where Palladio and Vignola were producing an architecture based on a completely different set of stylistic and cultural imperatives. Even while Hardwick was being designed and built, however, the independent lines of development of English and, to a lesser extent, other northern European architecture were coming to an end.

Sebastiano Serlio had written his *Tutte l'Opere d'Architettura* in 1537, and Palladio his *I Quattro Libri dell'Architettura* in 1570. Both these works, which became widely translated and available, contributed to the spread of the principles of architecture developed in the Italian Renaissance, and the comparative independence and vivacity of English architecture came to an end with the work of Inigo Jones. Jones had been in Italy just after 1600 and his entirely different approach changed English architecture completely. We have only to compare the classical calmness and serenity of the Queen's House at Greenwich of 1616 with the Smythson work of just twenty years earlier to see the change.

the consolidation of technique

The arrival of Italian Renaissance architectural thinking in northern Europe wrought a radical and irreversible change in architectural morphology. As the sixteenth century came to an end, the powerful impact that glass had on late Gothic, English Elizabethan and Jacobean, as well as Dutch architecture as a significant part of the conceptual thinking behind it (what might be called the architectonics and the deriving of form), gave way to the consideration of the material as part of a broad syntax, in which the quality of manufacture became more important than the part it played in building elevations. The use of glass became less a conceptual driving force, and more a matter of the incorporation of a quality product into an overall programme.

This subordination of glass, as it became incorporated in the new morphology, was paralleled by its spread into the improvement of building generally, and not only for the very rich. It is inevitable, in a book which relates the inspirational and technical impact of a material on a field of human endeavour such as architecture, that the story is told in terms of the peaks of achievement. The charting of the way in which glass has periodically driven architecture to great conceptual heights must not, however, lead to a disregard for the increasing use of glass in more commonplace buildings. The extension of glass use is similar to the development of the computer in our own century, from the high-powered, large and expensive machine to the spread of the pocket calculator and desktop computer. As with the computer, not only did the expanding market represent the democratization of glass and its delivery of the controlled transparent enclosure; it also contributed to the all-important, self-sustaining spirals of price reduction, quality and availability. This is a characteristic phenomenon in the incorporation of technology and innovation into design and the market it serves, and one of the more cheerful lessons that history has to teach us: the preserve of the rich in one generation is the commonplace of the next. The quantum leaps in the use of glass in architecture are only oscillatory peaks in an ever-upward curve which describes the development of the window. It is too simplistic to consider glass in architecture in the sixteenth and seventeenth centuries as the preserve of the Palace and 'Prodigy' House. Sansovino reported the sixteenth century claim that every house in Venice had glass; furthermore, in more northern climates, glass was becoming a generally available commodity.

Venice was the great and early home of the drive for quality, and its place in the history of glass has already been referred to. While the northern Europeans were creating their architecture of glass in the great age of Gothic, the Venetians were enhancing the product to new levels of quality, and the guild of glass-makers was founded in 1291, on the island of Murano. The use of the island was originally related to the avoidance of the fire risk, but was to serve the Venetian glass-makers well as they guarded their art. The Venetians not only possessed great skills at forming glass, they also improved its transparency with their use of pyrolusite. The manganese content of this mineral oxidizes iron and produces very clear glass, until it oxidizes itself to produce the characteristic purple seen in old glasses in Belgium and the Netherlands.

By the end of the fourteenth century, Venetian glass was being brought into northern Europe, as signified by the permission given by Richard III for importing duty-free glass from Venetian ships in the Port of London, a permission renewed by Henry IV in 1400. The spread of the Venetians north and west was accelerated after the capture of Constantinople by the Turks in 1453. Dwindling trade with the east pushed the Venetians northwards, leading to a domination by them of high-quality glass-making until the end of the seventeenth century. The Venice of the early sixteenth century was one of the greatest cities in Europe, a centre for architectural magnificence as much as for glass. Sansovino became chief architect to the city in 1529, and was joined in 1530 by Sanmicheli, who subsequently became the city's chief engineer. At the time the late Gothic windows were going in to King's College Chapel in Cambridge, Sansovino was building his library of San Marco, completing the Piazza. It was in this Venice that Sansovino recorded the proud and universal use of glass. The incomparable Venetian glass-makers not only served their own city, but quickly

28. Medieval glass-making. This print is from an eleventh century manuscript, showing glass blowing. It probably originates from a German manuscript dating from the ninth century. The three parts of the process which characterize all glass-making can be seen in the design of the kiln: the furnace itself at the bottom, the melting pots in the centre, and the annealing (cooling) chamber at the top.

29. Fifteenth century glass-making in Bohemia. This shows the whole glass-making process. At the back is a man digging sand. Ash flux and fuel are being carried in baskets and sacks. At the right of the front of the picture is a boy tending the furnace, and the glass blowers can be seen gathering and blowing the glass. The man on the left is removing the glassware for annealing.

30. Sixteenth century glass-making in Germany. This shows a furnace as described by the scholar Georgius Agricola in his book *De Re Metallica* published in 1556. The furnace is again in three parts, with the entry to the annealing chamber presumed to be at the back. Marketing seems to be going on in the building behind.

installed themselves wherever they could. Thus, although eight Muranese workers had to be held in England in 1550 on the pretext of having debts, by 1575 a twenty-one year licence had been granted to Giacopo Verzelini to make drinking glasses in Broad Street in London.

This internationalization of glass-making was not just restricted to the Venetians. Jean Carre of Antwerp obtained a similar licence to make window glass in England under Elizabeth I in 1565, conditional upon his training of local English glass-makers. His workers settled in the south of England, probably to make the brilliant crown glass. As fuel for the furnaces became exhausted, the industry moved west into Hampshire, Somerset, and up through Gloucester to Staffordshire – much to the chagrin of the English craftsmen who competed for it. Paul Tyzack, one of Carre's contractors, founded the famous

Stourbridge industry, and may have been the first to use to coal furnaces.

The spread of glass-making throughout Europe, and the comparatively free trade in products and skilled craftsmen, ensured both an increase in the sophistication of the market as quality became widespread, and the increase in its size as a larger number of less wealthy people wanted glass for their houses. A significant aspect of the new architectural vocabularies of the seventeenth century, whether for a Renaissance palace or a humbler home, was the need for simple sheets of high-quality glass to replace the existing subdivision of the window into small sheets of often uneven and questionable quality.

This drive for quality produced responses in the glass-maker, and the sixteenth and seventeenth centuries saw new efforts in the industry to make a better product. In the sixteenth century, the choice in window glass remained that between spun glass, known as crown, and blown cylinder glass, known as broad sheet. Although the skills deployed were much greater, this was essentially the same choice that lay open to the cathedral builders in the eleventh and twelfth centuries. Of the two, crown was generally considered the superior product: in the middle of the century, crown from Normandy was chosen for the glazing of the windows in the Escorial Palace in Spain, beating competition from Spain, Burgundy and Lorraine. As discussed earlier, the advantage in spun over blown cylinder glass lay in its brilliance, and (given a very skilled craftsman) its evenness.

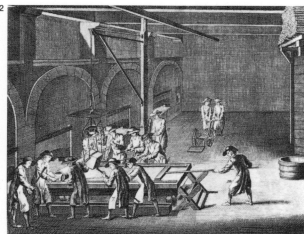

31. Spinning crown glass in the eighteenth century. The upper part of the picture shows the blown bulb after it has been opened, being spun in front of the 'glory hole'. The lower part shows the disc flattened by centrifugal force. The glass was heated at the furnace throughout the process, giving it the characteristic 'fire' finish.

32. Casting plate glass in the eighteenth century. Glass is shown being poured from the square cuvette on to the table below. The width of the sheet is governed by the spacing of the two iron bars on each side of the table. The two men in the back-ground are pushing the trolley used to transport the cuvette from the melting furnace. The roller on the left was used to flatten the glass into a sheet in under a minute. The hot sheet was then pushed into the annealing ovens, seen on the left-hand wall, where they cooled for ten days. Grinding and polishing were then carried out.

33. Venetian glass-making skills, as seen in this mirror, were essential to the creation of perfectly flat glass, until the invention of plate glass in France in the 1680s.

Blown cylinder glass continued to be made in the way described by Theophilus early in the twelfth century. Crown glass, such as the Norman crown used for the Escorial, was also made with the same essential technique handed down over many centuries. As with broad sheet, the first process involved blowing. The viscous glass was pipe-blown whilst its mass was rolled against a slab of stone, iron or wet timber. The combined action produced a pear shape, eventually the shape of a huge ship's decanter. A pointed nipple was formed in the centre of the bottom as the blowing and rolling process went on; the nipple was then attached to the end of an iron rod. The blow pipe end was snapped off by a touch from a cold iron bar. The spinning then began, widening the hole at the end where the blow pipe had been. Spinning the dish, with its rim in the flames, was continued until, suddenly, the rim flipped over to be in the same plane as the flat bottom.

Remarkably, this technique converted the glass into a circular plate of approximately even thickness. More importantly perhaps (in terms of its competition with the cylinder glass) its virtually continuous contact with flames during formation, and the absence of contact with rolling or flattening tables, gave it the characteristic of a fired finish. Once formed, the discs were annealed slowly and carefully in an annealing oven, standing on their edges and separated to permit air flow. By the nineteenth century, this technique

was developed to produce discs nearly two metres in diameter, with remarkably little wastage at about ten per cent. The pane sizes were always, and inevitably, less than those available with cylinder glass, but the fired and unmarked finish often led to preference, particularly in England.

Both the two principal sheet glass methods of production in currency at the end of the sixteenth century, spun and cylinder, had their advantages and disadvantages. The high polish on spun crown came with a limit on size, which did not concern those accustomed to large windows being made up from small panes in lead calms. The larger sheets (up to about 1,300 mm in length) available in blown cylinder were characterized by an uneven thickness and flatness, and a dull, sometimes marked, finish.

33

The expanding markets for carriage windows and high-quality mirrors were not easily satisfied by either technique, however, which, in the case of mirrors, had the effect of bolstering the dominance of the Venetians and other Italians. The making of large mirrors particularly defied the skills of the glass-blowers whose expertise produced the basis both for spun and cylinder glass. The cylinder method could produce something like the sizes called for, but the material was not of high enough quality for the growing sophistication of rich and noble clients. Polishing blown glass was extremely difficult given its intrinsic fragility, and the making of thick flat glass was effectively impossible using blowing because of the weight of the material. Thus it was, in a sophisticated market such as that in England, that while mirrors of reasonable quality were being made at Vauxhall in London in 1620 in the glass factory founded five years earlier by Sir Edward Zouche, the craftsmen making it were, characteristically, Venetian. Zouche had been given a monopoly in glass-making, using coal-fired furnaces, in 1611. Sir Robert Mansell bought this monopoly in 1618, and England saw glass being made for windows in many centres: in Tyneside, Stourbridge and southern Scotland, and still in Broad Street, kept open for 'Venetian' glass.

The spread of glass, and requirement for quality to which this spread contributed, led to an increasingly demanding clientele which had developed a taste for large panes of strong, fine glass; not satisfied by the

34

34. The Palace of Versailles, near Paris, 1669–85, Le Vau and J H Mansart. The development of Versailles was an on-going celebration of the power of Louis XIV. In producing the Hall of Mirrors, J H Mansart trebled the frontage of the building and wonderfully exploited plate glass, the new French invention. The light flooding in through the great windows was amplified by the matching progression of mirrors on the other side of the Hall. Thermal control was less successful – wine and water froze on the dining table in the cold winter of 1695.

thin and distorting crown, brilliant but small in size and fragile, or by the larger 'broad' panes, with their own distortions and imperfect surfaces. A world that had spent centuries perfectly happy with compromise between size and quality, was ready for a new way of fulfilling its increasing demands.

This new way was finally developed in about 1670. In 1665, the King of France, Louis XIV, gave Nicholas du Noyer a monopoly to manufacture flat glass in Orléans. Unfortunately for this initiative, it was based on the skills of craftsmen inevitably imported from Venice, and duly failed when they decided to go back to Murano. The Venetians were not the only glass-makers in Orléans, however; it was also the home of Bernard Perrot, whose family was Italian, from Liguria, but who was himself properly settled in France.

In 1676, the French government gave its support to another initiative to make strong, flat, polished glass; no doubt they were becoming tired of either

importing it, or having to bring in the skills to make it. By 1687, Perrot had developed a process for casting and polishing glass, and a year later his process was published in the French Académie des Sciences.

Despite Perrot's authorship, the King gave sole rights to a favoured lawyer, Abraham Thevart, who brought to Paris the glass-maker Louis Lucas de Nehou from Tourlaville, near Cherbourg in Normandy. The first works of the new venture were on the site of what is now the Musée d'Orsay, but by 1693 the casting tables had been moved to the Château de St Gobain, thus logging a new name in the history of glass manufacture. By 1695, the works had become the Manufacture Royale des Glaces de France, thus receiving the imprimatur of Louis XIV, the King for whom the new Château of Versailles was built as, perhaps, the greatest and most extravagant of palaces.

The new technique, the first innovation in glass-making for many centuries, completely revolutionized the skills needed to make glass. A large pouring pot was heated in the furnace and the molten glass poured into it. The pot was moved with mechanical assistance over to the casting table and poured into the mould which had been prepared. (The casting table was originally made of masonry with a copper top, until the stronger cast iron was introduced in the middle of the nineteenth century.) The mould was made specifically for each piece of glass using iron bars; the thickness of the iron bars set the thickness of the glass. The

treacly mass was then rolled with a heavy copper or iron cylinder. The resulting hot glass plate, once set, was taken to an annealing oven where it stayed for several days. The temperature of the annealing oven was gradually reduced until the plate reached room temperature. This simple, and very economical process produced plates of any required size and thickness, without the inherent constraint implicit in the spun crown or blown cylinder process. However, the glass surface was marked by the contact with the copper table surface and the roller. This necessitated the complicated part of the process, grinding and polishing.

Polishing was a technique known to the cylinder glass-makers, who used it to remove the blemishes caused by the flattening process. However, giving a fine surface to a cast plate necessitated much more complicated techniques, and a great deal more time. The cast plate was laid on a bed of plaster of Paris, supported on stone slabs. Above this was mounted a wheel, to the underside of which were cemented small pieces of glass. The mounting of the wheel above the table had to be set perfectly to ensure that they were parallel with each other. As the wheel was spun above the plate, water and sand were poured into the interface, using gradually finer sand as the grinding proceeded. Polishing was then carried out using jewellers' rouge (hydrated ferric oxide powder). When polishing was finished, the glass was turned over and the reverse side treated in the same way.

It may be imagined how long this process took, and how much skill was needed to avoid breaking the glass, or damaging its surface. This more than offset all the advantages gained from the cheap casting process itself, and the product was very expensive, particularly so until steam power was introduced at the end of the eighteenth century.

While it is perhaps stretching a principle to claim that the creation of polished plate glass was a result of a client demanding a product, it is true to say that the Versailles of Louis XIV made wonderful use of the new material. At Versailles we see the French version of the English houses of Smythson, built by an immensely ambitious and powerful monarch. Here, unlike at Hardwick or Longleat, it is subordinated to the discipline of ordering of the Italian Renaissance, but glassy it certainly is. Norberg-Schulz has described Versailles as a glass house, linking the transparent structures of the Gothic Age to the great iron and glass buildings of the nineteenth century. It is symptomatic of the disposition of Louis XIV that the most significant use of glass in this most sumptuous of all palaces was in the Hall of Mirrors. Louis minister, Colbert, tried unsuccessfully to import Venetian glass-makers to make the mirrors; two of them died mysteriously. Despite this, the remarkable glass room was completed and, with its huge windows overlooking Le Nôtre's gardens and its echoing line of arched mirrors, it is surely one of the greatest rooms in Europe.

France was not alone in having patrons who were willing to pay for the new material, and the period saw the

35. The new wing at Hampton Court, 1689–96, Sir Christopher Wren. The fenestration of the new building was designed in accordance with conventional hierarchies, with the largest panes in the central part, and with a reduction in pane size elsewhere. The large sizes in the centre, however, are a manifestation of the architectural potential of plate glass, just as the smaller sizes are an acceptance of its cost.

migration of all techniques, both the improved traditional methods and cast plate.

In 1692 the Company of Glassmakers, founded only a year earlier, was advertising 'all sorts of exquisite looking-glass plates, coach glasses, sash and other lustrous glass for windows and other uses'. Its speciality was the new cast plate. Although very expensive, there was a market for it, such as for the mirrors at Chatsworth installed in 1687. Its quality made it a sign of status and it was, therefore, naturally used in the larger windows in Christopher Wren's new apartments at Hampton Court installed between 1689 and 1696. The biggest panes here, many of which still survive, measure 750 mm by 245 mm. It is worth noting, however, that the high cost of the new cast plate meant that it was only used for eighty-four of the windows in Hampton Court, at a cost of £4,600; 250 were glazed in crown, at a much cheaper rate, costing £600. The use of glasses with such a large price differential is a measure of the cost of the new glass, and of the value placed on it.

Certainly both Versailles, designed by Le Vau in 1669 with additions by J H Mansart in 1678, and Christopher Wren's new Wing at Hampton Court, exemplified the use to which improved glass technology could be put in providing very large windows, just as they demonstrated how the Italian Renaissance had taken root in northern Europe.

In England, by this time, the rich and noble were not the only people to

35

benefit from the increasing availability of glass. Manufacturing advances, such as the coal-fired reverberatory furnace, contributed to the large-scale extension of the glass market in England between 1670 and 1700. During this period glass became almost universally available across the social scale, with glass being sold in a variety of price ranges; twelve different types were available in 1700.

At the top end of the market remained Norman crown, which was used in addition to cast plate in the new type of wooden sliding sash windows installed in the royal palaces of the period. Given its value and prestige, it is not surprising that English manufacturers became trained so proficiently. In 1679, Henry Richards went to France specifically to learn the art of crown glass-making for the newly

invented sash windows, and by 1684 English commercial crown was being made at Bankside, Southwark in London by John Bowles's company.

Cylinder glass, too, was made in better qualities in England at this time, and John Evelyn reported a visit he made to the Vauxhall Works in September 1676. He claimed that the blown plates he saw there were superior to those imported from Venice. In the early 1690s, the Vauxhall plant moved over to the new French casting process, thus providing the English market with an industry producing every type of glass.

The eighteenth century saw the new and improved materials assume a natural place in the architecture of the time. Glazing and fenestration became simply part of the overall assembly of the external wall, expressed as a hole in it rather than as a membrane filling the space between structural members. More significantly, perhaps, in technical terms, the window had not only to be of a sufficient size, it also had to open. Size was a function in the need for light and view; the commentator Isaac Ware, in his *A Complete Body of Architecture* of 1756, said that 'as much glass should be seen, and as nearly a continued body as possible'. When the problem of opening is added to this ambition for size, the side-hung casement presented problems.

The invention of the vertically sliding sash window overcame the problem in side-hung windows of weight and hinging. The problem of weight was, of course, exacerbated by the new glasses, particularly cast plate. With the vertically sliding sash, northern Europeans could have large windows, glazed with strong glass in large panes, and still be able to open them. Just as important perhaps, the new window could be opened a small amount for ventilation in wet weather without much risk of letting the rain inside.

The issue of size was critical, and Sir William Chambers, writing his *Treatise on Civil Architecture* in 1759, set out the concerns as he saw them. 'The first consideration with regard to windows,' he says, 'is their size, which depends on the climate and the extent of the rooms they are to light.' Chambers refers to Palladio's rules, that the width of the window should be between one-fifth and one-quarter of the width of the room, with a height twice and one-sixth

their width. Palladio had realized the problems created by different room sizes, of course, and proposed that all the windows of any particular floor should be the same size; he suggested, as a compromise in illumination terms, that window sizes should be based on rooms whose length-to-breadth was in the ratio of five:three (one of his favoured harmonic proportions). Thus deep rooms are the basis for window sizes.

Having considered window width, Chambers went on to expound the Palladian view on the space between windows, suggesting that the interval should be between the window width itself, and twice this as a maximum in 'dwelling houses', partly to ensure that the rooms are 'sufficiently lighted', and partly to avoid the house looking 'like a prison'. This advice on proportion extends through to the glazing within the window, which should be three panes wide and four panes high. The problem with these proportional rules is that they could be at odds with another of Chambers's recommendations. As he said: 'The purpose for which the building is intended should likewise be considered, and regulate the quantity of light introduced. In dwelling houses, and all places where pleasure is the main purpose, there cannot be too much.'

As Raymond McGrath (who refers to these quotations) has pointed out, the problem with Palladian fenestration is that it suited the Italian climate more than a northern European one, where light was at a greater premium. The actual glazed area in Palladian windows could be quite small, requiring graphic

compensation in the form of large architraves and surrounds to produce suitably generous features on the elevations. In England at this time, the strict principles of the Palladians were leavened by the Georgians, who were (in true English style) far more relaxed and pragmatic. With the Georgians, the sash window became more refined, so by the Regency period of the early nineteenth century, glazing bars had been reduced from the early two inches (50 mm) to about half an inch (12 mm) in width.

The graphic, and sometimes practical problem of the vertical sliding sash window was the necessary horizontal framing member half way up it. A ventilating opening window designed to slide vertically was essentially two windows sliding past each other, and a horizontal member, which provided a meeting line for the frames, often inevitably occurred at eye level, below door head height. The sliding sash did not lend itself to use for doors at all, of course, which also presented problems for ground floors and upper storey balcony access (not necessarily a large problem in a cool and sometimes rainy climate). The French overcame this by widely ignoring the vertically sliding sash, and adopting the *croisé* window. This comprised a pair of inward-opening glazed doors with a fixed or opening light above. A pair of louvred shutters allowed the windows to open in hot weather while providing control of glare and solar penetration. These two window types formed the basis for fenestration in European architecture from the early eighteenth

century onwards, each with its own advantages and disadvantages, but each adopted to suit the climate to a degree, and each exploiting the continuously improving quality of glass available, and the glass sizes that could be produced.

The eighteenth century saw great oscillations in terms of popularity of use between crown, broad and plate glass. In England for example, the sash window was linked to the gradual commercial supremacy of crown glass. In 1730, cylinder 'broad' glass was the material most commonly used. However, despite continental technical improvements, by 1780 only half as much broad as crown glass was being made. The dominance of crown lay in the local skills available to make it and, more significantly, on the imposition of an excise duty system in 1746. This duty distorted the use of glass in England for a hundred years. Perhaps most significantly, casting seems to have all but disappeared by about 1750, giving a new lease of life to blown plate, which was being made in ever-increasing sizes. By this time, the normally accepted maximum size of blown plate was about one metre square (taken from a cylinder with a diameter of just over 300 mm). However, in 1773 the Cookson Company of Tyneside was making plates 84 in by 52 in (2,135 mm by 1,320 mm), well beyond this size, and very expensive: a plate 60 in by 40 in (1,530 mm by 1,015 mm) cost £35.10s in around 1775, or about £24 per square metre.

The difficulty of producing blown plate in sizes beyond one metre square by the cylinder method then led to a renewal of cast plate manufacture in England, only twenty-five years after its virtual disappearance, to resist the importing of French cast, which was producing import bills of up to £100,000 per year in value by 1770. The British Cast Plate Glass Manufacturers company was formed in 1773, at Ravenhead, Lancashire. Skilled artisans were brought in from France to assist in the creation of an indigenous English cast plate industry for the second time in a hundred years.

This time, the technique took root properly. In this context it is one of the great ironies of glass history that the glass for I M Pei's Pyramids at the Louvre (which had to be cast rather than produced by the float process, because of its unique water-white mix) could be cast in France, but had to be ground and polished in St Helens, Lancashire, the only place in Europe which still had the old 1930s automatic grinding and polishing machines.

In 1789, a steam engine was introduced to grind and polish the plates, and in 1792 new management consolidated manufacture and large-scale production. By 1794, polished plate glass was offered to the British public in a vast range of sizes, from 6 in by 5 in (152 mm by 127 mm) to 75 in by 117 in (1,905 mm by 2,972 mm), in prices ranging from 5d to a staggering £404.12.0 per plate. This latter price was a measure of what the sophisticated upper end of the English market was prepared to pay, not necessarily for a window pane, but more likely for a piece of fine quality glass for a mirror.

36. The Palm House, Royal Botanical Gardens, Kew, London, 1845–8, Richard Turner and Decimus Burton.

Eighteenth century Europe saw enormous advances in the technique of making glass, of the windows which it went into, and of mirror work which relied on it. However, eighteenth century architecture is, to a large degree, dominated not by technology and materials, but by the formal preoccupations of the Italian Renaissance which took root in as many different guises as there were cultures and climates to nourish it. The importance of the window in all this was, of course, paramount as the primary element in elevations, which is why it occupied such an important place in the canon of Palladio. But the glazing was subordinate to the overall design, and fenestration became an elevational device. In the word fenestration is the clue to the attitude of the seventeenth and eighteenth century architects and their patrons. Fenestration was one of the principal elements of elevational pattern making, along with the orders, the hierarchical disposition of rustication and fine ashlar, and the arrangement of columns, porticos and pediments. One cannot use the term fenestration to describe the glazing of King's College Chapel or Chartres Cathedral, while the work of Smythson was virtually entirely fenestration.

However, at the same time as glass was being perfected and subordinated to form part of Renaissance regulation and form making, it was being put to another use in northern Europe, which was to revolutionize our attitude to it.

the conservatory

The development of the conservatory, from the end of the sixteenth century to the middle of the nineteenth century, is one of the important stories of Western architecture. The conservatory brought together two strands of horticultural thinking; the wish to 'over-winter' plants, and to preserve and exhibit the trophies of oceanic exploration. The difference between the two is fundamental. Failed over-wintering simply leads to trying harder next time. Failed 'hospitality' for an exotic stranger may lead to an irretrievable loss in scientific or prestigious investment: the control of the environment in such a case is critical. The creation of the large glass buildings as homes for plants became a celebratory experience which was to transform architecture, particularly as their social significance became clear.

The idea of growing plants out of season, or away from their natural habitat, is very old, and indeed was an early Roman practice. The use of glasshouses to foster plant growth was certainly current in the Middle Ages. McGrath quotes a letter of 1385 relating that 'at Bois le Duc … they grow flowers in glass pavilions turned to the south'. However, it was not until the sixteenth century, the time of Hardwick and Antwerp Town Hall, that the idea of over-wintering delicate plants under glass was developed, in Italy as well as the Netherlands and England. The great explorers, such as Sir Walter Raleigh (who has the reputation for bringing both tobacco and the potato to Europe), brought plants back from their voyages; and Raleigh himself,

whose voyages took place in the 1580s, imported orange seeds to England to be planted on the estate of Sir Francis Carew in Surrey: growing in an unprotected environment, they died in the hard winter frost of 1739–40.

By 1587, Leyden University Botanic Garden was founded in the Netherlands to provide a home to plants and seeds from the East Indies. Unfortunately, its glazed wintering gallery faced north – the principles of passive solar energy and the 'greenhouse effect' were yet to be learned. However, the idea of the warmed conservatory, originating in the Roman 'forcing houses' of Martial and Columella, was reborn. During the seventeenth century, many Dutch forcing houses were built to the Leyden pattern, often with proper glasshouses.

The early ideas of collecting exotic plants were as much related to the exhibiting of wealth as to the scientific examination and conservation of species, and it is in this distinction that the creation of the conservatory as an important architectural form derives its significance.

Edible fruits were particular prizes and the importance of preserving exotica is evident in the orangery. A curious fascination for the orange developed in European aristocracy, and by 1620 Salomon de Caus had designed his orangery for the Elector Palatine in Heidelberg. His idea was simple and two-fold: to build a timber and glass shelter, about 85 m by 15 m, for over 400 trees for erection each Michelmas (at the end of September), and to keep them warm during the winter using four

37

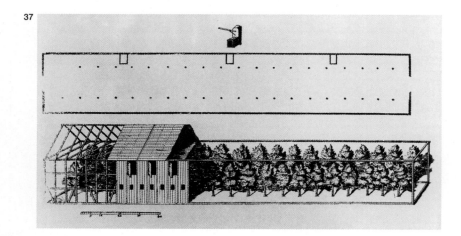

37. Orangery for the Elector Palatine, Heidelberg, Germany, 1620, Salomon de Caus. The needs of botany provided the incentive for this portable building, an early essay in the idea of the prefabricated structure, capable of being dismantled and re-erected each year.

38. Drawing from *Remarks on the Construction of Hothouses* by J C Loudon, 1817. This was Loudon's proof of the need for conservatory architecture to be derived in accordance to different principles to those used for conventional buildings. The use of scientific method and the analysis of performance to derive construction, underwrites the importance of the conservatory in the development of all architecture in the nineteenth century and onwards.

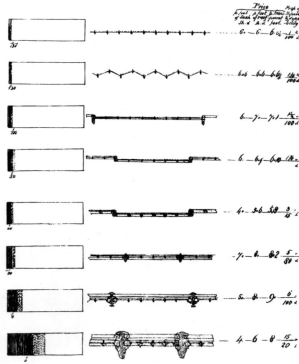

furnaces. At Easter time, the conservatory could be dismantled, leaving the trees uncovered for the summer. Following the success of this building, which gave the Elector a beautiful winter walking space, a permanent building with stone walls was built.

The Dutch made significant developments in the design of glasshouses in the late seventeenth and early eighteenth century. The principal elements of a passive solar energy conservatory were in place in these Dutch forcing frames by the beginning of the eighteenth century; with their massive masonry, high thermal capacity back wall containing heating flues, and sloping glass wall on the south side. The glazing was openable to enable plants to be put in or taken out, and to provide ventilation at times of potential overheating. Crude 'double-glazing' consisted of an inner frame incorporating oil paper. It was with such conservatories that George Clifford set up the controlled gardens at Hartekamp in Holland, where the great Swedish naturalist Linnaeus worked. It was Linnaeus who, with the aid of these early glazed structures, was able to cultivate and classify exotic plants.

The early orangeries or winter-gardens were by no means always dedicated to horticulture. Following the precedent of Salomon de Caus, Christopher Wren, assisted by Nicholas Hawksmoor and John Vanbrugh, designed the Kensington Palace orangery for Queen Anne in 1704. At about the same time, the Duke of Devonshire had an orangery built at Chatsworth where the new and expensive mirrors referred to earlier had been installed. Other great eighteenth century winter-gardens and orangeries include that at Wye House in Maryland, USA, and Richard Bradley's 1718 proposal for an 'Architectural Conservatory' at Cambridge with corinthian columns. Bradley was the Professor of Botany at the University, but still broad-minded enough to promote the benefit of the building for summer parties.

As horticultural experience grew, the advantage of the slope on the glass became evident. The early Dutch forcing frames experimented with almost vertical glass walls, and others set at 30° or less: the flatter angles increased the amount of sunlight (direct or diffused), and although requiring greater protection, they gave great benefit. The importance and advantage of what were effectively glazed roofs gradually became clear. By the middle of the eighteenth century, Philip Miller had initiated and completed the reconstruction of the glass conservatories at the Chelsea Apothecaries Gardens, which had received such support from Sir Hans Sloane in the 1720s. Miller gave the conservatories vertical glass faces and a 45° glass roof. By the time the great J C Loudon was writing in 1817, he was able to categorize types of conservatory design, and comment on glazing and orientation, referring specifically to the desired glass slope for a latitude of fifty-two-and-a-half degrees north, which was 14°30'.

This interest in horticulture and exotic plants might have had no impact on the development of architecture, but it

39

40

41

42

39–43. The international evolution of the conservatory is a fascinating combination of the interests of horticulture and the collection of exotica, overlaid with the differing objectives of private enthusiasm and public amenity and pleasure. The eighteenth century saw practicality and emerging botanical science embodied in the Dutch forcing house.

The architectural pretension of the Orangery is exemplified by the building shown here at Wye House, Mills River Neck in Maryland, United States (39). The Jardin des Plantes in Paris (40) of 1854 and the Great Conservatory at Chatsworth of 1836 (42), demonstrate the international nature of the competition in the nineteenth century to create large glass structures. Turner's Glasnevin Conservatory at Dublin's Botanic

Garden, built in 1847 (41), gives an indication of what was to come at the Palm House in Kew (36), and Hector Horeau's Jardin d'Hiver (43) completed in 1848 showed the effect of subordinating planting to public amenity; it was a clear and acknowledged pointer to the Crystal Palace of three years later.

43

was, in fact, one of the great influences on the change which took place in architectural thinking in northern Europe in the nineteenth century. The strength of this influence was a result of the happy coincidence of patronage and technology. In the age before the flourishing of university botany departments and socially-funded botanic gardens, the clients for the early conservatories were usually the same rich landowners and patrons who were constructing great houses.

Two hundred years after Bess of Hardwick's time, her equivalent in society would be more likely to build a Renaissance palace or villa with a glass orangery; it was from these elegant adjuncts to the main houses that the great glass architecture of the second half of the nineteenth century was to develop. Once the glasshouses had been removed from the realm of pure scientific botany and placed in the world of 'society', appearance began to assume a significant role in their design.

The development of conservatory design in the late eighteenth and nineteenth centuries was a wonderful mixture of gradually formulated science and design intuition, slowly informed by success. A typical early design by Sir George Mackenzie was submitted to the Horticultural Society in London in 1815, in the form of a quarter sphere of 4.5 m radius, set up against a pedimented brick wall. Loudon said he liked the appearance, but he gave the proposal a vigorous scientific criticism, and came up with a 15 m high bell-shaped alternative.

Not only was Loudon quite properly concerned with the science of conserva-

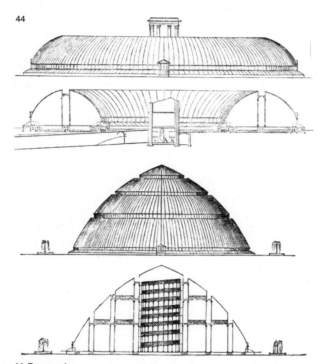

44. Proposed alternatives for the Glasshouse for the Birmingham Botanical Horticultural Garden, 1831, J C Loudon. It is a tragedy of the history of conservatories that many of the greatest examples were either not built, or have been destroyed. The project was never built, but Loudon's preference was for an enormous conical dome over 30 m high.

tories, he was also concerned with how they were made and their architectural significance. His 18 lb wrought-iron glazing bar, which could adopt a curve, steered the newly-developing glass architecture significantly in an important direction. Loudon realized the importance of the manufacturers in his work, and used his own property, Bayswater House in London, to market his innovations. The Bayswater House conservatory was a constructed catalogue of techniques. His originality in understanding the science and construction of glasshouses was matched by an appreciation of their architectural potential. He looked for a new architecture that 'may be beautiful without exhibiting any of the orders of Grecian or Gothic'.

He continued, 'may not therefore glass roofs be rendered expressive of ideas of a higher and more appropriate kind, than those which are suggested by mere sheds or a glazed arcade.'

The first half of the nineteenth century in northern Europe saw the flowering of the conservatory, both as an architectural type of great beauty, and as a form of significance for the future of architecture itself, as the expertise to create the buildings brought a new sort of designer into the profession.

Great architects, such as Nash and Soane in England, Schinkel in Germany and Percier and Fontaine in France, were creating what was conventionally known as 'architecture'. This was the time of the London terraces, the Rue de Rivoli and the Ecole des Beaux-Arts in Paris. However, it was also the time that designer/gardeners, such as Loudon and Henry Phillips in England, Mackenzie in Scotland and Rohault de Fleury and Hector Horeau in France, produced masterpieces in glass architecture which were to lay the formal and technical foundations for a new generation of buildings. These were made to serve not only horticulture and recreation but, more significantly, the need for large covered and daylit spaces which the new industry and commerce was to demand as the century developed into the railway age.

Many of the early examples were private, and built by enthusiasts excited into patronage by the opportunity to house and show off exotic plants, and to provide themselves with glass-covered winter-gardens for walking and entertaining. By the early nineteenth

century, conservatories were popular domestic architectural adjuncts, and many were to be seen in an urban setting in Belgravia, the new smart section of London. Outside London, English conservatories on a more expansive scale could be seen at Alton Towers in Staffordshire and at Syon House just west of the capital.

The adoption by the cultivated elite of a new form of architecture led to many early uneasy stylistic marriages. A conventional architect would instinctively associate architecture with the use of ordained, often neo-classical, grammar. As a result, these early conservatories were often dressed in the prevailing styles of the period. At Alton Towers, for example, the Earl of Shrewsbury employed Robert Abraham to build a large conservatory (and a smaller one), designed very much as a glazed classical building on Bradley's model of a century earlier. The Camellia House below Smythson's Wollaton Hall is similarly designed, as was Jeffry Wyatville's Belton House Orangery in Grantham of 1820.

These 'architectural' glass buildings were a long way from the glasshouses of Loudon, with their much more scientific design basis. In 1827, a large conservatory at Bretton Hall in Yorkshire demonstrated the potential of the Loudon principles of design and construction. The conservatory was taken down in 1832, but Loudon described the building in *An Encyclopaedia of Cottage, Farm and Villa Architecture* of 1832. His description sets out briefly, but perfectly, the key ingredients of the principles behind the design of the building: 'there were no rafters or principal ribs for strengthening the roof besides the common wrought-iron sash bar … This caused some anxiety, for when the iron-work was put up, before it was glazed, the slightest wind put the whole of it in motion from the base to the summit … As soon as the glass was put in, however, it was found to be perfectly strong'. This passage will strike a chord for anyone interested in the history of structures, as well as those tracing the history of glass. Loudon is describing a stressed skin, in which the apparently fragile transparent membrane is the element which gives strength and stability to the frame. The greater significance of this passage can easily be understood when it is seen in the context of the drawing in which Loudon demonstrated the light-transmitting benefit of the new metal glazing bars. At one extreme, we see 'architecture' blocking out light; at the other is shown the minimal and fine detail of an iron-framed membrane. Together these combined to give a new architectural syntax: the fine, light-transmitting frame, working with the idea of the stressed skin, showing the potential of the new glass architecture freed from the baggage of conventional architectural form.

In the two decades between 1820 and 1840, with the influence of innovators such as Loudon, the idea of what constituted a reputable and successful conservatory began to change. There is some confusion about the date of the Bicton Garden Palm House built early in these decades near Budleigh Salterton in Devon. Its date, however, is insignificant

45. The Palm House, Bicton, near Budleigh Salterton, Devon, c 1820–40, architect unknown. This small building, with its astonishingly slender metal support system, demonstrates the potential of the new glass architecture, and the immense skills already developed in minimal structures using glass, by constructors, independently of architects.

45

when considered in terms of its elegance, and importance, as a possibly unconscious conceptual 'trial run' for the great Palm House at Kew.

The building comprises the glass envelope only, terminated at the north end by a brick wall following the profile of the roof. Tiny glazing bars, at about 180 mm centres, flow up and over this roof, holding the overlapping fish-scale pieces of glass: it is only the glazing that keeps the structure stable. The small size of the panes avoids the appearance of faceting, and enables the curved profile of the envelope to be maintained. The structure, and what was hitherto known as 'architecture', is nowhere to be seen. Extremely slender columns support equally insubstantial arches of iron, and the whole support is effectively invisible. The concept is of a glass bubble using the techniques of Loudon, incorporating the curved iron glazing bar, turned into a beautiful envelope by the makers, W & D Bailey, and subsequently by their successors D & E Bailey. The purity of form and construction reads like a truncated

46. The Great
Conservatory,
Chatsworth House,
Derbyshire, 1836–40,
Joseph Paxton. An
early photograph of
the glazing in
progress illustrates
the enormous scale
of the building.

prototype for the later, and much larger, building at Kew. It is a beautifully shaped and constructed, if modest, masterpiece.

It is important to register the crucial contribution made by the constructors in a building such as Bicton; the makers were to have an essential impact on the development of the large span, lightweight buildings which flowed from these early prototypes. Baileys, with or without Loudon, created the first all-glass enclosures of real significance, including the 33 m diameter domed conservatory at Bretton Hall, Yorkshire of 1827.

In 1831, Loudon himself was furthering the cause of the great glass building in his (sadly, unbuilt) proposals for the Birmingham Horticultural Society's Botanical Garden, sited at Edgbaston. The Society's plans were extremely ambitious, and were also intended to be partially self-financing by means of a nursery to satisfy the perceived demand for plants by the public. Loudon produced two optional designs. The cheaper of the two was a large ring of glass; the more ambitious option offered was an amazing proposal for a great pointed dome. Its diameter was to be 200 ft (61 m), and its height of 100 ft (30.5 m) was enough to incorporate a central glass cylinder 30 ft (9 m) in diameter, to contain tall tropical trees. The dome was to be divided into four by radial walls, to produce four different climates.

While Birmingham was promoting its Botanical Garden, a similar venture was being implemented in London, with the creation of the new 'theme park' for the Royal Zoological Society. Edward

46

Cross, the client, employed Henry Phillips to lay out the garden, which opened in 1831. The project included a glass structure proclaimed as the largest conservatory in England. Unfortunately, the gardens are now gone: the conservatory was demolished in 1856, and the area is now built over by the encroaching sprawl of southeast London. Henry Phillips was also at work further south in England, in Brighton. After a false and under-funded start in Brighton in 1827, Phillips's 'Antheum' was eventually built in 1832 in Hove. This glass structure was in the form of an elliptical dome 60 ft (18.3 m) high, comprising cast-iron ribs spanning 170 ft (51.8 m). The building goes down in history as one of the more important elements in the 'learning curve' of the new space-defying structures (rather as the attempts at Cluny Abbey did in the eleventh century).

Inadequately assessed in terms of stability, it relied for its strength and shape on the longitudinal ribs, and on light cast-iron purlins acting as the latitudinal horizontal connecting members. The structure was stable as long as the timber scaffolding below was in place, but clearly needed diagonal bracing to prevent a twisting collapse. This was apparently as clear to the original designer as it would be to an engineer today, but the structure had not been designed to take the weight of the extra diagonals, and the contractor refused to bear the expense of providing them. The removal of the scaffolding resulted in catastrophic and dramatic collapse. When the thirty year old Paxton (already established at Chatsworth for five years),

visited the project in July 1832, it was nearly complete, and must have been inspirational. Two months later it had collapsed, leaving a disastrous object lesson in the dangers of the new lightweight long-span structures.

The new ideas for the designs of winter-gardens were not, of course, restricted to England. The fashion for the form was international, and designers and patrons travelling to and fro across Europe kept an eye on the competition, and ensured that the next venture would be built on what could be learned from the last. Exactly contemporary with the unfortunate Hove structure was the conservatory at the Jardin des Plantes in Paris. Its architect, the aptly named Rohault de Fleury, started the project in 1833, and was sensible enough to the potential difficulties inherent in creating it to make a fact-finding visit to England a year later as the structure progressed. At the same time, Paxton visited the Jardin des Plantes with his employer, the Duke of Devonshire.

Sigfried Giedion, in *Space, Time and Architecture*, refers to the building as 'the prototype of all large iron framed conservatories', and 'the first large structure consisting mainly of iron and glass'. This accolade paid little heed to the earlier English structures, but the building seems to have been a considerable influence on subsequent buildings of the same type in Liège and Ghent. John Hix refers to another project at the Jardin des Plantes which highlights the great significance of the conservatory in architectural development of the mid-nineteenth century. None other than

Gottfried Semper, the great German architectural thinker, proposed a huge portable glass roof for the Jardin.

In 1836, three years after his visit to Paris, Paxton produced his own first great conservatory, at Chatsworth. Like so many of these early glass buildings, the Great Chatsworth Conservatory is no longer there for us to see: having proved too expensive to run, it was tragically blown up in 1920. However, at the time it was one of the most ambitious and beautiful glasshouses, 277 ft by 123 ft (84.4 m by 37.5 m), with a 67 ft (20.4 m) high roof, it contained a world of micro-climates and garden events, with exotic birds in the air and tropical fish in the pools. The micro-climatic aspect of such a building, and the extensive mechanical engineering designed to sustain it, was the key to its success, and fundamental to its importance as a building type. It brings home to us its roots in the imaginations of the great gardener/product designer/constructor/engineers and their patrons. The building was visited by Queen Victoria and Prince Albert in December 1843, which could have done no harm to Paxton's cause during the machinations surrounding the design of the Crystal Palace at the end of the decade.

A comparison between Bicton and Chatsworth, or between the techniques promoted by Loudon and Paxton, demonstrates how different in construction these buildings could be. Unlike Loudon's conservatories, Paxton built his out of laminated timber; unlike Bicton's surface membrane of glass, Chatsworth was glazed with

47. Jardin des Plantes, Paris, 1833 onwards, Rohault de Fleury.

47

the ridge and furrow promoted twenty years earlier by Loudon himself to ensure that the sun was more or less perpendicular to at least one glass surface for much of the day. The furrows also served to collect water and condensation, and were thus an important component in Paxton's later, greater structure in Hyde Park.

The ten years after the completion of the Chatsworth Great Conservatory saw yet more beautiful examples of the nineteenth-century conservatory, and the appearance of new names who were to go on to make considerable contributions to the architecture of the century, as the impact of the new glazed structures made itself felt.

Paxton himself designed and built conservatories at Capesthorne Hall in Cheshire, and Darley House near Chatsworth. Both of these gave him important experience and confidence, as precursors and proving grounds for

his ideas for the Crystal Palace to come. His employer, the Duke, had become president of the Royal Horticultural Society in 1838. Having already built Paxton's Great Conservatory at Chatsworth, he proposed a new conservatory complex on the site he leased to the Society in 1821, and this was started in 1840. It was never completed due to the high cost created by the duty on glass, which was by now acting as a significant brake on the development of glass structures.

Despite this financial hindrance, the mid-1840s saw the perfection of the conservatory, and the creation of projects in Ireland, England and France, as each country produced its own version of the new glass architecture. In France, two winter-gardens were built on the Champs Elysées in Paris. The first proved too prosaic and unambitious for the Parisians, and the architect Hector Horeau designed a replacement to be

erected in 1848. This was 300 ft (91.4 m) long by 180 ft (54.8 m) wide, and 60 ft (18.3 m) high, with a raised peripheral walkway, fountains, cafés and wonderful planting. Horeau designed a similar project in Lyons at the same time. In Ireland, the great engineer Richard Turner was creating his first important projects, based on his Dublin Works. Following his supplying of the cast iron for Charles Lanyon's Belfast Palm House in 1839, he went on to design a Palm House himself at Glasnevin in Dublin in 1842 (see figure 41). This was glazed on the Bicton model, with glass laid in curved planes rather than the ridge and furrow preferred by Loudon and Paxton.

In 1840, the newly 'Royal' Botanic Society asked Decimus Burton to design a winter-garden on its new 18 acre site in the middle of Regent's Park in London. Burton had worked under Nash on the Regent's Park Terraces. He had already developed expertise in conservatory design, having worked on the details and working drawings for Paxton's Great Conservatory at Chatsworth. Burton designed a vast conservatory 315 ft (96 m) long by 165 ft (50.3 m) wide, with timber framing, employing the ridge and furrow configuration for the glazing (as had been used at Chatsworth). After five years of inaction, the timber framing was changed to iron, and tenders invited. Cubitt submitted a price for a timber option, but Turner's tender was in iron and glass, and lower. After some negotiation on the final form, Turner's price was accepted, and the Regent's Park Conservatory was completed by May 1846.

Meanwhile, a dramatic event had taken place which was to have a radical effect on the development of glass architecture in England: in 1845, the duty was removed from glass. This was to have an impact on all uses of glass in buildings, of course, but its most immediate and historic effect on the story of glass architecture was related to two projects which were to happen in the next five years. The greatest and most architecturally significant of these was Paxton's Crystal Palace; but the first was the Palm House at Kew.

Kew Gardens, in west London, had for a century been a horticultural centre with royal connections. Following the decision to build a new palm house, Decimus Burton was approached, and prepared a design proposal in 1844: the director of the Gardens, William Hooker, and the curator, John Smith, objected to the number of columns and rejected the design. Turner then arrived from Dublin with a model and full estimates. The client team was sufficiently impressed to ask him to proceed to full drawings. Burton, who was evidently in a strong enough position to make his influence felt, suggested that improvements could be made, particularly with regard to the inner row of columns, the proportions, and 'Ecclesiastical or Gothic styling'. In 1844, he produced a signed sketch showing the section of the building as he preferred it. Turner, the contract safely in his hands and underway, generously accepted the advice and wrote to the director happily accommodating the change, and duly crediting Burton with the improvement.

48. The Temperate House, Royal Botanical Gardens, Kew, London, 1860 onwards, Decimus Burton. Another enormous glass structure covering over 5,000 square metres. The plan-form, orthogonal geometry, and incorporation of conventional stone architecture at ground level show a marked difference from the curved virtuosity of the Palm House.

49. The Palm House, Royal Botanical Gardens, Kew, London, 1845–8, Richard Turner and Decimus Burton.

With the general arrangement of the building agreed, Turner proceeded to carry out the detailing and fabrication. The result is, to this day, one of the most beautiful experiences to be had in the world of glass architecture – a result of scale, simple form and fine and appropriate detailing.

The building is huge. The overall length is 326 ft 6 in (99.5 m), and the central section 137 ft 6 in by 100 ft (41.9 m by 30.5 m); the height of this section is 63 ft (19.2 m). As usual with such structures, the vital engineering which maintained its interior climate was concealed. Boilers beneath the floor were connected to a coal-yard and chimney 550 ft (167.6 m) away by smoke flues and a railway line for the delivery of coal and the removal of ashes. Although the Palm House is large, it is not so much its size which gives it its impact on the beautiful landscape at Kew, but its form. Whilst the section suggested by Burton has the apsidal shape of the Great Conservatory at Chatsworth, the plan is cruciform, symmetrical on both axes, with a low 'nave' and 'transepts', and a central elongated dome to accommodate the largest trees. The predominance of the lower part of the building enables it to present a form which hugs the landscape at the height of the tree line in the gardens around it.

The structure comprised curved wrought-iron ribs supported on cast-iron columns and brackets, the whole assembly being braced with post-tensioned wrought-iron tie rods, and cast-iron tubes brought into compression by the post-tensioning. Rainwater was taken down the cast-iron columns in the (by now)

conventional manner. The glazing was smooth and in simple curved planes rather than ridge and furrow, with the glass draped over the iron glazing bars, relaxing into a natural curved profile. It is this which gives the Palm House its purity of form: ridge and furrow glazing would have given the building a serrated profile, and presented us with a saw-tooth silhouette in the landscape. As it is, it exists as a perfect model for all such buildings, and a supreme expression of the glass it exploits. From a distance, particularly on a slightly misty morning, it appears as a delicate formal cloud settled mysteriously into the trees; closer to, it can be a reflective machine, or a transparent and almost non-existent bubble.

Turner was both an engineer and a constructor, and it may be fanciful to ascribe too much aesthetic intention to his selection of the smooth Bicton skin for his greatest work. Nevertheless, the result in the Palm House at Kew is still there for us to see. Now re-glazed, it is the apotheosis of the glass conservatory, and is arguably the most beautiful glass structure in the world. As with many such structures, its authorship is complex, and the Palm House had its roots in an earlier project which brought together the two collaborators, the Regent's Park Winter-Garden. The comparison between the Palm House and Burton's later Temperate House, which is twice as big and has much more conventional 'architectural' form, indicates the power of Turner's influence. Turner himself was to go on to produce one of the top three proposals for the Crystal Palace competition, eventually won by Paxton.

The Crystal Palace, and the exhibition which it housed, was the great mid-century manifestation of British industrial pre-eminence. Before we go on to look at it and the buildings which followed it, it is worth reviewing the important changes in the glass industry in Britain which took place in the period between 1800 and 1850.

This period was not only a time when a new realm of formal and constructional potential was opened up in the form of long-span glazed conservatories. It has been argued that the history of flat glass-making in England in this period ranks in importance with the Elizabethan/Jacobean and late Stuart/Baroque periods of 200 years or so earlier. The emergence of iron as a material for use in building from the eighteenth century to the nineteenth, and the general impact of industrialization in England, the birthplace of the industrial revolution, was mirrored by activity in the glass-making industry. The industry which could supply a project like Paxton's Crystal Palace was fundamentally different from that which existed in 1800.

The changes were both organizational and technical, and took place in a continuously varying taxation environment, which itself profoundly affected the nature of glass production and marketing. Moreover, they took place at a time when scientific knowledge was being expanded and clarified, in glass as in all other areas of chemistry. In 1612, the great glass-maker Neri, working in Pisa, Antwerp and Florence, was able to make very clear glass crystal, and he

48

49

knew that manganese was important as a decolourizer. Even he, however, did not understand the function of lime and magnesia. Bradshaw's English recipe book of 1778–9 gave a typical materials content for flint glass; 20 lb of purified potash from wood ashes, 70 lb of red lead, 60 lb of washed sand from Lynn, $\frac{1}{2}$ oz of magnesium oxide and 4 oz of arsenious oxide. Such a mix was still empirical. The next fifty years were to revolutionize ways of thinking about content. In 1787, science had a systematic nomenclature for materials after Lavoisier's work; compounds were given in symbols. This was followed by the work of J J Berzelius in 1808 which led to the adoption of chemical formulae. By 1826, Samuel Parkes was able to write an important historic statement in his *Chemical Catechism*, that: 'The art of making glass is entirely chemical, consisting of siliceous earth with alkali and oxides of lead. The Manufacturer will be enabled on chemical principles to ascertain the exact quantity necessary for any fixed portion of silica.' This statement lays the conceptual foundations for all subsequent glass-making. By 1830, Dumas wrote his article which set out the preferred proportions of glass in terms of durability and ease of manufacture: by weight, one part sodium or potassium oxide, one part of calcium oxide and six parts silica: this equates to six molecular parts of silica, and one part each of sodium oxide, calcium oxide and magnesium oxide. The modern glass mix was thus defined.

As the chemistry was being determined, so the industry was being set up.

51

In England, for example, three large producers emerged providing the 'critical mass' necessary to implement technical change in terms of production technique: Chances of Stourbridge, James Hartley of Sunderland, and Pilkington-Greenhall of St Helens, Lancashire.

Technically, the main change consisted of the slow swing from crown glass manufacture to that of cylinder glass, reversing the trend at the end of the eighteenth century. This was a result not only of technology, but substantially of the coincidence of excise duty reductions and the recession of the 1840s. Excise duty, based on weight, was an important source of government revenue in England from the seventeenth century onwards, increasing by a factor of seven between 1776 and 1808, as the American War of Independence and the Napoleonic Wars were financed. The tax favoured the thinner crown glass, but was gradually reduced from 1819 to 1845, when it was removed altogether. This put sheet glass in a continuously improving position to compete. Furthermore, however hard the crown glass

50–52. The Palm House, Royal Botanical Gardens, Kew, London, 1845–8, Richard Turner and Decimus Burton. The building has recently been reglazed, but was originally clad in a yellowish-green copper oxide glass to prevent sun scorch.

manufacturers tried to increase pane sizes, they were constrained by their own technology. By the middle of the century, discs could be made up to 66 in (1,676 mm) wide or even larger. However, the standard available size remained stuck at around 48–54 in (1,220–1,372 mm). Contemporary cutting guides (such as William Cooper's of 1835) show how panes were limited to 22 in by 14½ in (559 mm by 368 mm).

Crown glass, the material so favoured for the Georgian sash window, was suffering from unacceptable limits in size for a market increasingly interested in large panes, and its artificial price advantage, distorted by excise duty, was being eroded. By 1845, the construction and commissioning of crown glass furnaces had stopped in England, and Pilkington, the last major producers, ceased their manufacture of it in 1872.

A major contributor to this swing to sheet glass from crown was the improvement in its manufacture in Germany in the eighteenth century, and the important refinements made to this in continental Europe and England in the nineteenth century. Following the invention of cast plate glass in France in the seventeenth century, manufacturers were continuously seeking ways of improving the quality of blown plate, so as to avoid the inherent problems of weight, price and finish associated with the cast product. What became known as 'German Sheet' (actually originating in Bohemia in the last quarter of the eighteenth century) was thinner than conventional blown plate, and was not ground and polished after flattening. It was thus cheaper than

the thicker, polished blown plate; but it had a hammered appearance on one side, which caused understandable prejudice.

By the 1830s, new broad glass was available using a larger cylinder than hitherto, created in Lorraine and Germany by swinging the globe of glass in a deep trench. The elongated cylinder extended to between 1.2 and 1.8 m, with a diameter of 300 mm to 500 mm. The resulting opened-out plate could be around 1.5 m², with one dimension potentially even longer. Around this time the English were still hanging on to their beloved, shining, crown glass, with all its limits on size.

Despite this English prejudice, both the Chance and Hartley Companies started to to make large-size blown plate in England in 1832, mainly for export to Europe. Then, in 1838, J T Chance invented his 'Patent Plate' by implementing a technique for polishing blown cylinder glass which was thin enough to be classified under the 'blown plate' definition of the excise regulations. His technique was simple but effective, relying on a wet resilient leather backing to the glass as it was polished. By 1845, Chance was producing 10,000 sq ft (929 m²) a week for mirrors, coach windows and

52

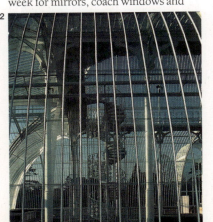

glass to cover pictures.

Also during the 1840s Chance's competitors, Hartleys of Sunderland, developed another type of patent plate by introducing a rolling stage into the traditional French cast plate method. This patent rolled plate could be produced down to a 3 mm thickness, and put Hartleys in a position to be able to bid for Paxton's Crystal Palace at a price only slightly higher than Chance's early version blown broad cylinder glass.

In referring to his glass as 'Patent Plate', Chance was relating his material to the more expensive cast plate, which in England went back to the founding of the British Cast Plate Glass Manufacturers at Ravenhead in 1773. Cast plate was still the only method of making large panes in the early eighteenth century. Ravenhead's production included plates up to 12 ft by 6 ft (3.6 m by 1.8 m). This size compares with the maximum manageable blown plate size of about 4 ft by 2 ft 3 in (1.2 m by 0.68 m). Until the demise of crown glass in England through the first half of the nineteenth century, and the increasing acceptance of patent plate, cast plate was the only material suitable for very large glass panes: larger, that is, than the 22 in by 14½ in (559 mm by 368 mm) crown cuts, or the blown plate panes, which could double both these dimensions, but still not produce a good size mirror. Thus while the Crystal Palace was eventually made of patent plate (selected in competition), a proud exhibit displayed in the building was a cast plate 19 ft by 10 ft (5.8 m by 3 m), a piece equivalent to the largest stock size of float available today.

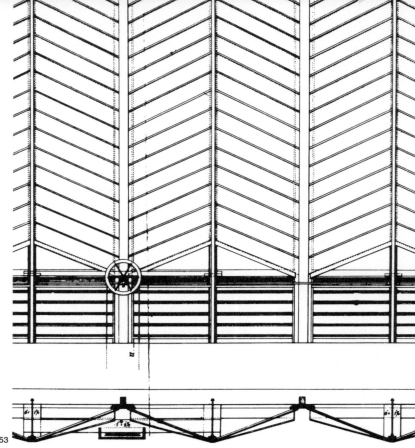

cathedrals of commerce

The story of the Crystal Palace is one of the best known, and most often told, in the canon of western architecture. Its importance in the developing story of glass in architecture is central. Just as the Palm House demonstrates the power of innovative *a priori* thinking in architecture, free of stylistic baggage, so the powerful ingenuity of Joseph Paxton, combined with his political position and skills, was significant in the creation of one of the world's first 'modern' buildings.

In 1845, the Royal Society for the Encouragement of Arts, Manufacture and Commerce (now usually known as the Royal Society of Arts), with Prince Albert as its president, conceived the notion of an international exhibition to celebrate industry and manufacturing. In 1850, a Royal Commission was set up to produce it, and an open competition was initiated; 245 entries were submitted in April of the same year. With the opening date set for 1 May 1851, most of the entries posed problems, notably in terms of speed of execution and ease of removal.

Paxton, an eminent politician and businessman, as well as a gardener, dropped hints in high places that the project was running into potential crisis, and on 11 June produced his own sketch design. Within ten days, a massive brick and iron scheme by Brunel was in the *Illustrated London News*, and Paxton was showing his design to Charles Fox of Fox and Henderson, who were primarily railway equipment manufacturers, and to Robert Lucas Chance, whose blown

53. Detail plan and elevation of the transept roofing of the Crystal Palace.

54. The Crystal Palace, The Great Exhibition Building, Hyde Park, London, 1851, Joseph Paxton with Fox and Henderson.

53

plate had been used in the Chatsworth Conservatory. He had already had the opportunity to show the design privately to Robert Stephenson, one of the Commissioners, on a train journey the same day: Stephenson's reported comment was 'admirable'. On 29 June, Paxton, Fox and Chance agreed to submit a joint bid by 11 July, the tender date.

On 24 June, with Brunel's building already getting a bad press, Paxton showed his designs to Prince Albert, who was impressed. Five days later, the Commission saw it again, but the majority was beginning to feel that 'changing horses' at this stage was difficult, and that they should settle on the design already proposed. Paxton then played yet another good card, and had his own designs published in the *Illustrated London News*. Such was the positive nature of the public reaction that the Commission agreed to accept it,

provided the consortium submitted a formal tender.

The designers adjusted their bay dimension from 20 ft to 24 ft to suit the exhibition brief, and then put in their bid: £150,000, or £79,800 if the tenderers retained the ownership of the materials. This was an offer which, in financial terms, was difficult to refuse, and the Commission also felt comfortable with Paxton's track record for his previous large glazed projects, which used very similar technology. An enormous advantage to Paxton at this stage was his experience in similar construction to that proposed. The ridge and furrow glazing was lifted from his earlier design work at Chatsworth, and the laminated timber arch was taken straight from the Capesthorne Conservatory. Furthermore, Fox and Henderson agreed to build *over* a group of popular elm trees on the site with a large transept, achieving the height with

a 'Chatsworth arch' quickly designed by Paxton. Thus by 15 July, about five weeks after his blotting paper sketch, Paxton was able to send a telegram to his wife to the effect that the Commission had approved his proposal.

What followed this decision was even more extraordinary than the work done to produce the tender. A building covering 772,784 sq ft (71,793 m²) of ground, 1,848 ft long (564 m) by 456 ft wide (139 m) had to be produced for opening in nine months. The secret lay in experience (particularly the use of the ridge and furrow glazing), prefabrication, and the very long hours which Victorian engineers and workmen were prepared to put into projects.

Team assembly and tooling up were virtually instant. Henderson employed the two Dudley firms of Cochrane and Company, and Jobson to supply cast-iron columns and girders. He also commissioned the timberwork from the Phoenix Sawmills. Chance, as a partner, increased the output of his factory to make the required 900,000 sq ft (about 83,600 m²) of 16 oz blown plate glass. By the third week in September, the first column was erected on site. Charles Fox, Henderson's own partner, had the job of designing all the components and assemblies, and supervising the construction; it was Fox, in fact who was the effective architect/builder, and he submitted the designs and calculations to the Commission member, William Cubitt. Cubitt himself acted as a very 'removed' technical client.

Paxton's contribution, other than the concept and the political skill and position needed to sell it, was primarily in the glazing system, in which his experience in conservatory design and construction was critical to success. Ingenuity and design skill ran right through the whole project: typical was the idea of the glazing wagon, which ran on wheels in the patent gutters; there was room for four men to sit and hooped metal arches were designed over it, enabling it to be covered so that glazing could progress in wet weather.

The real key to the technical and timing success, however, lay in the repetition of standard components and careful modular coordination, to ensure the successful on-site assembly of factory-made components. Dimensional coordination and repetition provided the basis for the simple and disciplined

55

generation of form. The two key dimensions were the 24 ft (7.3 m) required as an exhibitors' bay size by the Commission, and the size of glass pane available from Chance of 49 in (1.25 m). The form of the building comprised a stepped hall 408 ft wide (124.3 m) in five main bays, the outer bays being single-storey, the intermediate bays two-storey, and the main central bay three-storey, as in the blotting paper sketch.

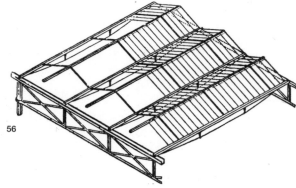

56

55. Glazing trolley designed for use during the construc-tion of the Crystal Palace.

56. Isometric drawing of typical roof bay.

57. The sash-bar cutting machine.

58. Sections through the middle and end of the trussed 'Paxton gutter', with central rain gutter and side channels for condensation.

Each bay was based on the 8 ft module (2.4 m) selected for the ridge-and-furrow dimension, producing an end elevation with a centre section 120 ft wide (36.5 m) and the others 72 ft wide (21.9 m). The main central nave had a structural span of 72 ft, and the other spans were 48 ft and 24 ft. A centre transept over the elm trees comprised an arch in laminated timber (as at Chatsworth), springing from a height of 63 ft, and spanning 72 ft.

The Paxton team divided the Commission's 24 ft bay by three to create a ridge-and-furrow dimension of 8 ft. All main setting-out dimensions were based on a grid of 4 ft. The biggest trusses, spanning across the nave of the building, were 72 ft long and made of wrought iron, as were the next size down having a 48 ft span. The typical repeating 24 ft trusses were in cast iron. All of them were 3 ft deep, thus simplifying the geometry of the roof structure.

The columns were in cast iron incorporating a sealed joint at the head for the passage of rainwater; 3 ft long collars enabled the main trusses to be

connected to the columns on site. All columns had the same diameter, so all the trusses could be the same length. Variation in column strength was provided by varying the column wall thickness. The columns were located at 24 ft centres down the main lengths of the building, and this dimension was subdivided into three by two intermediate timber columns, shaped to imitate the cast iron. These members provided a secondary support frame, and were held together with a decorative arched cast-iron assembly which provided the top bracing for the 8 ft bay system.

Whilst the structure and form of the building was a collaborative effort between all the partners, Paxton conceived and produced the cladding system which provided the envelope. Wall panels hung on the secondary framing comprised glass, timber boards, or doors, with a 3 ft band of galvanized sheet iron louvres at the top and a complementing band at low level, to provide ventilation. These louvres were operated in 108 ft banks by a wheel and cord mechanism located so as to permit the adjustment of a 216 ft length from one position.

57

The basis of Paxton's roof glazing system was a timber and iron rainwater gutter spanning 24 ft. The rainwater channel and condensation grooves were routed out from a 5 in by 6 in timber member. Into these gutters were connected the sash bars produced using Paxton's own machine already used for the Great Conservatory at Chatsworth. It was steam driven, and considerably reduced the price of the final section. The whole original section of timber

58

could be fed in at one end, and was then processed through a series of circular saws and cutting blades. About 4,500 m of bar were produced each day. They were painted with typical ingenuity: instead of the paint being brushed on, the bars were immersed in tubs of paint, and then pulled through an arrangement of brushes which removed the surplus paint. The flooring comprised boards with half-inch gaps between them (to facilitate cleaning), these boards having earlier been used to create the construction compound fence.

The building must have been a glorious sight well before the exhibits

59

arrived, with its structure 'colour-coded' to a scheme devised by the architect Owen Jones. The structure itself was pale blue, the cross bracing yellow, the columns blue and yellow, and the underside of the trusses red. The constructional innovation of the Crystal Palace was a direct result of the marriage of a critical path programme, and the essentially non-architect expertise which made the achievement of this programme possible. Fortunately for us now, it can be seen in wonderful detail in the publications of the time, both in Charles Downes's book of 1852, *The Building for the Great Exhibition*, and earlier in the *Illustrated London News*, which carried weekly drawings and lithographs showing progress in November and December 1850, only six months after Paxton's first blotting paper sketch. Calotype photographs show what it was like when completed.

The importance of the building lies not only in its architecture and construction, however. Its content, the purpose of its existence, was also of great significance, not least when seen in the light of the different opinions of the

59. The Crystal Palace : the enormity of its empty interior in a photograph shortly before it was dismantled

60. The Crystal Palace, cross bracing.

61. The Sydenham Hill reconstruction of the Crystal Palace.

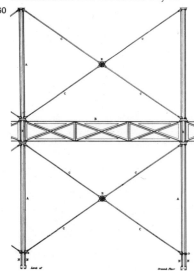

60

visitors it attracted. Many British visitors found the idea of the new machine age anathema. To one particular German visitor at least, however, it had great importance for the future of design. Gottfried Semper, the greatest German architectural theorist of his time, who had himself proposed the enormous portable glass roof over the Jardin des Plantes in Paris already referred to, visited the Exhibition, and in 1852 wrote 'Wissenschaft, Industrie und Kunst'. This essay, translated as 'Science, Industry and Art', embraced the idea of design in the machine age, and Semper went on to design an early (and unbuilt) museum project for the 'Museum of Practical Art' in London, the institution which developed into the Victoria and Albert Museum. Semper despised the tendency in Britain to want to return to pre-industrial hand-crafted design and manufacture, and Germany had already embraced the new industrial way of

creating architectural form, as in Schinkel's Berlin Bauakademie of 1835.

The British were more wary about the architectural implications of the Crystal Palace. In Ruskin's *Seven Lamps of Architecture* of 1853, he expressed a cautious view that, perhaps, new architectural laws could be established related to metal construction, but his overriding opinion was that the Crystal Palace proved that higher beauty was impossible in iron. Pugin went further, calling it a 'glass monster'. Thus did the leading theoreticians in Britain and Germany settle in relation to the new possibilities of metal and glass, to say nothing of the idea of a machine aesthetic. The Crystal Palace itself, of course, went on.

The building had been leased to the Exhibition Commission, not sold to it, and when the Exhibition was finished its removal was agreed after an extended stay in Hyde Park. Paxton tried to negotiate that the building should stay in Hyde Park as a winter-garden, but gave up when Parliament voted for its removal in April 1852. Within a month, Paxton had formed a company, underwritten by £500,000 of capital. His railway connections led to the chairman appointed to his company being Samuel Laing of the London, Brighton and South Coast Railway, and a 349 acre site was duly found close to the Brighton Line, in Sydenham. Its railway connection would, it was thought, increase the number of visitors, and Paxton's imagination took off once more.

The Sydenham Crystal Palace was even larger than that in Hyde Park, and

used many of the same components. The building became 1,608 ft (490 m) long, and received a glass barrel-vaulted roof. The glass area doubled, and the building contained huge trees, courts simulating the architecture of different periods, and a huge, tiered concert platform. The glass itself was 21 oz rather than the original 16 oz. The newly re-created building was placed in extensive landscaping and

61

pleasure gardens. The requirement for heating (not installed at Hyde Park) led to the need for a large heating plant, and fountains were designed which required two huge water towers, designed by Brunel, to provide the head of water necessary to produce the 120,000 gallons of water per minute.

The building was certainly popular, but the escalating costs created continual financial difficulties. The capital cost of the gardens, as well as the buildings, made the project difficult to service in financial terms, despite its success in housing huge concerts and other events.

The building's end came on
30 November 1936 when, it is thought,
someone dropped a cigarette into one
of the half-inch gaps between the
floorboards. The resulting fire could
be seen in Cambridge, over sixty
miles away.

The Crystal Palace, in both its
forms, set precedents for many of the
overlaying characteristics of the new
architecture to come in the subsequent
fifty years and beyond. In terms of
construction, materials, morphology
and procurement, it staked out new
architectural territory. Konrad
Wachsmann put the historical
importance of the building perfectly
in the opening chapter of his book,
The Turning Point of Building of 1961.
'What [Paxton] built was not only a
demonstration of fresh insight but
also a symbol of the new spirit of the
times. From reason and logic, intuitively
embracing the thought of the new
age of technology, there arose a
beauty, such as had never before been
known, appraised or experienced.
The Crystal Palace was a work of art.'
As a precursor of the new glass
cathedrals of industry, however, it was
only a start.

62. Proposal for the St
Cloud Exhibition
Building, Paris, 1861,
Joseph Paxton. This
was intended as
repeat performance of
the Crystal Palace,
but with the addition
of domes, the largest
of these was to be 360
ft high in the centre of
the structure. It was,
sadly, never executed.

63. St Pancras
Station, London,
1865–67, W H Barlow
and R M Ordish.

64. Palais des
Machines, Paris,
1889, Dutert, with
Contamin, Pierron and
Charton. St Pancras
and the Palais des
Machines demon-
strate different ways
of resolving long span
structures. The
buildings were for
different purposes,
but the design
imperative is the
same: large free
spaces that need
daylight.

62

By the middle of the nineteenth
century, cast-iron columns and wrought-
iron rails, used in conjunction with
modular glazing, had become the
standard technique for the rapid
prefabrication and erection of the
new large warehouses, market
buildings and railway stations needed
for urban distribution.

The commercial and technical
products of the industrial revolution
generated a need for building forms
which did not exist in the conventional
architecture of the time. A series of new
requirements produced a new 'brief' for
architecture, with a need for very large
volumes, as uninterrupted by columns
as possible, often lofty (to enhance the
spatial experience, and to dissipate the
smoke and steam of the railway trains),
and daylit. Many new project types
required such a brief: the creation of
the extensive railway systems and their
termini in Britain, Europe and America;
the expansion of national and
international trade and the resulting

64

requirement for large distribution
market halls; the idea of the glazed
shopping arcade to shelter the new
urban consumer; and the series of
international exhibitions organized to
celebrate the development of commerce
and invention in the second half of the
nineteenth century. As Konrad
Wachsmann has said, the new iron
and glass age generated its own
architecture out of the *Zeitgeist*.

After the success of the Great
Exhibition in Hyde Park, other great
cities in the Western world rushed to
produce their own versions. In 1851,
New York had a project underway,
having invited entries for an
architectural competition. This was
won by Carstensen and Gildermeister,
both New Yorkers. Concern about
snow loads led them to avoid glass
roofs, but the building was completely
walled in glass. In 1853 it was the turn

of Dublin, where John Benson produced
a mainly timber structure slightly
larger than the Crystal Palace. The
converse to the New York approach
appeared in the Palais de l'Industrie in
Paris by Cendrier and Barrault of 1855;
here the walls were masonry, but the
roof entirely glass.

In 1861, Paxton himself designed
another exhibition building for St Cloud
outside Paris, which would have been
even more ambitious than the Crystal
Palace. This was not built, but six years
later the Second Universal Exhibition
in Paris was the reason for yet another
immense display of iron and glass
architecture in a building designed
by J B Krantz. This comprised seven
concentric galleries in the form of a
'pulled out' circle.

Exhibition buildings, then as now,
were structures erected as part of the
wish for cities and nations to compete

for prestige in the new world of international trade. They have mostly been demolished or destroyed by fire, and many of the projects for them were never realized at all. However, those that were built were manifestations of the extension of trade and industry which resulted from the creation of the railway systems installed in the period. Railway engineers rapidly became part of the developing architectural scene, and designers like Turner crossed easily

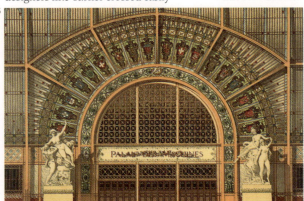

between the conservatory and the railway shed.

The new railway networks had enormous impacts on the cities they served. In London, the map in certain areas changed radically as, for example, Victoria Station was constructed, together with Victoria Street, carving great tracts through the existing urban grain. At the end of each system stood the new terminals, usually with a major statement of Victorian architecture (often a hotel), but also usually with a large glazed roof behind it. In 1852, Lewis Cubitt completed the twin arches at King's Cross Station in north London,

65, 66. Palais des Machines. The facade on the Avenue de la Bourdonnais. In wondering at the size and brilliance of these structures, it is easy to forget the care with which the finest details were considered.

67. Cross section through the main truss, Palais des Machines.

68. Pennsylvania Station, New York, 1905–10, McKim, Mead and White.

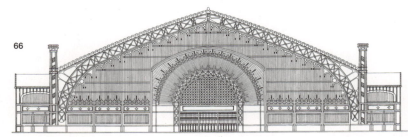

each with a span of 105 ft (32 m) and a length of 800 ft (244 m). A year later, work was progressing on another station in north London, at Paddington. The timing of this slightly later station enabled some of the lessons of the Crystal Palace to be employed. The design was led by Brunel, the great engineer for the Great Western Railway, who had served on the Commission for the Great Exhibition. Three spans covered the station area of 240 ft by 700 ft (73 m by 213 m). The glazing was Paxton's ridge and furrow design, and the whole structure was constructed by Fox and Henderson,

the builders of the Crystal Palace.

In 1866 came St Pancras Station, next to King's Cross, and serving the competing rail network, which had Paxton on its Board. The neo-Gothic Midland Hotel by George Gilbert Scott stood in front of the enormous glazed single arch of William Henry Barlow's train shed. Barlow, who had helped Paxton in the early days of Crystal Palace, had originally intended to roof across the platforms in several spans, but eventually opted for a single span of 245 ft 6 in (74.8 m) to enable vaults to be constructed below the concourse.

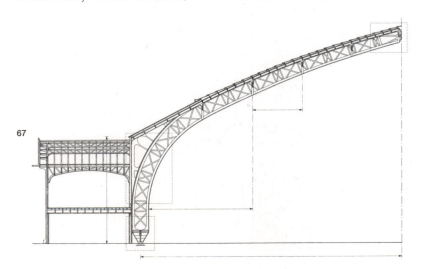

Paris, again, saw perhaps the final masterpiece of this nineteenth century building type, in 1889. The Palais des Machines, by Dutert as architect, and Contamin, Pierron and Charton as engineers, was a structure of a different order from Crystal Palace. Paxton's structures were grand in their overall impact, but were based on the repetition of comparatively small spans. They were not really major works of engineering. In the Palais des Machines,

however, the main span was 115 m down a length of 240 m. This span was half as big again as the St Pancras Station arch of 1866, and was constructed of pairs of curved trusses, pin jointed top and bottom. The roof was of translucent blue and white glass. It is a tragedy that it was taken down in 1910, and that only its original companion on the site, the Eiffel Tower, remains to this day.

Fifty years later, when Pennsylvania Station was built between 1905 and 1910, the same dichotomy between the old and new architecture, as was seen at King's Cross and St Pancras, endured. Here in New York, McKim Mead and White provided a colonnaded entrance facade in the true neo-classical manner; the trains, of course, entered the station in tunnels, so the great glazed train shed was unnecessary. However, the passenger concourse provided a wonderful display of steel and glass; three enormous groin vaults flooded the area with light.

The new glazed roof structures could do more than provide daylit covered spaces for the new railways.

They also provided the necessary technique for shopping arcades which became popular from the middle of the nineteenth century onwards. The glass-roofed shopping arcade as an architectural type operated at the other end of the distribution chain from the railway station – it covered, protected and illuminated the final consumer. The architectural idea of the shopping arcade was simple, but important. It was not a building interior with a glass roof.

69. Galérie d'Orléans, Palais Royale, Paris, 1829, Fontaine.

70. Galleria Vittorio Emmanuele II, Milan, 1865–7, Giuseppe Mengoni. This is one of the world's great meeting places, and always comfortable whatever the weather.

71. The Imperial and Royal Post Office Savings Bank, Vienna, 1904–12, Otto Wagner.

72. The Gage Building, Chicago, 1898–9, Holabird and Roche, and Louis Sullivan. Sullivan designed the facade of the tallest of the three buildings, on the right, but did not work on the other two, which are simpler, and more in the style of the emerging, practical tradition of Chicago architecture.

It was an internal street, with real street facades down each side fronting real buildings, and a glass roof providing protection from the weather. Usually open at the ends, it was a creation of micro-climate rather than a building.

The first shopping arcade of significance was built in 1829 in Paris, the glass barrel-vaulted Galerie d'Orléans, by Fontaine. This was sadly demolished in 1935 during the restoration of the Palais Royal. The greatest, however, was the Galleria Vittorio Emmanuele II in Milan of 1865–7, built at about the same time as St Pancras Station in London. The Galleria, which is as much a piece of urban design as it is a building, brought the iron and glass technology of northern Europe south to the warmer climate of Italy, where it could provide shelter from the sun as well as the rain. Moreover, it was not only the design ideas that were imported; so were the entrepreneurial skills, and the iron and glass, all brought south from England. Here, a glazed barrel vault roofs over a building based on a cruciform

pedestrian internal street. The long axis linked the piazza in front of Milan Cathedral to the square in front of La Scala Opera House. The architect was Giuseppe Mengoni, who designed it in 1861.

The Galleria in Milan provided a model for the generations of buildings to come, culminating in the shopping malls of the latter part of our own century. Its spatial and environmental quality is vastly superior, however, compared with the mean internal spaces of most modern shopping malls, where we see what the impact of twentieth century cost accounting leads to.

A glazed internal space of another sort was created forty years later in 1905 by Otto Wagner at the Post Office Savings Bank in Vienna, where the aesthetic of the early twentieth

century is perfectly suited to the glazed roof and floor of this masterpiece. Wagner brought to the concept of the glazed hall the philosophical and aesthetic principles of the great architect, with the view that modern life should be reflected in modern materials. The Post Office Savings Bank begins to cross the divide between the glass-roofed *galérie* and the modern atrium, and incorporates a glass floor to provide light to the level below. The Viennese work of this time, including that of Wagner and Loos, is both prophetic and seminal in relation to the European architecture of the next forty years. Wagner's steel and glass hall is a clear statement of the importance of glass in this architecture.

frames and skins: the new morphology

Historically parallel to the development
of these glazed halls, with their wonderful transparent walls and roofs, another
exploitation of the marriage of iron and
glass was developing: the iron, and then
the steel structural frame, and the glass
wall that came with it. Again, it was the
imperatives of function and commerce
which drove the formulation of technique, with a desire for free interior
space interrupted only by columns.
This in turn, and with the same rationale
that had led to the Gothic glass wall,
opened up the facade into a framed
opening; this time, however, the frame
was metal, not stone.

The first uses were in mills, warehouses, factories and other utilitarian
structures where 'architecture' did not
matter. James Strike has pointed out the
difference between the quality of buildings such as a typical mill of the 1790s,
with its six per cent glazed area, and the
Stanley Mill at Stonehouse of 1813,
whose frame permits a forty per cent
area to be devoted to glazing. As Strike
says, 'it was only when the iron frame
eliminated the need for external fabric to
be loadbearing that the potential for
large window areas could be fully
achieved'. In Britain similar developments took place, with very beneficial
effects for the workforce. In this principle lay the seeds of the curtain wall and
the building skin which were to develop
a hundred years later.

Buildings of this type appeared both
in Europe and North America in the
middle of the century. In the work of
James Bogardus in New York, for exam-

73

ple, we see the potential of the new 'fire-proof' cast-iron frames. His factory of 1848 at the junction of Duncine Street and Centre Street is an excellent demonstration of the cast-iron frame and a metal and glass facade system. Bogardus went on to design the store for Harper Brothers in New York in 1854, with its ornate exposed cast-iron frame. Harpers retains the *parti* of a Renaissance palazzo, with orders (of a sort) and arches and pilasters. It is nevertheless an iron and glass building, both in terms of construction and expression. In 1856, Bogardus extended his ideas into his pamphlet *Cast-Iron Buildings*.

By the middle of the nineteenth century, the time of the Palm House, the Crystal Palace and the Galleria in Milan, the thinking embodied in these buildings was manifesting itself on the high street. In the Gardner's Store in Glasgow of 1855–6; designed as a warehouse on Jamaica Street by John Baird, we see a fine example of what could be done,

73. Carson Pirie Scott Store, Chicago, 1899–1904, Louis Sullivan. One of the greatest masterpieces of the iron, steel and glass architecture of the first Chicago school.

74. Gardner's Store, Glasgow, 1855–6, John Baird.

75. Oriel Chambers, Liverpool, 1864–5, Peter Ellis.

76. Reliance Building, Chicago, 1894, D H Burnham and Company. The projecting bays of the building exploit the large areas of glazing to produce shifting reflections, articulated by the terracotta sheathing.

built, as the *Illustrated London News* of March 1856 said, 'entirely of cast iron and British plate glass'. The facade exploited the potential of the fully-glazed wall superbly, and the building still stands as a testament to the architectonic prowess of its architect. Just as powerful was Oriel Chambers in Liverpool, designed by Peter Ellis and built in 1864–5. Here there are plate glass oriel windows and detailing which would bear repetition now, 150 years later. Echoes of it appear in Michael Hopkins and Partners' design for Bracken House in the City of London in 1992.

The real birthplace for the new iron- or steel-framed structure was far from Europe – in the Midwest of America. The downtown area of Chicago suffered the most terrible destruction by fire in 1871. This fire demonstrated the vulnerability of cast iron amongst other things, but it provided a wonderful, and historically unique opportunity for a generation of architects, with the newly-invented 'elevator' at their disposal. Elisha Graves Otis had first shown his elevator at the New York Fair of 1853–4; in 1880, Siemens had invented the elec-

74

75

tric elevator and by 1887 the first permanent electric elevator had been installed in Baltimore in the USA.

The architects of Chicago used the resulting urban *tabula rasa* to tremendous and historic effect. The 1870s and 1880s saw an unprecedented series of buildings in Chicago exploiting the possibilities of the frame in which the glazing gradually occupied a larger and larger proportion of the facade. We see the shape of things to come in William Jenney's seven-storey Leiter Building of 1879 (now known as 208 West Monroe Building). Here, floor beams span between piers, and a three-bay cast-iron mullion system was designed simply to get as much light into the offices as possible. The same thinking was evident in the nine-storey Willoughby Building, said to have been designed by the self-proclaimed 'inventor' of skyscraper construction, Leroy S Buffington. By 1890, William Jenney had gone on to design the sixteen-storey Manhattan Building, which was one of the first Chicago buildings to use skeleton construction throughout. By the time of Burnham and Company's Reliance Building of 1894, the glass skyscraper had effectively arrived. The same year saw Adler and Sullivan's Chicago Stock Exchange.

Louis Sullivan, in *The Autobiography of an Idea*, set out the basis of the new high-rise aesthetic perfectly, as he recognized the interdependence and mutually interactive power of the high-rise building and the steel frame; he also put his finger on the critical issue of the facade:

'It became evident that the very tall masonry office building was in its nature economically unfit as ground values steadily rose. Not only did its thick walls entail loss of space and therefore revenue, but its unavoidably small window openings could not furnish the proper and desirable ratio of glass area to rentable floor area.'

Sullivan was not a commercial architect, and his aesthetic was decoratively rich: we have only to look at his part of the Gage Building in Chicago of 1898–9 compared to the buildings by Holabird and Roche next to it, to see the difference between the latter's 'stripped down' utility and Sullivan's embellished 'architecture'. However, he saw very well the essential driving forces behind the new building form. The rapid development of the type is to be seen in Holabird and Roche's Cable Building of 1899, a tough ten-storey building sadly destroyed in 1961, and in the unparalleled power of the Carson Pirie Scott Store by Louis Sullivan built between 1899 and 1904. With its powerful horizontal double-square windows, and its differentiated lower two storeys, it turns the corner for architecture into the twentieth century just as beautifully as it turned the corner between Madison Street and State Street.

76

michael wigginton   **glass in architecture**

The second half of the nineteenth century not only saw the development of the large-scale all-glass envelope as an element of architecture, whether for walls or roof; it also saw, as a natural consequence of this development, market demand for better and larger glass panes, but little real improvement in the manufactured product.

What might now be called the 'mass market' was well catered for. The Crystal Palace, for example, was a showcase not only of the exhibits inside it, but it also represented the largest single glazing contract ever attempted. Chance Brothers won the contract with blown sheet, and in doing so further reduced the appeal of crown in the market. About three million panes of 16 oz sheet glass, 49 in by 10 in (1,244 mm by 254 mm), were produced for the building between July 1850 and February 1851. This was over 956,000 sq ft or about 89,000 m². Chance's claimed that this amount was produced without interruption to their usual production.

However, what was good enough for the Crystal Palace was not necessarily good enough for an increasingly sophisticated window market. An article in *The Builder* in England of 14 April 1860 deplored the lack of availability of good quality window glass to suit the '... present style, namely squares about 46 by 30, or 40 by 32'.

As has already been noted, this was twice the size in both dimensions that could be obtained in good quality crown. The problem with the blown sheet available in such sizes was '...

77. Hyam's Store, Birmingham, 1859, J J Bateman. Architecture such as this may seem ill-formed and insignificant, but good quality, flat, strong glass was as much a prerequisite for a shop front in Birmingham as it was for the great buildings of the Chicago school and the flowering of the glass architecture that followed in the next century.

78. This early design for a plate glass door by J B Papworth is 3 ft 9 in wide by 7 ft high and dates from 1828. The potential for large plates is fully realized here.

77

whether the glass is made in this country or in any other, it is all alike having a hammery-looking surface, consequently driving us to the expense of plate glass'. The article went on to plead: '... cannot manufacturers give sheet glass the even appearance of crown glass?' The sheet *The Builder* was talking about was from cylinders blown to diameters of 32 to 36 in (813 to 914 mm).

The state of the market in England was clear from the nature of the industry itself. By the mid-1850s, seventy-five per cent of all the country's window glass was being made by three firms, and Pilkington, one of the three, were selling about the same amount of blown sheet as crown; and, by 1872 they had stopped producing crown altogether. However, the poor quality of blown plate or sheet led to discriminating buyers using polished cast plate,

provided they could afford it, and here size did not normally present a problem for most buildings.

Both the French and the English could make polished cast plate glass in very large sizes by the middle of the nineteenth century, as demonstrated by the large piece in the Crystal Palace Exhibition. A huge expansion of the English plate glass market had been experienced between the 1820s and the 1840s, accompanied by a drop in price of about sixty per cent to five shillings per square foot.

This expansion continued into the 1850s and 1860s. By 1866, ten years after Gardner's Store in Glasgow, the weekly output of polished plate glass had doubled from its 1847 figure to 140,000 square feet. In consumption terms, this could be added to the very competitive French and Belgian glass. Prices also fell further at this time, by another fifty per cent. Between 1852 and 1854, Paxton himself had installed enormous panes of plate glass in the ground floor of Mentmore Towers in

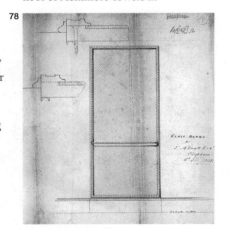
78

Buckinghamshire, but plate glass was ceasing to be the preserve of wealthy private customers. In particular, the idea of the large glass shop window was becoming very attractive to the high street retailer. Charles Dickens himself remarked on the vogue for plate glass in London; the fashion quickly spread. A print from 1859 shows large plate glass windows in Birmingham about 6 m high, and at this time plates 8 ft high by 4 ft wide (2.44 m by 1.22 m) were common.

George Gilbert Scott noted in 1858, in his *Remarks on Secular and Domestic Architecture*, on the blessing of plate glass as providing glazing as undivided as possible and '... one of the most useful and beautiful inventions of the day'. Moreover, plate glass did not have to be flat. As had been recognized early in the century, it could also be curved – a great advantage in shop windows.

As the century drew to a close, the conditions were effectively in place for the realization of a new architecture, in which metal and glass were to play a central role. Large-span structures in iron and steel, and all-glass roofs and walls had been conceived and developed to serve the demands of new architectural forms: halls, microclimatic enclosures and multi-storey commercial buildings to serve the newly-emerging citizens of a brave new industrial world.

This could not easily take place without a change in the way that sheet glass was made, but this, too, was on the horizon.

glass architecture and the
modern movement

The turn of the century, while not being
the sort of precise trigger for renewal
that the historian might like, did come at
a time of revolution in art and culture
such as had not been seen since the
Renaissance. What is more, the revolution happened very quickly.

Unlike the nineteenth century's
romantic revolution, the early twentieth
century version was iconoclastic and
often brash; serious underneath, but
challenging and often ironic and con-
trary on the surface. This was the age of
Space–Time, the aesthetics of movement, dislocation and excitement with
the machine. As Cecily Mackworth said
in *Apollinaire and the Cubist Life*, 'These
first decades of the twentieth century
[were] a century in which man's existence suddenly became far more con-
densed as well as far more complicated.
The invention of trains and motor cars
meant that modern man was already reg-
istering impressions at an infinitely
greater speed than a man of the eigh-

79

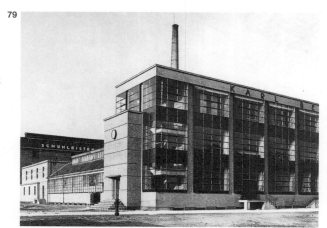

79. Fagus Factory,
Alfeld-an-der-Leine,
1911–12, Walter
Gropius and Adolf
Meyer.

80. AEG Turbine
Factory, Berlin, 1909,
Peter Behrens.
Behrens used glass in
his building for AEG
as an important
material in his
abstract composition
of forms, which
rely on conventional
ideas of solid corners
and structural
containment. At the
Werkbund Pavilion
(81), Gropius and
Meyer were happy to
reverse the principle.

80

teenth century could ever have done.
This resulted in a rupture of forms,
which had been brought about first by
scientists or engineers, and was next
translated into visual art and later into
literature.'

The parallel changes in architecture,
which mirrored this cultural revolution,
were perhaps most evident in Germany.
The differences in the attitude to architecture, industry and the machine
between Britain and Germany at the
time of the 1851 Exhibition have
already been referred to, and there
followed a continuous thread of
consistent thinking between the
writings of Gottfried Semper and the
origins of the Deutsche Werkbund;
for example, Friedrich Naumann's essay
of 1904, *Die Kunst in Maschinenzeitalter*
(Art in the Epoch of the Machine), took
a position in direct contradiction to
William Morris' Arts and Crafts argu-
ments concerning the alienation of
machine culture. The foundation of the
Deutsche Werkbund by Peter Behrens
and others in 1907 established a group

dedicated to the fusion of art, design
and production. In the same year,
Behrens was appointed architect and
designer to the young, but now enormous, German Electrical Company,
Algemeine Elektricitats Gesellschaft, AEG.
Behrens's own architectural work for
them was a tough monument to industrial culture, although he was as much a
'stylist' for AEG as a technical designer
(a role that has persisted in industrial
design to this day).

The Werkbund itself, however, progressed to a new form of vision, made
manifest by the Werkbund Exhibition of
1914. Two buildings in this exhibition
not only signalled the way forward, they
also had glass at the centre of their concept. They were the model factory by
Walter Gropius and Adolf Meyer, and
Bruno Taut's Glass Pavilion.

The model factory turned the hitherto conventional massing of a building on
its head. The end terminations of the
form are not a containing masonry mass;
instead, glazing is wrapped round spiral
stairs, dissolving the corners. This building was an extension of the thinking
already seen in the Fagus Factory in
Alfeld-an-der-Leine of 1911. Here, large
panels of glass were set forward from
brick piers, a reversal of the normal
device of stretching glazing between
structural members (the window convention from the Gothic cathedral to the
sliding sash). The glass wall is a slightly
projecting glass plane, clearly stated as
the primary architectural surface on the
elevation: Behrens's AEG building in
reverse. The Werkbund factory extended
this surface around the corner.

Taut's Glass Pavilion, by contrast,
was fanciful and almost expressionist.
However, its creation was an even
greater manifestation of the importance
glass was to play in the new architecture
than the factory. Aphorisms were
inscribed around the building, as
though to make sure that the aesthetic
message of the building was firmly
understood. Its intellectual basis was a
belief that glass was the central and most
vital material symbolizing the architecture of the future. Central to this thinking was Paul Scheerbart, a Bohemian
poet and novelist. In 1914, the year of
the Werkbund Exhibition, Scheerbart
published *Glasarchitektur*, which sets
out in 111 'chapters' (some of which
are only four or five lines long) a
programme for the use of glass in the
new architecture. Read today, this
book's agenda for the future and
potential of the material still represents
an extraordinary imaginative leap,
covering an enormous range from
multiple glazing to glass fibres.

Chapters One and 111, the opening
and closing texts in the book, make
its essence clear. Chapter One sets out
the philosophy:

*...we live for the most part in closed
rooms. These form the environment
from which our culture grows. Our
culture is to a certain extent the product
of our architecture. If we want our culture
to rise to a higher level, we are obliged,
for better or for worse, to change our
architecture. And this only becomes
possible if we take away the closed character from the rooms in which we live. We*

81

can only do that by introducing glass architecture, which lets in the light of the sun, the moon, and the stars, not merely through a few windows, but through every possible wall, which will be made entirely of glass – of coloured glass. The new environment, which we thus create, must bring us a new culture.)

As we will see, Scheerbart's belief that glass was in a unique position to represent and facilitate social and spiritual change was shared by many architectural theorists after him. Relating transparency to openness was a powerful temptation in the new social age. Chapter 111 reiterates the optimism of this new culture:

After all the above, we can indeed speak of a glass culture. The new glass environment will completely transform mankind, and it remains only to wish that the new glass culture will not find too many opponents. It is to be hoped, in fact, that glass culture will have ever fewer opponents.

Taut's Glass Pavilion, with its clearly expressed polemic, was a celebration of

81. Werkbund Pavilion, Cologne, 1914, Walter Gropius and Adolf Meyer.

82. Proposal for an office building in Friedrichstrasse, Berlin, 1919, Mies van der Rohe. The courage of this design lies in its flouting of the competition conditions and in setting out a new agenda for the architecture of the tall building, and for glass architecture.

83. Model of the Glass Skyscraper Project, Berlin, 1922, Mies van der Rohe. This entirely conceptual proposition, with its amoeboid plan, was an essay in the aesthetic potential of glass.

84. Glass Pavilion, Cologne, 1914, Bruno Taut.

this potential, and was made as entirely of glass as was possible at the time.

After the Great War, this enthusiasm continued unabated, and the architect Adolf Behne said in 1918: 'It is not the crazy caprice of a poet that glass architecture will bring a new culture. *It is a fact.*' So, too, continued the spirit of the Werkbund itself in an alliance led by Behne, Gropius and Taut, the *Arbeitsrat fur Kunst*. In his introduction to the 'Exhibition of Unknown Architects' in 1919, Gropius wrote what amounted to the first draft of the Weimar Bauhaus programme of the same month.

In November 1919, a corporate manifesto was started in the form of the notes and sketches created by a group of Berlin-based artists and architects. This chain of correspondence was called *Die Glaserne Kette*, the Glass Chain. The chain did not last long, and began to break up in 1920, but the spirit of the movement, with glass at its centre, went on.

The impact of glass on architectural thinking accelerated. In 1914, Mies van der Rohe had been the classical/vernacu-

83

lar architect of the Villa Urbig. After the war, like so many other German architects, he began to subscribe to the new aesthetic thinking, and became a directing member of the radical *Novembergruppe* which included amongst its numbers Arthur Korn, the painter Hans Richter, and J J P Oud as a foreign member. The links with *Die Glaserne Kette* created a completely new view of aesthetics in him, and by 1919 he had designed an entry for the competition for the Friedrichstrasse in Berlin. Mies's angular glass tower represented an amazing shift, both for him and for architecture.

In an interview given in 1968, he described his idea: 'Because I was using glass, I was anxious to avoid dead surfaces reflecting too much light, so I broke the facades a little in plan so that light could fall on them at different

angles: like crystal, like cut crystal.' The tower represented the physical embodiment of Scheerbart's thinking.

In 1922 came another proposal, the glass skyscraper, of which Mies said: 'I tried to work with small areas of glass, and adjusted my strips of glass to the light, and then pushed them into the plasticine planes of the floors. That gave me the curve … I had no expressionist intention. I wanted to show the skeleton, and I thought that the best way would be simply to put the glass skin on.' The plan of this building is as 'amorphous' as the structure of glass itself, and this time a model demonstrated the idea. The glass technology implicit in this tower was not available for half a century, but it is a testament

84

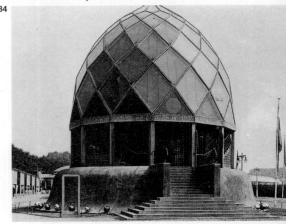

to the power of the concept that it was still vital when Foster Associates created the Willis Faber & Dumas Building in the mid-1970s.

The combination of design, theory and pamphleteering was endemic to the development of the Modern Movement at this time. The Berlin magazine *G*,

carrying the subtitle *Material zur ele-
mentaren Gestaltung*, was typical. Its first
issue was published in 1923, and Mies
van der Rohe was a contributor to it.
Kenneth Frampton has ascribed to *G* an
attitude which combined 'constructivist
objectivity with a Dadaist feeling for
chance'. It certainly purported to be
anti-art, using the word art in its specifically 'fine art' sense. In its drive towards
a new art, it was parallel in tone to the
Dutch magazine *De Stijl*: indeed, as the
original members of *De Stijl* fell away
(except Van Doesberg) they were substantially replaced by *G* group members.
A typical Mies van der Rohe *G* slogan
was 'we reject all aesthetic speculation,
all doctrine, all formalism'. The *G* group
made the Bauhaus look almost arty, and
it was *G*-type thinking which seems to
have inspired Arthur Korn's sequel to
Scheerbart, *Glas im Bau als
Gebrauchsgegenstand*. Korn repeated the
eulogy of glass written by Scheerbart a
decade earlier:

*A new world of glass has been opened
that concedes nothing to the windows of
the Gothic world in beauty. But we have
secured a great advance over them ... in
making an independent glass skin. No
more wall and window, even though the window might be the dominant part – the window is the wall itself, this wall is itself the
window ... In this new dispensation the outer
wall no longer makes itself visible ... And
therewith appears the truly unique quality of
glass compared to all materials hitherto in
use: it is there and it is not there. It is the
great mystery membrane, delicate and
strong at the same time.*

85. Hallidie Building,
San Francisco, 1918,
Willis Jefferson Polk.

Nor was Korn only a propagandist
for glass. It was his deep appreciation
of the material as a designer that led
him to use non-reflecting glass in a
shop window he and Konrad
Weitzmann designed.

Mies van der Rohe's propositions
of this time, which were referred to in
Glas im Bau, were essentially and
inevitably rhetorical. The technology
did not exist to produce the frameless
thirty-storey suspended glass wall
implied by his model with its top
hangers. In any literal sense, the curtain
wall as a suspended assembly was not
possible. However, three years before
in San Francisco, a more practical culture was already at work to produce an
entire multi-storey wall of glass. Willis
Jefferson Polk's Hallidie Building was
a reinforced concrete structure with
a glass curtain wall carried by cantilevered floor slabs three feet in front
of the column line. The architect of
the Glass Tower of 1922 and the technology of the curtain wall of the
Hallidie building were not to meet
for over thirty years, but the origins
of much of the architecture which
followed World War II were clearly
evident in the early 1920s.

The essentially different approaches
in the pragmatic curtain wall (a constructional solution to a technical proposition) and its conceptual equivalent
(derived from a more abstract and
metaphorical position) were fundamental, and in opposition to each other. The
working out of their programmatic
implications is a key part of the story of
post- World War II architecture.

85

The aesthetic and polemical expressions surrounding the use of glass in architecture would have remained just that, had it not been for the technical and production revolution which was taking place at the same time. Until the turn of the century, flat architectural glass was only available in the three basic forms: blown sheet or plate, spun 'crown' and polished castplate.

The new century saw one last effort to improve broad cylinder glass when the American Window Glass Company introduced machine blowing, using John Lubbers' invention of 1896. In this process, enough molten glass for one cylinder was ladled from the furnace into a heated pot. A blow pipe terminating in a flared disc was lowered into the glass, which solidified around the edge of the disc. The whole blow pipe was then raised and air blown in at the same time. Careful control of pressure and drawing speed, and the design of the whole apparatus, created the required thickness and diameter. The cylinders created had potential faults such as ripple marks, but they could be 9 m or so long and up to 600 mm in diameter, giving a girth of about 1.8 m to create the flattened-out sheet. This size advantage over hand-blowing gave them immediate currency, and the patented principle was introduced into England by Pilkington in 1910, where they were in use until the 1930s.

However, the mechanization of broad cylinder glass only slightly prolonged its long and central role in the history of glass-making. In 1904, the Belgian glass-maker Fourcault took out his first patent for the manufacture of sheet glass by 'drawing'. In this technique, the molten glass was drawn

up from a slot in the so-called 'debiteuse', itself pushed down slightly into the melt by a series of rollers. The process had to be started using a bait, but once started it could be continued as long as raw material was provided to the melt, and the rollers kept turning. This amazing invention produced the first new way of making thin flat glass for 250 years, and in its thinness lay its advantage over cast plate. Size ceased to be a problem, as did the hammered surface of blown plate. The width of the machine as developed delivered glass between 75 in and 90 in wide (1.9 and 2.3 m). The thickness depended on the speed of drawing, which was 120 ft per hour for 24 oz (680g) glass. The process suffered mainly from the problem of the glass which remained adhered to the rollers, demanding regular stopping to clean the plant and remove the devitrified glass.

One year later, in 1905, the Colburn or Libbey-Owens process was patented in the USA. This used knurled rollers rather than a debiteuse, and turned the glass horizontally after the initial drawing. Again, the maximum width generally produced was 90 in. The problem with this process was the slight damage to one surface done by the rollers. This was avoided in a later American process developed by the Pittsburgh Plate Glass Company which was similar to the Libbey-Owens process, but retained the vertical draw of the Fourcault principle, thus producing sheet glass with a much better surface.

Plate glass, too, benefited from techniques developed immediately after World War I. The first was the Bicheroux rolled plate process, in which the glass was produced by squeezing it between

two rollers prior to grinding and polishing, as in the figured glass-rolling process already in existence. The result was reduced waste and much less difficulty in the achievement of a flat polished surface, although up to half the thickness was ground off to obtain a 6 mm plate. The Ford Motor Company, with its tendency to mass production and its early demand for automotive glass, refined the process by inventing a continuous feed for the glass melt, rather than using pots. Ford also mechanized the grinding and polishing process and made it continuous, a typical piece of 'production line' thinking. This mechanized approach was picked up in England where, by 1923, experiments were going on to try to produce plate using the Ford technique, but in greater widths to suit the building industry. It took until 1938 for Pilkington to develop its automatic twin grinder and polisher for architectural glass.

Just as sheet and plate glass became developed products in the 1920s and thirties, so did the idea of toughened glass finally become realized as an architectural material. By a felicitous accident of history, the late 1920s also saw the development of the long elusive technique for heat-strengthening glass, essential not only for the new shop fronts and large areas of glazing, but also for the realization of the glass architecture to come. The phenomenon of Prince Rupert's drops had been known since the Middle Ages, and was more a glass-maker's game than a product: if molten glass is dripped into water it produces a tear-shaped drop which is very strong at the head, but shatters into safe grains if the tail is broken.

Around 1870, De la Bastie had tried to produce a 'tempered' glass by plunging red-hot glass into a bath of linseed oil and tallow, but the product, if it survived, was usually warped. A later Siemens method, using cool cast-iron plates to hold the glass as it rapidly cooled itself, went some way to producing toughened glass, but it was not until 1928 that the French finally developed the material we now know.

The Compagnies Réunies des Glaces et Verres Spéciaux du Nord de la France produced 'Securit' by heating a suspended glass plate to a high temperature in an electric furnace, and then rapidly chilling it by blowing cool air on to both faces. As in all previous (but unsuccessful) techniques, the cooling of the surface contracts it faster than the inner body of the glass, but then, as the inner body slowly cools, it pulls the contracted outer surface into compression. The resulting plate is up to four times stronger than annealed glass, and when shattered, breaks into pieces with rounded, safe shapes.

This product, occurring at the peak of interest in glass between the wars, not only provided the basis for strong and safe doors and shop windows; it was to form the basis of all the developments in structural glazing which were to take place after World War II. It is the material which eventually made possible the realization of Mies's 1922 tower in three-storey form, which is Foster Associates' Willis Faber & Dumas Building of 1975.

So, in the 1920s and thirties, with the new architecture in full flood, the industry created the products it needed to make the new dreams come true.

The 1920s saw wonderful exploitation of the new materials in the achievement of the new aesthetic. The houses and small projects produced by Mies van der Rohe in the decade demonstrated the change of attitude flowing across Europe and America after the war. Both the Tugendhat House of 1928–30 and the Barcelona Pavilion of 1929 derived their architectural form from the attitude to free-flowing space, and the only way to obtain the continuous flow of space as well as enclosure was by using glass, with as little interruption from framing as possible. The somewhat bourgeois label 'picture window' derives from this view of

86. The German Pavilion for the International Exposition, Barcelona, 1929, Mies van der Rohe.

87. Tugendhat House, Brno, Czechoslovakia, 1928–30, Mies van der Rohe.

88. Cité de Refuge, Paris, 1930–31, Le Corbusier.

glazing so perfectly exemplified by the Tugendhat House, where the glazing could actually be lowered electrically and removed completely. The house also included rudimentary air-conditioning, and its cost was that of eight luxury apartments, but it showed what could be done.

The Barcelona Pavilion, now beautifully rebuilt on its existing site, carried through the free and open wall arrangements of the Brick Country

House of six years earlier, when Mies had still been designing vernacular houses (like the Villa Mosler of 1924). It shows us now, over sixty years later, how Mies had created a perfect new architecture of his own in about five years (albeit with a great spatial indebtedness to Frank Lloyd Wright).

At this time, Walter Gropius was creating the Bauhaus, which drew its spirit from the Grand Ducal School of Arts and Crafts in Weimar directed by Henry van der Velde. Gropius, the architect of the Fagus Factory and the model factory at the Werkbund Exhibition, produced an architecture of glass walls and free form for the new buildings at Dessau of 1925–6.

However, it was a contemporary of Mies's days in Peter Behrens's office who produced a different sort of glass architecture as the decade ended. Le Corbusier, who was born in 1887, worked in Behrens's office

for five months in 1910.

Le Corbusier, too, had produced a small-scale masterpiece in 1929, the Villa Savoye at Poissy, but here the 'picture windows', with their huge pieces of plate glass, were subsumed into a piece of plastic formalism in which pure geometry led the concept. The formal principles used by Le Corbusier were similar to those of Gropius at Dessau (elevations built out of white planes and long horizontal windows), but he did not have a school to run like Gropius, and a series of great projects was flowing from his office.

One of the greatest of these projects incorporated some of the ideas of Scheerbart fifteen years earlier. The Cité de Refuge in Paris was conceived as a hostel for the poor. With a typical lack of modesty matched by commercial guile, Le Corbusier obtained the commission by

proclaiming his own importance '…at the head of the Modern Movement in architecture', and also offered a forty per cent fee discount. It helped that the Princesse de Polignac, for whom he had designed a house, was paying for the building.

Le Corbusier's objectives were extremely ambitious. The idea (explained perfectly by Reyner Banham in *The Architecture of the Well-Tempered Environment*) was to produce a '*mur neutralisant*'. This was a multiple glass wall within which tempered air flowed, neutralizing the effect of the cold or solar heat outside. Unfortunately Le Corbusier's control of budgets was not as good as his control of concepts, which led to the inner glass skin and the refrigeration plant being omitted. The result was an environmental catastrophe, leading to the enforced introduction of opening windows in 1933. We have had to wait until Richard Rogers Partnership's Lloyd's Building, built in London in the 1980s, to see the idea properly used, this time with fifty years of experience behind it.

Le Corbusier's *mur neutralisant* may have been a technical failure, but (typically) it pointed the way both

89

89, 90. Maison
Dalsace, the Maison
de Verre, Paris, 1931,
Pierre Chareau and
Bernard Bijvoët. One
of the great glass
buildings of the
twentieth century.

to the concepts of a future glass
architecture, and its hazards. The idea
of an architectural skin with a multiple
function (vision, screen, duct, blanket)
exploited glass in a wonderful new way,
quite different from Mies's seductive and
shimmering aesthetic of ten years earlier.
However, in the way it fell into the
greenhouse overheating phenomenon,
it was an early warning of what could
happen when glass curtain walls were
installed without compensating
engineering.

At the same time that Le Corbusier
was creating his flawed masterpiece
in Paris, a building of a completely
different order of size, but enormous
technical virtuosity, was being produced
in a small street in the Latin Quarter. The
Maison Dalsace was completed in 1931.
Its architect, Pierre Chareau, was four
years older than Le Corbusier, and had
developed into one of the greatest
designers of his time. His perforated

metal screens and metal staircases of the twenties and thirties would fit well with the detailing of today's 'high-tech' avant garde. The commission for the house, which was to become known as the 'Maison de Verre', and on which he worked with Bernard Bijvoët, is one of the most seminal works of the twentieth century.

With what Kenneth Frampton has called 'an obsessional and superfluous

91, 92. Van Nelle Factory, Rotterdam, 1927–9, Brinkman and Van der Vlugt.

93. Boots Pharmaceutical Factory, Beeston, Nottingham, 1930–32, Owen Williams.

94. SC Johnson and Son, Racine, Wisconsin: Administration Building, 1936–9; Research Tower, 1947–50, Frank Lloyd Wright.

95. Peter Jones Store, London, 1936, Slater and Moberly, with Professor Reilly and W Crabtree.

use of glass', Chareau created a project which used glass in an exemplary way. The site was a typical small Paris courtyard, and the brief was to create accommodation for a doctor while retaining the second floor dwelling of an elderly lady above it. Chareau's solution a steel supporting structure and a translucent glass brick wall, was a perfect response. The wall gives privacy and light, and in the evening the building becomes a lantern for the courtyard. The wall is claimed as the precursor for the sparkle glass in the Lloyd's Building fifty years later,

described in detail in a case study in this book and was the external manifestation of a work of rich and ambivalent genius.

Apart from the use of glass which gave it its name, the Maison de Verre makes an illuminating comparison with Le Corbusier's ideas of house design. Le Corbusier's *machine à habiter* was more metaphorical than literal; the Maison de Verre, on the other hand, is a real machine.

Both Mies van der Rohe's tower of 1922 and the Cité de Refuge were statements of grand and ambitious intent for a new glass architecture. But other work of the time demonstrated a new glass architecture with (literally) more 'street credibility'. Erich Mendelsohn had been a member of *Arbeitsrat fur Kunst*, the precursor of *Die Gläserne Kette*. In 1927, he designed the Petersdorff store in Breslau, in which the great horizontal planes of floor-to-ceiling glazing sweep round the elevation between enormous expressed bands. The use of curved glass to terminate the elevation is a powerful and typical Expressionist image.

This bringing of glass architecture to the street in the form of a metropolitan department store was mirrored by its use in the great Van Nelle Factory in Rotterdam of 1927–9 by Brinkman and Van der Vlugt, for which Mart Stam was the project architect. The

glass and metal facade was an inspiration to Le Corbusier, whose Cité de Refuge was to follow it. In its open and frank showing of structure through the glass wall of the packing building, and the dynamic raking glass-clad conveyors, the building was not only aesthetically courageous and committed, it was also a manifestation of the social attitudes incorporated in the League of Nations building by Hannes Meyer of 1926–7. As Meyer said: 'No pillared reception rooms for weary monarchs but hygienic work rooms for the busy representatives of their people. No back corridors for backstairs diplomacy, but open glazed rooms for public negotiation of honest men.'

This sort of wall also appeared in England, in the new Chemicals Building for the Boots Pharmaceutical Company in Nottingham of 1930–32, designed by Sir Owen Williams. This used 32 oz (907g) glass in steel frames. Owen Williams was also the designer of the

curtain-walled Daily Express Building in Fleet Street, London, of 1932.

This association between the transparency of glass and the social transparency of democracy was as important an ethical determinant of the 'honest expression' of function as the glass of the Mies van der Rohe tower was an aesthetic determinant, and the *mur neutralisant* a technical one. The socially symbolic, aesthetic and technical opportunities of glass were together a potent combination, and inspired the work of a wide but loosely coherent group of committed international activists who spanned across continental Europe.

In the USA, too, the potential for new technology in general, and glass in particular, was creating a new mood directly parallel with the ideas across the Atlantic. The following text from Frank Lloyd Wright's Kahn lectures at Princeton, given in 1930, make his attitude to glass clear. The lecture was called 'Style in Industry':

94

Glass has now a perfect visibility, thin sheets of air crystallized to keep air currents outside or inside. Glass surfaces, too, may be modified to let the vision sweep through to any extent up to perfection. Tradition left no orders concerning this material as a means of perfect visibility: hence the sense of glass as crystal has not, as poetry, entered yet into architecture. All the dignity of colour and material available in any other material may be discounted with permanence. Shadows were the 'brush work' of the ancient Architect. Let the modern now work with light, light diffused, light reflected – light for its own sake, shadows gratuitous. It is the Machine that makes modern *these rare new opportunities in Glass.*

In the Johnson Wax Administration Building in Racine, Wisconsin of 1936–9, Wright created a tour de force of glass technology, with a membrane

96. The Crystal Pavilion at the Century of Progress Exhibition, Chicago, 1934 by George and William Keck. An astonishing demonstration of virtuosity in steel and glass. The glazing comprised translucent ripple glass for the ground floor, tinted glass for the middle floor and clear glass at the top.

of borosilicate glass tubing producing a wonderful translucency. Wright himself describes his technical solution in the caption to a photograph of the interior:

Glass tubing laid up like bricks in a wall compose all the lighting surfaces. Light enters the building where the cornice used to be. In the interior, the box-like structure vanished completely. The walls carrying the glass ribbing are of hard red brick and red kasotsa sandstone. The entire fabric is reinforced concrete, cold drawn mesh used for reinforcement.

Great architects point the way and take the risks, but it is too simplistic to see the history of architecture as a matter only of the work of the 'masters', particularly so when we are considering the use of such a universal material as glass.

With the new products on the market, glass became part of the new architectural scene at every level.

95

96

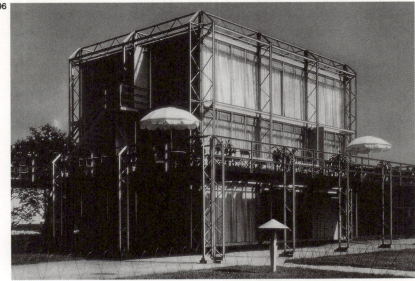

The idea of the 'picture window', epitomized in Mies van der Rohe's Tugendhat House and Le Corbusier's Villa Savoye, was added to the vocabulary of domestic architecture, and the plate glass shop window, uninterrupted by framing, became the natural instrument for marketing wares on the high street. The curtain wall became the easy way to clad the new multi-storey commercial buildings. Peter Jones Store in Sloane Square, London of 1936 may not constitute a major statement in architecture; but with its free form in the urban setting, its elegant use of the curtain wall, and its enormous shop windows, it demonstrated how good architecture using the new techniques was beginning to make itself felt in the street rather than in the manifesto.

The Keck Brothers' Crystal Pavilion for Chicago's Progress Exhibition in

1934 gave a foretaste of the architecture to come. With glass occupying a central part in the thinking of the great pre-war designers, and with new products and technologies making high-quality glass a key material in the development of simple, good street building, glass architecture was poised to move into new and larger roles after the profound disruption of World War II.

Before we embark on a study of this, however, it is important to pause in consideration of the place of glass in modern architectural history, and look at the material itself. In this age of science and technology, it is increasingly our knowledge of its physics, chemistry and performance which is enabling us to exploit the true potential of this wonderful material, about which Scheerbart, Korn, Mies van der Rohe and Frank Lloyd Wright wrote hymns.

02   glass technology

1–3. The manufacture
of glass products in
the 1950s continued
centuries-old
processes:
'Gatherers' at work
during the
manufacture of high-
voltage insulators at
Ravenhead, 1945 (1).
A 'gather' of glass
being manipulated for
a blown cell prior to
machine blowing,
Ravenhead, 1953 (2).
A blown cell being
placed in an
annealing kiln,
Ravenhead, 1957 (3).

the technology of primary glass

It is one of the central tenets of design
theory that a knowledge of, and
sympathy for, materials lies at the heart
of successful artistic creation. It is no less
true that product and industrial design,
and technical specification, demand a
full understanding of materials: how
they are made, and how and why they
perform in the way they do.

The unique physical properties of
glass, deriving from its chemical
composition and the way it is made,
have led to it being adopted and
exploited in many, very diverse ways.
For the designer in architecture, it is its
performance characteristics in terms of
radiation transmission, combined with
its hardness and resistance to
weathering, which make it so central to
the unfolding of architectural history.
However, glass is a very beguiling
material. Its visual ambiguity and beauty,
and its associations, have led to it being
used inappropriately, and often foolishly,
particularly in our own century.

Remarkably, the chemical
composition of glass as it is used in
building has remained similar for two
thousand years. However, developments
in the way it is made, and in particular,
the evolution of secondary
manufacturing and processing
techniques, have revolutionized
applications in our own century, and in
the process have changed architecture.

Technology is at the root of these
changes, and only by understanding the
technology of glass, its physics and
chemistry, and the technologies
associated with its manufacture, can the
designer become fluent in its use. By
looking at what it is, how it is made and
what its properties are, we can judge its
potential and its limitations.

In particular, by studying its
remarkable relationship with light we
can understand and manipulate its
transparency. We can then begin to see
how we can develop the palette by
combining it with other materials, and
producing the rich and complex
variations which hold so much promise
for the future.

1  3

2

the constitution, chemistry and physics of glass

Glass is an inorganic product of fusion which has cooled to a rigid state without crystallizing. This technical definition has less appeal than its common description as a super-cooled liquid: molecularly it is amorphous, like a liquid, but it is actually solid.

The solidifying of an element or compound is normally accompanied by its becoming micro-crystalline and opaque. Fortunately for man and his architecture, not all materials behave like this. It is a characteristic of the oxides of silicon, boron, germanium, phosphorus, arsenic and certain other compounds, that when heated to the point of fusion, and then carefully cooled, they maintain an amorphous, non-crystalline and transparent state. These are called 'glass formers'. Glasses are not the only transparent solids we know; in our century, we have seen the appearance of many transparent plastics to join glass. Glass is unique, however, in its rocky hardness and resistance to weathering.

Glass formers on their own have never been able to produce glasses of the

4, 5. Molten glass. The basis for all glass-making is the melting of silica or a similar compound, with a mixture of other ingredients, and the careful cooling of the melt to manipulate and control viscosity and crystallization.

5

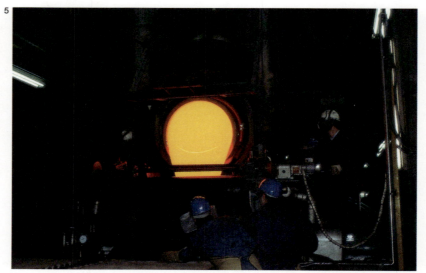

required sort at an acceptable cost, and have usually been obtained from raw materials containing lots of impurities. Moreover, glass-making techniques have historically needed the addition of other materials to assist in its manufacture. These, in turn, have amended its properties.

The eventual properties of glass are dependent upon the glass former used, the impurities in it, and the other materials added to aid manufacture and improve performance. The history of glass-making has been characterized by the search for suitable mixes. The starting point has, until the twentieth century, been the prime glass former, silica, the oxide of silicon. Silicon is one of the most common elements in the earth's crust, its most usual form being in silica, which we know as ordinary sand. As with most materials obtained by extraction, the form in which silica is available in sand is very impure, being mixed with

other oxides such as iron and the so-called 'earth' oxides. Whereas the photon absorption (the measure of its effective inhibition of light transmission) of pure silica glass is negligible, the impurities have photon absorptions which are very high in certain parts of the spectrum. Just one gram of iron oxide in a kilogram of silica gives glass the characteristic green tint. Removing this is expensive, and explains why 'water white' glasses, which are completely clear without the green tint of common soda-lime glasses, are not in common use. The extra absorptivity of iron to infrared radiation actually helps in the melting process since the glass containing it absorbs heat better. For this reason, it is sometimes added to help maintain constant colour and to reduce the cost of melting.

While the glass-maker thinks of the impurities in extracted silica as unfortunate but virtually unavoidable contami-

nants, he is very keen to add certain materials which facilitate the making of the material and improve certain aspects of quality. First, he needs fluxes to reduce the melting point. The melting point of pure silica is over 1,700°C, but the introduction of materials such as sodium oxide, potassium oxide and boric oxide reduce this to around 1,600°C. This reduction in temperature makes an enormous difference to the technology needed, and to the energy costs involved. In addition to these chemical fluxes, broken glass itself is an excellent flux material, and cullet, as it is called, is a normal constituent of glasses. Other materials are introduced as melting and refining agents, which help keep the glass free of defects and air bubbles. Avoiding crystallization is one of the historic problems of glass-makers, and crystallization preventers, such as alumina (aluminium oxide), assist in this aim by increasing the viscosity of the glass. Other additives include stabilizers which help improve chemical durability.

So, in producing what we have come to know as window glass, glass-makers have spent centuries refining the mixes developed empirically by the Romans into a precise and measured process, in which minute proportions of carefully selected materials are added to the molten material to produce the hard transparent product as economically and effectively as possible. The result of their work is soda-lime glass, seen in its early version in ancient Rome, and now produced all over the world with an international recipe which is remarkable in its consistency.

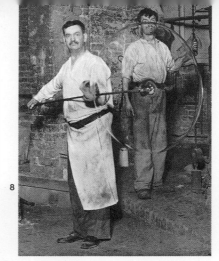

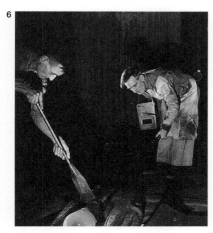

6

glass-making

Glass is by no means simply the result of its chemistry. Glass-making is a triumph of technique over viscosity, and over the difficulties of controlling chemical structure during the making.

To say that 'glass is the inorganic product of fusion which has cooled to a rigid state without crystallizing' is to refer to a process which has taxed man's ingenuity for centuries. The critical words here are 'cooled to a rigid state without crystallizing'. As has been said, glass-making materials differ from other materials by being easier to cool without the formation of the crystals which destroy the transparency. 'Easier' is not the same as 'easy', however, and the avoidance of crystal formation during cooling is one of the central skills of the glass-maker.

Glass-making is essentially very simple and involves three steps: melting, forming and carefully controlled cooling. Melting creates a molten mass in which the various constituents are completely mixed. Forming is carried

6–8. Forming in the 1950s. Up to fifty years ago traditional methods were still used, as seen here in the manufacture of coloured sheet glass; the molten glass is rotated in a mould before being blown into a cylinder (6). The viscosity of the cooled glass enables forming to be carried out at room temperature (7). A crown table being spun at the end of a punty (8).

9. Rolling glass. Rolling has remained a technique for forming flat glass for many centuries, and is still used to make patterned and other glasses.

out as the temperature of the hot 'melt' falls, and its viscosity gradually increases to the point where it can be shaped. The final process is commonly called 'annealing' in the glass industry, which properly means the process of controlled heating and cooling to achieved a desired physical state; to the glass-maker, however, annealing generally refers to the process which is principally concerned with a controlled drop in the temperature across the 'transformation temperature', that small zone in the cooling curve during which the glass effectively solidifies without crystallizing. The glass-blower's real skill lies in moving his artefact through these three stages in one continuous process.

In Chapter One we saw how the early glass-makers developed the two primary hand techniques of blowing and spinning, and established the need and function of the constituent materials by empirical means. We also saw how the advances of technique involved gradual improvement, helped only occasionally

7

8

by significant new advances, such as the invention of cast plate in 1685.

Glass-making for industries other than construction evolved significantly towards the end of the nineteenth century, a period which also saw the change of manufacturing technique from an empirical set of crafts to technologies informed by science as the processes and the chemistries became understood.

Pressed glass (the basis for the manufacture of glass bricks) was the subject of an American government report in 1884, and this period also saw the rapid development of mechanical bottle-making by manufacturers such as Michael Owens, who joined the W L Libbey and Son Company in 1888 and thus founded one of the great names in glass manufacture, Libbey Owens. Rolling glass was also a technique developed towards the end of the nineteenth century. Mason and Conqueror's glass-rolling machine also dates from this time, being patented in 1884: within ten years, single- and double-rolling was being used to make products such as wired glass and glass carrying patterns on both sides.

The attempts to draw flat glass in thin sheaths in the late nineteenth century, eventually led to the successful development of several competing technologies, notably the Belgian Fourcault method, the American Colburn/Libbey Owens

method, and the method developed by the Pittsburgh Plate Glass (PPG) Company which essentially combined the other two techniques, all described in Appendix Two.

The first half of the twentieth century, one of the great eras of glass architecture, saw glass-making improve with the evolutionary developments in technical and industrial improvement, but no new technologies. By the middle of the twentieth century, the glass industry had three complementary ways of making flat glass. Thin glass was made

9

by drawing, thicker glass (for larger, stronger panes) by casting, and rolling produced patterned and wired glass.

The post-World War II era quickly saw developments which were to transform glass-making, and the products available. In 1950, sheet glass was the predominant product used for simple building glazing, with just over seventy per cent being made by the Fourcault process, twenty per cent on

Colburn machines, and the rest by the PPG process. Then, in October 1952, Alastair Pilkington began to experiment with the idea of using molten metal to support the glass ribbon.

The principle employed was simple and beautiful. It involved the floating of molten glass on to a molten metal rather than a rigid bed. This, it was argued, would enable both sides of the resulting sheet to be flat, smooth and finished. Because the supporting liquid metal would itself be intrinsically flat and smooth, no subsequent treatment would be needed for it. As Alastair Pilkington said, 'Because the surface of the metal is

10. Cutting a continuous ribbon of glass into large plates prior to polishing, Cowley Hill, 1957.

11. Removing a finished plate from the continuous polishing table.

12. A float process plant. The high tower contains the batched raw materials located at the front of the process.

13. The use of computers is central to the whole process, from the control of the thickness, to the cutting out of defective glass and the final cutting of the ribbon into standard sizes for warehousing.

dead flat, the glass is dead flat too. Natural forces of weight and surface tension bring it to an absolutely uniform thickness.' All that was required was the selection of a metal with an appropriate melting point, preferably below that of glass (so that the molten glass helped keep the metal molten) and a density high enough to prevent any tendency for the glass to sink – the glass had to float on its bath of metal. Ideally the ponding depth of the molten glass on the metal would be a dimension which was about that of a glass window pane: thick enough to be self-supporting when its surface area was a few square metres, but thin enough to be economical in terms of the use of the material.

Tin was selected as the ideal metal, with its melting point of 232°C and its density of 7,285 kg/m³, compared with 1,726°C and 2,650 kg for silicon oxide, the basic raw material of glass. The inventors realized the importance of strictly controlled temperatures, as well as control of the constituents of the gaseous atmosphere above the glass and metal to prevent oxidation, and the design of the plant to create such an

environment for glass production was critical. By 1954, a pilot plant was running, and the float process was a commercial proposition by 1959.

The natural ponding depth of about 6 mm of molten glass on molten tin meant that this thickness of material became the first float glass marketed, thus moving it into competition with plate glass; but within five years, techniques of damming and pulling the glass in the float bath had combined to

make possible a wider range of thicknesses. Float glass soon replaced cast plate as the process for making thick glass, and by the mid-1980s, thirty years after the original invention, Pilkington were producing thin sheets by the float process, thin enough to replace the material used by the automotive industry. This effectively signed the death warrant of the drawn sheet glass industry in the developed world.

The float process provides the almost-perfect production system. When it eventually became feasible to use it to produce thin sheets, with a thickness of 4 mm or less, it replaced sheet as a way of glazing comparatively small areas with

thin panes. The floated sheets do not have the brilliant fired quality which results from the older sheet processes; the side which has been in contact with the tin is inevitably slightly dulled. However, the flexibility in available thickness, and the benefit of continuous production inherent in float, has led to its domination of glass production.

The process, which is more fully described in Appendix Two, is carried out in a fully-automated, computer-controlled factory, converting one of the cheapest and most readily available materials on the planet into an almost immaculate light-transmitting plate. Although the inherently high capital cost of the plant (around £100 million) inhibited the universal use of the float process to start with, the technology is now so good that float plants are installed worldwide.

However, the float process also has its disadvantages. As originally conceived, it had to run twenty-four hours a day, seven days a week, throughout the year. Stopping it implies the solidifying of the tin and the seizing up of the plant. An even greater disadvantage is the time it takes to vary the content of the mix to produce glasses of different colours. To make a tinted glass by the float process, which requires the inclusion of less than half a per cent by weight of a few ingredients, can take several days' worth of ribbon creation to produce a glass of consistent colour. The only alternative is to have a dedicated float line for each colour, which places great demands on production programmes in terms of predicting the

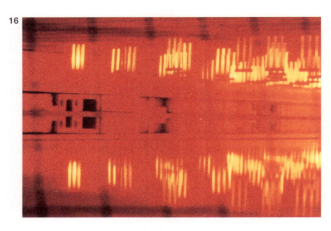

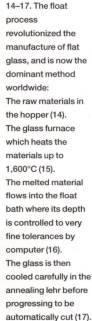

14–17. The float process revolutionized the manufacture of flat glass, and is now the dominant method worldwide: The raw materials in the hopper (14). The glass furnace which heats the materials up to 1,600°C (15). The melted material flows into the float bath where its depth is controlled to very fine tolerances by computer (16). The glass is then cooled carefully in the annealing lehr before progressing to be automatically cut (17).

market for each colour. These difficulties meant that for a building like the Pyramids at the Louvre in Paris, discussed as a case study later in the book, the water-white glass had to be made by the old cast plate process.

Other attempts to enrich the colour palette of float glass have included the so-called 'electro-float' technique whereby current is made to pass through the glass to the tin beneath, permitting the implanting of metallic particles in the surface. Such is the refined, or perhaps fickle, nature of the glass market that these glasses have failed to establish themselves.

The required continuous flow of glass through manufacturing plants has, until recently, implied a seemingly unavoidable creation of glass material flowing off the production line at about 15 m per minute, or up to half a million square metres of glass a week per float line. The establishment of realistic marketing and pricing mechanisms to sell such production is obviously difficult. However, a new generation of short-run float plants is now in production, and already having an impact.

The difficulties in establishing a clear, quantified market need for body-tinted glasses, together with the increasing sophistication of the market in respect of spectral and radiation transmission performance, have limited the amount specified and installed. For example, designers realized in the 1960s and 1970s that body-tinted glasses produced a very undesirable exclusion of light, particularly when the greys and bronzes

elicited complaints of thundery aspects from occupants. The logic behind the claim that tinted glasses reduced solar loads was often found to be specious, particularly in cooler climates.

The flat glass-makers accordingly had to look elsewhere to produce added value and more selective performance, and the comparatively new coating technologies quickly came into their own. Manufacturing of soda-lime flat glass has thus increasingly been concerned with the production of very high quality, uncoloured glass – a basic

product for the glazing designer to incorporate into ever more carefully considered glass skins – and the substrate for thin film application. The time is now ripe for the primary glass-makers to concentrate on the flexibility of the process, and the improvement of mechanical properties. The introduction of short-run plants, the development of processes to coat the ribbon as it leaves the float tank, and the floating of borosilicate glass, are all indications that the float process is entering a new stage.

physical properties

It is not surprising, given the remarkable nature of its chemistry, and the manner of its making, that glass has properties which are themselves out of the ordinary. However, glass, as dealt with in this book, is a building product, and as such has to deliver performance in terms of construction just like any other. Of particular concern in architecture are those relating to its thermal and mechanical properties, especially its strength.

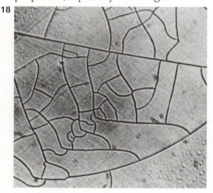

The thermal properties of glass in general, and soda-lime glass in particular, are fundamental to the way it performs, and to the way it fails. It has a thermal expansion co-efficient of about $10 \times 10^{-6}/°C$, compared with $11 \times 10^{-6}/°C$ for carbon steel and $22 \times 10^{-6}/°C$ for a typical aluminium alloy at 20°C. The impact of the additives in the glass is very significant: pure silica has a thermal expansion co-efficient twenty times less than soda-lime glass.

While the expansion properties of soda-lime glass are broadly similar to other building materials, its thermal conductivity is very low at about 1W/m °C, compared to over 200 for a

18. Griffith cracks. The smallest abrasions to glass are capable of creating surface cracks that can have a serious weakening effect.

19. Surface cracks on borosilicate glass. Cracks such as these are found on nearly all glasses, and are responsible for their comparative weaknesses.

20. A glass fibre. Glass fibres are immensely strong, but ironically ceramic fibres of carbon or silicon carbide are used to reinforce glass. Here a piece of glass reinforced with long ceramic fibres is being tested for strength. Such materials exhibit great strength without a tendency to brittle fracture.

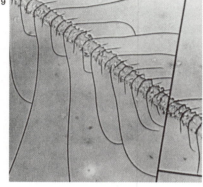

typical aluminium alloy and 60–70 for a typical carbon steel. It relates more closely to 0.6 W/m °C for water.

The performance of glass under rapidly changing temperature is a result of the interaction between these two properties in a material whose structure is not crystalline, and which generally has an imperfect surface at the microscopic level, being riddled with what are called 'Griffith cracks'. The significance of these cracks is covered in some detail as part of the discussion on strength which follows. The brittleness of soda-lime glass, taken with its thermal properties, make it a material which leaves much to be desired as a building product. Heating part of a glass pane causes conventional expansion, but the heat does not spread to surrounding areas, thus effectively making the expansion local. The intrinsic surface weakness of the material makes it very prone to fracture, although it has to be admitted that the ease with which it can be scored and snapped makes production and cutting a lot easier.

The other principal thermal property, specific heat, places glass in the normal

range for building materials. Specific heat is the measure of how much heat is necessary to raise the temperature of a substance, and the value for soda-lime glass is about 0.85–1.0 kJ/kg °C, compared to 0.9 for aluminium, about 0.5 for mild steel and 4.19 for water. It can be seen that glass 'holds' heat to about the same degree as many metals.

Many of the mechanical properties of glass are far more complex than the thermal properties, a product of the nature of the chemical and physical structure at a molecular level. Strength is a complex phenomenon, not described by any one property. A material that is strong in resisting one kind of stress may be weak in resisting another. Knowledge of this has led engineers to develop composite materials, and explains why reinforced concrete, a combination of steel and concrete, is such a popular structural material. Glass is conventionally considered to be strong in compression (it is very effective in a spherical form in deep water), and weak in tension. However, glass has also played a key part in the study of the strength of materials in the twentieth century, and detailed consideration shows that its structural properties are not simple.

We use the word strength about materials in a very familiar way, but the realities of strength and failure are very complex matters in the world of the materials scientist. In the case of glass, these realities are not only complex; they are also somewhat speculative. Before discussing glass, it helps to understand how engineers have developed an understanding about how materials

work, how to design with them, and how glass fails to fit the useful conventional patterns of behaviour.

Engineers, who tend to be those most concerned with strength and failure, rely upon predictability and analysis in their consideration of elements of construction, and the materials of which these are made. Given the inherent nature of materials, some have developed reputations for being 'structural' and other have not; this has been as much a matter of history, convention and habit as it has of 'real' properties. Thus steel and concrete might now be considered as 'structural', whereas stone, the basis for some of the greatest structures ever built, has now generally been demoted in the engineer's list of truly structural materials.

The nature of structural design requires the proposition of a configuration in materials of 'known' properties, followed by its analysis and refinement, often by a process of iteration. Critical to this process is the use of performance characteristics, generally related to the resistance of stress. The engineer is concerned with the ability of an element of construction to resist stress and change

of shape when loaded, and to do this in a predictable way. The development of the understanding of how materials work is very much a nineteenth-century phenomenon.

A key concept is known as 'Young's Modulus', named after the same English scientist, Thomas Young, who promoted the wave theory of light. Young was a typical polymath of his time, and published his ideas about the stiffness of materials in 1807. Such was Young's incompetence at expressing himself, however, that it took the French engineer Claude-Louis-Marie-Henri Navier to express the idea mathematically in 1826, in the simple equation: E (Young's Modulus) = stress/strain. This characteristic of a material becomes effective in structural evaluation once it is combined with the parallel concept of stiffness of shape.

To these two concepts, of the resistance to strain of a material, and the stiffness of an element, must be added the concept of failure, concerned with when an element ceases, for one reason or another, to serve its intended purpose.

Stiffness, strength and resistance to

21–23. Glass strength: 'Nomos' glass table by Foster Associates (21). Despite its reputation for brittleness, glass is still a very popular material for table tops. Glass ramp, Crescent Wing, Sainsbury Centre for the Visual Arts, Norwich, 1988–91, Foster Associates (22). Glass balustrade at the Queen's Stand, Epsom Racecourse, 1992, by Richard Horden Associates (23). In this balustrade, designed by Michael Wigginton and Richard Horden, the inherent strength of glass, particularly when assisted by an appropriate curved geometry, is exploited to provide protection with minimal visual interruption. The configuration was tested to an extremely high loading prior to installation, with virtually no deformation under load.

failure are all related to the internal structure of a material and, as has been established, the nature of its surface. Consideration of these, and of the overall idea of a 'strong' material, is very complex; all the more so when a material such as a metal alloy, or a composite such as reinforced concrete is examined. Thinking of strength as a manifestation of molecular bonding ceases to be useful, and the engineer has to rely on testing, tables, safety factors and other essentially empirical data.

Crucial in this understanding of how to design and evaluate structures is predictability, and it is in this realm, despite its stated resistances to compression and tension, that glass has thwarted designers' attempts to treat it structurally. Its brittle nature has led to understandable reluctance to subject it to structural analysis. Hence its low rating in terms of Weibull Modulus (which relates to the consistency of performance, allowing for variations in sample strength) referred to in Appendix One. However, by an accident in the history of technology, glass played a central part in the study of materials and structures, not so much as a study of itself, but as a material

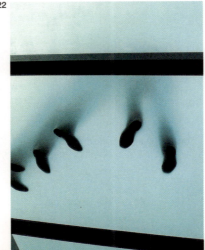

whose behaviour could exemplify structures in general.

The phenomenon of Griffith cracks has already been referred to in relation to thermal stress. When A A Griffith carried out his classic study of strength and fracture at the Royal Aircraft Establishment after the World War I, he chose glass as the material to study. As J E Gordon has pointed out, Griffith's work on the strength of glass was the basis for much later understanding of failure of large structures generally. In the knowledge that most materials do not extend indefinitely under stress, but eventually fail, Griffith's work was concerned with the causes of failure, and the relationship between surface energy, surface tension and strain, with the essential source of all strength, the interatomic forces, at the centre of the study.

The tensile strength of all materials ultimately derives from the bonding forces at an atomic level, and it is a characteristic of glass that the strength of large samples is much less than that of small samples (such as whiskers); it is also much less than theoretical calculation based on the internal forces would suggest. Griffith's work tested glass rods 1 mm in diameter, and he found that they failed at a tensile stress 100 times less than theory suggested. He tried the same tests with thinner and thinner fibres, and found that strength increased rapidly as he approached a diameter of 0.002 mm.

Griffith suggested that the weakness of glass was a result of solid pieces being full of internal cracks, these in turn resulting perhaps from the molecules

failing to join up properly as the glass cooled. Subsequent work by E N da C Andrade in 1937 showed the patterns of Griffith cracks on glass, although there is a possibility that the patterns seen were a result of sodium etching. John Morley, working in England in 1952, demonstrated that carefully made thick rods and fibres could have high strength, but researchers became aware of significant reduction in the strength of glass if the surface was scratched. This reduction did not occur if the outer surface was

protected by a sheath, and Griffith cracks became associated with the accidental damage to surface.

The problem with glass is that it not only suffers in strength from this surface damage, but also suffers from local crystallization. Making glass is a struggle against crystallization, as has been described earlier. If crystallization does occur, albeit in tiny areas, the local molecular arrangement becomes more dense and locally contracted. This process of 'devitrification' weakens the glass. With devitrification and Griffith cracks to contend with, the comparative weakness

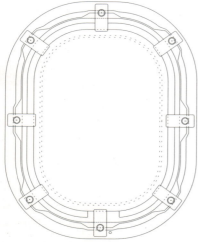

Elevation

24

Section

0   100mm

0   4in

24. Aircraft window cabin panel by Hawker Siddeley Aviation, 1975. Aircraft demand very light materials with high strength and impact resistance, and the development of alternatives to glass has been driven by this requirement.

25. Weathering of glass at Chartres Cathedral. The appearance of the glass at Chartres demonstrates two aspects of the qualities of the material: its dull exterior, which belies the interior brilliance and evolves a consonance with the surrounding stone, and its longevity.

of glass in tensile stress is to be expected. It is not surprising that the strengthening of glass by chemical or other means has been a preoccupation of glassmakers, particularly in the second half of the twentieth century.

Given the peculiarities and evident weakness of glass, it would be easy to dismiss it as a structural material. In fact, of course, although its brittleness is a defect, glass can perform structurally, and designers are increasingly exploiting its structural potential. From its use as cantilevered balustrading to load-bearing walls, roofs and beams, glass structures are appearing, invariably in the toughened form in which the surface defects are largely compensated for by placing the whole surface in compression.

In terms of application, strength is a problem related to another inherent difficulty associated with glass as a material for construction and product design: its weight. Glass is commonly perceived as a heavy material. There is an irony in this, related to the parallel (and in some ways real) perception of the weakness and brittleness of glass.

The density, or specific gravity, of pure silica glass is 2,200 kg per cubic metre, and that of soda-lime glass, with its additional constituents, is about twelve per cent higher at 2,470 to 2,490. This compares with 2,700 for aluminium and marble, and 7,900 for mild steel. Timbers vary greatly, but have specific gravities commonly between 500 and 900. The transparent plastics have specific gravities between 1,100 and 1,200, only slightly denser than water.

It can be seen from these figures that glass is 'lighter' than aluminium, and one-third as 'heavy' as steel. The problem with glass as a building material lies in its strength:weight ratio. Because glass is prone to damage failure, it has to be installed in thick sheets, whether for a table top or in a building. This is, to say the least, a pity. Its Young's Modulus is about the same as aluminium, but all architects are aware of the need for thickness in glass when large plates are considered. A 10 mm or 15 mm plate of aluminium is a very rare component indeed in a building, but quite usual for glass.

When we can make glass stronger, we will be able to remove its reputation for heaviness, particularly if we can involve the transparent plastics. The aircraft industry has already learned this lesson, as will be noted by any passenger in an airplane. Aircraft windows represent a classic reconciliation between the advantages and disadvantages of glass and transparent plastics. Those in the passenger cabin are much lighter than a conventional building window, but with a surface much more prone to scratching. The pilot's 'window' is a very sophisticated and heavy composite with coatings for heating.

Even with these problems of strength and weight, there are reasons to believe that, despite its nature, the structural properties of glass can now be better exploited without threat of catastrophic failure, and glass structures are appearing with increasing regularity. Several typical examples are included in the Case Studies section of Chapter Three.

25

Strength is an important property in a building material, and one which presents engineers and architects using glass with interesting problems of analysis and use. Some of its other mechanical properties, however, are both easy to define, and of known real value in resisting weathering: hardness and chemical resistance are both very important qualities.

Glass is very hard, with values similar to those of steel. In a material for which transparency is its greatest asset, hardness is fundamental. The cleanness of a transparent material is vital to its performance in viewing and illumination, and cleaning is an abrasive activity. Their inability to withstand abrasion is one of the major weaknesses of the transparent plastics. While the susceptibility of glass to surface damage of the order of magnitude of the Griffith cracks has been described, and is a cause of weakness, this does not detract from the inherent hardness of glass, and its ability to retain its finish over centuries if it is properly and regularly cleaned. Even without regular cleaning, the glory of Chartres Cathedral remains over 800 years. The windows were last cleaned, restored and re-leaded in the 1970s.

Of similar and related performance in its effect on transparency is its durability against chemical attack. Glass is very nearly that 'Holy Grail' of chemistry, the universal container. It can be used to

contain virtually anything without
chemical degradation or (equally important) without its own constituents being
leached out into the material contained.
Given enough time, glass will degrade;
long exposure to our polluted environment will eventually damage the surface
of a window which is never washed.
However, it will lose its transparency
through dirtying much faster than
through chemical deterioration.
Window glass, which is one of the
poorer glass materials in terms of corrosion resistance, only corrodes by less
than 8 micrometres (0.008 mm) per year
when attacked by water and sulphur
dioxide in our atmosphere.

   With all the mechanical performance
characteristics spelled out (the
Appendix provides more detail), it can
be seen that glass is both remarkable and
flawed. It provides one of the most
important performance properties
known to man in its durable transparency, but it has suffered ever since the
creation of its soda-lime version from a
propensity to failure. The beguiling brilliance of the polished glass surface
stands in contrast to the the dirty, broken
windows which are so often a testimony
to architectural and social neglect. It is in
relation to mechanical performance that
the need for treatments is most apparent,
as an alternative to the more radical
steps of selecting other chemistries. Very
strong primary glass materials exist, but
the difficulties inherent in their manufacture in sheet form, and the consequent cost, currently prohibit their
widespread use in the budgets generally
available in architecture.

26. 'Les Serres' of the
Cité des Sciences et
de l'Industrie at Parc
de la Villette, Paris,
designed between
1980 and 1986,
architect Adrien
Fainsilber; glass
installations by
Rice Francis Ritchie.
Recently architects,
and more usually
engineers, have
relished the capability
of glass to respond to
structural demands.

26

27 light and transmission:
the mystery of light

Historically, the prime performance characteristic of glass in relation to architecture has been in respect of the transmission of light. Indeed, one of Le Corbusier's great canonical statements was that architecture is 'the masterly, correct and magnificent play of masses brought together in light.' Light is truly the raw material of architecture, just as sound is that of music. The wonder of glass in architecture is that light can pass through it, as well as be reflected from it. At an aesthetic level it presents the architect with unique opportunities; technically, and in consideration of architecture as the provision of a protective envelope, its qualities are perhaps even more important, and have only recently been fully understood.

The way in which glass behaves in relation to light and energy is fundamental to its success, and sometimes its failure. In order to understand and manipulate glass in architecture, we must therefore understand how it interacts with light; but light itself is in many ways a mysterious phenomenon.

In our attempts to explain light, two theories are commonly employed which together also help us to use it and predict its behaviour. Light transmission has been variously described in terms of 'particle' or 'wave' theory. These two theories have been vying with each other for over two centuries, but now sit happily together in their late twentieth century versions, often used independently to explain different aspects of light.

The success of the particle theory before 1800 was undermined by the Englishman Young and the Frenchman Fresnel early in the nineteenth century, both of whom promoted the wave theory. This received powerful support from the ideas of James Clerk Maxwell, the great Scottish mathematical physicist, who postulated and developed his theory of electromagnetic radiation between 1864 and 1873. By the turn of the twentieth century, Max Planck had moved our understanding of the nature of energy forward, and concluded that it existed in distinct 'quantum' packages. This proposition, when developed, was able to unify the old wave and particle theories, acknowledging that light and other forms of electromagnetic radiation behaved both like particles and waves.

A detailed consideration of light and the nature of transparency is provided in Appendix One. In a brief discussion here, we can consider that the wave theory helps us understand how diffraction and interference work, just as they do with waves travelling across water, and that the particle theory helps

28

to explain the absorption or transmission of light by different materials. Energy 'waves' or particles are emitted by all bodies with a temperature above absolute zero (0 K, equivalent to -273°C), but radiation only becomes perceptible to human senses when quite high temperatures are reached. 'Hot' bodies (those with temperatures appreciably above absolute zero) emit radiation according to characteristic curves which correspond to their temperatures. The 'colour temperature' of a hot body is related to this characteristic curve, which has a peak in a specific place.

The sun emits radiation with a peak wavelength of about 500 nanometres (500 millionths of a millimetre), and this corresponds to the emission of radiation from a body with a temperature of 5,900 K, or 5,627°C. Our eyes respond to radiation at wavelengths between 400 nm and 750 nm, having evolved in relation to the sun's most powerful emission; 400 nm light is violet in colour, and 750 nm light is red. A very hot body like the sun will emit at all visible frequencies (as well as frequencies above and below them), and thus appear more or less white as they combine.

By a miracle of chemistry, glass is transparent in accordance with a curve very similar to the radiation of the sun. Its peak transmission is very close to peak solar radiation, and it also trans-

27. Structural glass prisms, designed by James Carpenter, 1985–7: the twentieth century inheritance of the great medieval tradition.

28. The sun, as often experienced in the damp air of temperate climates, its radiation modulated by the atmosphere to a diffuse white light, but still with a power at the surface of the earth of 50W/m² or more.

29. The wonderful colour at Chartres Cathedral is a result of the spectral modification of sunlight and daylight by the chemistry of glass, and of the paints applied to it as thin coatings.

30. All glasses reflect light impinging on their surface to a degree dependent upon their refractive index, unless they are specially treated. Light levels on each side of the glass affect the degree of visible reflection. In this photograph the interior can be seen clearly on the left through the glass, but as the angle of incidence approaches a glancing angle, reflection is all that can be seen.

mits fairly well as wavelengths increase into the so-called 'near infrared', which we perceive as radiated heat rather than light. Electric fires burn at red heat rather than white heat because at white heat temperatures they would melt.

The important aspect of transmission for a designer in glass is that, whether considered in terms of waves or photons, the real materials around us transmit or absorb light in accordance with the way their atomic structure passes or soaks up impinging photons of different energy levels. The appearance of conventional soda-lime glass as green is a direct result of the presence in it of iron oxide, whose atomic structure absorbs red light and transmits blue/green at the other end of the visible spectrum. The absorption of the red (and infrared) light makes 'green' glass good at absorbing radiated heat energy. This selective photon absorption is the basis for filter design.

Thus, whereas a perfect transmitter would permit the passage of all energy over the wavelengths considered, glass, in its various forms, and the coatings which may be applied to it, transmit light at different wavelengths in different proportions. Some of these are intrinsic to the chemical properties of glass and are virtually unchangeable, but as glass and window science has progressed we have become more concerned with describing and achieving required performances, whether in single sheet materials or in more complex layered assemblies.

colour and transmission control

The principal quality of glass is transparency, but transparency is not an absolute property. As has been explained, all materials absorb light to a certain degree and scales of transparency are essential indicators of performance. Transparency depends on chemistry and thickness, and varies wavelength by wavelength.

Transparency in relation to a pane of glass is complicated by the action of the surfaces which bound and define the material. Even light impinging on clean glass at an angle of incidence of 0° (what is known in optics as 'normal' to the surface) undergoes a certain amount of reflection at the surfaces, both on its way into the glass and on its way out again. Perpendicular or 'normal' incidence of light on a soda-lime silicate glass results in a loss of transmission of four per cent at each surface. As the angle of incidence increases from normal, so does the amount of reflection at the surface, starting to increase above 40°, and increasing dramatically above 70°, to almost 100 per cent reflection at a glancing angle. Given that daylight impinges on a window pane at every angle, this makes the mathematical assessment of transmission co-efficients, as part of the consideration of the apparently simple concept of transparency, rather complex.

Most glass manufacturers' catalogues provide transmission factors, but a standard measure, the Internal Transmittance, can be used to compare glasses without consideration of the problems of surface reflectance. Internal

Transmittance is defined as the ratio of radiant flux reaching the exit surface of a plane of parallel glass 25 mm thick to the flux which leaves the entry surface: in other words, it is a measure of the absorption of the light within the body of the glass only. Optical glasses, for which light transmission is a key property, vary in Internal Transmittance from about eighty to ninety per cent for wavelengths around 360 nm up to ninety-nine percent at 500 nm (this ignores surface reflection loss). Compared with these figures, typical daylight transmittances for soda-lime glass are about eighty-seven per cent for 6 mm thick float, dropping to about seventy-seven per cent for 20 mm material, so it can be seen that glass is by no means completely transparent. This is particularly the case in terms of its overall daylight transmittance (as opposed to how much we can see through it) because of the angles at which light strikes the surface and a small amount of internal absorption.

Transparency in terms of transmittance is dealt with in Appendix

30

One, and is a property with which architects should be more familiar. The important issue in considering the property is how it is defined by the manufacturer or authority who quotes it. It is critical to know whether the figure being given is in the visible wavebands only, or over all solar radiation wavebands, and whether it is for all incident light at whatever angle of incidence.

The other major optical property of transparent materials is the refractive index, which is a measure of the attenuation of light through the materials. Light is always slowed through materials and, as a result, a light ray striking a glass surface is bent as it goes through from one material to another. The phenomenon is well known to all of us who were shown at school a straight stick apparently bending as it is lowered into water. This refraction is the basis of optical lens design.

Without an understanding of what it means, it is of little practical use to know that the refractive index of soda-lime glass is 1.52, and that the indices of different common glasses varies between 1.47 and 1.56. A full explanation is given in Appendix One. However, the behaviour of light meeting the bounding surface between materials of different optical densities is of great importance, and is the basis of fibre optics, prismatics and other newly-developing technologies.

The optical properties of so-called 'clear glass' are only part of the story of the study of transmission, however.

31. The Seagram Building, Park Avenue, New York, 1954–8, Mies van der Rohe. The selection of the selenium pink-grey-bronze glass for the Seagram Building is an essential concomitant to the bronze used for the framing and spandrels. The glass has quite exceptional beauty, varying in its hue according to the time of day and the direction of the sun; it exploits the ambiguity of the material in a manner far beyond the use of its solar control capabilities, and has the effect of turning the building into an effective solid in daylight.

32. Lever House, Park Avenue, New York, 1951–2, Skidmore Owings and Merrill. An early architectural use of green heat-absorbing glass.

31

Having created the 'clear', virtually uncoloured product, the glass-maker's other preoccupation, from late Roman times onwards, has been the creation of colour. This has extended from the pictorial use of stained glass described in Chapter One, through to the use of radiation transmission modifiers as used in our own century.

The earliest tinted (as opposed to highly-coloured) glass used for its technical performance in the twentieth century was the pale green introduced in the USA in the 1930s. The purpose of this was to reduce glare in automobile windscreens, and in their concern to ensure good vision, the American Standards Authority was careful to specify minimum levels of light transmission. After World War II, as the new generation of commercial buildings began to appear in the USA and Europe, these body-tinted glasses became associated with a certain glamour as well as supposed technical efficacy.

The first tinted glasses in buildings used in any quantity were the green glasses derived from reinstating the iron oxide so painstakingly removed in the first purification process, but adding them back in very precise quantities. Iron oxide is very good at absorbing photons towards the near infrared, and thus reduces the transmission of solar heat.

After the green glass of Lever House in Park Avenue, New York of 1951–2, came the bronze glass of the Seagram Building of 1954–8 diagonally opposite it. While Lever House, by Skidmore Owings and Merrill, used a by then conventional and readily available tint, Mies van der Rohe, working with Philip Johnson, had a more ambitious aesthetic idea, to use a glass which complemented the bronze of the framing and panelling of the curtain wall. The selenium glass created for this building was an early example of the 'bronze' glass which was to gain so much favour in the 1960s and seventies.

The green and bronze colours were joined by the grey range, which used a variety of chemistries to produce slightly different greys as the proportions of cobalt oxide, nickel oxide and selenium were varied and added to the iron oxide picking off the right photons. The manufacturers were very competitive with their greys, as with the other colours, and each producer took careful note of the success or otherwise of a particular tone, as a sort of glass fashion

industry became established. However, two things conspired to limit the efficacy and widespread use of these tinted glasses after the first decade or so of their use.

The first was related to how poor and inappropriate their radiation transmission was across the visible solar spectrum, particularly in northern latitudes. Their use in the USA was ostensibly concerned with heat rejection, with the idea of reducing air conditioning loads. This had a certain credibility at most latitudes in the USA, even those as far north as New York at a latitude of 41 degrees. However, fifty-three per cent of all solar energy is in the visible spectrum, and it is by definition impossible to reduce heat gain much beyond fifty per cent without dramatically affecting light transmission. In southern climates, where glare might be a problem, heavy tints could be useful, though only in summer. In northern Europe, however,

32

with latitudes between 48 degrees and 60 degrees, the use of tinted glass was soon found to be counterproductive. The small benefits in heat rejection in summer were outweighed by the loss of light in the other three seasons, and simply gave gloomy interiors. The tinted glass in these buildings was in fact generally no more than glamour-wrap, which lost its appeal as soon as its shortcomings were realized (particularly by those who occupied the buildings). The problem here was essentially that most of the work to reduce heat

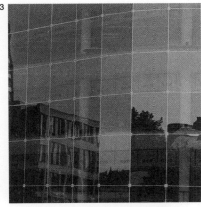

transmission was being done by the iron oxide. The other materials tended mostly to affect transmission in the visible spectrum. While this helped in reducing the overall transmission, the reduction in the light content is an inefficient way of controlling heat when light itself is at a premium.

The second reason for the short life of tinted glass as a generalized solution for the building envelope was the invention of the float process, described in detail in Appendix Two. The float process, developed by Pilkington in the

33, 34. The Willis Faber & Dumas Building, Ipswich, 1973–5, Foster Associates. This building completes one particularly thematic journey in glass architecture. The curvilinear plan form, and the suspension system, are both prefigured in Mies van der Rohe's 1922 Office Tower. However, Mies's early building was intended to be an essay in transparency, and Willis Faber & Dumas appears as a solid derived from the colour of its glass, in the same manner as the Seagram Building.

UK from 1952 onwards, was both the greatest invention in the history of flat glass-making, and the effective end of the idea of tailor-made body-tinting. While tinted plate glass could be produced in small quantities by virtually any mix desired by the glass-maker, the architect or the client, the float process is continuous, relentlessly floating its viscous mix down from the melt tank to the annealing lehr across the bath of molten tin. To change the colour and ensure an even tone using one float line takes three days to produce homogeneity in the mix, which amounts to a great deal of waste. The glass-maker's answer to this was to restrict colour availability, often dedicating a float line to each colour. The market was studied assiduously to establish whether one particular tone was preferred to another, but once selected, the colour was set. Apart from the problem of electing and creating a tint, the glass-makers had an enormous problem to deal with in terms of replacement: a broken tinted window requires replacement by exactly the same tone,

and the stocking and manufacturing problems of large ranges proved insurmountable.

So, with their intrinsic inefficiency in terms of light and heat transmission, with the gloomy interiors they gave, and with the palette limitations applied by the makers, it is not surprising that tinted glass buildings were not in vogue in northern Europe for long. This is not to say that extremely successful buildings using tinted glasses have not been made; the Willis Faber Dumas Building included as a case study in the next chapter is a very good example. It is simply that architects have learned how and when to use the materials, and architecture is all the better for it.

The essential reasons behind the difficulty in appropriately applying these modified transmission materials lie in the failure of architects to understand and apply the physics of transmission, which in turn is a result of their use by under-educated architects for the wrong reasons, without regard to their thermal and light transmission performance. The same is largely true of the application of the succeeding generations of modified transmission materials, the surface-modified and coated glasses.

Given the commercial problems of body-tinting glasses, the ever-resourceful and inventive glass-makers quickly came up with ways of modifying transmission performance without tampering with the melt. They developed techniques for affecting the surface only.

Pilkington created two such surface treatments in a period of only a few

years. The first was called Spectrafloat, and was made by driving metal ions into the surface of the molten glass using an electromotive force. The resulting glass was only a short-term success, not least because of the rationalization and success of body-tinted bronze float.

A second product, known as Reflectafloat, was created a few years later, and was made differently. Gas, basically a silicon hydride gas sometimes known as silane, was directed on to the float ribbon, which decomposed into silicon. This surface layer is silver in reflection and bronze in transmission. The process is still in operation, and is used to coat body-tinted glasses for use in hotter climates.

The comparative falling out of favour of these products is partly because they failed to persuade architects and building-owners of their performance and appearance, but partly because a new generation of products was beginning to emerge. In the sixties and seventies, coated glasses began to appear in the market. To begin with their use was principally in hot, sunny climates. The coatings were, in performance terms, essentially radiation shields, reflecting away unwanted solar energy. Visually they were, from the outside, mirrors, and 'mirror glass buildings' became almost a category of architectural typology.

The term 'mirror glass' was not only indicative of the visual effect of these new coated products; it also reminds us of the long history of coating as a technology. Mirror-making is an ancient skill, mastered by the Venetians, itself placing demands on the glass-manufacturing processes over centuries in relation to flatness and purity: only the best glass could be used for mirrors. Early mirror-making was essentially a coating technique, originally using silver; the product was, of course, opaque.

The last quarter of the twentieth century, however, has brought a range of techniques of applying materials to glass so thinly that their intrinsic crystalline opacity has been rendered transparent simply because of how few atoms were present in the layer to absorb the photons. As time progressed through the seventies and eighties, so technologies developed which enabled manufacturers to apply ever thinner layers. To begin with, performance and appearance were almost entirely led by manufacturing criteria rather than highly-developed performance demand.

A project designed by the author in the early seventies demonstrates the product range at the time. Visual and performance criteria based on a need for undistorted spectral transmission, rejection of unwanted solar energy and a neutral tonal appearance from

35

35. More intelligent applications of thin films than the thick oxides applied to architectural glasses have long been available in camera lenses, where they are designed to decrease reflections within a lens system, and increase the amount of light travelling through it.

36, 37. The Hyatt Regency Dallas at Reunion, 1976–8, Welton Becket Associates (36), and Dallas skyline at sunset – thin glamour-wrap (37). The development of reflective coatings for buildings has occurred over the last 25 years. The aggressive solar radiation in Dallas, which at 33 degrees is the same latitude as the Mediterranean coast of North Africa, makes radiation shielding by reflection appropriate.

the outside (so that reflections were correctly coloured), effectively ruled out many of the newly available products, which relied on metals or metal oxides. The metals concerned, selected not only for their performance and colour, but also because of their stability and adherence to the glass substrate, frequently produced the golds, coppers and blues which were so characteristic of reflective glass at the time.

Concern about the long-term stability of the few products available from Europe and South Africa, using metals such as chromium which were comparatively neutral in transmission and appearance, led to the selection of an American product because of its twenty-year warranty. Such was the concern of the American manufacturer about the installation of the product and the effect of the construction details on product life, that the detailing of the cladding system was subject to their criteria and comment, taking precedence over the advice of the TNO in the Netherlands, one of the most prestigious building research establishments in Europe.

Since this time, technology has revolutionized the application of thin films. The description of the various techniques available is described fully in Appendix One, but in this review the most significant issues to refer to are the congruence of two influences on thin film development. The first was the development of techniques which enabled thinner and thinner layers to be applied. The first coated architectural

36

products carried films which would now hardly be called thin at all: compared with the coatings applied to a camera lens, for example, they were almost plastered on. This had the effect, given their metallic nature, of making them mirrors. It also restricted the number of coatings which could be applied. It should be mentioned that the makers of architectural products had less freedom with the performance of their coatings than the camera lens manufacturers who were unconcerned about the appearance of their lenses in reflection: the character-istic 'bloom' on a lens is not acceptable in a conventional glazing application.

The second influence was the realization that performance should lead the product, rather than the other way round. Consideration of camera lenses is an indicator of the effect performance-thinking has on light transmission technology when performance itself is critical. The early post-war Leica Guide demonstrated the lens-maker's concern for transmission, not often shared by the flat glass-maker until several decades later. It is worth quoting the relevant paragraph from the guide:

A modern process for improving the performance of a lens consists of the application of a microscopically fine deposit of inorganic substance on the surfaces. This considerably reduces reflections between glass to air surfaces of the lens. In an Elmar [lens] for example, the loss of light due to surface reflection is about 35%, which can be reduced by coating to about 5%. Apart from the gain in speed of the lens, which may be about half a stop, it is of greater importance that the light scatter which impairs image contrast is eliminated, producing a more brilliant negative. Leica lenses made since 1946 leave the factory coated.

The importance of the ideas expressed in such a statement will not be lost on anyone who has worked with coated glasses over the last twenty years. As we have come to realize the importance of performance of glasses, and as technology has developed, so the efficacy of glazing has improved.

37

Particularly significant is the objective of the lens coating to increase light transmission, a vital performance property in a lens system.

Perhaps the most important recent manifestations of these two influences, of improved technique and performance awareness, have been respectively those of sputtering technology and the understanding of low emissivity. Sputtering enables coatings to be applied so thinly that none of them need be seen. The number of visible light photons absorbed with such a technique, in which many thin films can be laid down over each other only nanometres thick, is so small that the producer can begin to tailor their performance.

Low emissivity was, and is, simply a typical performance property in which the use of specific oxides or metals in thin films produces very low radiation emission. This means that a low-emissivity (low-E) glass warmed by conduction by the interior of a room can have its emission to the outside inhibited by coating the exterior surface with a low-E film. Double-glazing units using low-E glass have their typical U-values reduced to 1.9 W/ °C or below. The fact that emissivity and reflectivity are inversely proportionate to each other provides a degree of solar reflection as well, although consideration is complicated by the behaviour in respect of longwave and shortwave radiation. Low-E coatings are already made in several versions. Tin oxide-silver-tin oxide coatings can be totally transparent to shortwave radiation, or can have the silver layer thickened to reflect an

38. Business Promotion Centre, Duisburg, 1993, Sir Norman Foster and Partners. European work has created an approach to glass architecture suited to its latitudes and concerns with energy. Duisburg is one of an emerging series of buildings developing ideas of the energy-efficient wall.

increasing percentage of both visible and infrared radiation, giving both low-E and solar control in one coating. Other coatings include fluorine-doped tin oxide, which is harder than the sputtered tin oxide-silver-tin oxide version. These new low-E glasses are important additions to the glass palette.

There are many different forms of coating available as we progress towards the end of the twentieth century, and the real advantage with all of them is that they are applied as a secondary process to glass as a substrate, thus allowing the glass-maker to concentrate on other functions of melt chemistry, while passing to the coater the responsibility of transmission performance and other film functions (such as carrying electric current, for example).

Specialist coating companies working in the lighting and optical industries are now producing coated glasses by evaporation and other techniques in which up to forty or more layers 50 nm thick are laid over each other as interference layers in dichroic products, in which reflection and transmission are tailor-made to design. Although hard coatings are available, all coatings suffer to a greater or lesser degree from being vulnerable to damage, and are generally best applied to the side of a glass which will be protected in a cavity. However, properly adapted for use in buildings, these products could transform the efficiency of glazing in architecture and are the basis of what is called the 'smart window', the window of the future.

38

39

the developing palette

The last twenty to thirty years have seen a dramatic change in the way architects, designers and glass-makers have thought about glass. While it is true that most flat glass is still being used in its simplest form, single-glazed in simple installations, the increasing sophistication of the market, the spread of this sophistication down the market, and the developments in glass and associated technologies, have led to the proliferation of techniques to enhance performance.

Nor has flat glass been the only form of the material to have a major evolutionary impact on architecture. New technologies and the routine implementation of technology transfer have created a rich and expanding palette. The glass catalogue in Appendix One shows how the palette can be classified in terms of process and complexity, and a review of technologies shows how rich the palette is, and could be in the future.

The evolving technology is discussed here under four headings: Treatments, which take the primary floated (or rolled, or even cast) product and amend it by a secondary process; Other Glasses, the palette used by those involved in industries other than the flat glass industry, whose chemical content and form differ from soda lime, and which provide a rich source of ideas for architecture; Alternative Materials, the transparent and translucent plastics which have come to complement glass; and Composites, the rich and infinite range of products and performances which come from the combination of materials.

treatments

Fortunately for the designer in glass, the creation of the flat annealed product is not the end of the matter. Like most other materials, glass can be worked and treated to modify and develop its characteristics; these secondary processes can be fundamental to the effectiveness of glass.

The most important of these is heat strengthening, also termed toughening or tempering. In the UK, the term heat strengthening is used to describe the partial toughening process employed to produce a glass two to three times as strong as the annealed product. Fully toughened glass ('tempered' in the USA) is four to five times as strong as annealed glass. Of more significance than strength in this distinction is the fact that heat-strengthened glass breaks like annealed glass (that is the glass produced by the primary process and untreated). It thus cannot be described as a 'safety' glass.

The discovery that the use of heat and sudden cold could change the nature of glass was not a new one when it was finally perfected at the end of the 1920s. However, the development of the technique since then has gone some way to overcoming the problems of glass strength, and has contributed to new forms of expression. Like so many techniques in glass manufacture, the process of toughening is both beautifully simple and very effective. The annealed glass is heated up to about 625°C and then rapidly and carefully cooled. This cooling, which can only be applied to the surface, initially puts the surface into tension as it tries to contract over the still hot interior of the glass. Then, as the interior of the glass cools, it contracts and pulls the surface into compression. The differential cooling between interior and surface also puts the interior into tension, as the already cooled rigidity of the surface resists the cooling shrinkage of the central zone of the glass. A bending tensile stress as large as the surface compression stress can then be applied before the glass itself goes into tension.

The combined effect is to produce a stronger material in tension, up to five times the strength of annealed glass.

Resulting from the complexity of stresses in the materials an important side benefit occurs: failure leads to multiple crack branching due to the release of elastic energy, and the glass breaks into relatively safe pieces. Recently, the problems of glass imperfections, such as nickel sulphide inclusions which led to some dramatic spontaneous failures,

39. Glass door to Now and Zen Restaurant, London, 1991, Rick Mather with Dewhurst Macfarlane. The building incorporates beautiful uses of glass structurally, from the frameless revolving door to the glass plate pavement lights.

40. The architect of this Regency terrace in Brunswick Square, Hove, was rigorous enough to realize that the curved bays at the front of the house demanded curved glass rather than crude facets.

41. Curvature, together with the great strength, which comes from heat treatment, is now part of the aesthetic of vehicles such as this coach by Mercedes Benz.

42. The double curvature in the Eco Yacht, by Francis and Francis, doubtless owes something to the expertise developed by Martin Francis as the designer of the glass system at Willis Faber & Dumas, and as a Partner in Rice Francis Ritchie who designed 'Les Serres' at Parc de la Villette.

have now been substantially overcome by the process of heat soaking, which ensures that contaminated material does not reach the market place.

From its commercial development in the 1920s, toughened glass has become a material of great importance in the creation of large-scale glass assemblies, and suspended-glass walls are now commonplace, despite the fact that the glass cannot be worked or drilled after toughening.

While it cannot be said that the inherent weakness of soda-lime glass has been completely overcome, we now have available a very much stronger material. Of equal significance to architecture, new means of holding these toughened sheets in place have revolutionized architectural expression, as bolted fixings have permitted the removal of the window frame.

The idea of heating glass to change its character is not restricted to strengthening, however. Heat-softened glass is plastic, and heated glass can be

curved permanently to adopt simple shapes or even (to a lesser degree) double curvature. From the curved glass windows of Regency times to the aerodynamism of a bus windscreen, glass-bending has become an important process, particularly in vehicle manufacture. It is impossible to think of automobiles at the end of the twentieth century without the benefit of curved glass to maintain the lines of the vehicle. Since rapid chilling of the heated and curved material automatically produces heat strengthening or toughening, depending on the rate of cooling, with the potential production of a relatively safe material, the benefits are threefold. A very good example can be seen in Francis and Francis' Motor Yacht ECO, which demonstrates the potential for double-curvature and toughening in a unit with a girth of 1,600 mm by 1,050 mm, using glass 19 mm thick.

Tempering is not the only available way to increase glass strength. Chemical strengthening involves ion exchange induced in the glass surface by heating sodium glass in a molten potassium or lithium salt. Both these salts have larger ions than those in sodium. These larger ions change places with their smaller sodium counterparts, effectively compressing the surface. With an exchange zone of 0.1 mm the strength of the resulting material can increase by five or six times. Chemically-strengthened glasses are used in the aircraft and lighting industries, and for toughening ophthalmic lenses.

Transparency, as well as strength, can be amended by secondary treatment.

Perfect transparency is not always needed in a glass, and obscuration is a common requirement. Etching, using hydrofluoric acid, and sand-blasting are both ways of producing beautiful diffusing surfaces.

Finally, the idea of coating glass is not so much a treatment as an addition, and is discussed above in its relation to its prime role to amend transmission. It is also dealt with in some detail in Appendix Two. However, it would be wrong to leave a discussion like this without referring to the technique commonly known as 'fritting', in which specialist ceramic paints are applied in a pattern on the glass, often by the silk-screen process. This technique joins the ancient skill of 'flashing' which has served the glass-maker for so long.

As will be obvious from this brief review, the appearance of the primary glass plate from the annealing lehr need only be the beginning of its journey into architecture.

other glasses

When the history of glass in architecture is discussed, it is with an unspoken, but clear assumption that the glass being referred to is soda-lime glass, which has formed the basis of flat glass-making for thousands of years. Simple or doped soda-lime glass has consistently served architecture, and still does, with its advantages in terms of manufacture, and the comparative high degree of development in our techniques for making it to very high standards. With the arrival of a continuous float process tailored to it, the dedication of flat glass-manufacture to the soda-lime product appeared, in the 1950s and sixties, to be set for the foreseeable future.

However, soda-lime glass is only one of hundreds, if not thousands, of glasses known to the glass technologist. Many of these lie in the realms of optical science

43. Fritted window, Stockley Park, London, 1989, Foster Associates. Fritting is a technique that creates a printed pattern on a glass which is effectively fired into the surface, using specially constituted paints.

44. For high performance we must look outside the field of so-called architectural glasses. This small tungsten halogen lamp, the size of a paper clip, relies on the creation of very high brightness with a high corrected colour temperature, and a corresponding high filament temperature.

45. Specialist manufacturers have provided us with borosilicates, which have their origin in the creation of tubing for the chemical and pharmaceutical industries. This tube is made by Schott of Germany.

46, 47. The discovery of ceramic glass has led to its use to make kitchen hobs, and tiles for nose cones of space vehicles, where high re-entry temperatures had to be withstood.

or other worlds of technology and industry, such as lighting and radiation analysis. Some of these (to the architect) more exotic glasses are now finding their way into buildings. Given the deficiencies of soda-lime glass in terms of brittleness, low resistance to temperature change, thermal expansion and strength (to refer to only a few), it is clear that we should be seeking to improve or replace the historical product, and specific performance requirements are now increasingly entering the world of architecture and introducing new chemistries.

A fuller review of these is in Appendix One, but it is appropriate in this brief scan across glass technology to show how architecture is already enriched by the use of the enormously varied world of glass.

While the commonest use of silica in glass-making is as the prime constituent in soda-lime glass, silica makes a fine glass on its own, much finer in many respects than when 'contaminated' by the fluxes and other materials used in conventional flat glass-making. It is stronger, and more heat resistant. Its thermal softening and melting properties are about twice those of soda-

lime glass, which, of course, makes it much more difficult to produce. Silica, or 'quartz', glass is the material from which tungsten halogen light bulbs are made.

However, other 'exotic' glasses have proved themselves more amenable to manufacture as flat glass for architecture, and the most common of these is borosilicate. There are many 'glass formers': that is, materials which can be cooled to an effectively solid state without crystallizing, while remaining or becoming transparent. Boron is one of these, and boric oxide mixed with silica makes one of the most useful glasses currently in circulation. Borosilicate glass has temperature/viscosity/strength characteristics similar to those of soda lime. However, the reduction of its sodium content from thirteen per cent to four per cent and the introduction of twelve to thirteen per cent of boric oxide (B_2O_3) and two to three per cent of aluminium oxide (Al_2O_3) creates very significant changes in its thermal expansion, thermal conductivity and specific heat. The thermal expansion more than halves, dropping from 7.9 to 3.3. Thermal conductivity increases by ten per cent and specific heat drops by twenty per cent. This increases the ability of such a glass to withstand 'thermal shock', such as is experienced during cooking or in

fires in buildings. As one might expect, its low co-efficient of expansion makes it difficult to toughen thermally, since the 'prestressing' generated is directly proportional to the co-efficient of expansion.

The story of borosilicate glass is a model as a description of the transfer of technology over decades of development in production and markets. Otto Schott (1851–1935) was only twenty-five when he contacted Ernst Abbe, co-owner of the firm of Carl Zeiss of Jena, another great name in optics and glass. Schott founded the firm named after him in 1884, and after this time devoted himself to glass research. Early in the twentieth century, Schott was producing

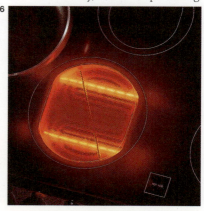

apparatus glass', and by the 1920s this borosilicate material was introduced into the household for cookware. The term Duran, the Schott trade name, became a household word, and parallel work by Corning in the USA gave us Pyrex. Borosilicate glass was first made for the building industry in the form of glass blocks, but by the 1970s flat borosilicate glass products were on the market, giving us a new effective fire-proof glass to join the well-established wired glasses. These have now been joined by the new clear ceramic glasses.

Ceramic glass is a discovery of the 1970s, and a family of glasses has since been developed, based on compositions in which materials, such as lithium and aluminium oxides, are added to the silicate base, together with titanium or zirconium. The comparatively exotic mix, made into a glass by careful heating and annealing, produces materials which have remarkable properties, with co-efficients of thermal expansion close to or even below zero. This property has proved essential in the design of the nose cones of space vehicles and cooking hobs, both of which have to experience enormous changes in temperature without significant changes in dimension or shape. Their resistance to thermal shock and their strength provide a profile of performance which is unique and of enormous potential value.

48. The Pyramid at the Louvre, Paris, 1986–8, I M Pei. The use of water-white glass had fallen out of general currency since its pre-war use as health glass, but Pei's insistence on producing a building which would allow a view of the stonework across the court without a colour alteration led to the re-creation of the chemical recipe. The material is now back in the catalogue of some major manufacturers.

49.The specialist glass-maker offers an enormous palette of materials of varying performance and optical properties.

The strength and resilience of borosilicate and ceramic glasses are complemented by the transmission qualities of the optical glasses. Optical glasses require very pure and perfectly made glass, with controlled refractive indices and dispersion. A high refractive index increases the light bending characteristics so important in lenses, particularly in spectacle glasses where a high index enables a lens to be thinner. The cost of such a material is very high, as any purchaser of high index spectacles will know. The dispersion defines the degree to which different colours are bent. Two classic families are recognized: crown glasses with a low

dispersion, and flint glasses with a high dispersion. Soda-lime glass has quite a low dispersion, whereas lead-alkali-silicate glasses have a high dispersion. The search for a high refractive index and a low dispersion has led to the development of dozens of glasses with 'optical positions' extending across the graph matrix, producing 'heavy' (high refractive index) and 'light' (low refractive index) materials. Combinations of barium oxide or phosphorus produce heavy flint, or heavy crown, glasses, and the use of rare earths, aluminium oxide, fluorine and many other materials has produced an enormous palette for the lens-maker.

The stage is now set for other glass products, like the ceramics, to follow the example of borosilicate and migrate across from specialist use into the building industry. From the optical glasses, with their great purity and precise optical behaviour, to the glass ceramics, a palette of chemistries is available which remains largely unexploited in architecture. There are the inevitable problems of cost and demand related to use, but we must remember the exorbitant price of plate glass used by Christopher Wren in the early eighteenth century. A water-white glass was used in the new Pyramids at the Louvre by I M Pei, 1986–8, and Pilkington have introduced 'Optiwhite' as a low-iron glass in thicknesses from 4 mm to 10 mm. The decades and centuries to come will surely use a wider range. This broad horizon is explored in Chapter Four.

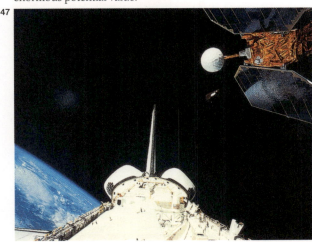

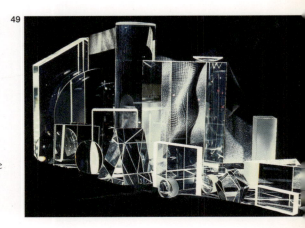

Meanwhile, we need to note that flat glass products are not the only range which are in use in architecture. Other materials, such as glass fibre and the more sophisticated optical fibres in which properties other than transparency are used, are just as important. This book, for obvious reasons, concentrates on flat glass and other building components made of glass. However, the intrinsic durability of glass, combined with the high strength it has as a filament described earlier in this chapter, make it ideal as a fibre. Glass fibres have claimed an essential place in product design and architecture.

The term 'glass fibre' generally refers to filaments of diameters below 0.1 mm. Glass fibres fall into two important main groups in terms of glass used, method of manufacture and purpose. A critical distinction needs to be made between the 'blown wool' forms, which are intrinsically 'damaged', and continuous filaments, which can be made to exploit the very high strength of glass in such a form. The first of these is the fibrous form used as wadding, often known as fibreglass. Insulating glass fibres are usually made from soda-lime glass and spun centrifugally or produced by air jets, hardening from the molten state as they meet the air. The resultant wadding provides an insulating 'wool', and can also be used in compressed form to make panels and mouldings, typically using a resin as a matrix. The wool derives its properties from the inherent strength of the glass, which stops it crumbling, and the air trapped within

50, 51. Fibre optic cables. Optical fibres, the thickness of hairs, are combined in harnesses to form the cables which have revolutionized telecommunications, and are now being used increasingly as light carriers. The strength of glass in fibre form is the key to success in these materials.

50

it, which give it excellent insulating properties equal to those of many foamed plastics.

A more carefully made form of glass fibre produces fine strands which exploit the great strength available from glass when it is finely drawn, referred to already in this chapter and in more detail in Appendix One. Glass fibres have a tensile strength up to six times that of mild steel, with the advantage of being inert and resisting corrosion.

Unlike glass wool, glass filaments and glass staple fibres – the two categories of this strong form of glass – are made from special glasses designed to suit the matrix material they are intended to reinforce, often an alkali-free alumino borosilicate glass.

Glass-reinforced plastics appeared in the early 1940s, comprising mats or other configurations of glass filaments used to strengthen plastics such as polyesters and many other plastics. Glass-

reinforced cement appeared twenty years later when a glass was developed which resisted attack from the alkali in the cement. Given the long currency of Georgian wired glass to maintain structural integrity in the sheet material, it is tempting to speculate on the potential for glass-reinforced glass.

The other main class of glass fibre, optical fibres, is of a fundamentally different character. Using the properties of refractive index and surface reflection, these have revolutionized telecommunications and are creating a significant family of light carriers in the field of illumination. Seen simply, optical fibres are light tubes, produced with diameters as low as that of very thin wire. The search for an effective 'light pipe' is over a hundred years old: the first patent was applied for in the USA in 1880. It took until the 1960s for two technologists working for the British Post Office to complete the idea of a light pipe using the phenomenon of internal reflection in glasses with very high transmission properties. Between 1970 and the mid-1980s, the length over which a light beam could be transmitted grew from 600 m to over 150 km.

The keys to the success of optical fibres are the immense strength and flexibility of glass in this finely drawn form, the creation of glasses of very high transparency, and the remarkable technology involved in making a fibre in which the glass type is carefully varied across its cross section of about 120 microns. In the advanced 'gradient fibres', this diameter typically incorporates a core of pure silica surrounded by a material of gradu-

ated refractive index to ensure that the signal sent in at one end reaches the other end in a coherent state.

It is an irony that the light pipe has, in a sense, been hi-jacked by the communications industry, but recent developments in lighting technology have reclaimed it, and uses for genuine light guides are being found. These take advantage of the ability of a light guide to separate the source and delivery of light. A hot incandescent lamp can be in one location, at one end of the pipe, so that the place being illuminated can be remote and does not have to receive the thermal impact of the source. This is of enormous value, for example, in surgery, as well as in the illumination of a food counter. Given the recent development of very high intensity light sources, there is an obvious potential application in the illumination of many locations from one source, with light source located in a place where its heat is not troublesome.

51

alternative materials

Glass, then, serves us in more than one way with its transparency. Not merely can it transmit light as a sheet material across one surface to another; it can also be used to transmit signals from one side of the planet to the other at the speed of light.

This quality of transparency is not restricted to glass, however, and it would be unnecessarily exclusive in a book on 'glass' to fail to refer to the other materials which provide transparency in architecture, sometimes on their own and sometimes combined with glass.

The potential for plastics as complements to glass is so great that Appendix Five is dedicated to them. Plastics are very much materials of the twentieth century, and clear plastics owe their origin to developments right at the beginning of the century, as Otto Rohm in Germany started work on the acrylic acid derivatives first developed sixty years earlier by Redtenbach. It is a measure of the difficulty of plastics manufacture that it took until the mid-1920s for Bauer, working in Rohm's laboratory, to make the first small quantities of methyl methacrylate, the precursor of polymethylmethacrylate (PMMA), now known as acrylic, Perspex or Plexiglass.

Subsequent developments in the plastics industry have eventually given us four main transparent plastics usable in building: acrylic (PMMA), polyvinyl chloride (PVC), polystyrene and polycarbonate. All these materials share the common internal structure of plastics, of being polymeric chains, often derived from hydrocarbons. They also share common properties of lightness and easy

52. The IBM Travelling Pavilion, 1982–6, Renzo Piano Building Workshop and Peter Rice. The development of transparent plastics has opened a new palette for architecture. When these materials are used as ersatz replacements they often prove unsatisfactory. When used to their full potential, as formable and lightweight light transmitting sheets, they release a whole new vocabulary of forms.

52

formability. The densities of the four materials are between about 1,100 and 1,400 kg/m³, with PVC the heaviest, polystyrene the lightest, and PMMA and polycarbonate about the same at 1,200 kg/m³, about half the density of soda-lime glass at 2,500 kg/m³. The light attenuating properties of plastics extend over about the same range as the glasses themselves. The refractive index of clear PMMA is 1.49, and that of clear polycarbonate 1.58, compared with 1.52 for soda-lime glass.

The properties of PMMA and polycarbonate have led to them being the preferred clear plastic materials for architects, with their comparatively high softening points, strength and resistance to yellowing. For all this, they only compete with glass as materials to be used on

their own in limited instances. Their maximum working temperatures (80–90°C for PMMA and 120–135°C for polycarbonate) are high enough for most purposes in building, and they are quite strong; the tensile strength of PMMA is between 55 and 75 N/mm², and that of polycarbonate 62.5 N/mm². Their thermal expansion co-efficients of about 70×10^{-6}/°C are 20% or so more than glass.

The problems with plastics, particularly clear plastics, for architects lie in their characteristic lack of hardness and durability when compared with glass. While the manufacturers of clear plastics may claim that their products have been successfully in place for twenty-five years or more, this does not compare with the known life of a glass window of

many centuries. The plastics manufacturer would argue, with some justification, that the very youth of the plastics industry has not given the materials time to prove themselves. However, their organic chemical nature leads to concern over long-term durability and the maintenance of properties, including those of brittleness and colour. Also their intrinsic softness compared with glass means that they must be dealt with and maintained in a much more careful way. Coatings have considerably enhanced abrasion resistance but few materials can compete with the hardness of glass. However, their flexibility and lack of brittleness have led to them taking a firm place in architecture, where their lightness, formability and low thermal conductivity are important properties.

composites

The arrival on the architectural scene of alternative materials is important, not so much because of their potential to replace glass, but for their ability to be combined with it. It is appropriate to complete this chapter on glass technology with a review of the way in which architecture is served not by one, simple, product, but by intelligent combinations of materials.

In his book *Glasarchitektur* of 1914, Paul Scheerbart mentions 'double walls' in glass (chapters four and 33), 'glass fibres' (chapter seventeen), 'materials which could compete with glass' (chapter 72), and 'unsplinterable glass … in which a celluloid sheet is placed between two sheets of glass and joins them together' (chapter 110). The greatest historical proponent of glass architecture fully realized that glass in rich combination was what gave it its potential power and importance. 'Double walls' of glass have extended between Le Corbusier's brave *murs neutralisants* of the Villa Schwob of 1916–17 and (more famously) the Cité de Refuge of 1930–33, and the conventional double glazing of today, itself a development of the 1920s.

The use of even the most basic composite glazing presents the designer with enormous problems. The creation of a window comprised simply of two glass panes and a cavity immediately creates problems with the quality of air in the cavity, in terms of its cleanliness and dryness. Damp, dirty air, either occupying the cavity at the time of manufacture or seeping in later, creates degradation of

53, 54. Balustrade at the Post Office Museum, Frankfurt, 1990, Gunther Behnisch. Laminates often remain hidden, providing safe and unobtrusive protection. Occasionally they emerge into the limelight.

55. Apple Computers Building, Stockley Park, London, 1990, Troughton McAslan. This building uses one of the most successful current translucent insulation products, Okalux, made from small acrylic tubes forming a honeycomb structure across a cavity between two sheets of glass, with a sheet of glass fibre tissue against the inner leaf to remove optical distortion and provide diffused light. The advanced forms of this system, which use 3.5 mm diameter tubes, are claimed to provide eighty per cent radiation transmission, and U-values of 0.8 W/m² °C.

the surface (even if only visually) through dirtying and condensation. One answer is to make one of the panes openable, but this is expensive, and troublesome in presenting twice the cleaning problems of a single pane. The obvious answer is a glass-to-glass unit (with a fused glass edge), or a well-sealed system. Glass-to-glass units were marketed by Pilkington in the 1960s and 1970s, but problems of sizing, ordering and stocking led to them being dropped in favour of the sealed unit we now know.

Even this is difficult to produce, and it is only comparatively recently, in the last decade or so, that the sealed unit has provided a reasonably stable component, with its aluminium perforated spacer, its desiccant to dry the air and its sealing system. The failure of such a unit by moist dirty air getting through the seal after, perhaps, one or two decades, is still a recurrent nightmare of manufacturers and designers alike. However, the creation of relatively well-sealed units has revolutionized glazing. A dry, clean, protected cavity permits the use of comparatively delicate films and other optical components, as well as providing a blanket of thermally insulating air. So confident are manufacturers of double-glazed units that gas-filled units are now on the market, using argon or the more expensive krypton which have improved performance by ten per cent or so.

The preceding parts of this chapter provide a demonstration of the rich palette of materials available to us, and Appendix Two describes the details

of manufacture and a large number of composites currently in use or under development. These include laminates, cavity glazing and an important and expanding range of cavity-filled systems.

Laminates represent an important category of glazing systems. The material used is not the celluloid referred to by Scheerbart in 1914, but polyvinyl butyral, supplied in flexible sheet form on a roll. The sheet is laid between two plates of glass, and pressed and autoclaved, which converts it into a tough, clear (or tinted) adhesive layer, the basis of bandit-proof glass. When laminated to annealed glass, the layer maintains the geometrical integrity of the pane in

breakage – a huge advantage over a toughened glass. When combined with one layer of toughened glass (as in a glass roof) such integrity is essential. Other versions of glass laminates include resin-filled units, which enable less smooth interfaces to be bonded together. Several manufacturers have developed diffusing glazing using interlayers of glass fibre, and there are now a few insulating systems which incorporate (for example) tiny acrylic tubes packed as spacers. These glasses produce panels

56

of high strength and with beautiful light diffusing qualities as well as good U-values. Recently, liquid crystal interlayers have been put onto the market which can be switched electrically from translucent to transparent and back again.

Among the cavity composites are systems incorporating refraction materials. These usually comprise an optical system (often made with acrylic, for reasons of weight) in sheets or tiles, set between the two panes of a double-glazing unit, which provides the necessary protection from the elements. This uses a precision-made acrylic moulding to redirect light from the whole of the visible skyvault to the back of a room, without distortion of vision or loss of light.

These composites represent the materials of the future. However good the glasses we create in the decades or centuries to come, a single pane will still only create a thin membrane as a barrier between the interior and the environment outside (until, that is, we can neutralize the boundary condition of a building). With the variety of glasses, treatments and coatings now available, a designer can genuinely begin to use glass as a rich palette rather than

56. Swanlea Secondary School, London, 1993, Percy Thomas Partnership with Hampshire County Architects. Okasolar, used here in the roof, has been developed by the same manufacturer who created Okalux. The configuration in this system is comprised of carefully formed curved reflectors within a double glazing unit, which act as reflecting solar shades. Here, the design of the roof slope and the internal reflectors provided sixty-two per cent solar penetration for the much welcomed low angle winter sun, but only twenty-five per cent during the summer.

57. Lloyd's Building, London, 1986, Richard Rogers Partnership. Lloyd's epitomizes the exploitation of glass technology, from the use of a special rolling to produce a designed sparkling optical translucence, to the use of the glazing as an air cushion to control the thermal environment, and to the creation of a great cathedral atrium, complete with glazed termination.

a simple light-transmitting device which keeps the weather out.

It is inevitable, in temperate climates, that we should develop complex systems of composites, and the limits of these are only constrained by our imaginations and the laws of physics. Chapter Four looks at some of the component materials and systems which will contribute to the evolution of glazing and the building skin in the twenty-first century and beyond, particularly as we learn to design nanometrically. The age of high technology in glass has only just begun; the last chapter shows where it could be taking us.

Before we look at the future of glass in architecture, however, we need to see how architects since World War II have exploited, and sometimes failed to exploit, the materials the industry has provided for them. At the beginning of this chapter the beguiling nature of glass was referred to, and much of the early fascination of the material in the twentieth century was the result of a love affair between architects and the material, not always matched by a technical understanding of its potential, or its defects. The story of glass in architecture since 1945 has been one in which architects have only slowly caught up with the progress made by the technologists, and which is central to the development of late twentieth century architecture, as the despised 'glass box' evolved into the rich catalogue of the 1990s.

57

1, 2. Library and
Administration
Building Project,
Illinois Institute of
Technology, 1942–3,
Mies van der Rohe.

3. The Farnsworth
House, Plano, Illinois,
1946–51, Mies van
der Rohe.

renaissance in chicago

The rise of fascism and Stalinist totalitarianism had a crushing effect on European culture. The communist regime in Russia, and the fascists in Germany and Italy had a fundamental distrust of the Modern Movement, and in Germany this was accompanied by racist and nationalist fervour which helped destroy cultural activity. The social and economic causes of World War II, its actuality and its aftermath, had a profound effect on architecture as on most other realms of human activity.

The decade before the outbreak of war saw the departure of some of the great names of European culture to the USA as life became intolerable for them. Walter Gropius, the founder of the Bauhaus, left for England in 1934 and arrived in America in 1937 to become the professor of architecture at the Graduate School of Design at Harvard University. Mies van der Rohe, after a four-year effort to keep the Bauhaus open, eventually proposed its dissolution on 19 July 1935. In 1938, he and Ludwig Hilbersheimer left for America, and both settled in Chicago.

Mies became the director of the architectural department of the Illinois Institute of Technology in 1938. In March 1936, he had been invited by John Holabird to head a reborn Armour Institute, and an appointment was eventually confirmed during a trip to the USA. The visit was made at the invitation, and expense, of Stanley Resor and his wife to design a vacation home for them at Jackson Hole in Wyoming. This house, which spanned across a mill race, with a

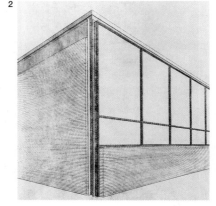

central span clad entirely in glass, took up an idea explored in the House on a Hillside of 1934, designed for the Tyrol. The IIT post was an unplanned but historically important result of this unfulfilled commission.

One immediate result of the outbreak of war in Europe in 1939 was that building activity, along with most other forms of peaceful industrial activity, ceased; architecture simply stopped. However, America remained untouched initially, and Mies was able to settle into his position at the Illinois Institute with a great new architectural commission; to design a campus for the Institute itself. During the next ten years, which saw World War II begin and end, Mies's work flourished in the creation of some of the most influential work of the twentieth century. These buildings were all essays in steel, glass and sometimes brick, at the same time rational and poetic. They were very much in the late nineteenth century Chicago tradition of Holabird and Roche, and Adler and Sullivan, as maintained in the twentieth century by Christian Eckstrom's Liberty Mutual

Insurance Building of 1908, and George and William Keck's wonderfully simple University Building of 1937, which, like much of their work, could easily have been designed in any decade since then up to today.

Mies embraced wholesale one of the main streams of American architecture, that of Howe and Lescaze in Philadelphia and Raymond Hood in New York. Hood's McGraw Hill Building of 1931, and Howe and Lescaze's Philadelphia Savings Fund Building of 1932, demonstrated the potential of simple framed exteriors in skyscrapers in a way not seen in Europe. These buildings had more complex forms than those of Mies, who brought to the genre a strictness, formal purity and vocabulary, with glass at its centre, which he was to build on for the next forty years.

Many of these works in the period up to 1950 were the natural successors of the great unbuilt prototypes of the prewar years, particularly the Reichsbank proposal of 1933, the House on a Hillside of 1934, and the subsequent Resor House at Jackson Hole in Wyoming of 1937. Pavilions and skinned towers were to be the two forms studied endlessly by Mies up to his death. The use of glass in these buildings is as fundamental to them as it was to the Gothic cathedrals. They are explorations of both the potential of pure transparency and, very differently, the formal potential of the glass skin first experimented with in 1921.

Mies started work on the new IIT campus immediately, and the first project was drawn and modelled in 1939.

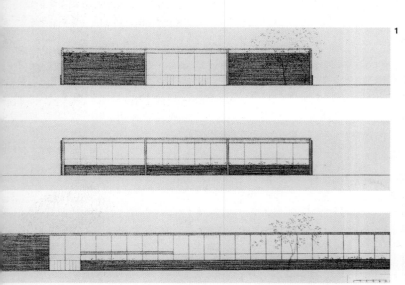

This incorporated, on a masterplanning scale, the essential characteristics of the spatial freedom of the Barcelona Pavilion and the Brick Country House of 1923. At IIT, this flow of space was modulated by rectangular blocks expanding away from a central symmetrical 'square' on the cross axis of the enormous site to the south of Chicago. In this first master-plan, the Library Building and a separate Administration Building faced each other across the square. A revised project was then produced, with the library and administration in one building on one side of the square, and the auditorium and Students' Union Building facing it on the other.

As the buildings appeared, the constructional vocabulary could be seen developing, as though the buildings were the syllabus for the students of architecture eventually to be housed fifteen years later in Crown Hall. First came the Minerals and Metals Research Building in 1942, whose design was

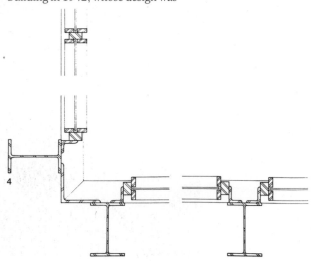

4, 5. Horizontal section through external wall, and view of Crown Hall, Illinois Institute of Technology, 1954–6, Mies van der Rohe.

predicated on an expressed, but flush steel and concrete-frame structure with brick infill, and a great flush-glass surface, redolent of the detailing just apparent in the drawings of the Reichsbank project in Berlin of 1933. Next, in 1945 and 1946, came the Alumni Building, the Metallurgy and Chemical Engineering Building, and the Chemistry Building. The expression here was significantly different. The building skin is located outside rather than within the main structural frame, and comprises a secondary frame made up from a system of 'H'-section 'secondary' steel mullions spanning the two- and three-storey heights of the buildings.

The details of all these buildings are shown in the exquisite drawings produced in Ludwig Hilbersheimer's book of 1956. The metal sections are not what we now know as rolled universal sections; they are crisp and precise. Their location, beyond the structural grid, forms the frame to the skin which extends outside the structure (unlike the Minerals and Metals Research Building). The elegance of these details has never been surpassed. In some ways they are perhaps not 'rational', but they have an internal logic which makes them seem inevitable, and very expressive. They also give a depth and gravitas to the skin of the building, and it was this aesthetic which Mies was to carry forward in the subsequent projects at IIT and elsewhere.

The 1944 drawing of the corner of the projected Library and Administration Building in Hilbersheimer's book highlights the tragedy of its non-

realization. The canon of 'glass architecture' cannot claim such a building as its own, perhaps, but in the size and expanse of the glazing, we see glass exploited to the highest degree. The undivided panes, about 18 ft by 12 ft (5.5 m by 3.6 m), share the exterior expression with meticulous brickwork, and would have been the largest in America up to that time. The curtailment of expression enunciated by Mies in a plate glass prospectus of 1933 is replaced by liberation, and glass comes into its own again.

The campus buildings which were built in the 1940s were followed by the Chapel in 1952 and the Commons Building in 1953. The Chapel, with its completely elementary form, is a perfect use of transparency in such a building; the altar is at one end, and at the other, a glass wall with very large panes, opens the small room of the building to the

space outside. The two-storey Commons Building, built a year, later repeats the constructional aesthetic of the buildings of 1945 and 1946.

As though to repay us for the loss of the Library and Administration Building, we have one late, great compensation at IIT. Crown Hall, of 1954–6, is one of the undisputed masterpieces of twentieth-century architecture; and, given the uncompromising nature of the working through of a formal idea, it is also one of the most controversial. Mies determined on a design for the building which was an enormous version of the '50 x 50' House of a few years earlier, described below. The main volume is 220 ft by 120 ft (67 m by 36.5 m) contained in a glass box, the roof of which is suspended from large beams spanning the full 120 ft depth of the building. This produces a column-free space, interrupted only by the characteristic central, symmetrical dividing walls, also seen in the '50 x 50' House and the Farnsworth House, described below. These walls follow the space-controlling rules developed by Mies in his earlier work; they are not permitted to meet to create solid corners, and their expression in plan and in space is of free ends. Two long, parallel central walls create an exhibition area, and provide a line for stairs to descend to the basement below. It is an interesting reflection on the overriding importance of this ground-level plan that in Hilbersheimer's book, published just after Crown Hall was completed, only this level is shown.

6, 7. The Farnsworth House, Plano, Illinois, 1946–51, Mies van der Rohe.

8. 50 x 50 House Project, 1950–51, Mies van der Rohe.

Large structural mullions 27 ft high (8.2 m) span the full single storey of the 'room'. The building envelope is entirely of ¼-in (6 mm) plate glass, divided horizontally at door head height, over which are located large panes 10 ft by 11 ft 6 in (3 m by 3.5 m). These huge upper panes are in clear glass, while the lower zone of glazing is translucent, using sand-blasted glass.

Whilst the pure expression of glass and steel is archetypal, some of the design decisions seem questionable and represent the dichotomies inherent in the organization of the building, also seen in many of Mies's later 'pavilion' buildings. 'Function' is sacrificed to 'form' in spatial terms throughout. Workshops and offices are relegated to the basement and lit by clerestory windows, again glazed in translucent sand-blasted ¼-inch plate glass. The use of sand-blasted glass ensures visual tidiness and coherence from the outside by concealing the student activity in the ground-level drafting rooms, but also prevents a view out. Although the continuity of space in the studios behind the glass is absolute, the spatial flow between the inside of the building and the outside, normally so sought after by Mies in his writings, is sacrificed to the aim for a pristine quality in the building's appearance. Thus, while Crown Hall is a paradigm for the glass pavilion and a perfect piece of abstract architecture, it incorporates ambivalent attitudes to what the glass pavilion can do as a building type, and in its translucent enclosure is inherently less satisfactory than the house designs of the time which Mies was producing.

Mies's work in Chicago of this period was not solely concerned with his post at IIT. His first American commission had been a house, and his interest in creating a house as an architectural prototype was not diminished when he arrived in America. As the first major buildings at IIT were being finished, he produced perhaps the greatest minimalist statement for a house in

history up to that time; the Farnsworth House of 1946–51.

The commission for the Farnsworth House at Fox River was a wonderful gift of circumstance in which site, topography and architectural idea met perfectly. Its location in a wood meant that conventional problems of privacy were absent, and the problem of siting the house on a flood plane required Mies to lift the building off the ground. The morphology of the house is thus as purely elemental as architecture can be. Two identical rectangular planes are held, one above the other, by steel columns. These planes contain the space of the dwelling entirely on their own. The glass is almost superfluous, serving only to mediate between the environment outside and the occupied space within: air curtains would almost have served the same purpose. Privacy and light exclusion are achieved by curtains. Nothing touches the external glass walls: the only enclosed space is (as

in Crown Hall) a 'core' formed by walls, separately expressed and sliding past each other.

The Farnsworth House is an important piece of architecture for many reasons. It represents the idealized minimum expression of contained space in a landscape. It is both 'site specific' and a platonic form idealizing the creation of space by the inference of planes. It is, as Hilbersheimer clearly states, 'meticulously worked out' in detail. However, with its single glazing at a latitude of about 42 degrees, not far from the 'Windy City', it is environmentally disadvantaged, to say the least, with about the same ability to withstand and modulate the elements as Hardwick Hall over 300 years earlier. It is an architectural statement made in terms of the limited environmental attitudes and glass technology of its time. As a conceptual model, however, it remains supreme.

As this was being completed, Mies produced another house project in 1950–51 which is the 'grounded' version of Farnsworth, but no less beautiful for that; the 50 x 50 House. This unbuilt house, which is actually 48 feet square, is just as pure a statement as Farnsworth, both structurally and in terms of enclosure. Four columns are

located at the centre of each elevation, thus freeing the corners. The model, always seen in photographic montage in its wooded setting, makes the aspiration clear. There are no mullions or framing to the glazing, only two fine vertical posts defining the doorways. The implied glass sizes are 24 ft by over 9 ft (7.3 m by 2.7 m), twice the area of the largest panes at Crown Hall: this still, today, represents an unachievable size for the float process (but only just). James Freed, who studied with Mies van der Rohe at IIT from 1948, has reminded us of the allegation that the 50 x 50 House was intrinsically unstable, with its four 'mid-span' columns. In fact, as Freed says, with its rigid plane roof and the welded joints,

stability would present no difficulty to an engineer even before the intrinsic stiffness of the glass, acting as a stressed skin, was taken into account.

Although the 50 x 50 House was never built, Mies's great admirer, Philip Johnson, had already completed a smaller version for himself in 1949. In Johnson's House, there is no attempt to resolve the

9. Glass House, New Canaan, Connecticut, 1949, Philip Johnson.

10. Eames House, Santa Monica, California, 1949, Charles and Ray Eames. A comparison between Johnson's house and the Farnsworth House or the 50 x 50 House show why Mies fell out with Johnson. Their approach to architectonics and detailing was diametrically opposed. When compared with the Eames House of the same date two completely divergent strategies for built form are apparent.

11. The Seagram Building, Park Avenue, New York, 1954–8, Mies van der Rohe.

problems of privacy and 'show', implicit in a house with no visible barriers between inside and out. The core elements are restricted to the sculptural cylindrical drum containing the shower room and fireplace, and the kitchen is vestigial, existing only as a bar. The 'bedroom' is a corner of the house defined only by a cupboard system. Privacy is provided by the site, and meals (as the author was told during a visit in the mid-1960s) are delivered on a tray. Unlike Mies's version, Johnson's House has a regular structure, with columns firmly planted in the corners, and the skin is located in relation to the structure in the same way as the later IIT buildings, that is, outside it.

Both these houses contrast intriguingly with the contemporary 'Case Study' House by Charles and Ray Eames being built across the continent in Santa Monica, California. It is tempting to relate the design principles behind this house to the difference in attitude between the platonic classicism of Mies, the European, and the relaxed environmentalism of the West Coast, the region of Soriano and Neutra (another expatriate European who had gone to the USA in the 1920s after working with Erich Mendelsohn). In fact, the principles behind the 'Glass House' – as the Eameses' house was called in the film doing the architectural school circuit in the late 1950s – were more complex. It was conceived as an 'off-the-peg' building, and used available, small steel-framed windows on the market in 1949. Its thesis was predicated on an agenda related to construction, and the use of well-designed and selected industrial

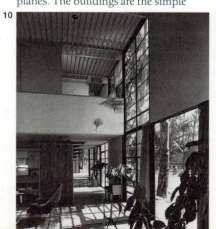

components put together to produce accommodating architecture with a light and elegant touch. This is as different from Mies's glass houses as is the furniture of Eames and Mies.

While Mies, Johnson and the Eameses were producing their alternative glass houses, and setting an important and rich agenda for post-war aesthetics, Mies was also producing buildings in downtown Chicago which were to have much greater, and questionable influence. At 860–880 Lake Shore Drive of 1948–51, Mies produced his first built 'skyscrapers'. Twenty-six-storeys high, these two rectangular solids are the first manifestation of the tall buildings in metal and glass that Mies was to design until his death twenty years later. The H-section mullions, created at IIT, are here shot into the sky as the strong expression of verticality. The rest is glass, with narrow set-back spandrels in the same plane as the window glazing.

In some ways, these buildings could not be more different from the meandering or jagged forms of the German projects of thirty years before. However, the corner transparency remains to give the observer the view of the expressed floor planes. The buildings are the simple

expression of orthogonal repetitive floors, immaculately detailed, with their prime properties being generosity of proportion and powerfully expressed technique, and are beautifully located next to Lake Michigan. Mies's followers, many of them educated by him at IIT, went on to produce similar works, with varying success, to create a new Chicago in metal and glass.

These glass skins produced by Mies in post-war America were not so much surprisingly new ways of 'skinning' a building as new conceptual constructions of an already established architectural element, the curtain wall. The idea of the curtain wall has already been discussed at the end of Chapter One. Mies's contribution was that of the supreme designer. The architectural potential for the sealed office tower had been established by Pietro Belluschi with his Equitable

Savings and Loan Building, completed in
Portland, Oregon in 1948. This used
green glass in double-glazing units.
Mies's aesthetic was quite different.

To see the difference between Mies's
idea of the glass wall and the post-war
curtain wall, we have only to compare
two New York buildings; Lever House by
the New York office of Skidmore Owings
and Merrill of 1950–52, and the Seagram
Building by Mies of 1956–8. Lever House
is a very fine building, inspired (it was
said at the time) as much by Le Corbusier
as by Mies. It represents both a well

12

conceived use of the curtain wall, and a
very idiosyncratic, purist and
controversial form in relation to Park
Avenue (though not as controversial as
Wright's Guggenheim Museum being
built at the same time on Fifth Avenue).
The curtain wall with its pale green
window glass (as used by Belluschi),
dark green spandrel glass and stainless

12. Equitable Savings
and Loan Building,
1948, Portland,
Oregon, Pietro
Belluschi.

13. 860–880 Lake
Shore Drive, Chicago,
1948–51, Mies van
der Rohe. Mies was
reported as saying
that the I-sections
were applied to the
facade because
without them the
building 'did not look
right'. The device
remained in all of
Mies's subsequent
work.

13

steel framing, with its delicate expression, still do credit to the named design partner Gordon Bunshaft, and the team of designers working for SOM in the fifties and sixties.

The Seagram Building, designed by Mies at the instigation of Philip Johnson, is fundamentally different from Lever House, both in terms of its massing and relationship to Park Avenue, and in the conception of its skin. The H-section mullions, already seen in Chicago, are here in that most aristocratic of materials, bronze, and are applied to the bronze-clad structure uni-directionally, spanning floor to floor. The glazing is in a specially-made bronze-coloured glass, with selenium added to the iron oxide present in the Lever House green. The colour of this glass performs two important tasks in the establishment of the aesthetic of the building. First, it turns the building into a solid; the transparency of the single-storey pavilions is replaced by a reflective surface. The objectives for glass architecture, set out by Mies in 1920–21, are realized, but in terms of a simple orthogonal form rather than the faceted multiple-reflection of the earlier proposals. Second, the colour of the building has a wonderful quality which changes from hour to hour, from pink to blue brown to bronze, as daylight and sunlight conditions change. It is fascinating to wonder whether Mies had anticipated this rich and variable colour quality in his building. The skin of the Seagram Building is about as far from the commercial curtain wall as can be imagined, and its expression was followed through by Mies in the subsequent tinted-glass towers in Chicago and Toronto.

14. Lever House, Park Avenue, New York, 1951–2, Skidmore Owings and Merrill. Lever House pre-dates the Seagram Building by a few years, but takes from Lake Shore Drive the principle of the pure metal and glass solid. The use of green glass for the vision panels and the spandrels was to become a much copied device, but rarely used as successfully as here.

Curtain wall buildings, such as Lever House, set off on a completely different track. To start with, the post-war American and European glass walls were often part of the developing vocabulary of the finest designers. In America, SOM was not the only American firm producing glass-walled buildings, for 1951–2 was also the time of the United Nations Building by Wallis K Harrison. With its tower and low-rise buildings reminiscent of Lever House, it was based, infamously, on the formal proposals incorporated in Le Corbusier's 'project 23A' of 1946. There is a sad and telling background to the eventual design of this building with its high glass-clad slab. Whilst Le Corbusier's belief in the *mur neutralisant* persisted, his experience on the Cité de Refuge described in Chapter One, and his intelligence led him to write to Senator Warren Austin, President of the Site Planning Committee for the United Nations, on 4 December 1947: 'My strong belief, Mr Senator, is that it is senseless to build in New York, where the climate is terrible in Summer, large glass areas which are not equipped with a *brise soleil*. I say this is dangerous, very seriously dangerous'. Le Corbusier realized from personal experience the problems which could inflict a building at a latitude of 41 degrees, the same as Madrid or Naples, compared with his own, much lesser difficulties in Paris, which has a latitude of 49 degrees.

Thus, at the beginning of the curtain wall in its post-war life, its intrinsic weaknesses had already been identified and called into question by one of the

14

15. General Motors
Technical Center,
Detroit, Michigan,
1948–56, Eero
Saarinen and
Associates.

16. The United
Nations Building,
New York, 1951–2,
Wallace K Harrison
and Associates.
Roche and Dinkeloo's
UN Plaza Hotel is
seen on the right.

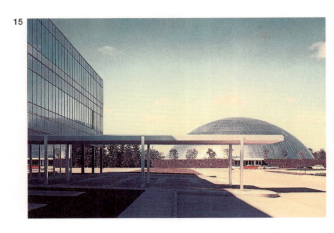

great European architects. Despite this, the curtain wall was soon seen as an ideal component in the newly expanding sector of commercial office development. The office building as a type came of age in the post-war period, partly because of the burgeoning demand for space for office-based activity, partly because of the development of the rental sector in office accommodation (with a concomitant requirement for 'universal' office space suitable for a wide variety of users), and significantly because of the programmes of urban regeneration which took place in some of Europe's major cities after the war. The property, or 'real estate' sectors in Europe and America became major players in the economies of most 'developed' countries, with the office building as their major stock in trade. The design of an office building based on the financial needs of this sector evolved as a result of carefully judged investment calculations, as much as considerations of architectural content or urban contribution. For those commissioning such a building, the curtain wall, with its slenderness, cheapness and off-the-peg quality, was an ideal way to clad their square miles of 'floor plate' (as the office floors came to be called).

The emerging problems in architecture posed by the commercial curtain wall, with its ubiquity, blandness and poor performance, became an important and negative constituent of post-war architecture, and are discussed in the second part of this chapter. However, the first decades after the war saw elegant explorations of the glass envelope, often

17

17. Manufacturers Hanover Trust Building, New York, 1953–4, Skidmore Owings and Merrill. SOM rejected the ziggurat section prompted by the New York zoning regulations (as did the Seagram Building). This building consists of a pure glass and aluminium box, uncompromised by the upper set-back floors: a generous act on a valuable site. The size of the largest panes is even now at the upper limit of what is possible, given normal stock sizes.

18. Pepsicola Headquarters, Park Avenue, New York, 1958–9, Skidmore Owings and Merrill. This building arrived in Park Avenue as a supremely reposed and detailed masterpiece of its genre. SOM translated Mies's I-section columns from dark steel or bronze into silver aluminium, framing the pale green glass. This limpid aesthetic still offers one of the most beautiful combinations of material available to us.

in commercial office buildings.

At the same time as Lever House and the UN Building were going up in New York, another expatriate European was building a masterpiece in the Midwest. Eero Saarinen's General Motors Technical Center of 1948–56 expressed another version of the glass skin, somehow more pragmatic and appropriate to the technology of the industry it served (see figure 15). Saarinen, whose work demonstrates a very broad attitude to form-making, and who was ostensibly as happy designing evocative, expressionist buildings like the TWA Terminal at Kennedy Airport, puns such as the Chicago Law School and the Women's Dormitories at the University of Pennsylvania of 1957–60, and strange compromises such as the American Embassy in London of 1955–60, also produced some magnificent glass walls. General Motors was the first of these, and also the first building of significance to use neoprene gaskets to fix the glazing (very appropriate for a building serving the automobile industry).

Skidmore Owings and Merrill's work of the 1950s extended the glass ideas of Lever House significantly. SOM was one of the first, and perhaps the greatest of the post-war corporate firms who demonstrated that fine architecture did not have to be created by single architects. None of the three named partners held a significant design position when the powerful buildings of the fifties and sixties were being created. Their design teams were led, and manned, by architects who were bound by a belief in the same way of thinking about architecture,

and notable for their willingness to remain 'unnamed'. Their own corporate nature matched the corporate organizations for whom they worked.

In the New York office, Gordon Bunshaft, and then Roy Allen, produced glass buildings with an almost Scheerbartian passion. The Warehouse and Vinegar Plant for H J Heinz in Pittsburgh, Pennsylvania, of 1950–52, used flush curtain walling inserted into the steel frame. The aluminium mullions are bright, anodized and support

18

specially rolled hammered-finish glass, with a blue tint to provide solar protection. Curved-corner opening lights provide ventilation. The Gunners' Mates School at Great Lakes Illinois, of 1952–4, extended the aesthetic by locating the blue-tinted heat-absorbing glass outside the steel frame. The Manufacturers Hanover Trust Company Bank on Fifth Avenue, New York of 1953–4 represents the 'glass building as

19. Jospersen
Office Building,
Copenhagen, 1956,
Arne Jacobsen.

20. Albright Knox
Art Gallery, Buffalo,
New York, 1958–61,
Skidmore Owings
and Merrill. This is
a remarkable
conception in glass,
and an example of
the creative ability
of SOM to exploit its
great range. The room
enclosed by the glass
box is an auditorium.
The dark grey tint
permits the use of the
projector in daytime
even with the
curtains open. The
dark abstract
monolith shares its
podium with the neo-
classical building to
which it is an
extension.

bank'. This building, which is only
four-storeys high in a context of
skyscrapers, is based on the principle
that transparency is the best security.
Powerful aluminium mullions frame
glass panes, the largest of which are
are 22 ft by 9 ft 8 in (6.7 m by 2.7 m) in
½-in (12 mm) plate glass.

SOM's glass architecture progressed
into the second half of the 1950s. The
transparent bank was followed by the
transparent plant building: the entry to
what is now Kennedy Airport in New
York was dominated by the fully-glazed
Central Heating and Refrigeration Plant
Building of 1957–8. SOM's Inland Steel
Building in Chicago was built at the
same time and was a development of the
high-rise curtain wall building first seen
at Lever House, but with refinement of
detailing and, it must be accepted, a
much more elegant and articulate plan.
A clear span office building sits next to a
separately expressed service tower. The
curtain wall, appropriately enough for
the client, is in stainless steel framing

green-tinted glass. The marriage
between the steel and the glass, and the
simplicity of the form, make it possibly
the most elegant high-rise building ever
designed by SOM.

The same sort of aesthetic was used
by Gordon Bunshaft and Roy Allen in the
SOM New York office for the Pepsicola
Building of 1958–60 on Park Avenue, a
few blocks up from Lever House. Here
the detailing is pure 'Mies', with H-section aluminium extrusions producing
glazing 13ft wide by 9 ft high (3.9 m by
2.7 m), using ½-in green-tinted polished
plate glass. The objective of maximizing
the glass size led to the creation of a parti-
tion-to-glass detail which relied on a
neoprene gasket to form a seal. These
SOM buildings of the late 1950s represent the apotheosis of the curtain wall in
the USA, and were accompanied and followed within the office by other, larger
buildings, such as Union Carbide and
the Chase Manhattan Bank, both built in
New York between 1957 and 1961.

This short and selective review of the
glass architecture of SOM in the fifties
and sixties would not be complete
without reference to two smaller glass
gems, more redolent of the houses and
pavilions of Mies. The Albright Knox Art
Gallery was built in 1958–61 in
Bunshaft's native Buffalo. The concept is
a stone-clad podium surmounted by a
glass box forming the auditorium. The
½-in thick grey glass turns the box into a
sublime abstraction. The Yale Computer
Center of 1960–61 uses the same
aesthetic to the same serene effect.

The America in which SOM was
working, with the wealth of its commerce

and industry, was inevitably an important
centre for architecture in the post-war
period, and the nature of corporate architecture in particular was considerably
influenced by the Europeans who had
arrived there before the war. The 'technical' architecture of glass, aluminium and
steel seemed entirely appropriate to the
air-conditioned, steel-framed, curtain
wall-clad buildings which corporate
America preferred at the time.

However, similar developments also
took place in the recovering Europe of the
same period. Egon Eiermann produced
some of the earliest and best German
post-war architecture, always with great
refinement, including the German
Embassy in Washington. His Linen Mill
at Blumberg of 1951 was clad in a light
glass wall of almost Scandinavian delicacy, a characteristic present in all his
subsequent work.

In Scandinavia itself, the Dane, Arne
Jacobsen, designed the Town Hall at
Rødovre of 1954–6, and the Jospersen
Office Building in Copenhagen of 1956.
These are both clad in clean, supremely
elegant glass skins. Transparent and grey
glass is combined to produce a beautiful
machine aesthetic, understated but
supremely articulate. In Italy, too, new
post-war corporate industry subscribed
to the aluminium and glass aesthetic, as
in the Olivetti Headquarters in Milan by
Bernasconi, Fiocchi and Nizzoli, of 1954.

Britain saw a sorrier interpretation of
the steel and glass aesthetic and the curtain wall. A 'New Brutalist' version of the
Miesian IIT vocabulary was designed by
Peter and Alison Smithson in their
Hunstanton School of 1949–54, but
subsequent British metal and glass architecture seems like a myopic copy of the
fine American and Scandinavian work.

the rise and fall of the curtain wall

Even as these carefully wrought buildings in Europe and America were being designed and made by good, and sometimes great architects, a more insidious form of glass architecture, similar in superficial appearance but fundamentally different in quality of concept, was being created. The period of post-war reconstruction was a time when the development industry began to find its feet. Its principal 'product' was the office building, and its area of action was, more often than not, the city. Glass became the unwitting ally of this enterprise, and the glass curtain wall effectively hi-jacked urban glass architecture.

The curtain wall, as a concept, has a long and distinguished history in the canon of architectural form. The idea of the curtain wall is actually ancient, and it is a term used to describe the heavy stone walls of medieval castles. In the new industrial age, the detachment of a light wall from the heavy structure behind became the means of producing an architecture in which framed structures could come into their own in a way which distanced them fundamentally from 'hole in the wall' architecture. With its vertical plane of glass expressed independently from, and hung on to, the structure, the Crystal Palace anticipated the curtain wall, as did many of the buildings in the Chicago School of the nineteenth century referred to in the first chapter, with their distillation of elevations into frame and glazed infill.

The twentieth century saw the slow but sure development of the curtain wall, both as a technology and as a means of architectural expression; early examples, such as Willis Polk's Hallidie Building of 1918, are referred to in Chapter One. Before World War II, curtain wall buildings developed simultaneously into two paradigms. The first evolved from architectural theory, and was based on a design principle which derived from the expressive separation of the external wall and structure. Walter Gropius's Dessau Bauhaus of 1926 was a perfect example, as were Mies van der Rohe's glass skin buildings. Such buildings were studied interpretations of a particular form of architectural expression. As such they invariably incorporated architectonic attitudes and detail corresponding to the considered objectives of their designers. Gerrit Rietveld's Institute for Applied Art in Amsterdam of 1956–68 is a case in point. The detail in such a curtain wall at the point where the floor edge meets the appropriate transom rails is reduced to the absolute minimum, and the section is cut back to obtain the maximum possible visual effect. Such detailing not only makes internal cleaning possible over the whole surface of the glass, it also makes it unnecessary to disturb the uniformity of the wall by the use of different glass (such as is necessary, for example, to conceal a downstand or suspended ceiling void, as at Lever House).

Such curtain walls have, as a clear objective, the expression of membrane. Before the invention of suspended glazing, these were rarely 'curtains' in any but a very metaphorical sense. They were as often seated as hung, and were really metal frameworks bolted to the

21. The Bauhaus Building, Dessau, 1926, Walter Gropius.

22. The Institute of Applied Art, Amsterdam, 1956–68, Gerrit Rietveld.

23. The Crystal Palace, The Great Exhibition Building, Hyde Park, London, 1851, Joseph Paxton with Fox and Henderson. A hundred years of development of the glass wall saw a sustained attempt to

reduce framing and mass. In multi-storey buildings the way that floor planes meet the wall has been of great importance in determining the final aesthetic, with immense efforts made to reduce the point of contact, as exemplified in Rietveld's Institute, with its cut-back detail. The Crystal Palace can be seen as the early progenitor of the twentieth century curtain wall.

structure behind, and glazed. However, the conceptual derivation drove the detailing, the selection of materials and the expression.

Contrasted to this form of wall was a much more prosaic form, not necessarily incorporating theoretical concepts of separation, elemental identity and expression, but merely exploiting technique. This is not to say that such 'pragmatic' curtain walls were not well designed or sometimes even beautiful: more to say that their origin lay in practical, rather than theoretical considerations.

In London, Sir Owen Williams' all-glass Daily Express Building of 1932 was followed by Peter Jones Store in Sloane Square, London of 1936 by Slater and Moberly, with Professor Reilly and W Crabtree consulting. Peter Jones still exists as a landmark in one of the most congenial squares in London. This was a classic 'pragmatic' curtain wall, with its ¼-inch plate glass held in pressed steel mullions with concealed fixings capped with bronze extrusions.

The development of the curtain wall in the 1950s and sixties became something quite different from that seen in the pre-war designs, and even more different from the beautiful versions designed by Mies van der Rohe, SOM, Jacobsen and the other architects lucky enough to gain commissions from clients who understood what architecture could be. This was the result of the congruence of interest between commercial developers and equally commercial curtain wall installation contractors, in which ideas of beauty and architec-

tural significance played little part. The developers, from London to Paris and from New York and Chicago to San Francisco, had as their objective the construction of buildings which would maximize rental return against capital outlay.

The origins of commercial developer architecture, particularly of the post-war office building as a 'type', have been touched upon earlier. The brief for such buildings was straightforward: it was to produce the maximum office floor area, with the greatest flexibility and 'lettability' of office use, with the greatest available window area, for the lowest cost. Exterior appearance, though important, was considered more critical in relation to its acceptability to planning authorities (to get the project accepted and built), than as expressions of anything in particular. The curtain wall played an important part in this. The planners, obliged for a variety of reasons always to restrict 'amounts' of building, lay down maxima in terms of gross building area, often generated by a 'plot ratio' calculation. The thin curtain

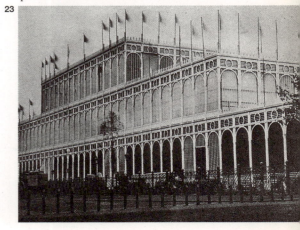

wall appeared in the market place as the ideal response to the needs of these clients and their architects.

Designers such as Eames, Saarinen and those in the offices of SOM, may have had high philosophical objectives for off-the-peg solutions, but rarely used them, of course. However, the section labelled 'cladding' on the shelves in office libraries quickly became filled, particularly in the 1960s, with curtain walling systems which offered ready-made, tested (not always thoroughly) assemblies of aluminium extrusions and glass which enabled architects to select their 'architecture' from a catalogue. For the developer clients, the simple attraction of the walls was their thinness and availability, producing a lettable area to within 100 mm or 150 mm of the outside wall of the building, and the building line. The buildings designed following this rationale were created in Park Avenue, New York in stark contrast to Lever House and the Seagram Building; their profiles hug the line of permitted building envelope, rising vertically until the City Code prescribes a set-back, and then dutifully retire as ziggurats in the sky.

The first notable examples of the curtain wall have already been referred to. At Lever House, and in many other buildings of the fifties, the curtain wall retained a memory of its theoretical and expressive source. However, subjected to the rigours of value engineering, the principle of the lowest common denominator, the need to produce a large market, the pressures of advertising, and the many other constraints which apply to

24. London Wall, London, 1960s. This development typifies the despised graph-paper architecture which the curtain wall engendered when dealt with in the worst commercial architecture.

commercial products, the curtain wall became quite another thing. The result was the so-called 'graph paper architecture' which became (rightly) so despised, and associated with the general opprobrium to which 'modern' architecture was increasingly prone in the sixties and seventies.

This 'instant architecture', so beautifully ridiculed by Jacques Tati in his film *Playtime* of 1967, attempted to produce the same thing everywhere as a result of the natural imperatives of mass marketing and production: a sort of 'International Style' without the style.

All this might not have been so bad had it not been for the intrinsic weaknesses in technology and performance which these walls incorporated. Amazingly, in the 'century of science', virtually every building referred to so far in this chapter, from Mies van der Rohe onwards, was single-glazed. Such an obvious defect did not seem to matter to

the new developers and their architects. As Reyner Banham pointed out in *Architecture of the Well Tempered Environment* of 1969, the uses of single glass skins in the USA was not considered an issue of concern in the nation of the low-energy-cost, air-conditioned environment. To quote Banham in relation to the UN Building mentioned earlier, 'Here, in New York, he [Le Corbusier, not Harrison] accomplished his dream of creating a great glass tower in an urban setting, and here in New York he also encountered the talents of the one man, in all probability, who could make it work: Willis Carrier'. With Carrier's Conduit Weathermaster air-conditioning system, the UN Building worked despite the omission of Le Corbusier's *brises soleils*, and despite the thinness of the skin.

The UN Building, however, was by comparison one of a higher breed of 'architecturally considered' curtain walls. At the mass production end of the

market, glass architecture was not so lucky, and a generation of glass 'heat sinks' appeared; high in their energy consumption, often cold in winter and too hot in summer, prone to condensation, and often poorly maintained and dirty (despite the ugly excrescences of window-cleaning equipment which perched on their roofs). These buildings, despite 400 years of technical development, were no better in controlling the thermal environment than the great Jacobean houses of the sixteenth century. They and their glass skins were not the result of considered and caring dialogue between user-clients and their architects about the nature of architecture or the beautiful integration of design and technology. The clients were often developers with a short-term interest in the project, who sold it on to an institution whose prime concern was its shareholders and investors. The users, the office worker occupants, were well down the chain of client interest and control.

Such architecture was an unenunciated conspiracy between absentee landlords (the institutional owners), uncaring architects, and indolent and ignorant planning authorities. As a result, modern architecture in general, and glass architecture in particular, got a very bad name. In the age of technology, architecture was simply failing to perform, with glass as an inert accomplice. If any good came out of the oil crisis of 1972–3, it was the increase in the realization that such thin glass skins were wasteful and inappropriate, particularly in 'advanced' countries such as the UK where fifty per cent of all energy consumption was in buildings.

glass and the architecture of energy

There is a beautiful and happy historical irony in the development of glass in architecture from 1940 to the 1960s. In the very same period as post-war glass architecture was giving us the Farnsworth House, Lever House and the commercial curtain wall, all of them single-glazed and environmentally inadequate, a new interest was developing in how to use glass wisely in environmental terms.

The 'greenhouse effect' of glass, derived from its transparency to shortwave radiation and its opacity to longwave low temperature radiation, fully explained in Appendix One, played an important part in the history of architecture. The impact of gardeners and horticulturalists who knew how to use this, such as Loudon and Paxton in the nineteenth century, has been documented in Chapter One.

The ancient use of glass architecture to defeat the vagaries of climate and encourage plant growth was paralleled by less botanically-derived work. De Saussure, the Swiss physicist who lived from 1740–1799, constructed the first glass thermal storage system using five layers of glass. Such concepts were categorically different from the gentle passive solar energy systems which constituted Loudon's conservatories: temperatures of nearly 90°C were achieved.

The early twentieth century saw significant efforts to use the sun's energy in architecture, and by 1931 Martin Wagner in Germany was able to produce his competition project 'The Growing

25. Sanatorium, Paimio, Finland, 1928–33, Alvar Aalto. Aalto shared with Le Corbusier and others an interest in environmental architecture, but with a characteristic passion for humanistic criteria. Paimio is instinctive, passive solar architecture.

26. The Peabody House, Dover, Massachusetts, 1947–8, Maria Telkes and Eleanor Raymond Peabody. This house followed the work of architects such as the Keck Brothers, but was the first real, occupied house to incorporate the essential features of passive solar energy use, including remote storage. The design derived from the conviction of

Dr Telkes, a research Metallurgist at MIT, that Glauber's salts could store energy collected by the sun. The house had mixed success, but was one of the essential pioneering projects in the new architecture.

25 House', in which a glass skin protected the outer walls of a building in a sheath, keeping the weather out, using incoming solar radiation, and reducing heat loss. The idea of, in some way, controlling solar energy by means of combinations of glass and mass took root, both because of the obvious financial and conceptual benefit, but also because of comfort and health. The tuberculosis sanatorium, with its large south-facing windows, was simply one manifestation of the building as sun trap. One of the most distinguished buildings of this sort was Alvar Aalto's Sanatorium at Paimio completed in 1933. This building is a perfect synthesis of orientation and form, and careful consideration of solar penetration. It is characteristic of this most humanitarian of great architects of the twentieth century that the relationship between architecture and the sun should be so caringly and sensitively treated.

This was also the year of the Cité de Refuge, where the *mur neutralisant* was examined by Le Corbusier in an attempt to overcome the environmental deficiencies in his beloved *pan de verre*, as exhibited in the earlier Pavillon Suisse of 1931. However, the idea of using glass as part of a solar energy collection system was quite different from that of the *mur neutralisant*, and did not really take hold until after the war. William Keck was developing solar houses in the 1930s, and by 1948 the first real 'solar house' had been built by Telkes and Raymond Peabody in Dover, Massachusetts, with eighty per cent of its heating requirement produced by solar energy.

In the late 1940s and 50s, as Mies van der Rohe, Philip Johnson and Charles Eames were producing their glass houses derived from considerations of space, form, constructional system and 'architectural principle', and while the commercial curtain wall was blighting the urban landscape, designers with few formal and conceptual preoccupations were laying the foundations for buildings which would rescue glass architecture from the inadequacies of the curtain wall.

Following the Peabody House in America, the first European solar houses were built in 1956 in England (not renowned as a sunny place) by Gardner and Curtis, to be followed in 1961 by one of the most important buildings of its kind anywhere, St George's School, Wallasey by A E Morgan. In this building, two glass walls 600 mm apart,

26

an outer clear system and inner panes which are generally translucent, shed diffused light into classrooms. Some of the inner panes are clear, and are backed by reversible panels, black on one side and polished aluminium on the other.

The solar wall system is designed to provide thermal control by the absorption and reflection of solar heat.

The south-facing solar wall presents a tall facade extending to the eaves of a roof which slopes down to the north. The structure is massive, comprising an insulated concrete roof and concrete floors. Heat is provided only by the sun, electric lighting and people. When the building got through a prolonged, very cold spell in the winter of 1962–3 without the boiler system being used, the heating plant was finally decided to be redundant. The low air-change rates implicit in the conserving of heat made the building smell unpleasant at times, but the passive solar collection quantities (up to 90 W/m² of wall averaged over twenty-four hours in the winter) indicates the potential for collection. Changes in external ambient conditions take about a week to register internally due to the high thermal capacity of the structure. The significance of this building lies in its location at a latitude of 53½ degrees, as well as its design.

This idea of combining a glazed solar wall with thermal capacity was also the basis of the system developed in France by F Trombe and J Michel, leading to the first French solar house built in 1962 in Odeillo in the Pyrenees area of France, at a latitude of 43½ degrees. The patented Trombe–Michel system used double glazing outside a black-painted masonry wall. Slots in the wall, top and bottom, allowed warmed air to circulate into the occupied space behind the wall in winter. In summer, the glazing was opened at the top allowing the solar heat

27. St George's School, Wallasey, near Liverpool, 1961, A E Morgan.

28–29. House at Odeillo, France, 1967, Jacques Michel and Félix Trombe. The patented Trombe–Michel wall consists of an outer glazed wall, 120 mm in front of a heavy concrete wall 600 mm thick. The concrete wall is painted black. Jeffrey Cook has set out the three ways such a wall provides heat to the building behind: as a passive heavy mass which becomes warm; as a passive convective loop, with air being allowed to flow past or through the wall; and as a fan-forced warm air supply system for storage elsewhere. Obviously the view out to the south is reduced or removed.

to be flushed away. The Lof House in Denver of 1961, with a latitude of about 40 degrees, used glass more remotely from the thermal store. Two glass collectors, one single-glazed, the other double-glazed, both contained several panes of glass partly painted black (to provide absorption). In the Lof system the heat is stored in rock.

Both the 'solar wall' buildings referred to, in Wallasey and France, leave much to be desired in terms of success as architectural forms. In the Trombe wall, a glass wall facing south with a black-painted wall behind denies one of the primary purposes of glazing: vision. Vision is also denied at Wallasey, where the glass is translucent rather than transparent (a defect it shares with Mies's architecturally more distinguished Crown Hall). Nevertheless, unattractive as these buildings were, they embodied the basis for correcting the careless (and often equally unattractive) curtain wall architecture appearing at the same time. The attitude they reflected meant that forms of architecture, and approaches to

design, were available when the new energy consciousness emerged at the end of the 1960s.

In April 1968, a group of thirty individuals from ten nations met at the invitation of Dr Aurelio Peccei at the Accademia dei Lincei in Rome. Their agenda was nothing less than the present and future predicament of man. The Club of Rome, as the group became known, published the The Limits to Growth in March 1972 after two years' study. In the same period, the sudden increase in the price of oil set by the Arab countries created, what at the time was called, the 'oil crisis', and focussed the attention of the rest of mankind on the importance of energy. In the same period, Ian McHarg published Design for Nature. The energy crisis, and the emergence of ecology as a relevant subject for architects, had a slow but profound impact on architecture. The immediate effect of the oil crisis on building costs led to a slowdown in construction, but of longer and more lasting effect was the new thinking about building performance which became essential,

particularly in climates which intrinsically required buildings to be extensively cooled or heated, and in countries where the price of energy was not held artificially low.

During the 1960s, these two streams of architectural activity, the curtain wall and the solar wall, progressed independently, complicated in the case of commercial architecture by the new glasses beginning to come out of the glass industry. Float glass had been invented by Pilkington in 1952, and by the 1960s previously rather exotic glasses (such as the pinky-brown glass of the Seagram Building) were being complemented by new tints.

28

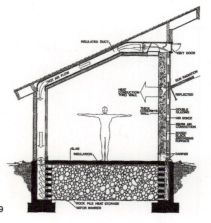

29

new generations

While the wholesale cladding of buildings in glass was, as often as not, a banal and blighting phenomenon, the arrival on the scene of new glasses in the 1960s did give an opportunity to the best architects to produce wonderful surfaces, redolent of the intentions declared by Mies in 1921. SOM and the Chicago School (many of whose members were fresh from Mies's teaching at IIT) were in the forefront of such architecture in commercial and large-scale public buildings.

One of the greatest of these was Eero Saarinen, who virtually created a 'school' of his own. His General Motors project of 1948–56 has already been mentioned. Saarinen's office recruited some of the best talent in the USA, including Gunnar Birkerts, Cesar Pelli and Anthony Lumsden; Kevin Roche became chief of the design staff in 1955–6, and General Motors was followed by the Law School at the University of Chicago, 1956–60. Then came the amazing Bell Telephone Corporation Research Laboratories at Holmdel, New Jersey, of 1957–62. This building must surely be one of the boldest and most inspiring projects of this

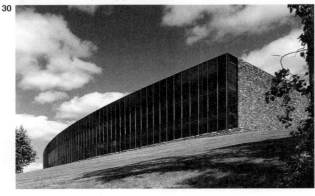

30. IBM Thomas J Watson Research Centre, Yorktown, New York, 1957–61, Eero Saarinen and Associates.

31. College Life Insurance Building, 1969, Dinkeloo and Roche. Dinkeloo and Roche inherited Saarinen's office, and his continued sequence of fine rhetorical statements in glass.

32. Bell Telephone Corporation Research Laboratories, Holmdel, New Jersey, 1957–62, Eero Saarinen and Associates.

century, with a scale reminiscent of Versailles. It is entirely inspired by the potential of glass. An enormous mirror glass box, 700 ft (213 m) long and five-storeys high, forms an overall climate controller and container for what are effectively independent buildings within. Such was the will in Saarinen's office to push glass technology that the building, on completion, was clad partly in grey body-tinted glass and partly in an experimental glass, pending the eventual installation of the final reflecting glass which was still being developed.

At the same time as Bell was progressing, the office produced the Thomas J Watson Research Center for IBM at Yorktown, New York, where a beautifully curving gasketed grey glass wall, 1,090 ft (332 m) long, forms the front face of an arc of building, contrasting with the masonry of the structure behind as it steps up the hillside. Yet another masterpiece followed this building in New York State, the John

Deere Building at Des Moines of 1957–63. This building used a palette of corten steel and a new gold-tinted glass to create a shimmering lattice of metal and glass.

Saarinen died in 1961 at the age of fifty-one, tragically failing to see the completion of what he considered to be his best buildings, but his firm was inherited by a new entity, Dinkeloo and Roche, who extended the repertoire to new heights of monumental, but supremely executed work, in which glass played a central role; such as the seminal Ford Foundation Building, mentioned below, and Cummins Engine Company Factory in Darlington, England of 1965. The firm's boldness soared to even greater heights in the project for the Federal Reserve Bank in New York of 1969, and the masterplan at UN Plaza of the same year. This had a great glass hall, hundreds of feet high at its centre, but has as its only manifestation the UN Plaza Hotel, a slim, elegant

and immensely tall shaft of glass opposite Harrison's project of nearly two decades earlier.

Even as the curtain wall was producing its dulling, insensitive and environmentally inadequate wrapping of commercial architecture, particularly in north America and northern Europe, new generations of architects were designing new buildings. Out of the dross of post-war commercialism, typologically definitive glass architecture developed wherever and whenever architects found a convergence between conceptual aims and the new, emerging materials and environmental attitudes. Sometimes, these new buildings were inspired by an environmental approach, sometimes by the inspiration of the material itself, and sometimes by the elegant fusion of the two.

The last twenty-five years or so have seen the consolidation of typological agendas in glass architecture. In the most sophisticated buildings these overlap, but they demonstrate nevertheless the way that architects have exploited new technologies in three distinct directions: environmental control, structural and constructional potential, and the sheer enjoyment of surface and ambiguous materiality that only glass can provide.

The potential for environmental control has delivered a variety of forms and techniques. At its most basic level of consideration it has given us the simple glass-covered court and the conservatory, but time and experience and, perhaps most significantly, the involvement of skilled environmental engineers, have given us the more recent sophisticated atria and energy-collecting and climate-moderating walls, all relying on glass.

The development of the atrium as an architectural form is one of the most important typological themes in late twentieth-century architecture, and is well documented. The obvious antecedents all date from the nineteenth century: the great conservatories of Loudon, Paxton, Turner and others which first exploited the radiation transmission characteristics of glass in large structures; the glazed urban forms of the great arcades such as the Galleria

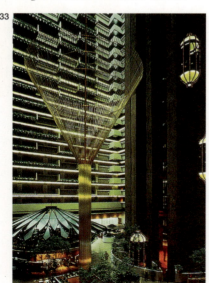

33. Regency Hyatt Hotel, Atlanta, Georgia, 1967, John Portman.

34. Building, University of Trondheim, Norway, 1978, Henning Larsen.

in Milan; and the huge arching roofs of the railway stations and exhibition buildings. More specifically relevant buildings include Barry's Reform Club in London of 1837: this building is a true 'atrium' with its central glazed 'courtyard' and its ambivalent internal/external quality.

The end of the nineteenth century saw some great American examples, such as John Root's Chicago Rookery Building of 1885, George Wyman's futuristic Bradbury Building in Los Angeles of 1893, and Frank Edbrooke's Brown Palace Hotel in Denver of 1893. This period also saw the GUM Store in Moscow of 1889–93 by Pomeransev. These were followed by Frank Lloyd Wright's Larkin Building of 1903, and in the same year, Berlage designed the Amsterdam Stock Exchange Building.

The atrium and shopping mall began to proliferate as a form after World War II. Early north American projects, like Victor Gruen's Midtown Plaza at Rochester, New York of 1956–62, were matched by Scandinavian examples, such as the two centres near Copenhagen in Denmark, at Rodovre (where Jacobsen had built the elegant glass Town Hall) and Lyngby. While the latitudes of Rochester, New York and Copenhagen are very different (about 43 degrees and 58 degrees respectively) their winter climates are similar, and the environmental control action of the glazed enclosures was derived from the same objective, well before the oil crisis of the early 1970s.

The subsequent proliferation of atrium buildings and glazed 'malls' was undoubtedly as much a result of com-

mercial interest and architectural fashion as of a considered response to an energy problem. However, the consideration of energy conservation and the idea of climate control, particularly in noisy and polluted cities, gave an extra legitimacy to the forms.

While the glazed, climate-controlling atrium was an important form in northern climates, the spatial and architec-

tonic potential was realized most effectively by John Portman, working in Atlanta in the warm south of the USA, who made the atrium idea his own in the early 1960s, as a response first to the need for public authority housing, and then, by the mid-1960s, as a form for hotels: the Regency Hyatt in Atlanta was completed in 1967. The idea was catching. While this building was on the

35

35. Ford Foundation
Building, New York,
1967, Roche and
Dinkeloo. This was
the first great New
York atrium building.

36. Winter Garden,
Niagara Falls, New
York, 1975, Victor
Gruen with Cesar
Pelli.

37. Newlands Primary
School, Yateley, 1979,
Hampshire County
Architects.

drawing board, Colin St John Wilson was designing a huge central atrium proposal for the, sadly unbuilt, Liverpool Civic Centre in 1965, and two years later, Kevin Roche and John Dinkeloo had completed the Ford Foundation Building in New York.

In the 1970s and eighties, atrium design became an increasingly important constituent of architectural thinking all round the world, particularly when its environmental and energy conservation benefits could be seen to be added to its obvious popularity. The social (and consequent commercial) advantages of the atrium, which were at the root of Portman's objectives in Atlanta, were extremely important: the spaces designed often represented the only twentieth-century volumes which provided that great feeling of uplift and soaring splendour given by the Gothic cathedral. However, as the importance

of energy design began to emerge, so did a new kind of glazed space.

Not surprisingly, northern climates provided the greatest rationale and genuine opportunities. In Scandinavia, the glass-covered street became a very attractive proposition. Fine examples were the High School at Sonderberg in Denmark by A5 Tegnestuen, and Henning Larsen's building in Norway at the University of Trondheim of 1978. These buildings were conceptually derived from the notion of climatic protection and energy conservation, and enabled naturally ventilated buildings to be provided with glass-covered spaces warmed by the sun, and by heat released into the space by conduction and convection from the main occupied spaces.

The north American shopping malls of the period derived from a different brief, but provided the same comfortable volumes. The Eaton Center in Toronto, by Bregman and Hamann and Zeidler Roberts Partnership, is one of the greatest and took from 1967, the year of its inception, to the early 1980s to complete. The nave of this twentieth century cathedral of commerce is 900 ft (274 m)

long, and has the generosity essential to such a building. Anyone who has experienced a Toronto winter will realize the enormous benefit of these great climate-controlling spaces.

The north American atrium, in the various guises of conservatory, courtyard or mall, was pushed into useful service in an enormous variety of buildings, from I M Pei's Kennedy Library in Boston of the early 1970s, to Arthur Cotton Moore's roofing over the courtyard of the old Post Office in Washington DC. In Europe, examples extend from the Hampshire County Architects' primary school at Yateley Newlands in Hampshire, to the Martin House at Heggbach in Germany by Mann and Partners, to the City Bank in Paris by Saubot and Jullien, to the Civic Centre at Chester-le-Street, County Durham, by Faulkner-Brown, Hendy, Watkinson and Stonor.

Many of the buildings discussed here defy categorization, but the idea of 'conservatory' is behind them all. Some were essentially conservatories, pure and simple. Cesar Pelli and Gruen Associates' Winter Garden at Niagara Falls was just that; a garden for the residents of the city to stroll through in their cold winters. Edward Larrabee Barnes' buildings for the Chicago Horticultural Society, and Ulrich Franzen and Associates' Boyce Thompson Institute for Plant Research at New York State College have more of a horticultural function, but were conservatories just the same.

Many of the early 'conservatory' glass buildings were simple descendants of a centuries-old tradition of botanical buildings or the late nineteenth century

atrium, but others were more overtly derived from an engineered attitude to energy, and the way glass could be used to conserve and optimize it by skillful control of the selective transmission characteristics of glass as between short-wave and longwave radiation, the so-called 'greenhouse effect'. Several of these were designed to a brief devised specifically to exploit energy collection, with the walls working as hard as the roof. Typical of such a building is the Program Support Facility for the Department of Energy at Argonne National Laboratories, Joliet, Illinois, by Murphy Jahn. This building was envisionaged as a pilot and demonstra-

37

tion project for passive solar energy use, future use of solar collectors and efficient use of daylighting. A similar objective lay behind the 'Prudential at Princeton' project also known as 'Enerplex', at Plainsborough, New Jersey, 1983, by the New York office of SOM. Like the Joliet project, the two buildings at Plainsborough represented an attitude to design responsibility as much derived from their clients' intentions as from a new overall approach to design.

36

38

38. Solar Dairy for
Indre Ostfold Meiri at
Mysen, near Oslo
Norway, 1980–81,
Arkitektkontoret
GASA. A very fine,
small essay in low
energy solar
architecture.
Monitoring has
demonstrated the
value of the glass
wall design.

39. Solar house in the
Landesgartenschau
1981, held in Baden-
Baden, by LOG ID.
The building was
dismantled after the
exhibition, but was an
early example of a
series of glass solar
projects by LOG ID
carried out since.

40. Meripolku Single-
Family Houses,
Espoo, Finland, 1978,
Harto Helpinen.

However, such client intentions require careful functional selection of systems and materials, without much self-indulgence. Significantly, the entire outer wall of the north building at Enerplex was glass, one-third being green and two-thirds clear. The inner wall was fifty per cent glass and fifty per cent plasterboard. On the south side, an atrium was designed with a hundred per cent clear glass to collect solar heat in winter. In the south building, windows were designed in size and shading characteristics to respond to orientation. On the north side, the atrium was designed with glass walls, with south-facing skylights. The whole project was conceived, designed and engineered to maximize the conservation of energy, with the sort of refined elegance to be expected of SOM.

A similar project was developed in the 1980s by the great Japanese company, Obayashi-gumi, for their technical research laboratories in Kiyose, Tokyo. Their brave objective was to produce the least energy-consuming building per

square metre in the world. The building was designed with a large active solar-collecting array over its roof, and with a double-glass skin on its south facade, carefully tilted to optimize passive solar collection.

The 1980s saw the proliferation of intelligently designed glass-walled buildings, in which the glazing was engineered to control or contribute to the creation of designed internal conditions. The Solar Dairy for Indre Ostfold Meiri at Mysen near Oslo in Norway by Arkitektkontoret GASA, of 1980–81, is an excellent example of such a building, as is the Occidental Chemical Center in Niagara Falls by Cannon Design, which is considered in detail as a case study; both used similar passive solar energy principles.

The creation of glass energy architecture is not the preserve of large building projects, of course. Many of the most innovative designs have been produced for private houses. Houses provide excellent bases for prototype design of all sorts, and the

39

40

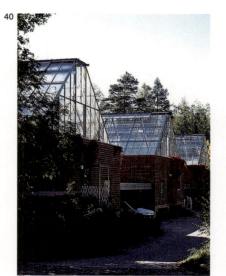

1970s and eighties produced a rich variety across the world. Domestic 'conservatories' of the 1970s included work emerging from the new 'green' movement in Germany. Typical of these are the whole catalogue of houses produced by the firm LOG ID, headed by Dieter Schempp, whose design proposition was clear from his generic title for these houses: 'Grune Solararchitektur'. Typical also are the house at Fluy, France by Ian Ritchie with Jocelyne van den Bossche Chrysalis Architects, the roof-lit Trombe wall in the house at San Juan Islands, Washington State by Morgan and Lindstrom, Kelbaugh and Lee's house for Douglas Kelbaugh at Princeton (which again used a Trombe wall), Harto Helpinen's houses at Lirislati in Finland, and Thomas Herzog's Richter Houses in Munich.

The idea of using the structural potential of glass is much more recent than the realization that it could contribute to climate control. It was not until 1928 that the basic material essential to the creation of glass structures, toughened or heat-strengthened glass, was invented in France as 'Securit'. Exploitation of the material was slow. Even in the 1961 edition of McGrath's great book, *Glass in Architecture and Decoration*, toughened glass is mentioned as a structural material only in relation to frameless doors. By this time, however, the French had already conceived the idea of the large suspended glass wall. The Hahn system, used in 1953–63 in the Maison de la Radio in Paris by Henri Bernard, used very large plates, two-storeys high, suspended by clamped fixings at the top and stiffened by glass fins perpendicular to the main glass plane. This idea became the basis for many similar systems introduced to provide dramatic, frameless glass walls in the 1960s.

It is one of the ironies of twentieth-century architecture that the great glass structures of the seventies and eighties came, not out of the cladding industry that promoted the 'curtain wall', but out of the passion of a new generation of architects and designers who were driven to exploit and enjoy technology in architecture, both to support their building concepts, and for their own sake. The key which unlocked this technology was the ability of toughened glass to maintain its integrity with holes drilled quite close to its edge, which enabled it to be suspended and carried on bolts. This, in turn, permitted assemblies of glass panels to be

41. 'Les Serres' of the
Cité des Sciences et
de l'Industrie at Parc
de la Villette, Paris:
Designed between
1980 and 1986.
Architect Adrien
Fainsilber; glass
installations by Rice
Francis Ritchie.

41

42

42. Roof over the
Montmartre
Funiculaire station,
Paris, François
Deslaugiers with
Marc Malinowsky of
Group Alto.

43. House, London,
1976, Michael and
Patty Hopkins. A
refined reworking of
the glass house,
twenty years after
Mies, Johnson and
the Eameses.

44. Broadfield House
Glass Museum, Glass
Pavilion, Dudley,
England, 1993–5,
Dewhurst
MacFarlane with
Design Antenna.

45. Ishihara House,
Osaka, 1978, Tadao
Ando.

created in various configurations, most simply as a set of adjacent panels connected in the same plane. The first assemblies used 'patch' fittings, which consisted of plates acting as connectors, but designers, and glass-makers, soon extended the vocabulary of fixing methods.

The Willis Faber & Dumas building in Ipswich, England, by Foster Associates, 1973–5 and considered as a case study in this chapter, is an excellent example of the obsessive desire on the part of a design team to seek a technical goal using the new techniques. The goal in question was a continuous, uninterrupted glass wall, just as that dreamt of by Mies van der Rohe in 1922. The early sketches demonstrate the design development from a metal support system to give stiffness to the glass wall through to the eventual genuine curtain wall suspended from the top of the building, each pane hung from the one above it, and the whole assembly stiffened by glass fins. The system used by Hahn for one plate was now used to create a multi-panel wall. The design took the, by now, conventional Pilkington patch fitting, in this case 165 mm square and in brass, and used it to create a new form of wall. One of the principal designers of the building,

43

Michael Hopkins, produced, in passing, a beautiful reworking of the glass house in London in 1976, in which he and Patty Hopkins set up their own practice.

The search was now on for the ever more discreet fixing of the glass wall. In 1980, Adrien Fainsilber, inspired by Willis Faber & Dumas, approached the engineer Peter Rice in connection with the creation of enormous glass enclosures at the Science Museum at Parc de la Villette, of which he was the architect. Peter Rice formed the practice Rice Francis Ritchie, thus combining with his own prodigious engineering skill the experience of two of the designers who had developed the glass wall at Ipswich. RFR removed the patch and the glass fin, and designed a four-way connector which reduced the fixing to the bolt itself. A system of spherical bearings and spring supports connects the glass wall back to a cable truss system, itself designed to minimize structural member sizes.

This wall revolutionized the idea of

hanging glass walls from point fixings, and bolt fixing systems have proliferated since Parc de la Villette. Glass manufacturers, such as Pilkington, have developed systems of their own, and engineering designers such as Mick Eekhout in the Netherlands, Marc Malinowsky in France, and RFR themselves, have devised ever more minimal ways of supporting and configuring glass walls and roofs. The fixing techniques have now been perfected for use with multiple-glazing assemblies, and using fixings embedded within laminated glasses.

The use of bolts relates particularly to the use of glass in tension: a glass panel is essentially hung from the bolt. Another line of enquiry, which has led to equally beautiful results, relies on the compression potential of glass. The strength of a stiffened, thick-glass panel is self-evident, if rather difficult to calculate in terms of quantity, and the last ten years have seen some remarkable developments in the idea of the glass load-bearing wall, the glass column and the glass beam.

It may seem perverse to use glass for functions which are more happily carried out by materials with more structural predictability, but the goal of transparency, and Buckminster Fuller's 'ephemeralization', have proved a great spur. It is a simple step from the use of a glass fin as a stiffener and bracing device to its use as a column, and this step is seen in Benthem and Crouwel's Sonsbeek Sculpture Pavilion of 1986. Equally structurally elegant was Benthem's own house in which the glass walls supported the roof. Both these buildings, considered as case studies below, use metal trusses to support the

44

roof, but subsequent developments have replaced the truss by a laminated glass beam; laminated to provide the benefit of redundancy which glass structures need. With the design of a mortice and tenon joint using three-ply laminated glass, the engineer Tim MacFarlane, of Dewhurst Macfarlane, has created very elegant, all-glass structures, with the architect Rick Mather in a conservatory in London, and with Design Antenna in the Glass Pavilion to Broadfield House Glass Museum in Dudley finished in 1995. The author, working with engineers Whitby and Bird, has designed a structural glass pavilion as part of a scheme for Stag Place in London, using stainless-steel beams bolted into load-bearing glass walls and supporting a bolt-fixed glass roof.

The structural design of these buildings is, to a large extent, empirical. The recommendations of the glass-makers with regard to the strength of their materials is naturally cautious, and development is generally based on the step-by-step design of prototype projects, almost analogous to the progression of stone architecture in the Middle Ages. Out of this experience will doubtless come new generations of glass structures.

The flowering of glass architecture in the **45** last twenty years has not only been concerned with serious issues of energy conservation and climate control, however, or the development of glass as a structural material. The beguiling nature of glass, particularly in its new forms as a coated material, have continued to fascinate the aesthetic sensibility of the new generation of architects, no longer restricted by the palette of the 1950s and sixties. The appearance of a glass building has long inspired the designer interested in the conceptual as well as, or rather than, the technical attributes of glass, and the products created by the industry have provided an ever richer palette.

In Japan and North America, the glass block has emerged to figure in fine buildings. The Japanese approach to glass is fascinating in its fusion of overtly twentieth-century, Western-adopted convention, and a traditional approach to architecture and light, particularly translucence. Le Corbusier's dictum 'the history of architecture is the history of the window', has particular significance when considered in terms of cultures with no history of flat glass-making. In Japan, with latitudes the same as the Mediterranean (between 30 degrees and 45 degrees), the climatic and environmental imperatives have traditionally not applied: the equivalent element to the Western window in traditional Japanese architecture is the shoji screen, and it is not at all surprising that the glass block has proved so attractive to many Japanese architects. It is tempting to suggest that the 'cause' of

46

the glass wall in the Maison de Verre of 1931, which was the need for light *and* privacy in densely-packed Paris, is the same as in many Japanese houses. Whatever the rationale, two of Tadao Ando's houses of the late 1970s, the Ishihara House and the Matsumoto House, employ the traditional Shoji screen re-created in the form of glass blocks. The Ishihara House has a glass block core as its central *tour de force*, and the Matsumoto House is an important essay in using glass blocks as a significant contributor to the spatial structure of the building.

On a larger scale, Fumihiko Maki's Central Building of the Faculty of Physical Education and Art at Tsukuba University of 1974 also used glass blocks to great effect. Arata Isozaki's Employees' Service Facilities for the Nippon Electric Glass Company used the company's own glass block as a translucent wall for the employees' dining hall, gymnasium and other areas, and also used NEG's 'Neoparie' in its entrance hall. This is a crystallized glass product which is remarkable for its toughness and resilient beauty.

Glass blocks were also used to great effect in the 1970s and early 1980s in several American buildings, not least because of the product development programme of companies such as PPG. The Wateridge Marketing Pavilion in San Diego, California by the WZMH Group used a solar-reflective glass block wall, producing a rippling mirror in dialogue with a reflecting pool. The Coleman A Young Recreation Center in Detroit, by William Kessler Associates,

46. Matsumoto House, Wakayama, 1980, Tadao Ando.

47. Ingot Café, Kita-Kyushi City, 1978, Shoei Yoh.

used glass block rather than flat glass because of the latter's susceptibility to damage. The resulting essay included a large barrel vault and glass brick columns and walls. A huge expanse of glass block created the walls of the Alfred C Glassell Jr School of Art at the Museum of Fine Arts in Houston, by Morris Aubry Architects, producing a glistening surface (particularly beautiful at night) and a well-lit (if somewhat cut-off) interior. A fine European use of glass block was in the Ferrari Company Cultural and Recreational Centre in Maranello in Italy, where a long, snaking glass block wall provided a 'free-form' entrance in an otherwise highly-geometrized building.

Japan has seen an approach to glass architecture very different from the Western emphasis on 'skin'. The work of Shoei Yoh has demonstrated a typical fascination with the material. In his Ingot

Café in Kita-Kyushi City of 1978, he created a glass crystal using chromium-coated multiple glazing which is metallic black by day and transparent by night. In the house he designed for Dr Shizo Matsushita in Nagasaki, glass and solid have been used with great wit. Shoei Yoh called the house a 'stainless steel house with light lattice', and grey glass was used to create a lattice of light around the insulated stainless steel panels: the light is a 'negative' metaphor for the joint. Both these projects are as much abstracted sculpture as they are works of architecture, and they exploit glass in a masterful way.

The case studies which follow, and close, this chapter span a period of over twenty years, but when considering twenty buildings in some detail, it is important to register the enormous number of buildings making significant use of glass in the decade since 1985. In

the UK alone, several buildings are published every month which could be acclaimed as representing the new glass architecture, and which expand the canon with designs of real ingenuity, technical innovation and beauty. Architects such as Sir Norman Foster and Partners, and Ian Ritchie and Partners in Britain, RFR, Dominique Perrault and Jean Nouvel in France, Thomas Herzog, and Petzinka Pink and Partners in Germany, and Herzog and de Meuron in Switzerland, are continuously expanding the boundaries of design in glass. A review of the glass architecture of this decade would constitute a book in itself.

But that is another story. Glass is at the beginning of a new chapter in the story of its contribution to architecture, and these buildings and designs, both in glass and plastics, show how wonderful this future might be.

47

case studies

The selection of a mere twenty buildings for study and celebration to describe a quarter of a century's worth of work in glass may seem a little invidious. Some sort of explanation is required concerning the way the buildings have been selected.

Since the early 1970s a gratifyingly large number of fine buildings using glass in an exemplary way has been built. When a review was carried out for an earlier version of this book, in the early 1980s, well over 150 buildings were identified which, in one way or another, demonstrated a new or unique way of using glass, and were dependent to a degree on glass for their concept.

In the last ten years in particular architects across the world have designed buildings which push the use of glass to new boundaries. Not surprisingly the so-called 'modernist' school have embraced glass as a key material with the same enthusiasm as did their forebears in the 1920s and 1930s, half a century before.

Several of the architects represented in this review of twenty buildings have themselves created many more than the examples selected, and many other architects are not represented. However, the inclusion of a building here is not intended to be some sort of accolade.

In selecting twenty buildings an attempt has been made to describe by example some of the most important aspects of the use of glass in architecture, both with an eye on its potential, and with a view towards the future. The intention of this book is to show that

opposite Roof of Waterloo International Terminal, London, 1992–3, Nicholas Grimshaw and Partners.

glass is a beautiful and beguiling material which, in the right hands, can create the most wonderful architecture. However glass is also the key to environmental performance, as the material most capable of transmitting energy, usefully or otherwise.

The twenty buildings presented demonstrate specific aspects of the use of glass. The first group uses glass as a skin, exploiting its variability, and in the technical sense incorporating it into architecture in a way that is fundamental to the concept of the building. The development of fixing techniques is evident in this group. European architects will look with envy at the endorsement of silicone 'structural' glazing techniques in the United States and in Canada.

This use of glass as a skin is extended into one great example of a glass roof. There are many extensive glass roofs in the world now of course, but the example chosen incorporates the essential qualities of the way in which such a roof can be designed and exploited at the end of our century.

One example of transparent plastic is selected, as an example of how the forming of such a material can create a fundamentally different morphology in the building skin, where lightness, and even weakness, are exploited.

The next group explores the use of the glass envelope as an environmental controller. The three examples chosen are different from each other, and are now only part of a developing canon of glass architecture, in which environmental engineering

principles are used to design glass skins which lay to rest the belief of the 1960s and 1970s, that glass was an intrinsically weak constituent of the architect's vocabulary in environmental terms. In the UK, Building Regulation has begun to accept that glass can actually be a fundamental help in saving energy, particularly when daylighting is taken into consideration, as it increasingly should. There are surely many buildings on the drawing boards and computer screens of architects now which take the principles of the *mur neutralisant* further forward, and use glass, carefully configured, to drive the environmental engineering of the building, including natural ventilation.

After this environmentally sensitive group of buildings come projects which explore another aspect of development in glass architecture, relating to how it is fixed. Suspended glazing has been with us for forty years now, and we must still look back to the use of the Hahn system by Henri Bernard at the Maison de la Radio in Paris of 1953–63 to see the use of huge uninterrupted glass panels. The manufacturers themselves have been instrumental in promoting these walls, and systems such as Pilkington's Planar have revolutionized glass architecture. Many versions now exist. The buildings selected here show a few magnificent exploitations of these systems, where the design depends on the synergetic combination of delicate steel structures and the use of the tensile properties of glass.

This group is followed by three buildings which use glass structurally

in a more total way, with the glass being used as a fully structural member. The intrinsic thinness of a glass panel if it is to exploit its transparency, to say nothing of its weight and cost, mean that glass used as a column or load-bearing wall must form part of a braced and stiffened structure. However, adhesives and a greater understanding the strength of glass have recently opened new possibilities. The involvement of the engineer in these structures is both inevitable and welcome.

Finally two examples are shown which celebrate glass in a small scale way, created by architects who simply relish its beauty and adaptability, with the enthusiasm which Scheerbart himself would have applauded.

The drawings which are used to illustrate these twenty buildings are produced with a view to enabling as complete an understanding as possible of how they are made, particularly following through the logic of their conception. In only four or six pages, however, the full story of a building cannot be told, and the author asks indulgence from all those architects whose buildings are shown. It may be a truism to state that the author is solely responsible for the images shown, but like all truisms, it is a matter of fact.

It is a cause for satisfaction that many recent buildings could be selected to replace those chosen here, and the author will enjoy being reminded of the fact by all those who would have selected others.

willis faber & dumas building

ipswich, england

architect foster associates
designed 1971–2
constructed 1975

1. Isometric drawing
through the perimeter
of the building.

2. The glass wall:
broken reflected
images are a prime
experience with the
building. 'Detailing' is
virtually absent,
texture relying on
reflection the glass
colour, and the small
punctuations of the
plates.

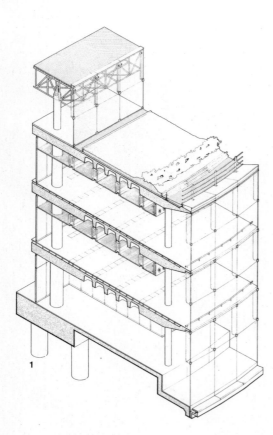

1

2

Now nearly twenty years old, the Willis Faber & Dumas building remains an icon in the architecture of the last quarter of this century, for several good reasons. Formally, it represents an idea about the workplace for office workers which is entirely different from those implicit in the towers, slabs and other monoliths which characterize post-war office building, from Lever House and the Seagram Building onwards. This derives from a separate, and generically more important distinction, relating to the attitude of the client. Like Hertzberger's great office building for Centraal Beheer in Apeldoorn, 1972, it demonstrates how an idea that a building can represent the culture of a company and its attitude to what it and its employees do, and that the selection of an architect, and subsequent collusion in the design of a building, is an essential part of its ethos. In addition to this, the architect's passion for a material has resulted in one of the century's great glass buildings.

The glass wall had featured in several previous buildings by Foster Associates: the Advance Head Office for IBM at Cosham, the Fred Olsen Lines terminal at Millwall Docks, both completed in 1971, and the architects' own offices in Great Portland Street, all include an entirely glass wall clearly conceived as 'seamless'. The fact that glass is only available in panels is played down, and the junctions are kept as small as possible. Willis Faber & Dumas has a more historic antecedent, however, in Mies van der Rohe's glass tower project of 1922. Mies's great meandering glass

wall, designed to exploit the possibilities of inter-reflection and changing angles of light, is now realized with the benefit of half a century of technology.

With the typical directness of the office, the plan form of the building is derived from the shape of the site. The perimeter is simply drawn along the building line, or as close to it as is appropriate. The resulting deep plan, reflecting the ideas of open office planning emerging at the time, is split by a central 'well' which accommodates the escalators which rise through the building. Solidity is imparted to the building by the use of a grey-tinted glass.

The character and significance of the building as seen from the outside derives from the way the glass wall is put together. Here, the term 'curtain wall' is a much closer description of how the wall is made than when applied to the devalued product of the commercial industry. An early version included a polished tubular mullion system using vertical edge support only, but Pilkington said they were prepared to offer their suspended glass system using solar tinted glass, and competitive tendering demonstrated that this was marginally cheaper. With Martin Francis (later to become a partner in Rice Francis Ritchie) as glazing consultant, the glass wall became a project in its own right.

The intrinsic high-tensile strength of the glass is used to permit the whole wall to be suspended from the top of the three-storey structure. Each 2 m (6 ft 6 in) wide panel zone is suspended from the roof level of the building by means of

a bolted clamping strip, and pane-to-pane fixing at each level is achieved by patch fittings. The proposal seen crudely in Mies's 1922 model (where the tapes used to suspend the strips of glass can be seen) is now realized. Stiffness is provided by 19 mm (¾ in) thick glass fins, and connections to intermediate floors give lateral restraint only. Sliding patch fittings allow for vertical thermal and building movement. The whole assembly is designed to accommodate a 50 mm (2 in) structural tolerance, and the rigour of the architects required that each panel was the same size, which is something of a challenge in a meandering glass wall without the benefit of cover strips.

The result is the shimmering and beautiful surface envisaged by Mies. The colour of the 12 mm (½ in) thick, toughened, bronze anti-sun glass gives density to the surface, and ensures that, during the daytime, the prime experience is one of reflection. The minimal glass-to-glass silicone joints ensure the vital visual continuity of the wall, and also ensure the evenness of weathering and cleanliness.

This building is single-glazed. As such it belongs to a category which might not receive total acclaim twenty years on. However, the very low wall-to-floor ratio is itself energy conserving. It remains a supreme model of a place of work, one of the great buildings of its time and a fine example of glass architecture.

WILLIS FABER & DUMAS LIMITED

3

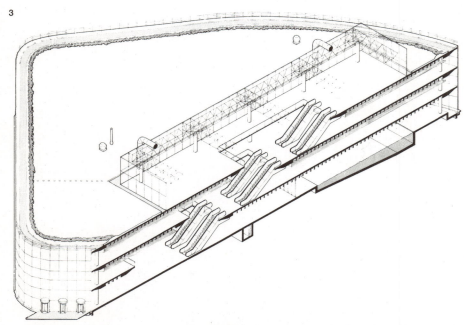

5

6

7

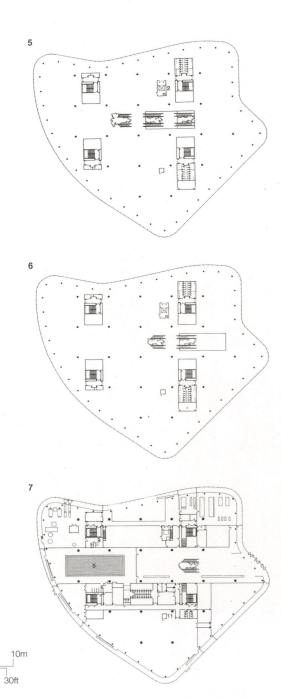

4

3. Cut-away
isometric, showing
the spatial continuity
between the entrance
hall and the roof, with
its lawn and garden.

4. At night the
inversion of the
lighting levels
between inside and
out convert the
building into a
lantern, and bring life
to the street: true
architecture of
transparency.

5–7. Floor plans, with
the ground floor at the
bottom. The
meandering wall
follows the site
boundary, maximizing
the area of each floor
plate, and thus
minimizing the height
of the building. The
concept of Mies van
der Rohe's 1922
office tower is joined
with a rationale based
on economy, relying
on the prevailing
environmental control
techniques of the
1970s.

0   10m

0   30ft

8

9

12

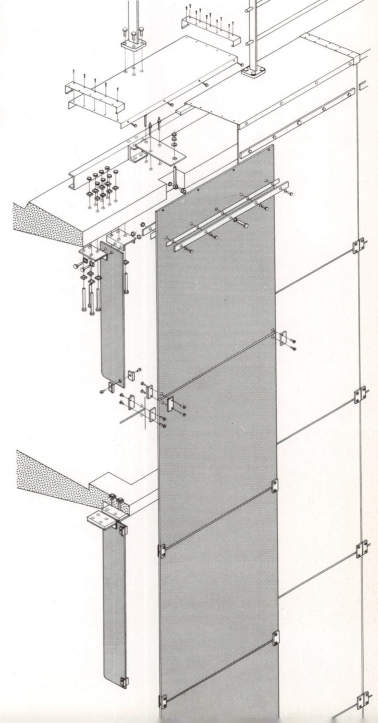

8. The interior perimeter zone, which serves as an ambulatory and buffer space. A wall which seems to be almost entirely reflective from the outside is completely transparent from the inside.

9. The half-storey height glass fins provide wind restraint. They are connected to the concrete floor above, and fixed to the glazing by sliding patch fittings.

10–11. The usual slot of a sliding patch fitting assembly is shown in 11. This was converted into a hinge by the incorporation of a cylindrical pivot shown in 10, which allowed the fitting to be used for the changing facets of the wall.

12. Exploded isometric of the glass wall. A single bolt carries the load of the storey height facet, with the load spread by the top clamping strips. The sliding patch fitting takes up thermal and building movement.

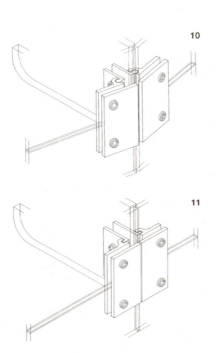

10

11

13

13. The glass wall.

14. The minimal
geometry of the skin:
the glazing grid was
devised to ensure
that each pane in the
meandering surface
had the same
dimensions.

15, 16. Top and
bottom details. The
traditional cornice
and plinth are
replaced by minimal
termination and an
implied continuity.

17, 18. Construction
details at 1:20. The
full section through
the skin shows the
simplicity of the
technical conception.
The bottom detail is
both elegant and
practical.

15

17

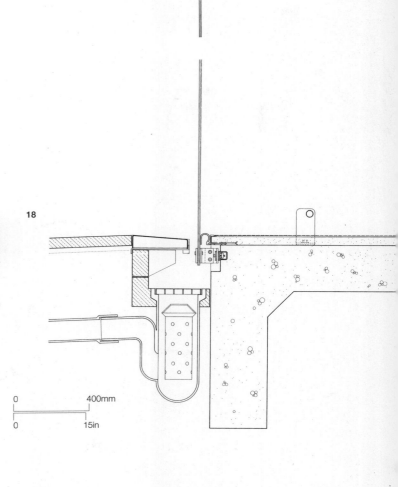

14

16

18

0   400mm

0   15in

corning museum

corning, new york

architect gunnar birkerts & associates inc
designed 1976
constructed 1980

1. The geometrically
generated freedom of
the plan.

2. The horizontal
periscope. The use of
mirror in Birkerts's
work is never facile,
and here it is
brilliantly employed
to protect and
enliven, as well as to
provide view.

Gunnar Birkerts is one a group of fine American architects who worked in Eero Saarinen's office in the 1950s, and whose work is characterized by conceptual innovation and formal courage, working within the general tenets of the Modern Movement. His colleagues working for Saarinen included Anthony Lumsden, who went on to produce some remarkable, expressive glass skins, and Cesar Pelli – whose work in glass includes the design of the Winter Garden at Niagara Falls (shown on page 101), and the Tower over the Museum of Modern Art in New York – as well as Kevin Roche and John Dinkeloo, who effectively inherited Saarinen's practice. The opportunities offered by the design of a museum for glass artefacts were given to an architect well qualified to exploit them.

The town of Corning, in up-state New York, is a world glass centre. Both the Corning Glass Works and Steuben Glass are located here, so it was an obvious place to create a major glass collection.

Birkerts's design is brilliant in concept and detail, and uniquely derived from the nature of glass. The swooping and apparently free curves of the plan are an expression of the amorphous molecular nature of glass itself, disciplined by the geometry of quarter circles. Birkerts has described the concept in poetic form:

The concept is already here
I search for words to express it.
It is the metaphor of glass
Appropriate
Free flowing and amorphous
When heated in the glory hole.
Crystalline and structured when cold
and formed.
The perimeter envelope is analogous to
the amorphous
The interior supporting structure
expressive
of the order
of the crystal.
Great contrasts.

The snaking perimeter is twice the length that a square enclosing the same area would be, and thus doubles the available space for the exhibits around the edge of the building. The section, too, is derived from one of the most ancient glass devices, the mirror. Birkerts created a horizontal periscope which produced a protective eyebrow for the building, while giving controlled view and light penetration. This exploitation of mirror is a favourite device for Birkerts, and is also seen at the Calvary Baptist Church in Detroit, Michigan, and the extraordinary underground library for the Law School at the University of Michigan. At Corning, 6 mm (¼ in) stainless-steel-backed mirrors are set at 45 degrees to produce a 930 mm (3 ft) overhang, at the back of which is the double glazing, conventionally fixed using very small purpose-made framing.

The innovative use of glass extends through to the materials used for the skin. The search for a soft perimeter for the building led to the creation of a rolled glass with a textured outer finish, and a stainless steel coating on the back. As Birkerts has said, 'This reflects light outwards without mirroring anything, and becomes a soft and poetic skin'. These glass panels are 6 mm (¼ in) thick, and about 1m (3 ft 3 in) wide, with heights varying from 1.74 to 2.54 m (5ft 6 in to 8ft 3 in) high. The continuity of this surface, so essential to the concept of the soft skin, is achieved by the frameless silicone detailing.

The result is a velvety surface, varying from black to deep grey to silvery, depending on how it is viewed and how the light falls. This soft surface undulates around the building making a wonderful contrast with the specular hardness of the mirrors of the horizontal periscope below.

2

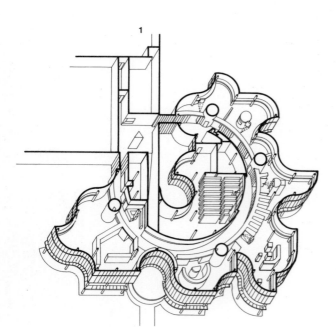

1

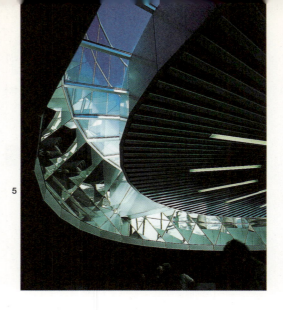

5

6

3

3. Exterior view, looking towards the entrance. Reflected light changes the colour from silver-blue to soft coppery gold.

4. The transformation of the grid: employing the simple use of the quarter and half-circle, disciplines the apparent arbitrariness of the wall.

5. Interior perimeter reflections.

6. The tight circular centre of the geometry.

7. A walk round the building reveals continuously changing form and interreflection, exactly as sought by Mies van der Rohe in 1922, but here relying on soft diffuse reflection.

8. External wall assembly drawing at 1:20.

9. The perimeter of the building has the quality of a fine mechanism, slid open to reveal its inner workings, like a highly polished subcutaneous layer beneath the outer skin.

4

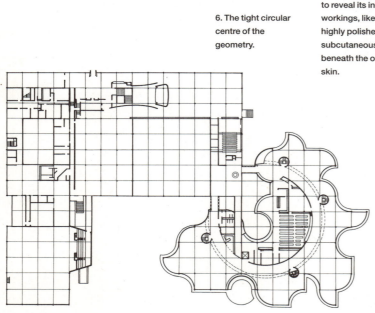

0   40m

0   120ft

7

8

9

0   400mm
⊢——————┤

0   15in
⊢——————┤

10, 11. The use of the meander: the configuration of the perimeter doubles the amount of space at the edge of the building available for exhibits.

12–15. Construction details at 1:5:
12, 13. Details through the upper glass cladding. The glass is 6 mm thick with a stainless steel coating on the back.
14. Vertical detail through the top of the horizontal periscope. The mirrors are 6 mm stainless-steel coated glass, constructed to produce a 930 mm overhang. The double glazed windows are framed in very small purpose-made extrusions.

15. Horizontal details through the double glazing and the upper glass cladding.

16. The Corning Museum is a perfect complement to the artefacts within it.

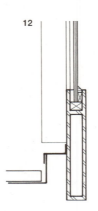

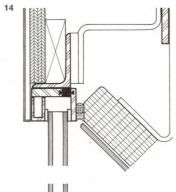

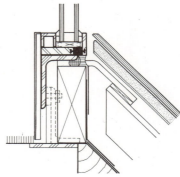

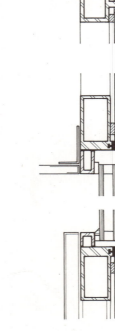

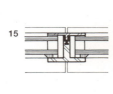

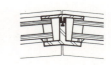

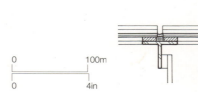

0   100m

0   4in

allied bank tower

fountain place, dallas
texas, USA

architect i m pei and partners
designed 1982
constructed 1983–6

1. Site plan.

2. One of the great
portals at the bottom
of the building. It is
characteristic of I M
Pei's office that the
pure and shapely
glass prism sits in a
beautiful urban
landscape dominated
by water, which varies
from informal
cascades to a
computer-controlled
water sculpture of
fountain jets drained
through its own
paving.

The Allied Bank Tower is the archetypal
Dallas building. The sight of mirror-glass
buildings shimmering in the heat is a
familiar one to anyone who flies into the
city, and the Allied Bank is the tallest
because the client wanted it to be. In
selecting I M Pei and Partners as the
architects, the client chose a firm noted
for its control of formal qualities fused
with immaculate and smooth detailing.
The shape and height of the building are
a testament to the bold and big attitude
for which the state is known.

The brief called for a distinctive
form, and this emerged from the twisting
geometry of the plan, derived from the
typical Pei device of the interaction
between an orthogonal shape and
intersecting diagonals. Here, the
interaction takes place in section as
well as plan, producing a sculptural
form which, from certain views,
appears to twist, and led to its nick-
name, 'the screwdriver'. It is a great
presence in the city, and sits next to
an amazing display of fountains.

The concept for the building is
formal, a large-scale, sculpted monolith,
which called for a smooth, two-
dimensional uninterrupted surface. The
skin of the building is thus a minimally
detailed glass sheath. It is this step, from
conceptual requirement to detailed
response, which characterizes the
work of I M Pei and Partners.

The detailing is entirely dependent
upon the technology of structural
silicone fixing, a technology which still
finds acceptance virtually impossible in
Britain, for example, where 'mechanical'
fixing (using the physical retention of
the glass pane by metal covering its
edge) is generally required.

On the face of it, the Allied Bank
might seem to be yet another wilful
attempt to produce an interesting shape
for an office building, to 'beat the box'.
In some way that is what it is, but the
triangulated geometry constitutes a
morphological device which is endemic
in Pei's office, and releases great
ingenuity in the detailing.

At the time it was built, it was the
largest structural silicone glass wall yet
constructed, with a surface area of nearly
42,000 m^2 (452,000 sq ft), and the
building itself is 220 m (715 ft) high.
The need for smoothness and lack of
interruption in the skin led to the design
of a very ingenious window-cleaning
system. The cradles are housed within
the building behind opening panels in
the glass. The cleaning procedure
involves the opening of the panel, the
emergence of a boom which carries the
cradle, and the connection of the cradles
to outrigger tubes fixed to the face of the
building, which constitute the only
features on its surface. These
are horizontal at the tops of the smooth
vertical faces, but are set at a very
steep angle up the diagonals on the
facade. The cradles move up these
angled tracks, providing access to the
whole face.

The glazing itself is simple single
glazing, in 6 mm (¼ in) heat-
strengthened, monolithic, reflective
green glass. There is no attempt to
produce an energy-saving skin here: the
budget did not allow it. When standing
behind the glass in the remarkable
spaces at the top of the building, with
the hot sun shining on to the elevation,
the radiant heat is very evident. This is
very much an air-conditioned building.

Although Allied Bank does not
feature in the list of great public work
in the oeuvre of the office, its technical
mastery is evident, and it occupies an
important place in the history of glass
in architecture, and the ruthless drive
for the smooth, seamless skin.

2

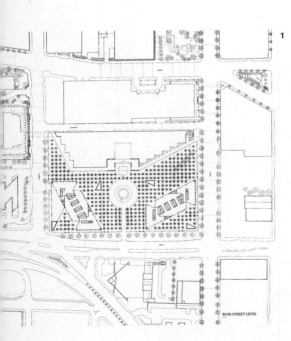

1

ROSS STREET LEVEL

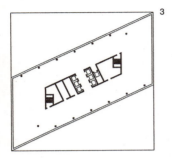

3

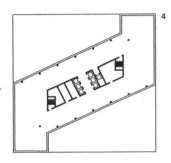

4

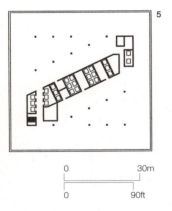

5

0   30m

0   90ft

6

3–5. Floor plans. The unique and eccentric form of the building, with its multi-storey wedges, is set by the diagonal configuration of the central service core.

6. The sheer glass surface. This surface is a testament to the single-minded achievement of objectives, in this case the creation of a seamless skin.

7. A client requirement for the building was that its form should be recognizable and unique. This gave the office the opportunity to explore the interpenetration of diagonals and slopes to create a tapering profile, exploited brilliantly again in the Bank of China Building in Hong Kong, started in the same year, but not completed until 1990.

7

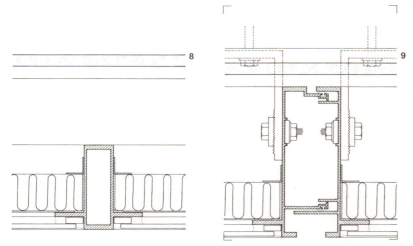

8

9

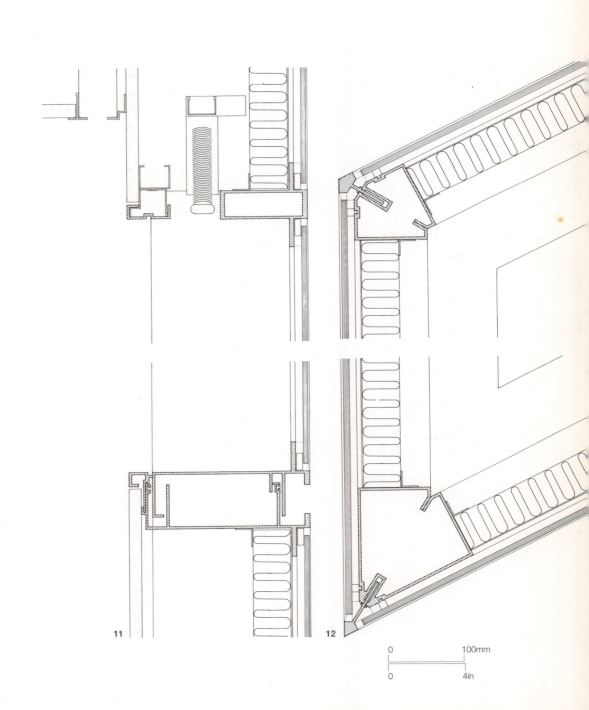

10

8, 9 and 11–12.
Construction details
at 1:5. 8, 9. Horizontal
sectional details,
showing the way in
which the flush skin
is achieved. Detail
9 shows how move-
ment is accommo-
dated and replace-
ment is facilitated.

10. The building's
main entrance.

11. Vertical section.
The building is glazed
in 6 mm heat-
strengthened
reflective green glass.

12. Horizontal
sections through
corners. The corner
extrusions are
designed to present
the same face width
at each position.

11

12

0   100mm

0   4in

the pyramids at the louvre
paris, france

architect i m pei and partners
with rice francis ritchie
designed 1983–5
constructed 1986–8

1, 2. Elevation and
plan: the pure
geometry of the
pyramid gives little
hint of the strenuous
efforts needed in its
realization.

3. View from inside
the central Pyramid,
out to the old building
of the Louvre, the
structure minimized
by the skill of the
engineer Peter Rice.

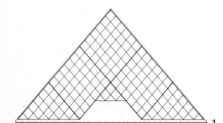

1

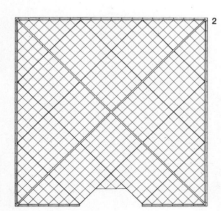

2

The Pyramids are one of the Grands Projets conceived for Paris in the 1980s, and constitute one of the most generally accepted triumphs amongst these sometimes controversial projects.

The project derives from the wish of the French authorities to renew the Louvre as a major gallery and centre for the arts, and to remove from it government offices which were seen to conflict with this objective. The idea was to provide much better public access to the collections by the creation of a below-ground concourse, top-lit by the central large Pyramid. The height of the water table on the site drove the architects to elevate the great form of the roof over this concourse, and the Pyramid was born.

The original idea of the project was to create a severe form, conceptually separate from the architecture of the Cour Napoléon around it. This form was to be totally transparent. One of Pei's early ideas was for a trellis without any glass at all. The architects experienced frustration in creating real transparency in a large glass form as the structure supporting it gets in the way. After early struggles, they approached Rice Francis Ritchie, who had already completed their work on 'Les Serres' at Parc de la Villette. The resulting structure incorporates much of what was learned there.

The glass itself posed equal problems of 'thereness'. The objective was to place the form as an almost completely transparent object in the space, with the beautiful stone of the Louvre visible through it. With this objective, transparency becomes a matter not only of the physical interruption of the structure, but also of the colour of the glass. It was clear that, with thick glass viewed generally at an angle, and with the shape of the Pyramid providing two faces to look through, only a very clear water-white glass would provide the transparency needed, without an overlay of the green tint given by a conventional iron oxide glass. These glasses abound in specialist manufacturers' catalogues. The architects found a German source for the chemistry, which was replicated in France using special sand from Fontainebleau. The problems of changeover, endemic in float glass manufacture, meant that this special mix had to be used to make plate glass; and then the architects hit a second problem. The only machinery in Europe which could grind and polish plates of the size concerned was in the UK. The plates were duly shipped over, polished, and shipped back again.

Having successfully solved the problem of colour, the architects had to consider the detailed concept of the surface, and rainwater. The conventional answer is structural silicone, as employed in the Allied Bank project, for example, and as used in Johnson and Burgee's Garden Grove Community Church. At the Louvre, however, the Pyramid glazing was going to be available for minute scrutiny by viewers very close to it, inside and out.

The issues of factory glazing, and the need to collect and dispose of rainwater, led to the creation of the section used to support the 21 mm (⅞ in) thick laminated glass. Structural glazing requires factory application to effect curing, and this is a major constraint on any flush glass skin, particularly when reglazing is considered: the glass has to come to site as a glazed panel, including its frame. Also, the nature of the silicone itself, and the way it meets the glass, is a constraint. As the architect has said, the use of silicone gives the designer an edge to work with, and also enables the viewer to see through the glass to the silicone behind: silicone is not conceived as an 'architectural' material. The design solution was to bevel, grind and polish the edge, and to apply a ceramic frit to the back of the glass to conceal the silicone (a method borrowed from the automotive industry).

The period taken to move from design concept, through detail to implementation, was two years. Much of this time was spent obstinately refusing to take no for an answer, and insisting on the achievement of materials and details which were themselves conceived by a highly refined sensitivity to glass, and enough knowledge to be sure of what was possible.

3

glass in
architecture

the pyramids at
the louvre

4

5

6

4. The great spiral stair, with its structural glass balustrade, showing the architect at right.

5. The prime objective in specifying the glass was to remove the green tint characteristically created by the iron in conventional soda-lime glass.

6. The space beneath the Pyramid. The pretext for the Pyramid was no doubt partly formal, but also related to the need to achieve height in a major public space, in a place where the water table set difficulties of depth.

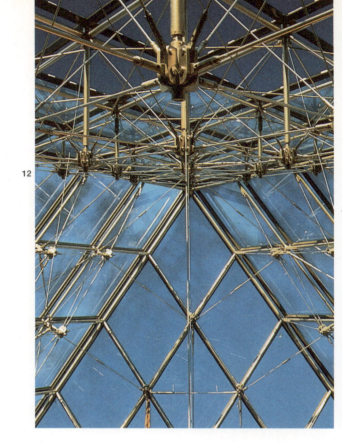

12

14

7. View looking up through the lattice structure supporting the glazing.

7

10

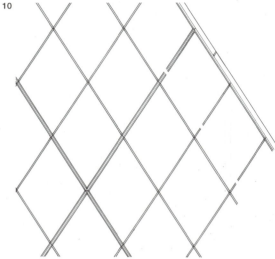

8, 9. Construction details at 1:5. The two sections show the major panel junction and the secondary panel junction. These details are always set on a slope. The glass is 21mm thick laminated.

10. Assembly elevation showing the distinction between main and secondary panels.

11. The top of the Pyramid.

12, 13. Detail of the structure: the designers talk of their early attempts to draw the Pyramid as a clear crystal form, which was always compromised by the structure as soon as the metal support system was added. The eventual finely drawn system reduces the structure to a minimum.

14. The central Pyramid in the Cour Napoléon. The use of water both protects the Pyramid and creates reflection.

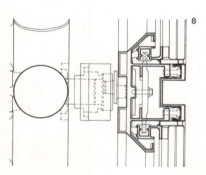

8

11

13

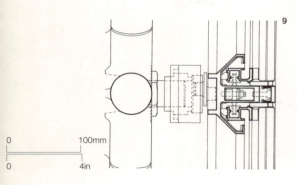

9

0   100mm

0   4in

garden grove community church

garden grove

california, USA

architect johnson/burgee architects
designed 1977–8
constructed 1978–80

1. Ground floor plan.

2. The skin.
Seen in the context of
many buildings
wholly clad in glass,
the pane size is quite
small. The fineness of
detail, with the gaps
between flush
framing members
almost appearing as a
brick joint, actually
contributes to the
continuity of surface.
The pane size also
makes opening
windows easy to
achieve.

Wonderful as glass is as an envelope,
to produce a skin for a building which
is entirely in transparent glass demands
a particular, and comparatively rare,
combination of climate and function.
The great conservatories of the
nineteenth century are obvious
examples of the appropriate use of a
complete glass envelope.

The Garden Grove Community
Church, known popularly as the Crystal
Cathedral, corresponded to the client's
wish to bond the experience of religion
with that of nature, and the building sits
as a miraculously-cut diamond, a daring
masterpiece in glass.

Mirror-glass buildings have
understandably received a mixed
reception when they have been located
in northern Europe and the northern
parts of North America. Their light-
absorbing nature has proved
inappropriate to climates where
predominant sky brightness is low.

In California, Texas and other
southern states, however, mirror glass
comes into its own. It still suffers from
the difficulties of the presentation of a
visually-impenetrable facade, but
environmentally it is perfectly suited to
the bright hot sun. The Crystal
Cathedral was a project for a huge
mirror-glass jewel, glittering in the
Californian sunshine.

The building is very large. Housing
a congregation of 3,000 people, it rises
as a four-pointed star to a height of 40 m
(130 ft). The reflective material used
creates an internal space surrounded by
a lacy structure and the sky. Even in the
climate of California (the building sits at
a latitude of about 34 degrees), the
building is high enough to be naturally
ventilated, with frameless operable
windows, and two enormous
motorized glazed doors, 27.5 m (89 ft
5 in) high by 4.5 m (14ft 8 in) wide.

The key to the building is its
detailing, which relies on single glazing,
factory glazed into aluminium framing
using structural silicone. The panels are
generally 610 mm (2 ft) high by 1,525
mm (5 ft) and 1,830 mm (6 ft) long. The
opening lights operate using a rack and
pinion system, and open to a maximum
of 45 degrees. These are fixed using a
simple bolt system through the glass,
and they close against a hypalon-coated
soft neoprene gasket. The skin is
designed to withstand the seismic forces
which can be experienced in California.

The glass itself is toughened in two
thicknesses: 3 mm (⅛ in) and 6 mm
(¼ in). It is also highly reflective, with a
silver coating providing eight per cent
light transmission and ten per cent total
solar transmission. These very low
transmissions are acceptable in southern
California where sky brightnesses and
radiation levels are so high.

It would be easy to dismiss the
Crystal Cathedral as a typically
Californian exaggeration, and a
pointless exercise in glass virtuosity.
In fact, the enclosure of a floor space
as large as this with an all-protecting,
naturally ventilated, comfortable glass
envelope is a triumph of technology
and environmental control, as well as
a supremely suitable building to serve
its ecclesiastical purpose.

2

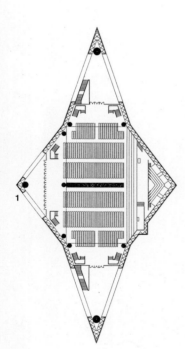

1

3. The interior
structure.

4–9. Construction
details at 1:5: as in the
two previous Case
Studies, the Crystal
Cathedral relies on
structural silicone
glazing.
4, 5 show fixed
glazing.
6, 7 show a beautifully
disguised opening
light.

10. The interior
volume. The eight per
cent light
transmission still
produces a high level
of light when exterior
levels are, on most
days, predictably up
to 100,000 lux. The
resultant source
brightness of the
envelope is still much
higher than the
European 'overcast
sky'.

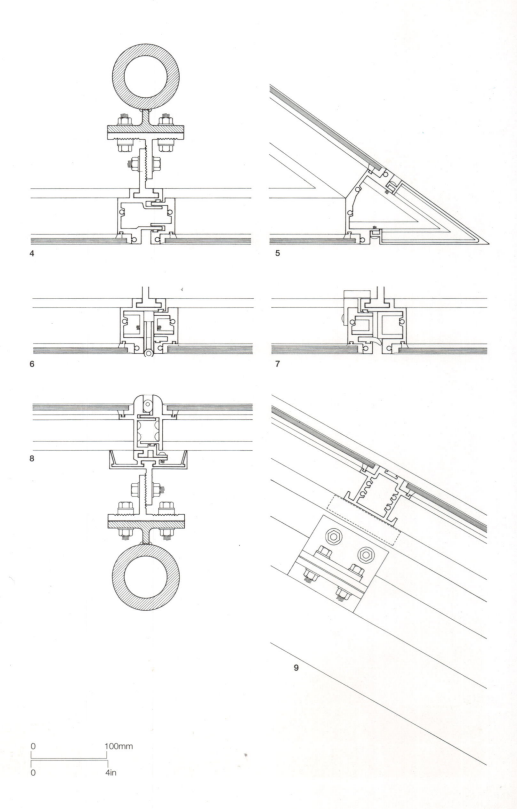

10

11

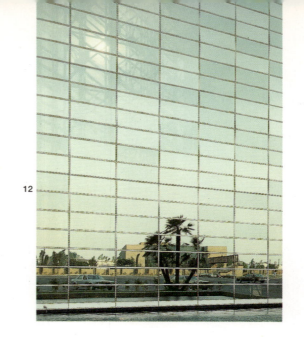

12

14

11. The tight grain of
the highly reflective
surface creates an
enormous glittering
solid, characterized
by sharp corners and
fine points.

12. The skin: a 'stack
bonded' and shining
surface.

13. The Crystal
Cathedral: a pinnacle
in glass.

14. The tight grain of
the recessed jointing
provides a great
reflective solidity in
the building.

13

provincial government offices and law courts complex

vancouver

british columbia, canada

architect arthur erickson architects
designed 1973–7
constructed 1977–80

1. Site plan.

2. A great public interior space. The success of the glazing is derived from the size of the panes, the detailing of the rainwater channels (remarkably similar to Paxton's for the Crystal Palace) and the carefully thought cleaning system. This produces a very simple configuration, quite different from the Louvre Pyramid.

The glass roof has one of the strongest pedigrees in the canon of glass architecture. From the great train sheds and market halls of the nineteenth century onwards, the idea of the protecting, daylight-providing roof has been a beguiling concept.

The number of projects successfully using such roofs is smaller than the power and potential of the idea suggests, and even when realized, is often carried out with clumsy and unsuccessful detailing. The reasons for this are not hard to find. The problems of producing water-tightness in a glass roof are not easy to resolve with complete success, and leaks are potentially disastrous for the owner, the architect and the contractor. The impact of a space covered by a glass roof is significantly reduced if the floor is littered with buckets. Of equal magnitude are the problems of cleaning both the upper and lower surfaces. Many glass atrium roofs are dirty, or have their elegance compromised by the appearance of ugly window-cleaning gear.

All this makes the roof over the Vancouver Law Courts complex a magnificent achievement. The Law Courts provide the southern anchor of Vancouver's large, three city-block, civic complex, with the old courthouse as the northern anchor. The climbing terraces of the complex slide beneath the great glass roof to form a courthouse, very different from the conventional and sombre monolith. The roof is conceived as a major symbol of 'publicness'. Its transparency invites people in, and allows people outside to enjoy views of the surrounding cityscape. At the same time, it provides an outdoor and open feeling to a major civic space, and allows daylight into many of the courtrooms. The roof is designed as a gently flattened 'saddle' section, with its longer, sloping side facing west. The roof area is 4,800 m² (51,667 sq ft), the same order of size as a football pitch.

The roof glazing comprises 870 modules of glass, each 3.56 m (11 ft 6 in) by 1.55 m (5 ft), consisting of panes of laminated glass structurally glazed with silicone into an aluminium frame. The laminated glass is typical for glazing in this sort of location, being 12 mm (½ in) clear annealed glass, and 6 mm (¼ in) green heat-absorbing heat-strengthened glass with a polyvinyl butyral interlayer.

Both the shedding of water and the window-cleaning are immaculately dealt with. The aluminium frame incorporates integral drainage channels and window-cleaning tracks set 200 mm (8 in) above the space trusses. The principle behind the detailing is the avoidance of miniature 'dams' to trap the water as it flows down the surface. The smooth surface produced by structural silicone detailing is almost essential in this situation.

The climate of Vancouver would be recognized by any northern European: its latitude of 39 degrees is about the same as that of Paris, and its weather is often similar. The lessons behind this building should not be lost on many cities whose climate justifies the creation of the great glass sheltering roof.

2

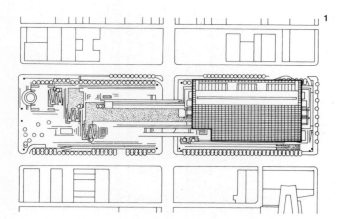

1

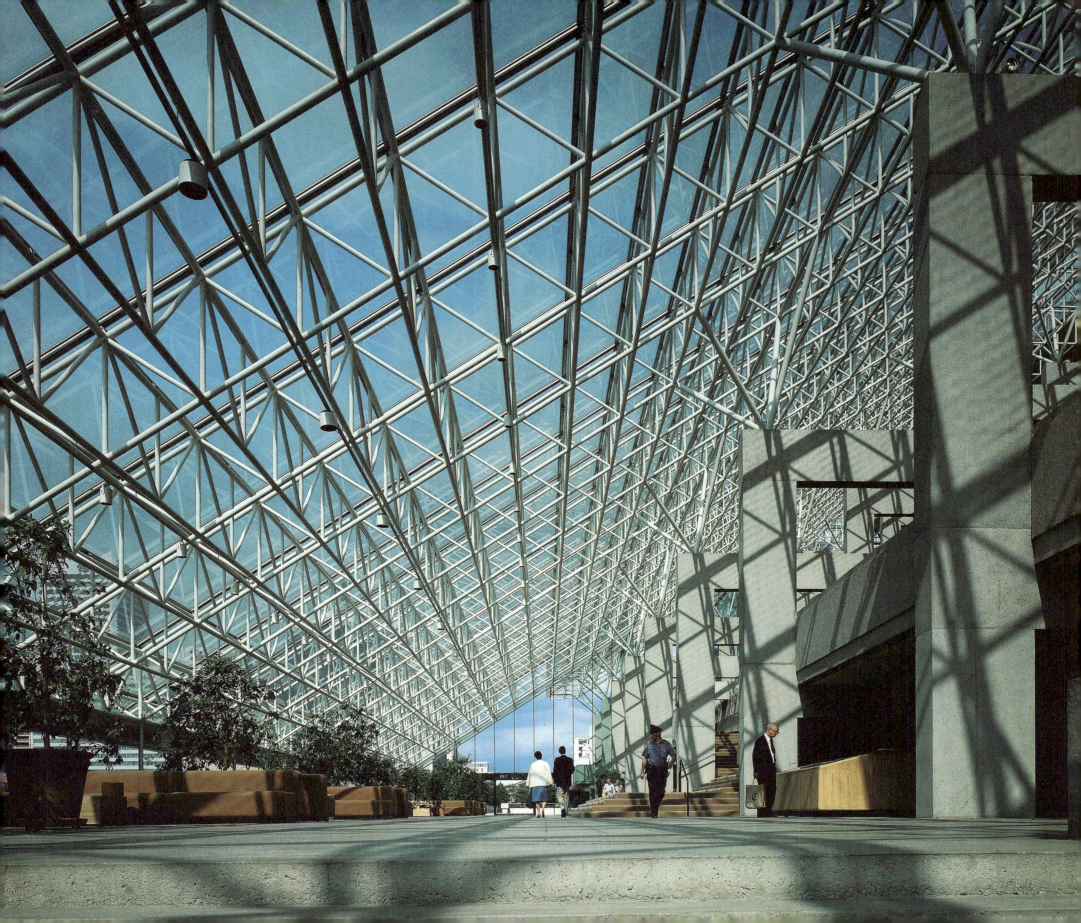

glass in
architecture

provincial
government
offices and law
courts complex

3

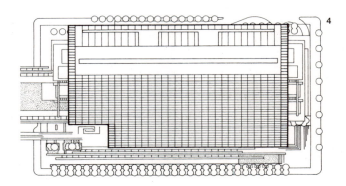

4

3. View from the
south. The roof
structure and its glass
surface is suspended
above the very
powerful solid
structure below.

4. Roof plan.

5. Cross section
at 1:500.

5

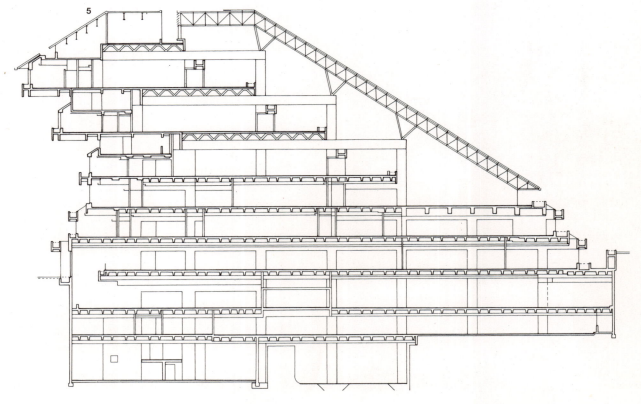

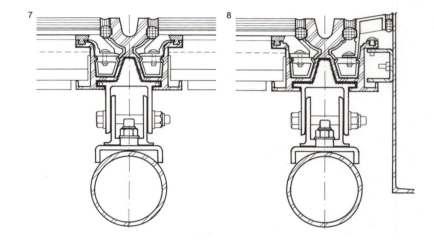

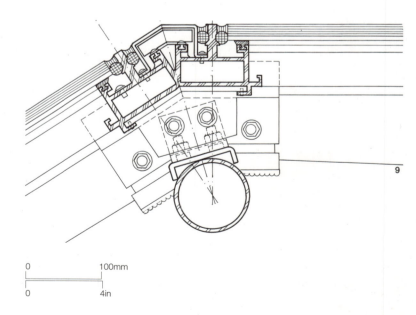

6. An upper terrace.

7, 8. Construction details at 1:5 across the slope, showing the drainage channels at a general location, and at the edge of the roof. The dimension at the edge, between the glazing and the channel section is remarkably small for such an enormous roof, and demonstrates the success of the rainwater shedding system.

9. Construction detail at 1:5 at the top of the roof slope. The details demonstrate the value of structural silicone detailing on a large roof like this. The flow of the water is uninterrupted by mullion caps or other physical obstructions, contributing to the self-cleaning aspect of the roof.

10. View from the west.

7

8

10

9

6

0   100mm

0   4in

IBM travelling pavilion

architect renzo piano building workshop
designed 1982
constructed 1982–6

1. Exterior and
interior elevations.

2. The design
successfully
juxtaposes the
visually soft
transparency of
polycarbonate as a
perfect complement
to timber.

1

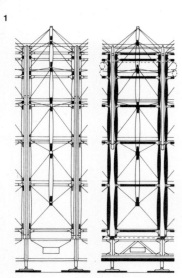

The IBM Travelling Pavilion exemplifies Renzo Piano's approach to architecture and detail. It is predicated on an unprejudiced and open love of materials, and a search for the appropriate. The term 'soft-tech' has been used to describe Piano's architecture, and this is perfectly represented in the Pavilion.

The client required a building in which information and computer technology could be exhibited in familiar surroundings, making it approachable to young people. The driving criteria behind the concept were therefore transparency, demountability and lightness: transparency so that the exhibition could always be seen in the familiar context of the site on which the building was placed; demountability to permit its easy erection and removal as it travelled Europe; lightness to make moving as easy as possible.

To these 'external' briefing criteria, the architects added two particular programme objectives of their own, which typify Piano's approach to design: that all components should act as part of the system of structural support, and that all details should clearly demonstrate their function. The design is a clear manifestation of these criteria. The building is a transparent tunnel consisting of a stressed skin acting with a system of laminated beech arches, configured to produce a rigid structure which is capable of accepting the movement induced by changes of temperature and loading. The skin comprises 6 mm (¼ in) clear polycarbonate sheets, formed to produce

pyramids whose size is derived from the maximum size of material available. Three pyramids are formed from each sheet, and each arch incorporates four of these triple modules, making twelve pyramids. The whole building comprises thirty-four of these, to produce a vault 5.3 m (17 ft) in radius.

The beech frame provides a double inner chord system with a radius of 5.1 m (16 ft 6 in), the framing members fixed at 1.2 m (4 ft) centres. The tops of the pyramids are connected with an upper chord system of laminated beech members set at a radius of 5.9 m (19 ft).

Polycarbonate is an ideal material for this sort of application. It is light, strong, has high transparency and is easily formed. However, it also possesses low stiffness and a high co-efficient of linear thermal expansion. These characteristics are the cause for much of the detailing of the Pavilion, and structural and thermal movement were the subjects of considerable study during the design and mock-up process. Rigid fixings are difficult in polycarbonate. This meant that the expansion from the surface temperatures experienced in sunlight (85°C) was difficult to accommodate. Failure to allow for movement would have led to compressive stress and potential buckling. Having tried springs between the pyramids and inner timber chords, and having found that this led to high bending moments, the final solution incorporated rigid stainless steel rods permitting circumferential movement.

The inner, base edges of the polycarbonate pyramids were designed

as the inner chords of the truss. These required stiffening, and the first proposal for this was glued polycarbonate channels. However, the stress cracking induced by the glued surface led to the use of a slotted aluminium channel with slotted holes. Given the nature of polycarbonate, it was decided that site installation should avoid direct connection to the plastic material, and the building is thus detailed with a wonderful array of nodes and movement connections.

Environmental control had to be effective on sites and conditions varying from the Mediterranean summer to the northern European winter. Solar overheating and glare were mitigated by shading devices and an acceptance of temperature layering. The Phoenics fluid dynamics programme led to modification of the diameter of the tunnel to ensure that unacceptable temperatures only occurred above a level of two metres, and solar shading is provided by the addition of inner, double-walled, white insulating pyramids and aluminium screens. Winter condensation was prevented by aircraft air nozzles served from vein-ducts. The building arrived in its purpose-made trucks complete with air-conditioning and heating plant.

The carefully considered detail and love of materials turns this simple building into a rich and elegant guest in the various locations it visited.

2

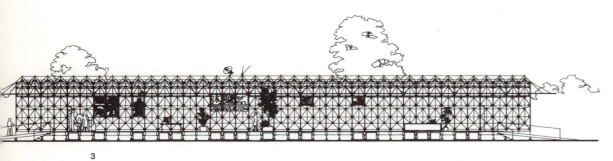

3

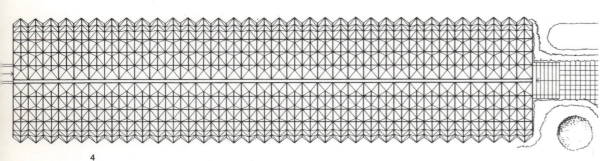

4

3. Elevation of whole
building.

4. Roof plan.

5, 6. Early conceptual
detail sketches: a
natural, proper and
characteristic
preoccupation with
the node.

7. Close-up view,
from inside, of the
clear polycarbonate
pyramid cladding.

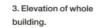

5

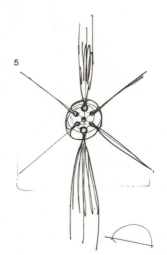

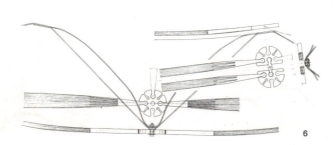

6

7

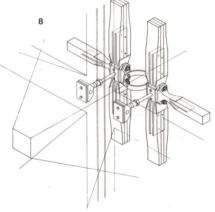

8

9

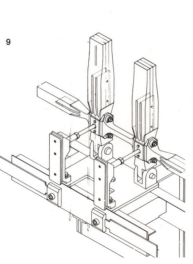

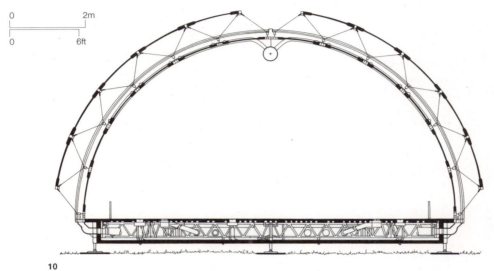

0   2m

0   6ft

10

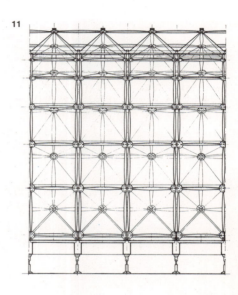

11

8–9. Isometrics of
junctions: the
generation of
grammar in detail
between metal and
timber.

10, 11. Cross section
and elevation at
1:100. The section
shows the deceptive
simplicity of a three-
dimensional truss
system.

12. Interior view.

12

13

13. Detailed view
from inside.

14. Reference cross
section.

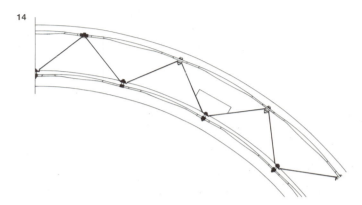

14

15–18. Construction
details at 1:5. These
four junction details
show the outer
connection of the
polycarbonate
pyramids, and the
two inner fixing
details.

19. The building on
site in a park in Milan.
It is the skill of Renzo
Piano to create high-
technology objects
out of materials the
form and detailing of
which evoke natural
forms. The pavilion
settles perfectly into
any context.

19

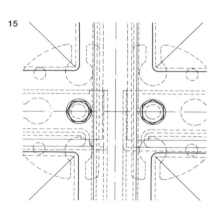

15

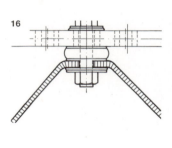

16

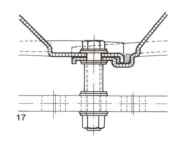

17

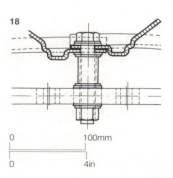

18

0   100mm

0   4in

lloyd's building
london

architect richard rogers partnership
designed 1978–82
constructed 1982–6

1. Service tower
elevation.

2. Detail of the
sparkle glass which
comprises the
general cladding for
the project. In a
building which
demands privacy the
use of a rolled glass
offers an ideal
opportunity to
generate multiple
reflection and
refraction at a very
small scale.

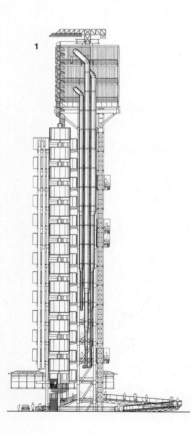

1

The Lloyd's Building is one of the icons of contemporary British architecture. It derives its form from the fusion of a simple atrium office building and the functional articulation of service towers in true adherence to Louis Kahn's principle of 'servant' and 'served' spaces.

The result is perfect, uninterrupted office space organized in a ring around the central atrium. Externally, the office floors are peeled away from the atrium to step down towards the lower scale of building to the south, leaving the tall barrel-vaulted atrium itself rising high and exposed.

The glassiness of this central element in the form is, however, only one of the multiplicity of uses to which the material is put in this essay in glass. The lifts are glass capsules in 15 mm (⅝ in) toughened glass boxes. The bridges providing means of escape are glass-clad using gel-filled laminated glass. On being heated by fire, this gel coagulates to form a thick insulating crust which stays in place adhered to the glass on the cool side. This material, which is now in common use in atrium buildings, solves the problems of means of escape across glass-clad routes.

The really innovative use of glass, however, lies in the glass walls of the office building. The sources for this can be found in two French examples of the early 1930s, both built in Paris: the *mur neutralisant* created by Le Corbusier for the Salvation Army Building, the Cité de Refuge of 1929–33, and the Maison de Verre by Pierre Chareau conceived and built at about the same time.

In the *mur neutralisant*, Le Corbusier aimed to create a multiple glass wall acting as an air duct to achieve environmental control. In the Lloyd's Building, the glazing consists of a normal double-glazed unit on the outside, a 75 mm (3 in) cavity, and a third layer of glass on the inside. Treated air enters the building from fan-shaped air terminals within the raised floor, and is extracted through the lights, where 50% of the heat is removed. It is then taken to the 75 mm (3 in) cavity, expelled at the base through an extract duct, and back to the plant rooms on top of the satellite towers. The building thus uses the glass skin to wrap itself in its own air.

The most significant and original use of glass, however, is in the 'sparkle glass', ostensibly inspired by Chareau's masterpiece. In the Maison de Verre, glass blocks are used to provide a beautiful obscuring, translucent wall, giving both light and privacy to the interior, and providing a glittering luminous surface to the courtyard at night. For the Lloyd's Building, the architects developed a rolled glass incorporating optically designed facets 6 mm (¼ in) across, amplifying the

translucent quality during daytime, and refracting light back to the interior at night from the artificial light sources. The rolled glass is made using a die engraved on case-hardened steel wrapped over the normal 250 mm (10 in) diameter roller. This produces a pattern about 785 mm (2ft 6 in) wide. The architects overcame the inherent problem of pattern continuity by introducing a selvedge to divide each 3 m (19 ft 9 in) high pane into four sections, with transparent areas for vision interspersed with areas of sparkle glass.

The performance of this complex glittering wall is such that 86% of the radiant summer component is removed by the combination of cavity and triple glazing. In winter, the inner wall is at room temperature, and in summer it is cool. The sparkle glass itself is an excellent example of the design of a material by architects who are fully in command of glass technology.

2

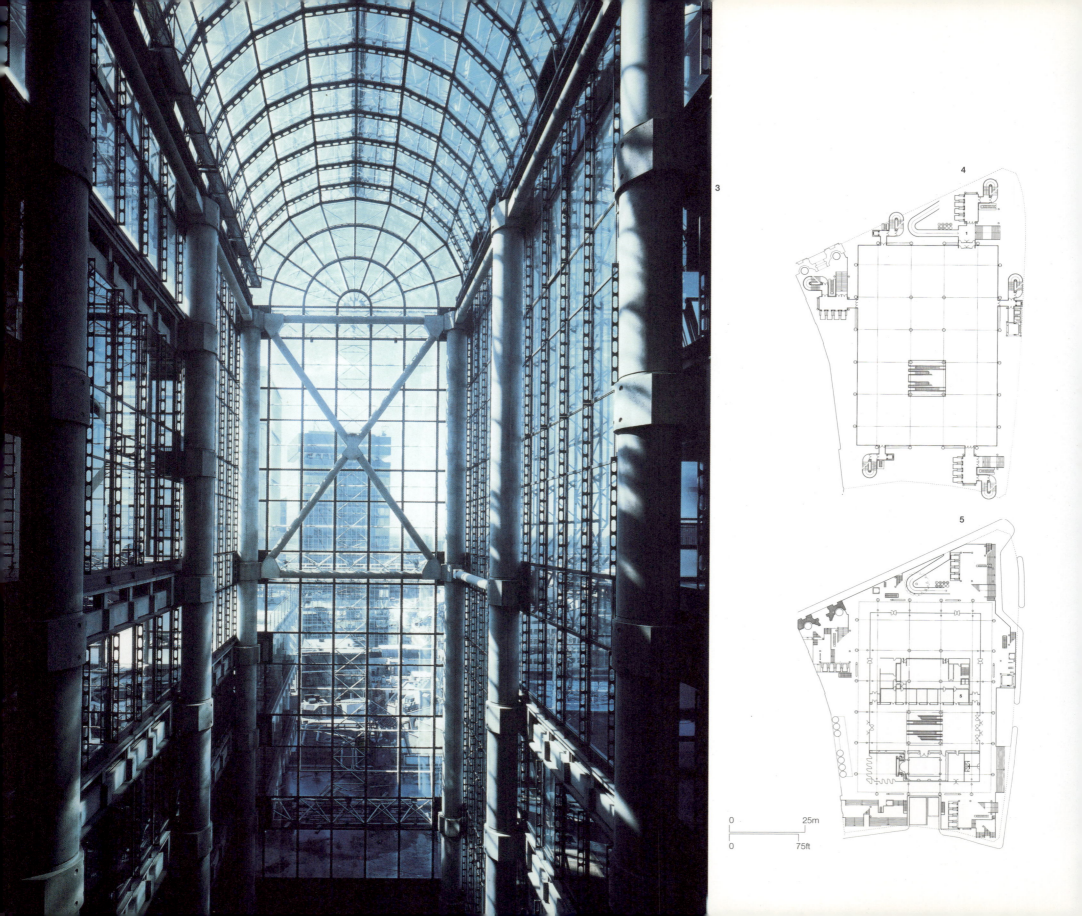

3

4

1

5

0   25m

0   75ft

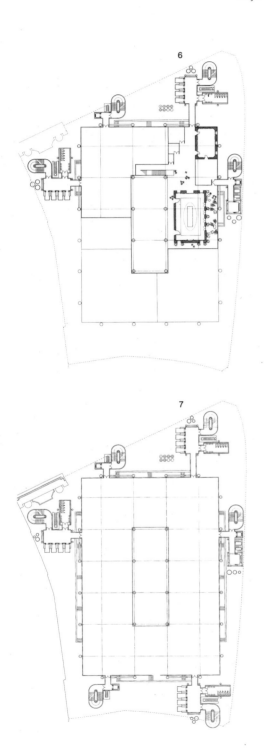

6

7

3. The atrium. This
space can be seen as
the nave of a Gothic
cathedral of the late
twentieth century,
complete with its
great end wall,
enriched by the
merging of medieval
space with the
glass roofs that
characterized the
'cathedrals' of
commerce of the
nineteenth century,
such as the Galleria
in Milan.

4–7. Floor plans: the
removal of vertical
circulation and
service space to the
outside of the
building releases the
centre of the site to
the production of
simple, flexible space
surrounding a large
atrium.

8. Cross section
through the atrium
at 1:600: the glass
wall is part of the
mechanical service
system which
dominates much of
this drawing.

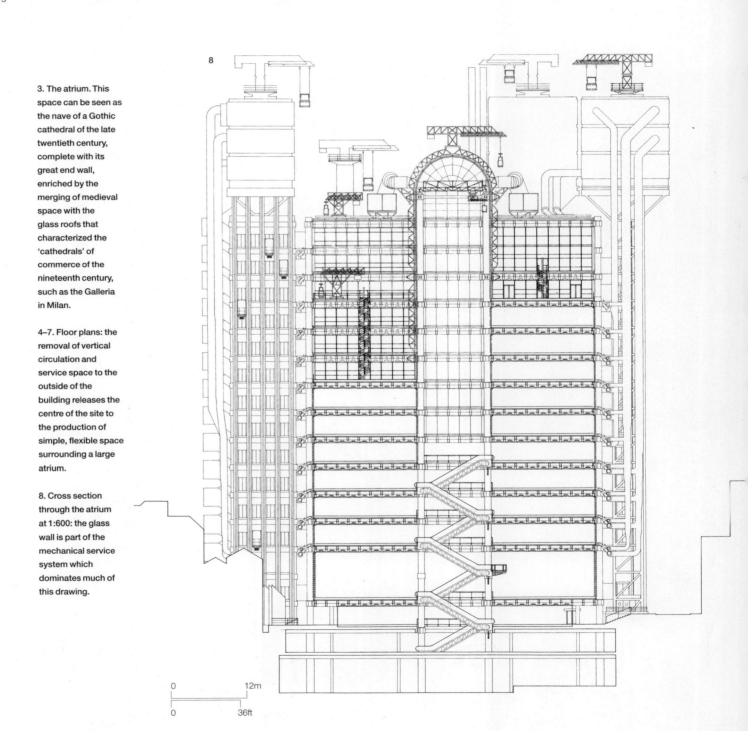

8

0   12m

0   36ft

9

9. The morphology of this building is perfectly suited to the need to peel away floors and provide light and space to neighbours. The simple boxiness of the glass towers of the 1950s and 1960s made such adjustment in plan and section impossible. Lloyd's is uniquely suited to the complex medieval street pattern of the City of London.

10. The external wall, with sparkle glass, and deep mullions. The holes cut in the mullions not only reduce the weight; they also increase the amount of light reaching the facade.

11. Detail section through external wall at 1:5. The inner panes can be opened for cleaning and maintenance purposes.

12. The facade, muscular and highly textured; it is a manifestation of the building in action.

10

11   12

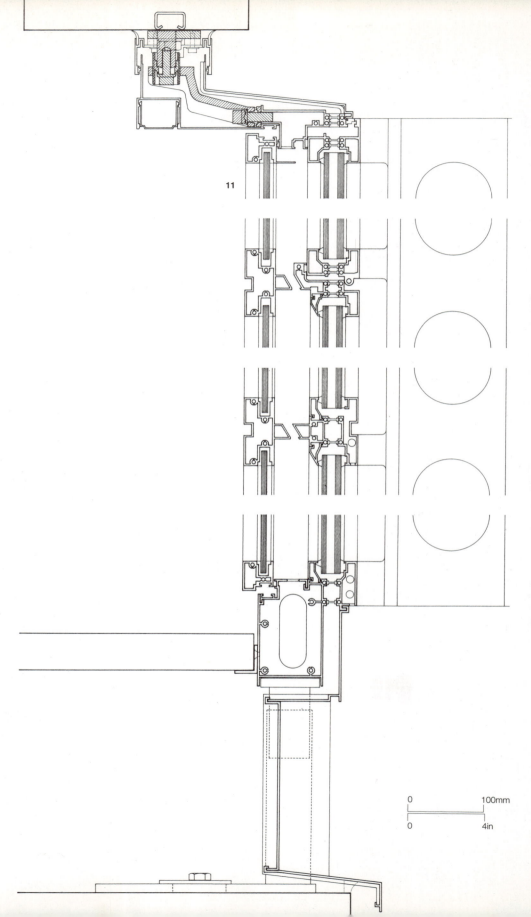

0   100mm
0   4in

occidental chemical center

niagara falls
new york, USA

architect cannon design, with
hellmuth obata and kassabaum
designed 1979
constructed 1980

1. The apparently
simple elevation of
the building belies the
intelligence which
went into the design,
and the intelligence of
the skin itself.

2. The solar wall. The
aerofoil louvre blades
are connected in
banks and rotate
automatically to
shield the building
and collect the sun's
radiation.

The Occidental Chemical Center,
originally named the Hooker Chemical
Building, represents a development in
the recent history of glass in architecture
which is of fundamental importance as
we approach the end of the century.

The problems of the inadequate
building skin have been stressed
throughout this book. Despite the early,
pre-war efforts of architects, such as Le
Corbusier, to create a glass skin which
could control the environment, it has
often been inadequately designed, and a
general perception arose that it was an
intrinsically poor performer. In the UK,
for example, limits were placed on the
area of glazing in buildings in an attempt
to conserve energy.

This perception is now changing as
clients, architects and engineers alike
are learning the potential benefits of
designed balance between heat loss
through glazing and the use of passive
solar energy.

The architects of Hooker faced an
apparent exclusivity of goals: first, to
develop a building which was highly
energy efficient, and second, to develop
a highly transparent building,
capitalizing on a location which affords
spectacular views of a great natural
wonder, the Niagara Falls. The result,
after comparative analysis of various
building skins, was (for its time) perhaps
the largest passive solar collector in the
world, and possibly the most energy
efficient office building in its climatic
zone (a latitude of about 43 degrees, the
same as Marseilles in Europe, but with
the climatic characteristics of the
American continental land mass and
very cold in winter).

An analytical comparison between
three different skin types led to the
selection of a 'dynamic' skin. This
included a proposal for adjustable
shading/insulating devices to eliminate
solar gain when necessary, or closed to
reduce heat loss during unoccupied
periods. A full-scale mock up of one
module was erected in Tempe Arizona,
at the College of Architecture of Arizona
State University, and the design tested
and validated. The final design
incorporates an outer double-glazing
system, and inner single-glazing one, the
two systems separated by a 1.5 m (5 ft)
gap within which are located aerofoil
louvres that respond to the sun.

The outer skin comprises a blue-
green outer pane and a clear inner
pane. The choice of the simple iron
oxide glass is the result of intelligent
selection, since it represents the
chemistry which maximizes light

penetration whilst limiting solar gain.
The glazing is very simply, and
unostentatiously, constructed with
mullions at 1.5 m (5 ft) centres and
transoms at about 1.8 m (6 ft) centres.
The inner skin is floor-to-ceiling single
glazing.

In the 1.5 m (5 ft) space between
these two glazing systems are banks of
linked 4.5 m (14 ft 7 in) long aerofoil
louvres, such as are used as dampers in
the air-conditioning and ventilation
industry. Each bank has one blade
carrying a solar cell at the back, which
registers when the sun falls on it and tilts
the whole bank out of the sun. This has
two effects: it prevents sun getting into
the building (unless over-ridden), and
causes the louvre itself to pick up the
radiative energy. This in turn creates a
stack effect which is exploited by the use
of grilles at floor level. The warm air
rises, to be thrown away at the top of the
building if unwanted.

The dynamic, quasi-intelligent skin
is linked to the building's automation
system. Monitoring the building has
demonstrated the validity of the
thinking behind its design, which has
been followed, of course, by others that
use the same principles. The design and
configuration present an interesting
comparison with the solar wall at the
Solar Dairy at Mysen in Norway, referred
to earlier in Chapter Three, which uses
venetian blinds in the same depth of
space, and which was actually being
designed at about the same time.

2

1

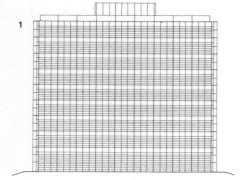

3

3. The whole solar wall: each facade is independently responsive.

4. Typical floor plan.

5. The elevation is as elementary as those of many curtain wall buildings of twenty years earlier, but here it is the outward manifestation of high performance solar engineering.

6. The entrance lobby.

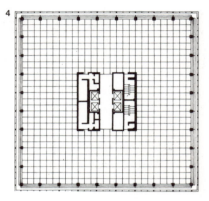

4

5

6

7

7. The base of the building at a typical corner. The grille acts as the intake to the fresh air supply at the bottom of the solar wall. This location for an air supply is possible here because the air is comparatively clean. The provision of fresh air at the bottom of solar walls in cities poses a particular problem.

8. Detail section through solar wall at 1:20. The floor level grilles provide cleaning access, and allow warmed air to rise to the top of the building.

9. Plan through solar wall. The glazing is conventionally framed, panellized into bays corresponding with the structure. Unlike Duisberg (p 162) and RWE (p 168) described below, the outer skin is doubled glazed.

8

9

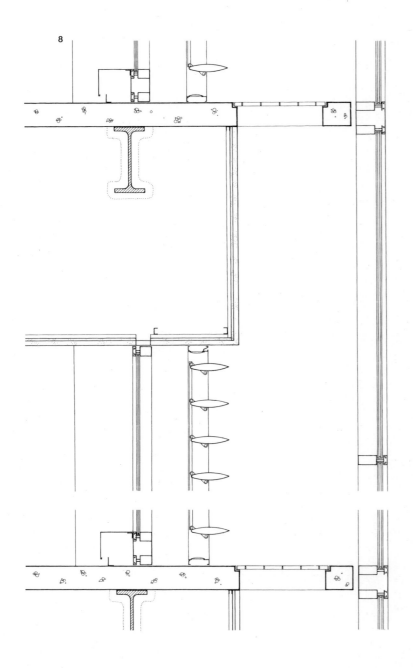

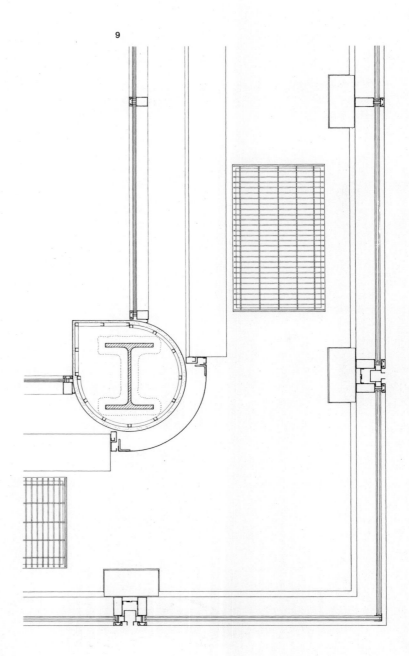

0   400mm

0   15in

business promotion centre

duisburg, germany

architect sir norman foster and partners
designed 1988–92
constructed 1993

1. Elevation.

2. This building, which is one of the successors of the Occidental Chemical Center, combines some of the engineering principles of that building with a more highly developed external skin. It has much less depth, and a single-glazed, bolt-fixed, exterior glass system.

The glass walls at the Business Promotion Centre in Duisburg represent the convergence and integration of two quite separate design preoccupations: the creation and exploitation of the seamless glass skin, and the development of the high performance environmental wall derived from Le Corbusier's *mur neutralisant*.

The plan form is in the shape of a lens, extruded up to a gently curving roof. This shape, which elegantly terminates a city block, is achieved at its skin by thirty-six faceted planes, each set at an angle of about two degrees to its neighbours, providing the shifting reflections characterized by Mies van der Rohe's tower of 1922 and Foster Associates' own Willis Faber & Dumas Building of 1975, p 110. The use of a bolt-fixing system enables the joint to be reduced to the width of the silicone seal. The full storey height panes, 1.5 m by 3.3 m (5 ft by 10ft 9in), are in clear float glass 12 mm (½ in) thick. There is no attempt to produce cosmetically devised colouring: the skin is driven by performance.

This single-glazed skin is the outer layer of a version of the 'breathing' wall, which is under great scrutiny as an engineering device in the 1990s, following the design of buildings such as the Occidental Chemical Center, p 156, and the Lloyd's Building, p 150, in the previous decade. There is a great deal of discussion between architects and engineers concerning the preferred configuration of these active glass walls, particularly related to the location of double and single-glazed skins. Issues of light and heat transmission, condensation, acoustic control, the need for cleaning and cost interact in a very complex way. Traffic noise and pollution are frequent determinants in the selection of sealed systems, and this is the case at Duisburg.

A critical consideration in all these walls relates to the mode and design of the ventilation system: the heating and cooling of fresh air for the occupants accounts for a very large proportion of the energy load.

At one extreme is the natural ventilation ideal, and at the other the entirely air-conditioned building. Natural ventilation poses great problems of noise and pollution in urban environments. At Duisburg the single glass skin is the outer envelope to a 200 mm (8 in) deep ventilated cavity, the inner skin of which is a double glazed argon-filled low-E system. The inner skin comprises side hung doors which are opening for cleaning purposes. Venetian blinds with a ten per cent perforation are located in the cavity to provide solar control and radiation collection.

Air is let (or if necessary pumped) into the cavity at a controlled temperature, taken from the building interior via the plant room. This generally obviates condensation on the outer pane, and removes the heat from the blinds, expelling it at the top of the building. The building's own ventilation system is separate. The benefit of a building with this sort of metabolism lies in the overall saving in energy, and particularly in the reduction of duct sizes. This enabled the floor-to-floor height to be kept down to 3.05 m (10 ft).

The building makes an interesting comparison with Willis Faber & Dumas of twenty years before. The earlier building with its tinted glass and very low wall:floor ratio, is characteristic of a different idea of environmental engineering. At Duisburg a wall:floor ratio of about fifty-six per cent, four times that of a deep plan building, demands a skin with a much higher engineering performance. What distinguishes it is the consistent passion for fine detail in the building, exemplified by the tiny pointed and polished stainless-steel tip which terminates each end of the glass wall. The concept of the outer membrane is as expressive as it is beautifully and quietly engineered.

2

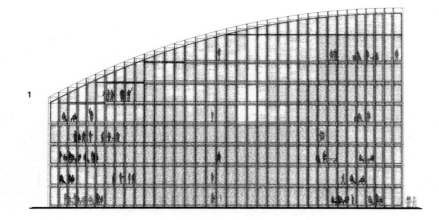

1

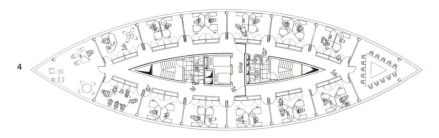

4

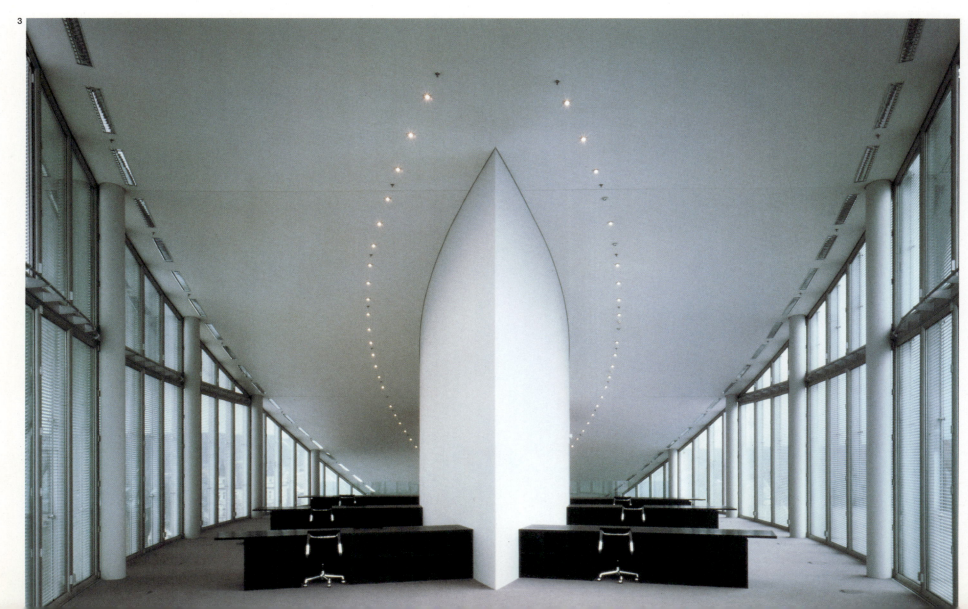

3

5

3. Interior view.

5, 6. Interior views.

4. Typical floor plan.
The shape represents
the last stage in an
evolutionary design
process which was
related to the turning
of a corner.

7. The exterior at
night. Like Willis
Faber & Dumas, this
building offers itself
to the city at night as
a living multiple
screen of activity.

6

7

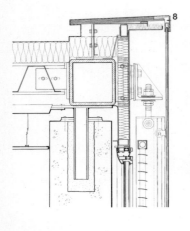

8

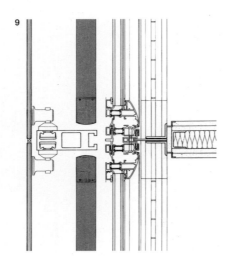

9

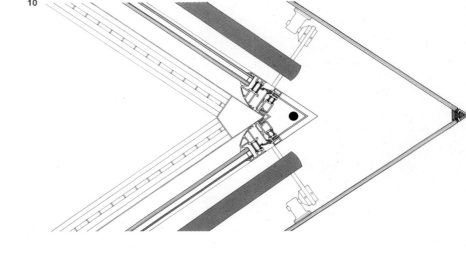

10

12

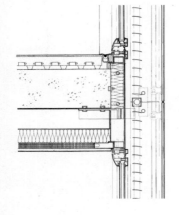

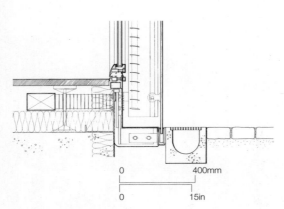

8. Detail section
through building
envelope at 1:20.

9–11. Horizontal
sections through
envelope at 1:10,
showing the
characteristic
commitment to the

resolution of detail in
the termination at the
corners.

12. A view of the
galleries at the lower
end of the building,
with their cantilevered
balustrades.

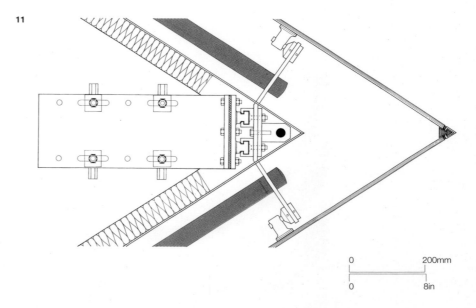

11

0   400mm

0   15in

0   200mm

0   8in

RWE AG headquarters

essen, germany

architect ingenhoven, overdiek und partner
designed 1991–4
constructed 1994–6

1. View of the model.

2. The facade: the simplest, clearest, rainscreen and first buffer layer.

1

The Headquarters of RWE AG in Essen is one of the most recent examples of the breathing glass wall.

The term breathing wall covers a wide and expanding range of envelope designs, the glass versions of which rely on the enhancement of the natural buoyancy generated in a glazed cavity by the integration of ventilation and thermal control. These walls fall within the general category called, with some legitimacy, 'the intelligent facade', and have become the subject of intense study at a theoretical level, and in real projects, particularly in northern Europe, where the urgent need for light has to be balanced with the concerns about heat loss (both through the fabric and as a result of ventilation), and solar gain. These concerns tend to be seasonal, but such are the vagaries of climate in the region that the designer has to produce systems which can respond to a wide range of weather conditions at all times of the year.

A significant decision in the design of such a wall is whether to design it primarily as a buffer zone, essentially disconnected in terms of air supply to the interior, or to accept the challenge of the integration of a 'natural' ventilation system with the air flows within the envelope. The parameters usually considered include the disposition of single and double glazing, the location and design of air inlets, the nature of solar shading (which is also radiation collecting) and the depth of the cavity, which is essentially a flue.

In the RWE building the designers have elected to design a thermal protection wall in a way which offers the integration of the external air with the interior in a real 'breathing wall'. This system is only one of a range of engineering strategies adopted to optimize the 'natural' use of the building to control the environment. A single glazed wall, fixed with bolts, forms the outer envelope to a shaft 500 mm (19½ in) deep containing a blind system, with the inner wall being double glazed. This is the same configuration as the Duisburg Business Promotion Centre, p 162, and the reverse of the walls at the Occidental Center in Niagara Falls, p 156. The glass used externally is 10 mm (⅜ in) thick Optiwhite, the comparatively iron free, high transmission glass produced by Pilkington's German subsidiary, Flachglas. The internal glazing uses 'Climaplus' white glass held in aluminium frames. The cavity is closed off at floor levels and at each mullion, and a flap system enables each cell of the facade to be naturally ventilated.

The integration of this buffer and thermal 'flushing' system with the interior is realized by the use of sliding interior glazing, which offers control to the occupants. In the summer, when solar loads are high, internal air can be exhausted to the cavity and lost to the exterior. In the winter the warmth collected by the cavity and its blind system can be allowed into the offices by the occupants opening their sliding windows.

In offering the opportunity for personal control by the occupants the building also confronts the challenge of maintaining the overall thermal balance of the building. This places responsibilities on those working on the building as well as the designers. Only by designing and constructing buildings like this, however, will the truly 'intelligent' building emerge.

The significant role the building plays in the canon of glass buildings at the end of the twentieth century is its demonstration of the resolution of the apparent conflicts between thermal conservation and daylight illumination in the use of glass as part of an engineering system. This is an essential item on the agenda for the glass buildings of the future.

2

3

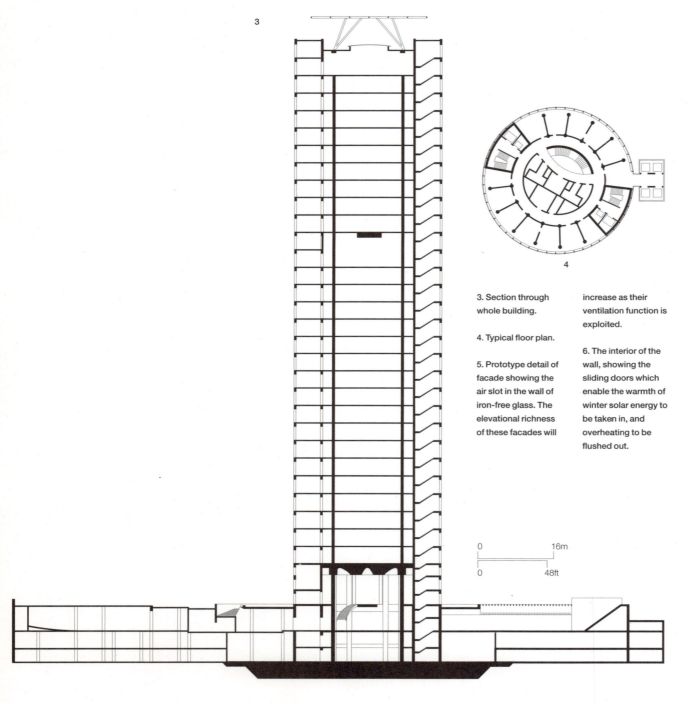

4

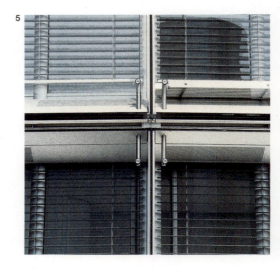

5

6

3. Section through whole building.

4. Typical floor plan.

5. Prototype detail of facade showing the air slot in the wall of iron-free glass. The elevational richness of these facades will increase as their ventilation function is exploited.

6. The interior of the wall, showing the sliding doors which enable the warmth of winter solar energy to be taken in, and overheating to be flushed out.

```
0          16m
0          48ft
```

7

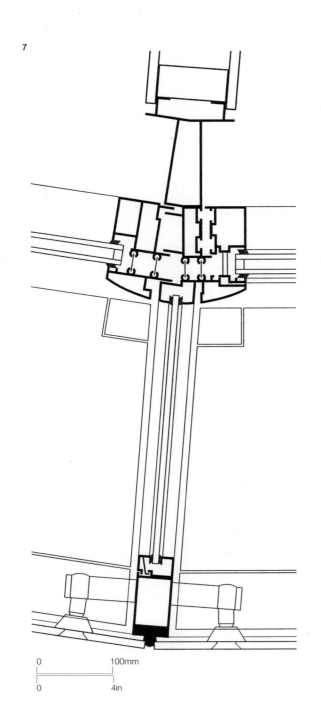

8

7. Horizontal section
at a mullion at 1:5,
showing the glass
division screen, the
outer single glazing,
and the inner double
glazed sliding doors.

8. The 'fish-mouth'
airflow valve detail at
1:10; a comparatively
sophisticated
component for a
building facade,
which controls the
airflow into and out
of the cavity.

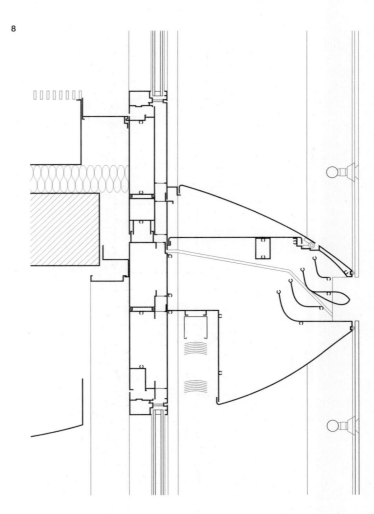

0   100mm

0   4in

0   200mm

0   8in

glass walls – 'les serres'
cité des sciences et de l'industrie
parc de la villette
paris, france

architect adrien fainsilber
with rice francis ritchie
designed 1983
constructed 1984–6

1. Isometric, showing
the 8 m square bays
and 2 m square
panes.

2. Detail view of the
facade.

The past two decades have seen great advances in the development of what is called structural glazing. This has been promoted by glass manufacturers themselves, as a natural result of the improvement of toughened glass and the better understanding of its strength. From the age of patch fittings and glass-stabilizing fins, which characterized the first projects using structural glass, we have seen the creation of walls which are more structurally responsive to the demands designers wish to put upon them, and the forces to which they have consequently been subjected.

Equally significant is the development of expertise as engineers and architects have understood that designing with glass was a little different from designing with other materials. One of the foremost teams associated with this sort of work is Rice Francis Ritchie (RFR) in Paris, founded in 1981 in order to carry out work at Parc de la Villette by three designers from across the Channel: Peter Rice, the great Irish engineer, Martin Francis and Ian Ritchie.

The decision to place three large glass structures on the park face of the exhibition building at Parc de la Villette gave the designers the opportunity to create their own objectives. Fainsilber's brief to RFR was to create enclosures as transparent as possible. To RFR this meant the reduction of structure, and

they therefore selected cable trusses. The experience of Willis Faber & Dumas, particularly for Martin Francis and Ian Ritchie while at Foster Associates, gave cause for confidence concerning the capacity of glass to adapt to a structure with considerable deformation, and the glass here is suspended as a curtain using small vertical connections fixed to bolts in the corners of each pane, inspired by Pilkington's work on their own Planar system.

The glass structure comprises 2 m x 2 m (6 ft 6 in x 6 ft 6 in) panels of toughened glass formed into 8 m x 8 m (26 ft x 26 ft) assemblies, all hung from the top. The mechanical assembly uses innovative point fixing details, which provide a flush exterior surface and centre the fixing load on the central neutral axis of the glass, using a stainless steel stud with an integrated spherical bearing set into a partially countersunk hole in the glass. Success for such fixings to glass relies on the creation of an appropriate contact surface, and an extensive testing programme was carried out to obtain statistically valid results. The use of materials here, the carefully chosen stainless-steel alloys and the aluminium alloy selected for its yield and work-hardening properties, were essential to the success of the detailing and the overall performance of the wall.

Large composite panels, such as those at Parc de la Villette, effectively act as one sheet partly because of the jointing action of the weatherproofing silicone. It is important that the 600 kg weight of the entire 8 m x 8 m (26 ft x 26 ft) glass panel acting under load is

always equally shared between the support points. A pre-stressed spring mechanism is incorporated into each support bracket, which ensures the spread of this load, and also acts as a shock absorber in the event of breakage.

The sheets of glass themselves are suspended in a chain from the springs using intermediate pieces which incorporate the potential for adjustment to take up tolerances, whether from the glass drilling or from the castings.

The structural ingenuity implicit in the glass walls is undeniable, but so is the transparency sought by Fainsilber in his commission to RFR. The amount of steel used to support the panels, and delicacy with which it is configured to produce the support, ensures that the impact of the walls is almost entirely that given by the glass. From the outside, the walls have the ambiguous quality inherent to all clear glass walls: angle dependent, sometimes reflective, sometimes transparent. From the inside, the view from low to high light levels ensures that the walls effectively disappear, provided they are kept clean.

In the search for high performance in glass walls, it is important to remember the prime property of the material, to provide true transparency. This is the lesson of 'les Serres' at Parc de la Villette.

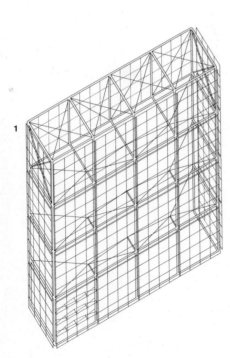

1

2

glass music hall

amsterdam, the netherlands

architect pieter zaanen with mick eekhout
designed 1988
constructed 1989–90

1. The glass
enclosure positioned
within its Berlage
room, showing the
'cello belly' devised
to avoid acoustic
flutter.

2. Detail of glass wall
and acoustic panels.

The Glass Music Hall is a highly original and unique application of glass. It is located in the former Stock Exchange of H P Berlage in the centre of Amsterdam, now converted for public use. The design problem involved the creation of an indoor acoustical envelope for rehearsals and performance, with an audience of up to two hundred, operating at the same time as an event for a further six hundred people in the adjacent Wang Music Hall.

A conventional solution to such a problem would have been the construction of a heavy, acoustically-separated box, but this would have meant a major insertion into the very fine architecture of Berlage's building. The solution adopted was the creation of a transparent enclosure within the existing brick volume. Structuring such an enclosure permitted Mick Eekhout to exploit his Quattro Glass Structures system.

Eekhout is an engineer working in glass: his activity extends across the divide between design and consultancy on the one hand, and installation contracting on the other. This expertise has put him in a unique position concerning the creation of glass structures. Quattro uses this design and practical expertise in a system combining nodes and tensile truss stabilizers. The key characteristics of the system are a rationalized minimalization of structure, as also seen in the work of RFR at Parc de la Villette, p 172.

Collaboration with acoustical advisers Peutz led to the conclusion that a 2,000 m³, 68, 656 cubic ft volume would provide the appropriate reverberation time, and a general shape for the volume of 20 m x 10 m by 10 m (65 ft x 32 ft 6 in by 32 ft 6 in) high was created, with unwanted 'flutter' resonance avoided by the development of a curve in one of the long sides. The analysis suggested 8 mm thick glass together with an area for absorption. A standard space frame, supported on six columns, provides the support for the trusses which in turn support the glass panels.

The two upper bolts carry the dead weight of five lower glass panels, each 1.8 m x 1.8 m by 8 mm (5 ft 10 in x 5 ft 10 in by 5/16 in) thick, with the Quattro nodes connecting four adjacent glass panels at the corners. The nodes are welded on short compression studs vertically stabilized by 10 mm (3/8 in) thick rods in two counterspanning 'bow-string' trusses.

Roof panels are also 1.8 m x 1.8 m (5 ft 10 in x 5 ft 10 in), and are in 10.2 mm (3/8 in) laminated annealed glass.

The wall thickness of 8 mm (5/16 in) leaves the walls comparatively resilient acoustically, and these are complemented by triangular absorbing panels and suspended acrylic domelight reflectors. The result is a two-second reverberation time. Musicians pronounce that they are very happy with it, the performances are very well attended, and the room is suitable for live CD recording.

Visually, the room is a great success. Pieter Zaanen decided to make the orthogonal walls grey tinted, which establishes them as a surface, and the curved wall is clear. As with all glass structures, the appearance of the room depends entirely upon lighting. When the lighting is directed at the yellow brick of the Berlage space, the glass room appears almost black. As it is entered, transparency is the overriding effect, and old brick walls become the effective perimeter of the space. Changing the lighting changes the nature of enclosure and the effective 'presence' or otherwise of the glass room.

The Glass Music Hall is one of the most ingenious uses of glass in architecture this century.

2

1

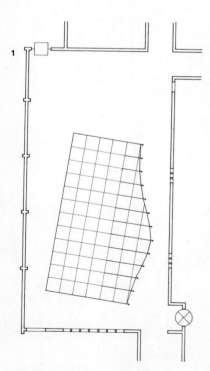

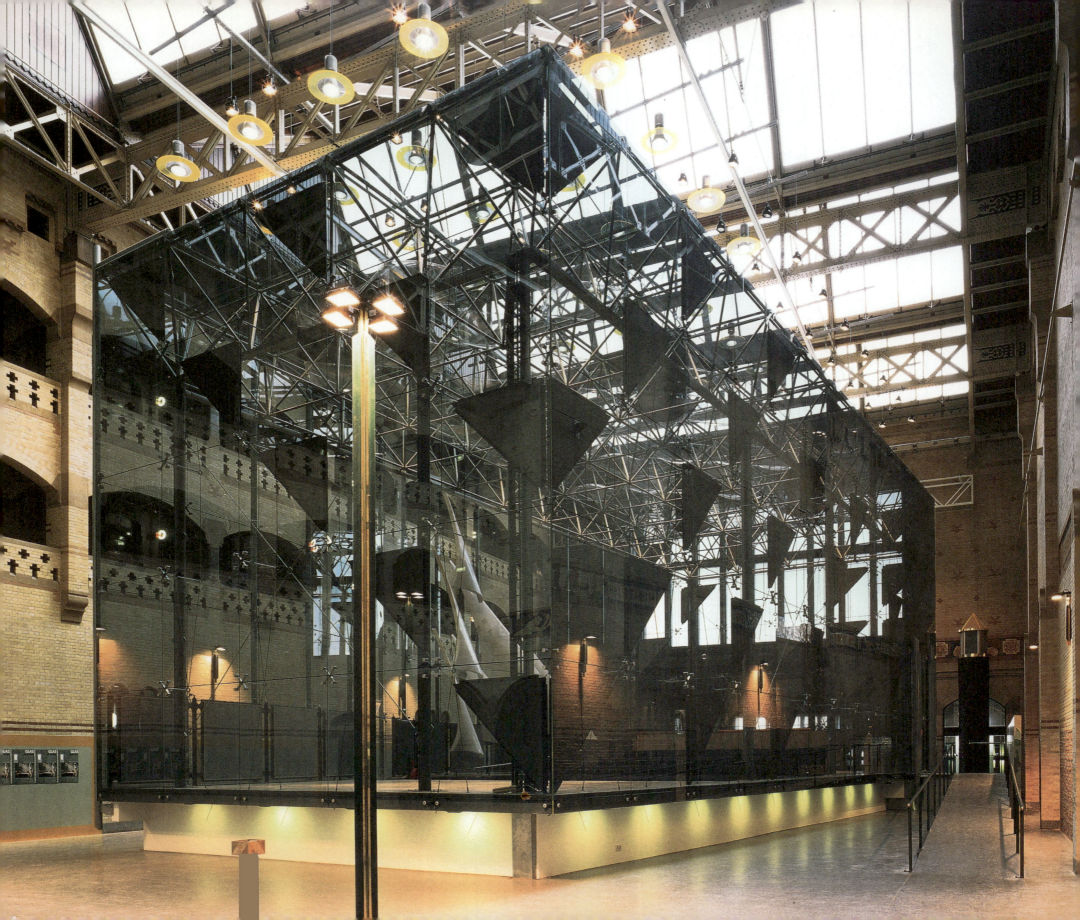

3   4

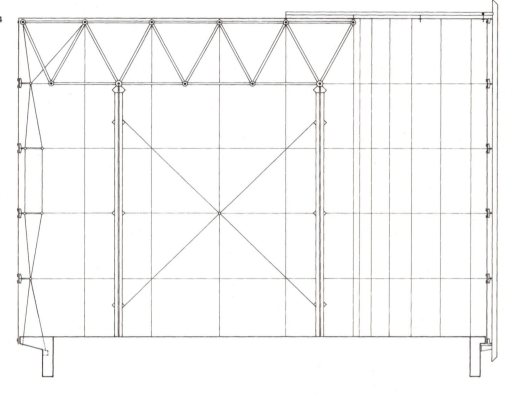

3. The glass structure in its context.

4. Section through the music room. The bow string and 'sprung' structure on the left contrasts with the more rigid structure on the right used to support the undulating wall.

5. Inside the music room: the invisible acoustic enclosure.

6. Outside the glass structure.

7, 8. Details of the bow string and panel assembly.

6

7   8

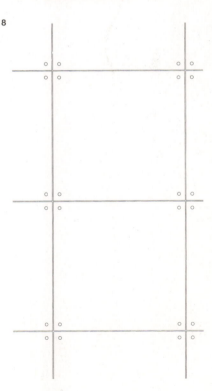

5

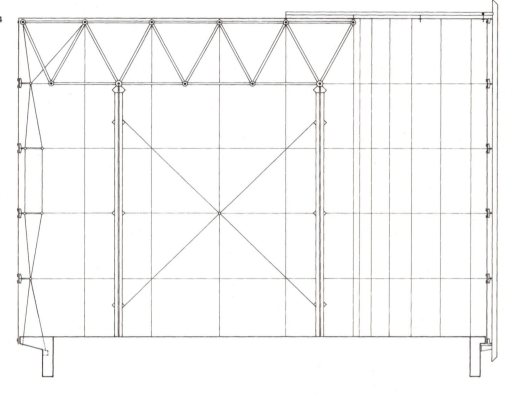

9. Construction
details across the top
of the structure at 1:5,
with the rigid fixings
to the right, and the
bow-string structure
to the left.

10. The interior,
showing the white grp
sails which further
enhance the
acoustics of the
room.

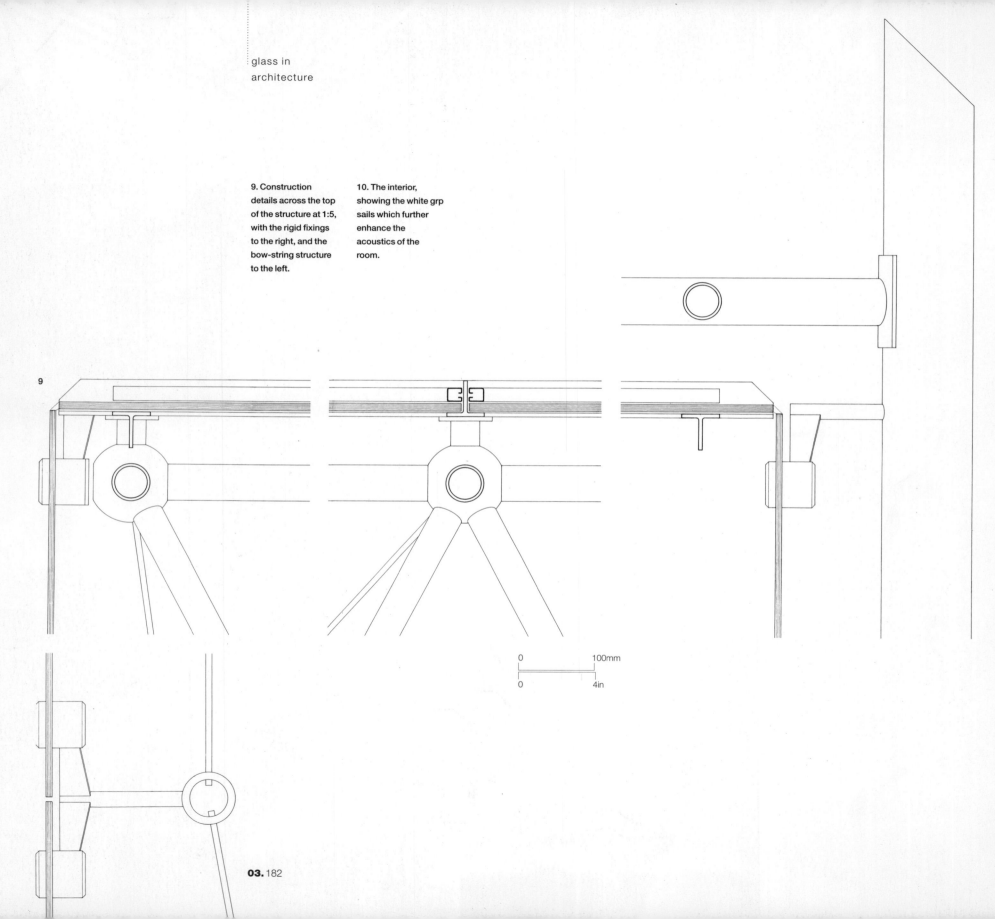

9

0   100mm

0   4in

banque populaire de l'ouest

montgermont, rennes, france

architect odile decq and benoît cornette
with rice francis ritchie
designed 1988
constructed 1989–90

1. Isometric. The four
front bays on the left
comprise glazing as a
facade to the
entrance hall: the
bays to the right
are the facade to
the office
accommodation.

2. Perimeter glass
support and roof level
shading: duplication
in reflection.

This building represents the extension of
the exceptionally light glass support
structure designed by Rice Francis
Ritchie for the glass facades at Parc de la
Villette, p 172, into the technology of
double glazing. The conceptual
objective is the extension of a
continuous glass wall, with consistent
(and minimal) detailing, across the
whole length of the 120 m (390 ft) long
facade.

The architects' design is a long
slender two-storey slab with a
completely glazed south face as the main
frontage of the building. Of the nine
bays comprising this facade four are
given over to the main entrance hall,
which is defined behind the wall by a
great curving masonry wall, which
penetrates the glass wall as it cuts
through it at each end. This hall is single
glazed. The remaining five bays of
the elevation are the glazing to offices
behind: the need for double glazing
to these offices presents the
technological challenge.

The creation of smooth glass office
walls, 8 m (26 ft) high, and
uninterrupted by framing when
experienced from the interior, led to the
decision to design an exterior support
system. This decision, which could
appear to be perverse, has a rational
basis given the requirement for wind
bracing and the need to protect the
exterior from the sun.

The essential structural principles are
based on the support of the weight of the
glass wall as a curtain suspended from
parapet-level trusses, with the
horizontal bracing and the wind load
being taken on a very light, and very
elegant, steel structure. This structure
consists of masts, at 12 m (39 ft) centres
and 2 m (6 ft 6 in) away from the glass
wall, supporting horizontal *sablières*
trusses at the top and three 'fishbone
trusses' 2 m (6 ft 6 in) apart aligned with
the joints in the glass wall behind. Small,
25 mm (1 in), articulated struts link this
structure to the glass wall, and support
the monobloc glass fixing and the
articulated bolt. Rigging cables hold the
whole delicate web in position.

The single glazing forming the facade
to the entrance hall reproduces most of
the technology already created for the
project at Parc de la Villette, with some
significant simplification in the way the
bolt is held in the hole in the glass.
However, significant development had
to be undertaken to make it possible to
employ the same detailing for the double
glazing. RFR's belief in the importance of
the articulated fixing, permitting
rotation of the bolt and relieving stress in
the glass at the fixing position,

demanded high precision and careful
prototyping and testing. The need for
exact alignment of the four holes in each
pane forming the double glazing unit
was complicated by the fact that some
of the 12 mm (½ in) glass is triple
laminated, thus requiring the perfect
alignment of twelve holes. This, taken
with the subtle adjustments to
configuration which such a wall
undergoes as it moves, placed very great
constraints on the manufacturers.

Overcoming these problems has
permitted the execution of a glass wall
which perfectly realizes the conceptual
aims of the architects and designers, and
coincidentally produces what is
probably the first fully suspended
structural double-glazed wall. The
layering of the building is completed by
the roller blinds which are controlled by
solar cells.

The building is a further
demonstration of the ephemeralization
of the support for the glass wall. The
location of the glass wall itself as an
element suspended between an external
structure and the building behind also
serves to dematerialize the wall, and
makes the project a landmark in the
development of glazing technology.

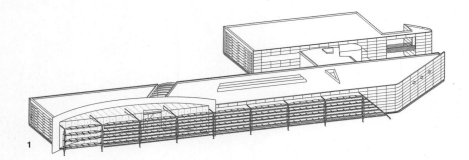

1

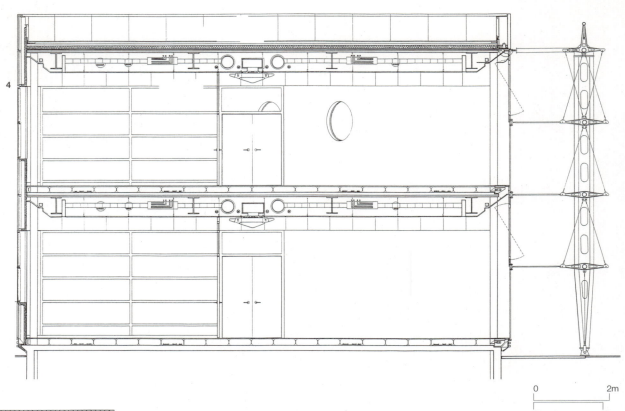

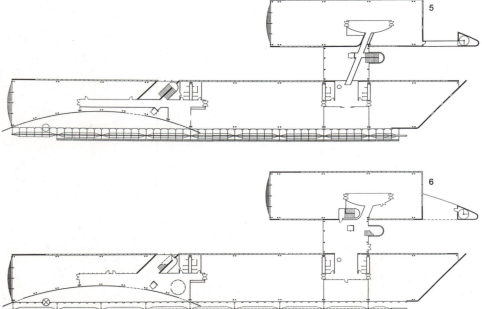

3. Front elevation.

4. Cross section at
1:100 showing the
dramatic offset of the
support system for
the glazing, which is
exploited to provide
solar shading.

5, 6. Floor plans at
upper and lower
levels.

banque
populaire de
l'ouest

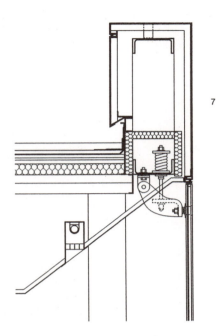

7

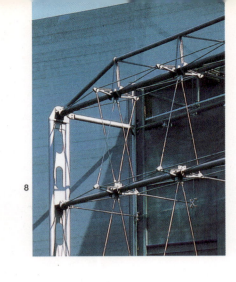

8

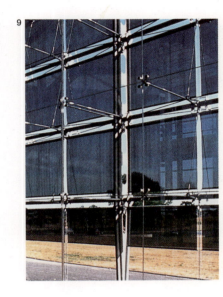

9

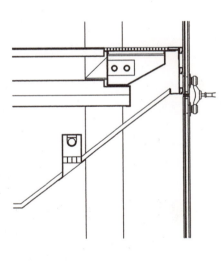

7. Vertical section
through the glazed
wall at 1:20, showing
the slant of the
suspended ceiling
created to clear top
detail of the glazing
below.

8, 9. The support
system. The location
of the structure
externally is not
merely rhetorical. It
enables the interior of
the office
accommodation to be
completely clear of
structure of any kind,
as well as providing
support to sun
shades.

10. Detail of the bolt
fixing design
assembly.

10

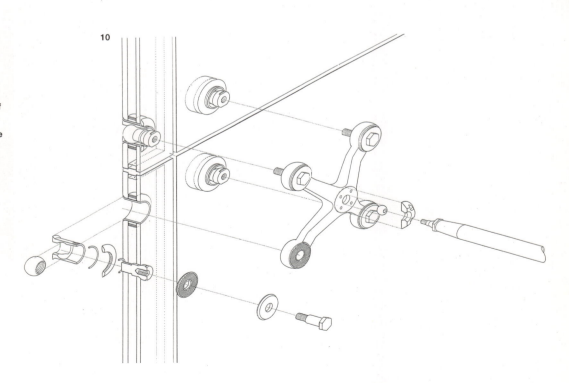

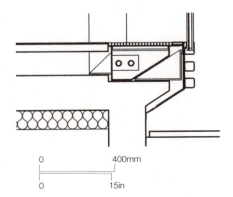

0   400mm
0   15in

11. The external
structure, a peristyle
in light metal.

12. View within the
tapering entrance hall
created in front of the
long glass facade
between the glazing
and its external
structural support.

11

waterloo international terminal

london, UK

architect nicholas grimshaw and partners
with YRM anthony hunt associates
designed 1991–2
constructed 1992–3

1. Aerial view.

2. View along the
platforms, clearly
showing the inversion
of roof structure, from
outside the glazing on
the left to inside on
the right.

The train shed has one of the best pedigrees in the evolutionary history of glass in architecture. From the earliest days of the railways, the need for lofty, glazed stations has been met by grand statements created by the engineers and glaziers of the nineteenth century, as they created the great vaults of Paddington, St Pancras and King's Cross in London, and the other termini of the newly developing railway companies. These enormous sheds tended not to be inspired or designed by 'architects'. To the architects of the time, they were matters for the engineer and those who worked for him and with him.

At St Pancras in 1866, the 'architecture' was put up by George Gilbert Scott as the Midland Hotel in neo-Gothic style. The train shed behind was by William Henry Barlow, a 'mere engineer', whose skills were necessary to create the 75 m (244 ft) span. The difference between these two structures stands as a testament to the architectural values of the time. The great shed at York of eleven years later introduced the curve into such a roof.

The maximum span of 48.5 m (158 ft) of Waterloo is not extraordinary in historical terms. It does, however, bring with it the technology of the late twentieth century in a wonderfully expressive form.

The nineteenth century train shed was a structural manifestation of its time: a straightforward high arch, or system of arches, simply supported. The new roof at Waterloo adopts a form which reflects the practical needs of a prescribed envelope, and the structural analysis of the late twentieth century. Two bow-stringed trusses, one effectively 'inside out', permit the curvature of the roof to change from a shallow curve to a tight one, to provide clearance over the trains on the outer track. The use of trusses like this gives the roof glazing more than the usual problems of movement to cope with. The springiness of the arches, combined with the movement created by the changing loads of the trains rolling in and out of the platforms below, add to the normal tolerance and movement problems experienced in all buildings.

With each pane having to be able to work independently to allow for movement, and with the twisted double curvature of the form, tolerances had to be much larger than usual. The joint at the sides of the glass sheets uses a folded 'concertina' neoprene gasket. The horizontal joints are open in structural terms, but the large gap is covered by a flexible gasket. The architects have pointed to the metaphor of the human hand with regard to the curved shape of the roof. This biomorphism is carried through to the scaly nature of the roof glazing.

The grammar of the bow-string truss and the accommodation of movement also characterize the great glass wall at the north end of the new terminal.

This encloses the edge of the old station, and effects the transition from it to the new platforms. The combination of bow-strings and bolted glazing is a fine example of an established method of creating such a wall.

Yet a third design in glass is used for the long west wall below the roof, separating the western access road from the public areas beneath the tracks. At first sight, the design solution appears conventional: glass fins stiffen a glass wall which is suspended from the concrete structure above. In fact, the problems to be solved here were, to say the least, unusual. Thermal movement along the length of the building is up to 55 mm (2⅛ in), and the arrival of a train causes the viaduct carrying it to deflect by up to 11 mm (⁷⁄₁₆ in), which is associated with a rise of 5 mm (³⁄₁₆ in) in the adjacent bay. The stainless steel pieces which make up the connection system are designed to respond to stress in a way which extends further the biomorphism of the building. The bone-like castings are bolted to the glass fins and support stainless steel rods which are left free to move within sleeves, and bolted to the panes of the glass wall.

The whole of Waterloo is a testament to will and ingenuity in the use of glass.

1

2

3

3. Exterior view from
the road access side
of the building.

4. Plan of the
supremely elegant
and expressive roof
structure.

5. Section through the
building at 1:250. The
realization of this
section is the view
shown on the
previous page. The
elevation of the trains
on their support
structure clearly
shows the need for
the accommodation
of movement in
structure and glazing
alike.

4

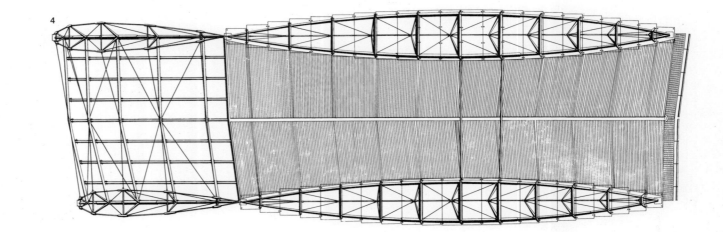

5

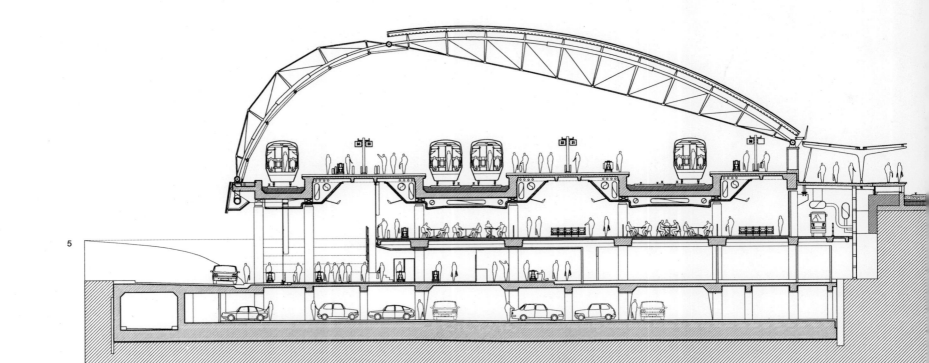

0   5m

0   15ft

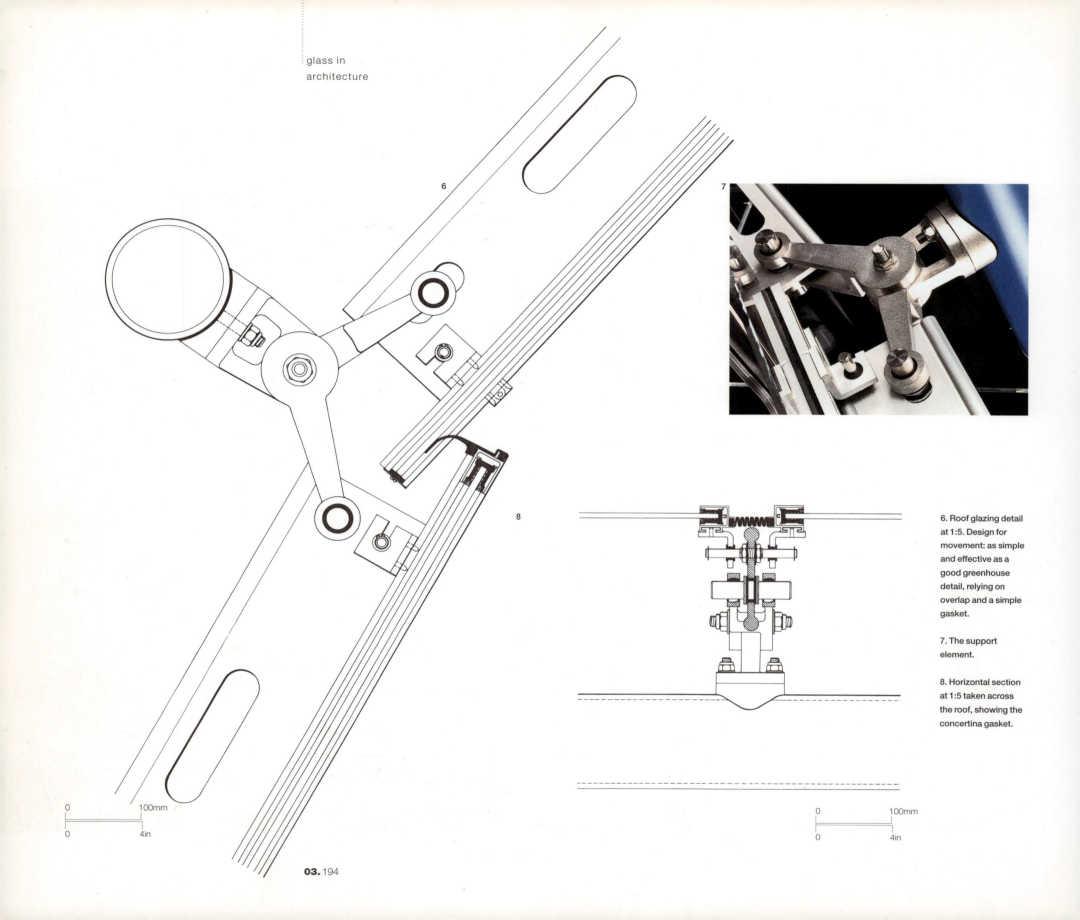

6

7

8

6. Roof glazing detail
at 1:5. Design for
movement: as simple
and effective as a
good greenhouse
detail, relying on
overlap and a simple
gasket.

7. The support
element.

8. Horizontal section
at 1:5 taken across
the roof, showing the
concertina gasket.

0   100mm

0   4in

0   100mm

0   4in

glass in
architecture

waterloo
international
terminal

9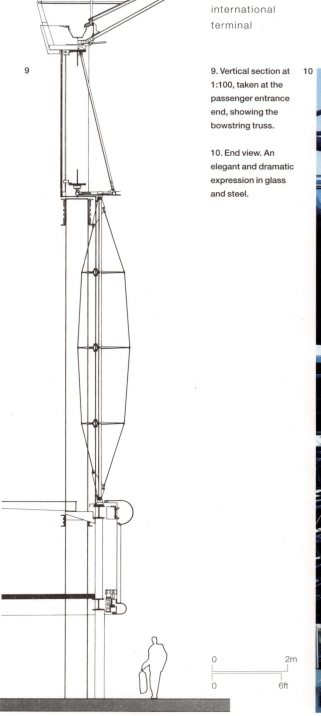

9. Vertical section at 1:100, taken at the passenger entrance end, showing the bowstring truss.

10. End view. An elegant and dramatic expression in glass and steel.

10

0   2m

0   6ft

western morning news building
plymouth, UK

architect nicholas grimshaw and partners
designed 1990–91
constructed 1991–3

1. North elevation.

2. Detail of
exoskeleton and
glass wall.

The use of glass in architecture as part of the image-creation process is as old as Hardwick Hall, and beyond. In the twentieth century, this process has become enriched both by technology and by social intent. Hannes Meyer's famous statement of 1926 has already been quoted in this book, but is worthy of repetition as the 'open' glass buildings of the end of our century are discussed:

No pillared reception rooms for weary monarchs but hygienic work rooms for the busy representatives of their people. No back corridors for backstairs diplomacy, but open glazed rooms for public negotiation of honest men.

The idea of an architecture which enabled the activity of the occupants to be visible to all, considered by Meyer to be a prerequisite of the socialist future, has developed into an art form in the age of advertising.

The idea of a building being a major source of information to the outside world about what goes on inside it, by means of its transparency, is now in common currency. The example of SOM's Manufacturers Hanover Trust Bank building in New York, 1954, and the Willis Faber & Dumas building of over twenty years later are prime city examples. In the case of office work and administration, what is seen may be fairly dull. It also places enormous strain on the domestic management of the office: if what is seen is overflowing waste bins and disorder, the transparency is counterproductive. However, in the case of manufacturing processes the transparency can work in very positive ways, in displaying the activity of the company inside it, and in the avoidance of the hostility and facelessness of the blank wall.

The Western Morning News Building continues the idea of displaying printing presses, already used by the architects at the Financial Times Printing Works, London, 1988. This latter building occupies a rather unprepossessing site on an eastern route out of London. The Western Morning News Building, however, sits on a hillside outside Plymouth, and exploits the site beautifully.

The concept of the glass wall is that of the minimal suspended structure pioneered by Rice Francis Ritchie (RFR) and Pilkington in the UK and Europe. Here, however, with a rural site, the problems of reflection, view and solar control are all important. The architects' solution, inspired both by an organic morphology and by considerations of reflection and transmission, is to tip the wall outwards. This is a vital step in the provision of transparency. All vertical walls on high open sites reflect the sky, simply due to the big change in lighting levels between the outside and the inside; the wall becomes a mirror. Once this is understood, the apparent whimsical nature of the boat-like form of the building is seen to have a more rigorous rationale.

The building is conceived as a set of platforms within an envelope. The wall is supported on an exterior array of 'tusks' which bend to follow the outward curvature of the glass wall. These carry the weight of the wall via stainless-steel rods which extend up to a fixing at the top of the tusks. The glass panels themselves are supported using Planar bolts on the usual four-node connector. Horizontal wind loads are taken by cast steel brackets fixed independently to the tusks.

The outward curve of the glass wall, with the structure conceived to support it, is as rational as it is evocative.

2

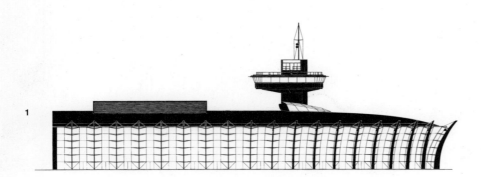

1

3

3. The building at
night.

4. Exterior view. The
inverted nautical
imagery is witty and
beguiling. The shape
is that of a ship, but
the structure is on the
outside, and in place
of a sheet steel hull is
a transparent
membrane.

5–7. Floor plans: the
editorial office
accommodation
is on the right of the
'bulkhead' and the
production areas are
to the left.

8. Detail of the great
outward-leaning wall.

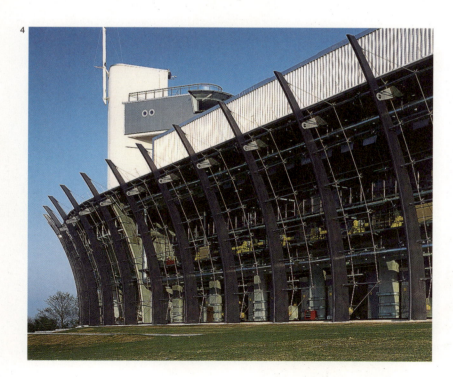

4

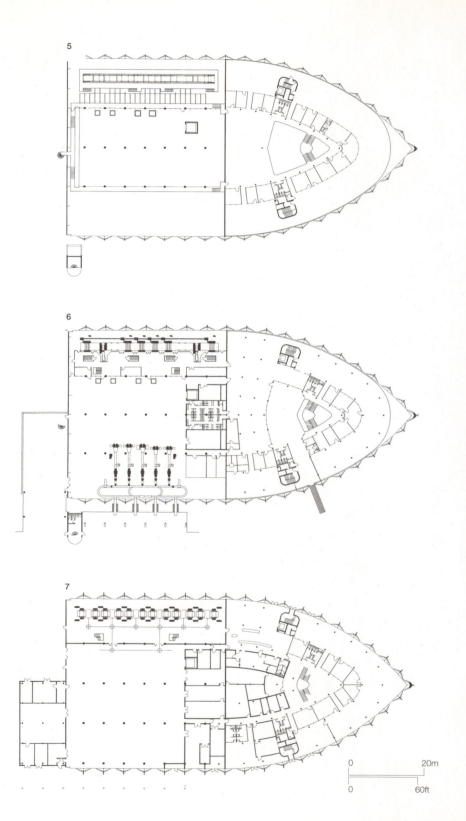

5

8

6

7

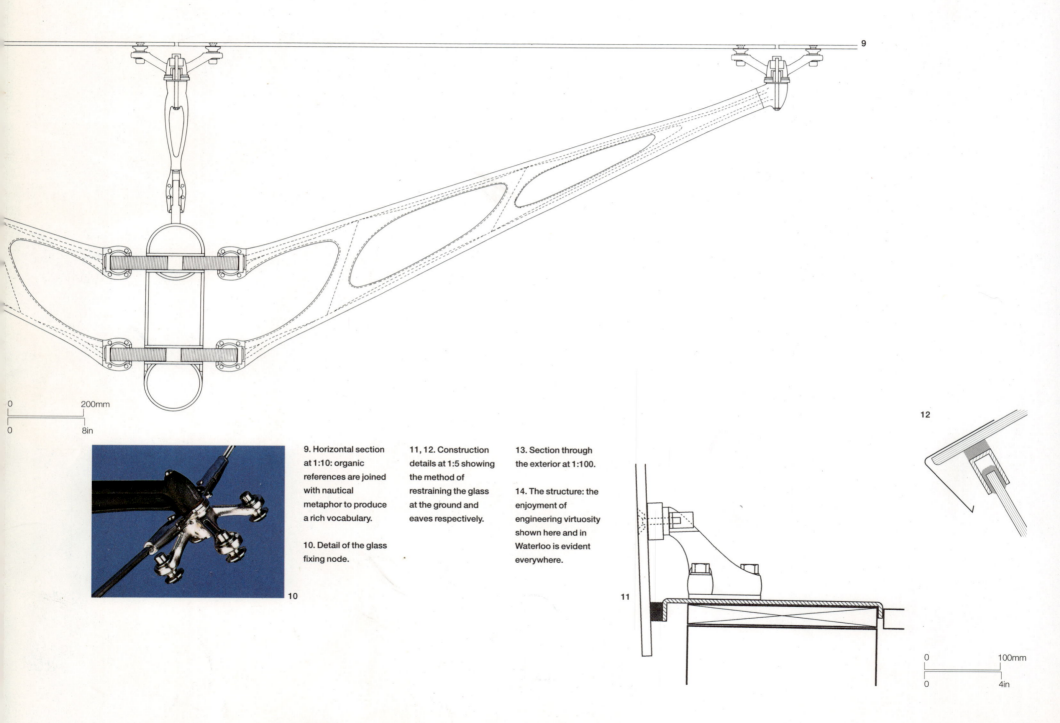

9

0   200mm

0   8in

10

12

11

0   100mm

0   4in

9. Horizontal section
at 1:10: organic
references are joined
with nautical
metaphor to produce
a rich vocabulary.

10. Detail of the glass
fixing node.

11, 12. Construction
details at 1:5 showing
the method of
restraining the glass
at the ground and
eaves respectively.

13. Section through
the exterior at 1:100.

14. The structure: the
enjoyment of
engineering virtuosity
shown here and in
Waterloo is evident
everywhere.

glass in
architecture

western
morning news
building

14

13

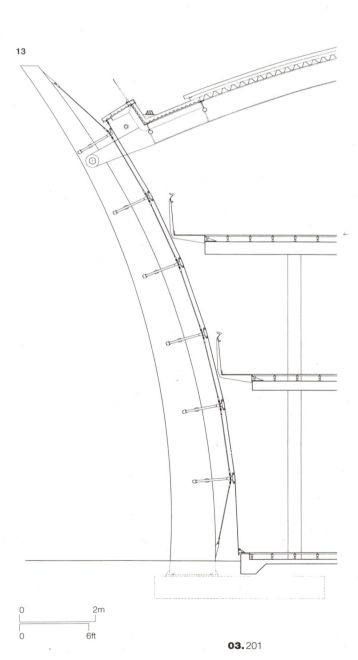

0 ———— 2m

0 ———— 6ft

03.201

benthem house

almere, the netherlands

architect benthem and crouwel
designed 1983
constructed 1984

1. Exterior view of the house.

2. The interior. The view out of this house is possibly the least interrupted of all glass buildings to date, a result of the glass acting as a load bearing wall, stiffened only by glass plates.

For most of its existence in architecture, the strength of glass has been considered as a defect. Its brittle nature has led to it being considered as an intrinsically weak material in the palette available to the architect, and this has not been helped by the way it has been made.

In the last two decades, the strength of glass has been exploited to much better effect, as the great suspended walls of Rice Francis Ritchie (RFR) at Parc de la Villette, p 172, and the work of Mick Eekhout and others have demonstrated. More recently designers have begun to use the compressive strength of glass to wonderful effect, in the glass load-bearing wall.

The key to the use of glass as a load bearer is the provision of stiffness. Glass is an intrinsically thin material, and when taken to a height of several metres, presents a problem of buckling shared with any sheet material. However, its strength is such that it can be taken to the full height available within current manufacturing limits provided it is properly braced. The result is the thin load-bearing membrane.

The house in Almere for Jan Benthem and his family incorporates such a wall, to wonderful effect. The Benthem House was one of the prize-winning designs for a temporary house. The temporary designation freed the designers from the constraints of regulation, and also imposed the condition that the building had to be removed after five years. This requirement for removal takes us back to that early great glass house, the Crystal Palace of 1851: having invested time and money in creating a glass house, it becomes an imperative that it is easy to dismantle and transport to another site for re-erection.

The architects' conceptual rationale for the building relates to the landscape of the Netherlands: as they have written, 'Holland's flat, uncluttered landscape with its capricious cloudy skies, hovering between land and water, has long been a major source of inspiration for many painters, writers and architects … Heavy solid structures that negate and disturb the landscape do not belong. Light transparent constructions allow for continuity and are a logical complement to this totally artificial man-made country'. The absolute validity of this manifesto does not need to be questioned; it is the starting point for a concept.

The house is a glass container held on a space frame 1.5 m (4 ft 10 in) above the reclaimed land. The spatial concept for the house is the same as for the Farnsworth House, two horizontal planes creating living space, but here there is no steel structure: the glass walls support the roof. The roof is made of corrugated steel, framed up with steel trusses and stainless steel cables and tensioners, held down to the floor by two cables. Glass fins, 15 mm (⁹⁄₁₆ in) thick and fixed by bolted connections, add stiffness to the load-bearing 12 mm (½ in) thick glass walls. The building is concerned with the use of tension to stop the roof blowing away, rather than the conventional carrying of weight to foundations by gravity. The only real 'detail' in the wall is the 5 mm (³⁄₁₆ in) gap between adjacent glass panels, which is filled with silicone.

The house was built by the members of Benthem and Crouwel's office, a procedure made possible by the use of pre-fabricated elements ready for assembly. The result is a glass enclosure of quite remarkable purity, with totally uninterrupted views from the interior.

It is self-evident that a building like this is not highly energy conscious. Heating and ventilation is by means of air ducted beneath the house. The house is not so much an environmental modifier as the simplest possible statement of construction, based upon the compressive strength of its most important material, glass.

2

1

3, 6. Interior views.

4. The plan: an exercise in extreme simplicity.

5. Section at 1:50: the only interior structure is the cable in the centre, designed to restrain the roof. The structural principle evident in this section is supremely expressive and taut.

3

4

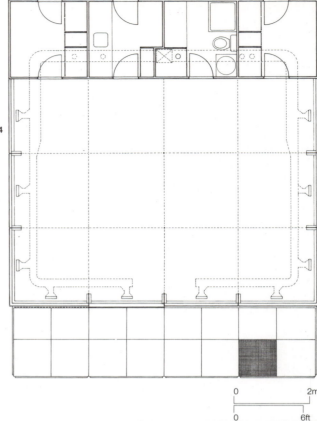

0   2m

0   6ft

5

6

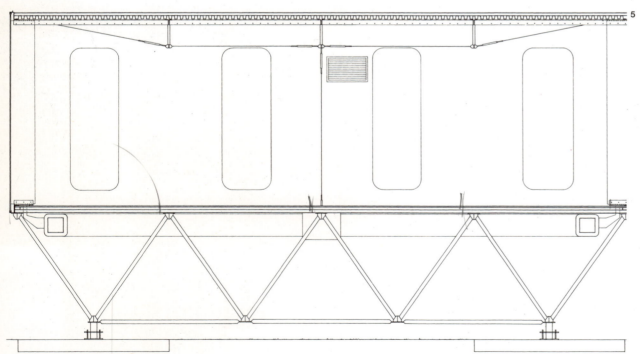

0   1m

0   3ft

7

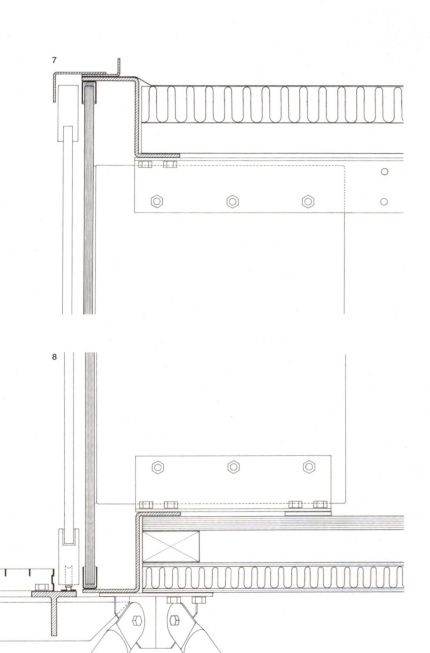

8

9

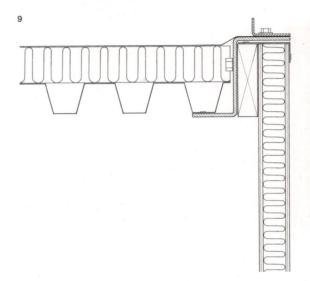

7–9. Detail sections at
1:5, showing the
sliding door outside
the glazing on the left.
The exceptionally
simple engineering of
the building can be
seen in the detailing
of the assembly on
the left: 'Z' sections at
the top and bottom
transfers the
compression loads,
created between the
roof and the floor, to
the glass, which is
restrained by fins.

10. Exterior view from
the entrance terrace
side of the house.

10

0   100mm

0   4in

11

11, 12. Exterior
views showing
stairway up to living
deck level.

13. View looking out
from the bedroom
area.

14. View looking
towards the cellular
service element of the
house, containing
kitchen, bathrooms
and other utility
spaces.

15, 16. Horizontal
detail sections at 1:5
of the external wall.

17. Exterior view
showing the house on
its raised structure.

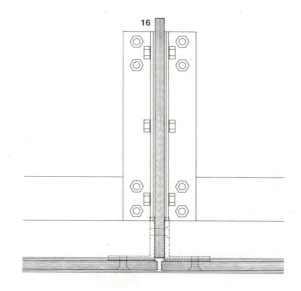

14

15

16

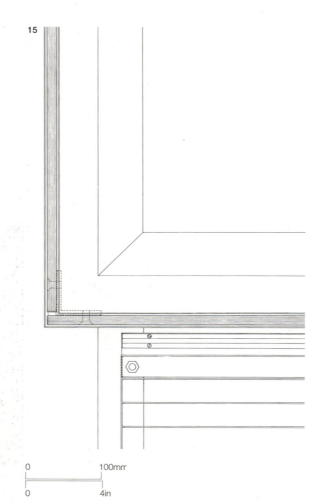

0   100mm

0   4in

12

13

17

sculpture pavilion

sonsbeek, the netherlands

architect benthem and crouwel
designed 1986
constructed 1986

1. Section and plan of
the pavilion.

2. Exterior view: this
'virtual' building
provides no more
than a sheltered route
for the study of
sculpture.

Two years after the construction of the
Almere House, p 202, Benthem and
Crouwel produced a second building
designed to exploit the structural
potential of glass. The building was to
house an international sculpture
exhibition, 'Sonsbeek '86', in Arnhem.

The intention was to create an
enclosure for the more fragile pieces of
sculpture which needed to be 'outdoors',
but also needed protection from the
wind and the rain. This simple
environmental requirement lent itself
perfectly to a piece of minimalist glass
architecture, exploiting not only the
principle of the load-bearing glass
wall, but also the glass roof. The design
is characterized by directness and
simplicity.

The building is conceived as four
square cells, 6 m x 6 m (6 ft 6 in x 6 ft 6
in) stepping up the slope, forming a

transparent tunnel. The support to the
roof is given, as in the Almere House, by
load-bearing toughened glass walls,
12 mm (½ in) thick, braced by 15 mm
(⁹⁄₁₆ in) thick glass fins bolted to them.
The wall panels are 2 m (6 ft 6 in) wide
by 4.6 m (15 ft) high, which is
approaching the maximum size available
from most toughening ovens. Steel
trusses are bolted directly to the glass
walls. The 600 mm (2 ft) step at each
change of roof level is equal to the depth
of the truss, and the glass sheet forming
the vertical closure at this point can be
opened to provide ventilation.

The solution to the problem of
rainwater shedding is as simple as the
rest of the concept. The ability of the
glass sheet forming the roof to adopt
curvature is used, and the trusses are
slightly arched, allowing water to flow
off the edge of the building.

The search for the all-glass structure
is now a well established one. Engineers
and architects on every continent are
exploring the potential of glass
structures, hampered by the lack of
information on strength and failure
which is so essential to them when
producing prediction and analysis. It
is a common plea that data is simply not
available, and this puts the engineer in
the position of the medieval builder,
relying to a degree on trial and error to
establish whether his structures are safe
or not. The real problem here is that
glass structures are still considered to be
exotic, and in a sense unnecessary.

The rationale for the glass structure
lies in the objectives expressed, for
example, by the design team at I M Pei

and Partners as they worked on the
Louvre Pyramid, p 126. Their stated
objective was to produce a genuinely
transparent, visually almost non-existent
enclosure. In this sense, the resulting
structure at the Louvre is a compromise,
albeit a very beautiful one.

If the full potential for glass in
architecture is to be exploited, given
that transparency is the greatest
characteristic glass has, the development
of all-glass structures is an important
element in the creation of an architecture
concerned with the disappearance
of enclosure.

In the absence of codes of practice
and real strength information, the
designer's first opportunity lies in the
world of the temporary building, and
Sonsbeek is an important example
of (nearly) all-glass architecture for
that reason.

It appears as a proposition awaiting
a technical solution, and in this respect
it is similar to Mies van der Rohe's 1922
glass tower project. The Sonsbeek
Pavilion was at least realized, but only to
be dismantled, and a sculpture cover is
only a sculpture cover after all. The
image remains, however, and in a world
where borosilicate, ceramic and other
very strong glasses are becoming
available, we are surely glimpsing
the future.

2

1

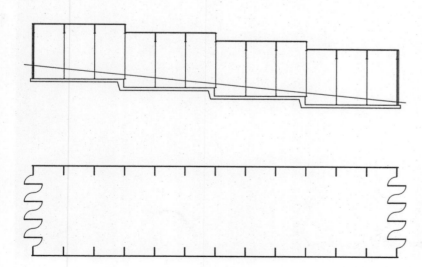

3

5

4

3. The detail between roof and wall, itself an elegant abstract sculpture of metal and glass.

4, 5. Exterior views.

6–9. Construction
details at 1:5:
The simplicity of the
details of the Pavilion
derive partly from its
concept as a rigid
tent, in which (for
example) thermal
performance was not
essential. However,
such a building
enables stresses in
such composite
structures to be
tested and evaluated
for more complex
proposals.

6. Vertical detail
section.

7. Vertical section
through metal truss.

8. Vertical section
through 'bulkhead'.

9. Horizontal section.

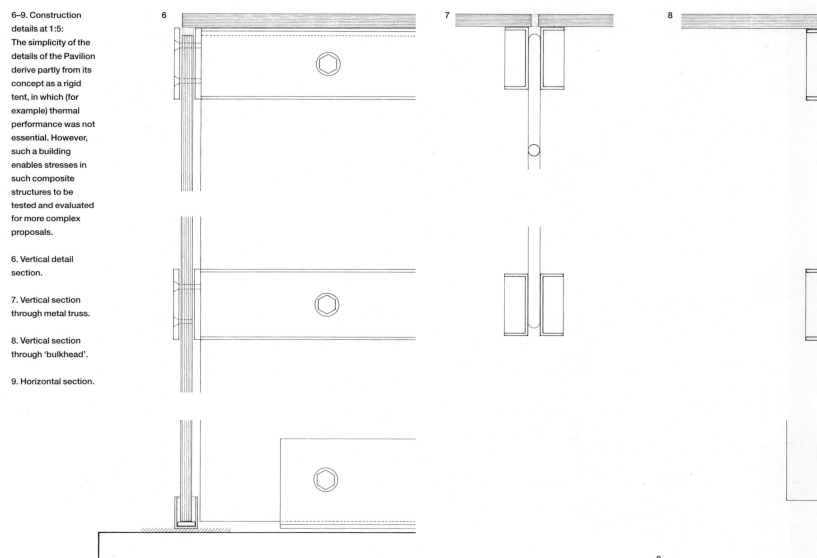

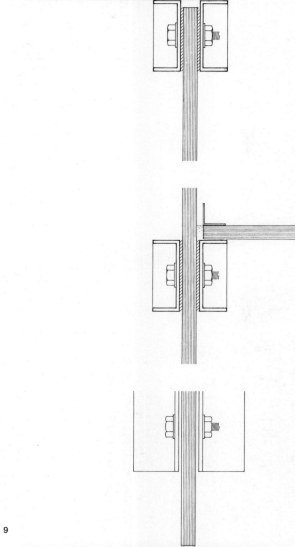

0   100mm

0   4in

house extension
hampstead, london

architect rick mather
with dewhurst macfarlane
designed 1990–91
constructed 1992

1. The glass wall: a
beautiful contrast
between the
refinement of the
glass and the stones
outside the
extension.

The idea of creating structures entirely out of glass has become a challenge to many architects and engineers. From considering the material as one which performed primarily in tension, projects are now appearing which use its strength in compression, and which treat it much more as a material with the properties of a conventional building components, capable of taking tension, compression, bending and shock.

Designers take comfort in the knowledge that glass is intrinsically (at a molecular level) a very strong material, but they also know that its fragility makes it prone to sudden and unpredicted failure. News of events such as the (at the time) unexplained spontaneous fracture of toughened glass, eventually found to be the result of nickel sulphide crystals, travel like shockwaves around the world of glass. Crystal imperfections have now been effectively removed as a problem by the expedient of heat-soaking, which establishes their presence and acts as a quality control mechanism.

Glass structures are developing rather in the way that stone structures developed in the Middle Ages, by pragmatism and trial and error. Engineers, who invariably have to stand responsible for structural failure, have no real codes or structural data to design with, and are forced into accepting the recommendations of the glass-makers, or into a programme of testing which demonstrates that a proposal is sound. This usually means the construction of prototypes, the cost of which may deter an otherwise enthusiastic client.

For this reason, many of the most ambitious ideas in glass architecture are carried out in small buildings, or temporary buildings, where all the participants can proceed with their eyes open, and with no significant long-term risk.

The work of Benthem and Crouwel in the Netherlands is paralleled in the UK by several architects and engineers. Rick Mather's house extension is a typical example, and one which takes the completeness of a glass structure further, while also responding to some of the environmental problems associated with all-glass enclosures.

The design intention of this project was simple: the creation of a structure entirely made of glass without the intrusion of any metal parts. The extension comprised main elements, a wall and a sloping roof, using sloping glass beams supported on glass columns. Not only were bolts and plates excluded from consideration; so were the aluminium spacers in the double glazing.

The engineering solution for all-glass structures suggests a fail-safe approach, using laminated glass, so that failure in one plate still left the other carrying load. Early two-ply solutions were rejected because of the problem of detailing the junction. The final design used 10 mm (⅜ in) toughened glass to make three-ply beams and columns, joined by a glass mortice and tenon joint fixed by silicone, with the outer layers of the beam taken past the centre ply of the column. The adhesive allowed the joint to act as a pin joint. The column base was bonded into a steel shoe, and the beam end was fixed with a friction clamp.

The double glazing is a German system using a glass spacer, which is glued between the two 10 mm (⅜ in) toughened glass sheets. The potential problem of condensation was overcome by the use of a Finnish heated glass system. This uses a sputtered dielectric coating to create a heated surface, sufficiently warm to act as a heat source. The outer pane is a low-emissivity glass which reduces heat loss and reflects the radiant heat back into the conservatory.

The glass panel components were made in Finland, and then shipped to Germany for the manufacture of the double-glazing units before being delivered to the site in Hampstead.

Night-time enhancement is achieved by the use of high intensity spotlights under the glass supports which cause the edges to glow, or by the use of back-lit etched glass panels running within the line of the glass supports.

1

3

2

2. Exterior view.

3. Detail view at the
junction of glass wall,
column and beam.

4. Ground floor plan:
the positions of the
glass beams are
shown dotted.

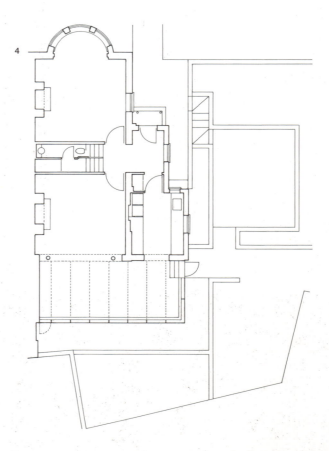

4

5

5. Interior view of the glass column/beam assembly.

6. Construction details at 1:5: the top details show the roof at the rear wall junction and at the front glazing. The centre detail is a composite horizontal section showing the glass 'column', and the glass beam with its connectors. The bottom detail shows the seating of the glass wall.

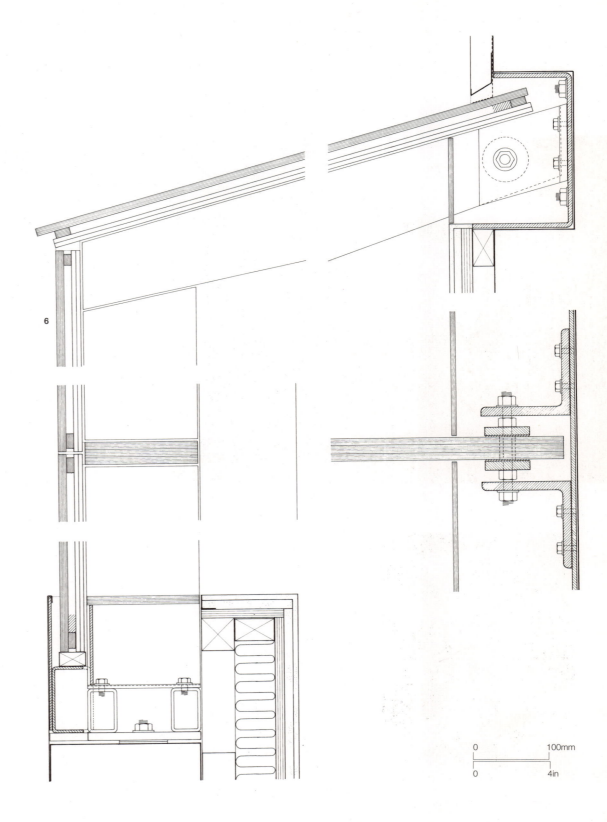

6

0   100mm

0   4in

joseph staircase
london

architect eva jiricna
designed 1986–88
constructed 1988/9

1. The staircase is the central element in the design of the shop, its own elegance complementing the beautifully designed artefacts created by the owner.

2. View upwards through the stair.

Staircases have long offered the opportunity for dramatic statements in architecture. From the Scala Reggia and the great Baroque staircases through to the sublimely simple staircase designed by Mies van der Rohe for the Chicago Arts Club, the stair has given architects the chance to demonstrate their control over the inevitable diagonal in a building. In mean and utilitarian architecture, the staircase may be relegated to a sightless shaft. In more generous architecture, the ascent and descent of the building can be one of its greatest joys. The shop has proved an obvious place for designers to create this kind of experience in the twentieth century.

Anyone who has ever designed a staircase will know the intricacies of geometry which dominate considerations of its setting out, its appearance from above and from underneath, and the creation of its balustrade. In the UK, Eva Jiricna has turned the intricacies of the metal and glass stair into her own preserve. In the London shops commissioned from her by clothes designer Joseph Ettedgui, she has created a developing grammar of staircase design which has increasingly exploited the use of glass and stainless steel.

The two major uses of glass are at 77 Fulham Road, a design dating from 1988, and at 26 Sloane Street of a year later. These two staircases provide great insight into the difficulties of using glass to make a stair. Not everyone is comfortable walking on glass, however, and in a stair the usual problems of insecurity are joined by the possibility of an increasing sense of vertigo, and by anxieties about modesty, given the possibility of those below looking up. The 'everyone' in a Joseph shop includes some of the most sophisticated people imaginable, but even they have been known to express concern, and the stair at 26 Sloane Street does occupy a large proportion of the floor area in one of the most expensive shopping streets in the world. This wonderful stair is currently undergoing an early enforced retirement and, at the time of writing remains in storage, awaiting relocation. The author has been advised that the same fate awaits the Arts Club stair in Chicago.

Perhaps the glass stair represents a late twentieth century example of what Scheerbart and Taut were promoting eighty years before: an idea conceived a little before appropriate technology arrived to make it easily possible. However, the idea of a stair which is to a large degree invisible is just too good to keep in store for long, and the new generations of glasses will surely make them as common as Scheerbart would no doubt have wanted.

2

1

3. Section through the
shop at 1:150.

4. Tread fixing detail,
at 1:5, showing the
glass seated on its
acrylic bed. To the
right is the balustrade
node at the centre of
its complex family of
rods and cross
bracing elements.

5. View from below.
What can appear as
an almost
incomprehensible
array of rods and ties
is in fact the rational
routing of forces to
produce spatial
sculpture.

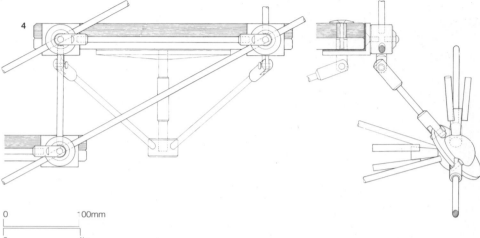

4

0   100mm

0   4in

5

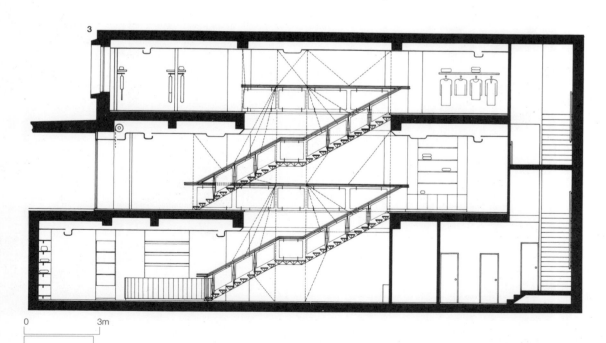

3

0   3m

0   9ft

6. Detail: an
expression of forces:
architecture as
jewellery.

7. Cross section
showing the cradle of
rods and ties which
support the stair
treads and the glass
balustrade. The side
balustrade trusses
are triangulated (see
below), as is the
horizontal truss
beneath each tread.

8. Plan through a
typical tread showing
the small triangular
balustrade truss and
the tread support
pads.

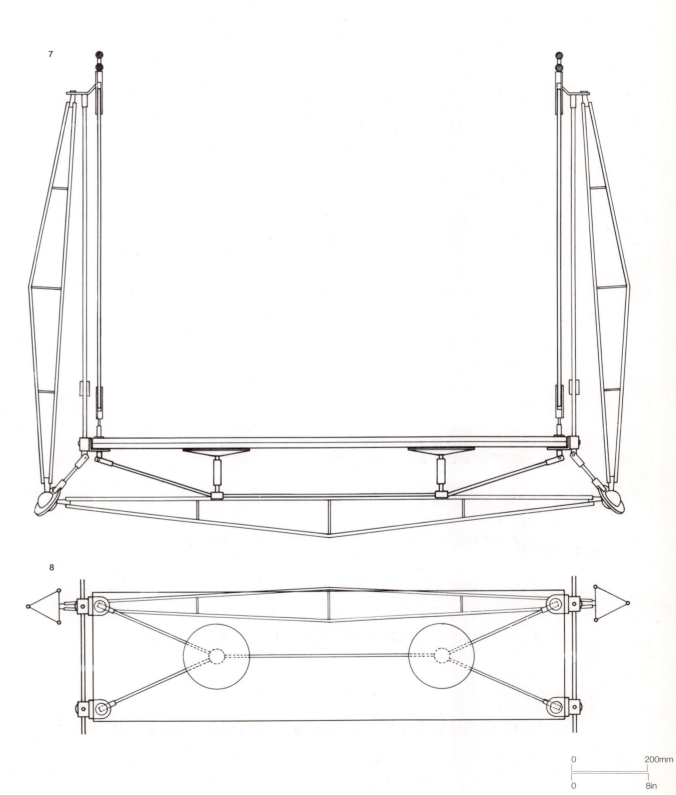

0   200mm

0   8in

04 the future: materials, intelligence and responsibility

1. Dichroic-coated fins in glazing of the Millennium project, New York, 1994, James Carpenter.

As we look forward to see where the technology race leads, we should ask three questions. What is possible, what is achievable, and what is desirable.
K Eric Drexler, *Engines of Creation*

Discussion about the future of technology is an intellectually hazardous affair. This is particularly so when the industries concerned have such enormous investments at stake and keep many of their programmes and objectives concealed.

The ancient habits of secrecy and process confidentiality die hard in the glass industry. The products which the industry provides are the result of extraordinary feats of technical imagination, with very high financial gearing in our own century between the raw material and the finished product. Competition between companies is vigorous by any standards and, as far as primary manufacture is concerned, restricted to a dozen or so main producers worldwide. With global production of one billion square metres a year, and about half of this going into secondary processing of some sort, often carried out by companies independent of the main glass-makers (and who can pick and choose between them), the drive to produce high quality, at a price carefully tuned to ensure market share, makes all manufacturers extremely cautious about what they make public.

Advanced and recently developed technologies have generally, in the recent past, been discussed by the industry in a particularly guarded way. For example, while the chemical contents of glasses are widely known, technical details of coating technologies are kept secret to the point where only a very few people at the top of a company, and the people directly concerned with the process, will know what the raw materials are and how they are used. In a new optical system for windows, being developed by the author at the time of writing, the tooling method used to create the optical device has not been patented because this is seen as a way in which the idea can be pirated, either now or after the expiry of the patent. The technologies are thus held in the minds of a very few people in the manufacturing company concerned.

In this context it may be imagined that the future of glass, in architecture or any other field, is the subject of enormous research and development budgets, conceived and expended in an atmosphere of secrecy akin to the defence or pharmaceutical industries. The communication of knowledge to a competitor can lead to commercial suicide.

This has all conspired to make consideration of the technical and architectural future of glass by someone outside the industry liable to be at best idle speculation, and at worst under-informed and misleading daydreaming. However, given information on technology which is freely, or not so freely available, and given also the identification of objectives which the industry and architects should set themselves, available futures can be described which are perhaps more likely to happen than not, or which could happen if willed hard enough, if only because they represent needs as well as practical possibilities.

1

To give structure to the consideration of the future of glass in architecture, it helps to consider it from two points of view. First, with regard to the aims which industry and architects might have concerning the performance of the material, and second, in relation to those avenues of research which seem to promise the greatest benefits.

This book is a celebration of one of man's most important materials, which is spread throughout an enormous range of his activities. Critical consideration of glass as a building material leads to the conclusion that, although it has many marvellous properties, it is not without its limitations. Unless treated, or made in a special and currently expensive way, it breaks easily and, when it breaks, is very dangerous. This problem, even when the glass is toughened, is a taxing matter to those whose job it is to worry about insurance and professional indemnity. A toughened glass window pane may break into small 'harmless' pieces, but such material falling from an extreme height could still do a great deal of damage and cause considerable injury.

Its strength (in the form and thickness of the ordinary annealed product generally preferred for windows) is extremely low given its known internal chemical bonding, and the problem of surface quality reduces an intrinsically strong material to one that breaks all too easily. In a fire it performs very badly unless used in a form specially and expensively developed for the purpose.

In its use as the extender of space and provider of view, it transmits not only

2. The space shuttle. The achievement of the space programme has been to demonstrate man's ability to define and solve problems of the utmost technical difficulty, covering materials science, energy collection, and many other areas of engineering and technology. Shown here is a photovoltaic array being unfolded.

light but also, in its all too frequent single-glazed form, a great deal of conducted heat, and its transmission of the spectrum in a controlled way has proved difficult to achieve. Also, by virtue of its transparency, it sets problems of maintenance almost unique in the building industry; with care glass will last thousands of years, but without regular cleaning it looks, and makes its context look, run-down and uncared for.

Add these defects together and you have one of the most depressing sights in architecture: the broken, dirty or boarded up window. You also have potentially the most uncomfortable zone in a building: the precious 'seat by the window' is the coldest or hottest place in a building, and the most uncomfortable for much of the year. When considered in the light of these deficiencies, it could be argued that the glass-makers have much to do before we have a safe and properly performing material.

The glass industry must now move forward and endeavour to provide us with materials which overcome these drawbacks, and exploit the new and

2

emerging technologies at an out-turn cost which proves acceptable in the building industry of the future. Many of the technologies which are needed to make these materials are with us now. Some are used regularly in other fields, and need not so much a breakthrough as modifications of technique and scale. Others, such as advanced coating technologies, are already in widespread use, but are clearly only at the beginning of their developmental potential.

In his book *Critical Path*, published in 1981, Buckminster Fuller described a mental attitude, and a management process, which harnessed the human imagination and made possible the achieving of objectives. Fuller was talking about how men got to the moon, but this attitude can apply to all human endeavour, which explains why Drexler commented similarly in his book on nanotechnology, *Engines of Creation*, of 1990.

In seeking to improve a material, and the design context within which it fits (the architecture of the twenty-first century and beyond), it is possible to scan the whole range of performance criteria and properties, write higher and tighter requirements against each one, and set the researcher to work on his new agenda starting with agreed shortcomings or goals. Seen alongside avenues already identified by the manufacturers as those likely to be fruitful in terms of their own technological progress, we have a real potential programme for the future.

Given the obvious benefits which must flow from such technical advance, for architecture and industry alike, we

should expect that, as we approach the end of the twentieth century, structured programmes would be created. It is therefore not surprising that the manufacturers have, in the last ten years or so, made great strides in their attempt to address the technological, and therefore conceptual and aesthetic, future for glass in architecture.

Initiatives such as the international 'Fenestration 2000' programme, sponsored by Departments of Energy in the UK and the US Department of Energy,[1] are a manifestation of the realization in the glazing industry of the central nature of their task in architecture. This is complemented by the Advanced Window Information System promoted by the TNO, the Dutch Building Research Establishment. The international nature of this effort is significant, taking advantage both of the intercontinental nature of research, and the interpenetration of the industry worldwide by the major glass-makers, many of whom now have part-ownership of each other.

Significant advances foreseen by the industry itself, as it contemplates the future include: the merger of the wall and window as a concept for the building envelope; the development of glazings with very low U-values involving transparent or translucent insulation; the exploitation of modified angular properties in optical devices; the further development of anti-soiling coatings; and the development of multiple-function glass walls which can be varied under control. In addition to these areas, which relate to the development of the building skin as an environmental controller, the industry is also interested in the use of the wall as an electroprocessor or microprocessor, using fibre optic or other signal-carrying devices and the development of light transport as a technology.

The immense value of these studies is the generation of an agenda for designers and manufacturers alike. Agendas can be as long or short as we like to make them, but any agenda for the future must include the following typical items:
— optical switching, using electrochromism, liquid crystals, suspended particles, photochromism and thermochromism, the use of wavelength selection, and the development of 'smart' materials.
— the improvement of daylighting characteristics, by the use of light-bending and modified angular property materials.
— the improvement of the insulating values in transparent and translucent materials, by the further development of aerogels, polymers and coatings.
— the improvement of the weathering characteristics of glass, by anti-soiling coatings and other means.
— the exploitation of light concentration and light distribution materials, using optical fibres, holographic and similar devices.
— the improvement of strength: the overcoming of the fragility and weakness of conventional soda-lime materials, with one objective being the improvement of the strength-to-weight ratio.
— fire resistance: the development of cheaper, lighter ways of preventing glass being the weak link in a fire.

— the advancement of manufacturing technology, concentrating particularly on flexible integrated systems.
— the rationalizing of size: the removal of the width constraint on glass (whether in the plant or by post-factory welding), and the co-ordination of size criteria of secondary processing.
— the better consideration of fixing: the development of glasses with fixing capabilities which obviate the difficulties of processes associated with thermally strengthened glass.
— the improvement of workability: the development of glasses which do not enhance performance at the expense of workability.
— the continued transfer of technological advance, particularly from automotive, aerospace and marine technologies, which traditionally, and still, require the solution of technical problems ahead of those in the building industry.
— the development of intelligent response: the extension of the 'super-window' idea to one in which glasses and their coatings and composite materials are combined to produce glazing which acts like a designed version of the human skin, in which different areas of the building surface can behave in different ways at the same time.

Such a list of areas of study is as extendible as the imagination allows it to be. The agenda which was implied in Scheerbart's book of 1914 was admittedly aphoristic, and in some ways fanciful, but

was almost ten times as long, and quite properly went into areas of aesthetics, human behaviour and concern for the human condition. However, the new technological and scientific possibilities for glass are beginning to become apparent to us, and, as we scan the horizon we can see clearly some of the potentialities for the glass buildings of the future, some of them closer than others, but all of them sufficiently defined to enable us to describe them.

the agenda
The property and performance characteristics which form obvious areas for research and improvement can be conveniently discussed under six headings:

— light transmission: its control and manipulation
— heat transmission: its control and improvement
— electronic glazing
— the transport of light
— power generation
— mechanical improvement: size, weight, strength, fire resistance and weathering

These can be considered independently, in terms of our wish to overcome the defects of glass as we use it, and our ambitions for performance. They can also be seen together, in terms of the complex composites of the future made by the newly developing manufacturing technologies, and exploiting technology transfer to the utmost, using design techniques made possible by computer modelling with the intelligent skin as the goal.

light transmission
Light transmission is the principal property of glass in architecture, and one which has proved difficult to master over the centuries. The great medieval stained-glass windows are examples not only of the aesthetic power of light transmission, but also of the way in which colour has traditionally been 'found' in a glass material rather than 'designed' for it. The development of body tints in the second half of our own century has proved essentially peripheral to our quest for designed performance in terms of spectral control. The aesthetic/cosmetic objectives of the sixties and seventies temporarily confused issues of designed wavelength transmission, and the result was tinted-glass buildings which cut out light and heat in often undesirable proportions.

Coatings, once introduced, were initially concerned with reflection. This was not necessarily as a prime design intention, but as a result of the intrinsic properties of the coating materials: this problem of the expedient use of available, but not always appropriate, materials has been described in Chapter Three. Refinement of coating techniques and a drive for performance has led more recently to the development of coated products in which transmission performance is the key criterion. The most significant of these are the low-emissivity coatings discussed in detail in Appendix One. By understanding the physics of heat transmission, a tailor-made performance in radiation emission has permitted the development of coatings in which it is inhibited, thus

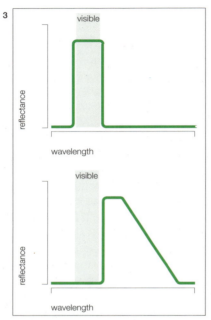

reducing heat loss. The importance of the principle of this idea should not be underestimated.

There is a large variety of low-emissivity glasses available, and many further types will no doubt come into use, such as gradient index coatings. These materials are of great potential benefit in reducing solar radiation (using the reflection properties), and reducing heat loss from the interior (using the low emissivity properties). This makes them useful as solar radiation protectors in car or building window designs in hot climates, and as low U-value materials in temperate climates. Motor manufacturers in the USA and Japan are at the forefront of development, as they strive to perfect the highly transparent, solar heat-rejecting windscreen.

3. Dichroic heat/light separators: transmission/reflection curves. These materials use multilayer hard coatings to produce designed, selective transmission and reflection, used as precision filters, beamsplitters, antireflection, and hot and cold mirrors. The upper curve shows the characteristic action of the system used in dichroic lamps, which reflects visible light but transmits near infrared. The lower curve operates in reverse, reflecting infrared but transmitting light within the visible spectrum.

4. Optical interference is common in nature, as with this soap bubble.

5. The tungsten halogen lamp reflector is a common product relying on dichroic materials. The light is reflected, but much of the radiation in the infrared is allowed to be transmitted back through the reflector, thus reducing the radiated heat emitted forward by the lamp.

The principle of wavelength-selective emission is shown equally well in a device which operates in the opposite mode. Radiative cooling coatings are designed to emit infrared, and take advantage of night-time cooling in hot climates. In theory a high emissivity surface under the right sky conditions can drop up to 50°C below ambient temperature with emission at 100 W/m², and in experiments surface temperatures have reached 15°C or more below ambient. Condensation becomes a problem in certain conditions, not only because of the occurrence of water and the consequent drainage and other related difficulties, but also because of the effect of moisture on emissivity. However, coatings developed by Granqvist, Eriksson and others in Sweden have been successfully produced, using silicon oxide-aluminium, silicon nitrate-aluminium, and polymer-coated metals. Although these materials are in their early stages in terms of long-term testing for degradation, weathering and stability, their eventual performance capability is enormous.

Another category of transmission-tailored coatings is that concerned with spectral splitting, with the regions of the

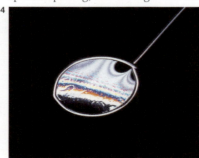

spectrum defined and designed for in terms of particular photovoltaic or photothermal needs. So-called 'cold mirror' coatings, which behave in an opposite way to low-E films, can provide high reflectance in the visible region, and high transmission in the infrared, so enhancing the efficiency of a photovoltaic system.

The new dichroic materials provided by multiple coating technology have also brought new possibilities in wavelength control, and are examples of the capability of multiple interference layers. The forty or so interference layers in a dichroic can be designed to produce a steep cut-off curve in transmission, occurring anywhere in the radiation spectrum. Thus, in a tungsten halogen reflector, visible light from 400 nm to 750 nm is reflected, but near- and far-infrared is transmitted, allowing heat energy to flow through the coating into the back of the fitting. This dramatically reduces the reflected/projected heat energy.

Design of layers can produce characteristic 'top-hat' curves. These could completely transmit energy from 400–750 nm, but block 0–400 nm and 750 nm upwards, and only transmit visible light. When combined with anti-reflection coatings, such a product would provide much better light transmission while halving heat transmission.

Multilayer interference coatings have very strong angular selectivity, which has a major impact on their use for glazing. For any dichroic-coated material, the filter action is such that wavelength is inversely proportional to the angle of incidence. Thus, as a beam striking the

surface rotates away from normal, the blocking action moves down in wavelength terms.

The coatings concerned are easily laid down on glass, but are not wholly suitable for plastics such as polycarbonate and, in particular, acrylic due to the low melting points and thermal expansion co-efficients, and the roughness of the polymer surfaces.

Dichroic and other filter glasses made in accordance with the technology could clearly be produced. However, large sizes, such as for windows, are viewed with concern given the coating technology, which is based on smaller sizes than those required for glazing, and the need for consistency. Despite this, manufacturers such as OCLI (Optical Coatings Ltd in the UK, and Optical

Coating Laboratories Inc in the USA) believe that the potential exists for dichroics to be used for infrared blocking windows. The remarkable, and very beautiful, optical properties of dichroics add a new dimension to the esoteric physics of selective transmission.

The manufacturers of dichroic materials are also involved in anti-reflection coatings. These may be less dramatic in their apparent effect than dichroics or waveband-splitting coatings, but must be seen in the light of the four per cent or so loss at the surface of most untreated glasses and polymers. The advantages of such coatings in photography have already been pointed out in Chapter Two: Leitz referred to them as an important marketing advantage in the 1940s. Automotive applications have also been important for many decades. The study of anti-reflection films is now well established following methods developed in 1986 by H A McLeod. A very large number of coatings are effective including sodium silicate, cerium oxide, magnesium fluoride and oxides of silicon and titanium. Some have colour correction, as used for Pilkington's K-Glass. New metal oxyfluoride coatings are becoming available which are especially interesting, given that they can be made by high-rate physical vapour deposition.

The use of anti-reflection coatings needs careful aesthetic and technical consideration. In principle, a non-reflecting glass is totally transparent in the sense that 'ghost' reflected images are avoided. These coatings will surely be commonplace in the future whenever their action accords with design objectives.

All of the materials described so far are related to the selective transmission of radiation without considering the angle of the beam. Of equal significance is the potential of angle-selective materials, and light-bending devices.

Angle-selection materials are surprisingly recent in their development given their obvious advantages. In Australia,

6. Angle 21. The photographs show images seen from different viewing distances through three different zones of the material, 2 m at the top, 1 m in the middle, and 300 mm at the bottom.

7. Serraglaze. SERRA is an acronym for Stacked Elemental Refractor/Reflector Array, and uses internal reflection in a light bending device. The overall thickness of the prototype material is about 1.5 mm, so it can be seen that the tiny slices of air which create the internal reflection are less than 0.02 mm wide. They must be accurate to within extremely fine tolerances to avoid distortion and unwanted optical effects, so precise, high technology manufacture is essential. The ray trace diagram shows how refraction and internal reflection are used to direct light impinging on the device at different angles and being redirected to where it is needed, by design.

following the lead of Granqvist in Sweden, work has been done on coatings with selective angle properties using magnetically-filtered cathodic arc evaporation and oblique evaporation. In Japan, Nippon Sheet Glass has already introduced its 'Angle 21' product using a polymer with an orientated column microstructure. This varies in its transmission from specular transmitting to diffuse scattering, depending upon the angle of the light beam. The polymer molecules can be orientated so as to give an angular-dependent crystal structure, and this has been achieved for dispersed liquid crystal films: this opens up the possibility of switching the angles electrically to produce the molecular venetian blind.

Another approach, in which the body of the glass is used, is exemplified by the product Louverre, by Corning, introduced in 1983. The grey louvres in the glass substance are created by the action of ultra-violet light and heat to 'fix' a photochromic material. Other

developments include the automotive product developed by Volkswagen and Vegla in Germany, in which a coated material gives forward transmittance of seventy-five per cent and upward transmittance of less than forty per cent.

A different line of research into angular control aims at enhancement of transmission rather than light-blocking. A product under design development by the author with Peter Milner and de Montfort of Lichfield known as Serraglaze, takes as its objective the use of the whole of that part of the sky vault 'visible' from a window (fifty per cent in the case of a conventional vertical window), by bending light towards the back of the room. This sort of objective has been the subject of study by daylighting engineers for a very long time. Prismatic glass was first used in the UK in the early 1900s. Early post-war efforts in the UK included the 'light shelf' invented as part of a study into natural lighting for hospitals; and so-called 'prismatic glazing' has been tried and marketed by Pilkington in the UK and, more recently, by Siemens in Germany whose Light System is on the market. Most of the systems available improve distribution at the expense of overall illumination. They also tend to be defective in terms of vision (slicing an image up or in other ways obscuring it), and often generate chromatic aberration of other unwanted effects.

What is needed is a device which achieves five technical objectives. First, the maximization of daylight penetration, taking daylight from as much of the sky vault as possible. Second, an even spread of daylight within the space

behind the window. Third, glare prevention, by controlling the amount of the sky vault visible from inside the room. Fourth, solar control. These four objectives taken together combine to present the eye with the least difficulties of accommodation, and the best delivery of light. The fifth is all-important in a window, that the glazing should provide undistorted vision from inside the room, without chromatic aberration. It is proposed that Serraglaze will use micro-tooling to produce a precise set of refractions and inter-reflections in an acrylic optical layer applied to a glass pane. The technology involved in the manufacture of these devices requires tooling accuracies measured in a few nanometres, and at the time of writing, embedded acrylic optics seem to offer the greatest possibilities.

All of the ideas described above relate to steady state, passive materials, which could separately or together improve transmission control dramatically. Removal of surface reflection, the design of selectively transmitting prod-

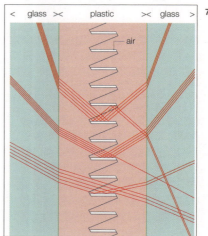

ucts, and the bending of light could clearly contribute enormously to how glass works for architecture. Their behaviour is fixed, however, and this places a fundamental constraint on their ultimate usefulness.

chromogenics: variable and switchable transmission

Variable transmission has been the subject of a great deal of research in the last few decades, and the development of thin film coatings has permitted a wholly different category of materials to be created, resulting from the capability of a film to carry an electric current.

The significant distinction to be made in variable transmission is between devices that are dependent on ambient conditions, and those that are truly switchable. Photochromic and thermochromic materials have been with us for some time. Photochromics, which rely on the presence of silver halides in the body of the glass, darken under the influence of bright light. This apparently beneficial phenomenon is useful for sunglasses, but can operate inappropriately in a window, when the need for light in the interior is often independent of the brightness outside. Thermochromics use glass coated with materials whose transmission is temperature dependent. This has meant that they have suffered from the same disadvantages as photochromic materials until the use of multiple-coating techniques made it possible to warm the material on demand: these include thin films which change from a semi-conducting to a metallic state when certain temperatures are reached.

8			
Description	Functional spectral range	Example of device	Solar usage
Changeable emissivity IR	F F V	Switchable	Research
		Absorptance/reflectance	
		Thermochromic/Electrochromic	
Tunable Solar IR	F V F	Electrochromic	Future glazing
Tunable Solar Visible	V F F	Photochromic Electrochromic SPD	Future glazing
Broadband IR	F V V	Thermochromic	Future glazing
Two-band adj VIS & NIR	V F V	None	None
Broadband Solar	V V F	Electrochromic liquid crystals	Future glazing
All band variable	V V V	None	None

8. Optical switching materials. This table sets out a theoretical agenda for optical switching. The left hand column is a performance description, further set out in the next columns by the spectral ranges concerned: the properties concerned may be fixed or variable, over different wavelength bands. The third main column describes which technology is appropriate to each.

In the table, the following codes are used:
F fixed properties over the range specified
V variable properties over the range specified
VIS the visible waveband: 390 to 770 nm
NIR the near-infrared waveband: 770 to 2,500 nm
IR infrared: 2,500 to 100,000 nm: these properties are largely dependent on the substrate, which are mostly opaque
SPD suspended particle device.

9. The design of an electrochromic device. The application of a voltage between the transparent conductor ions are moved by a uniformly distributed electrical field into and out of the electrochromic film. The charge-balancing counterflow of electrons remain in the electrochromic film as long as the ions are in place, changing its optical properties. The chemistry of such systems is described in Appendix One.

The use of films thin enough to transmit light, but capable of carrying current, combined with the properties of certain materials whose transparency can be made to vary by electrical charge or some other means, has produced research and development programmes worldwide. In the late 1980s and 1990s, work proceeding in Europe, the United States and Japan has produced collaborative efforts in what is now known as 'large area chromogenics'. The types of system currently under consideration can be categorized as 'discrete mass movement', or 'collective physical movement' processes, and include electrochromism, dispersed liquid crystals, guest–host liquid crystals, suspended particle devices, photochromism and thermochromism.

electrochromism

Electrochromism provides a change in the spectral transmission characteristics of a material by the switching of an electric current across it, thus changing its chemical structure.

The discovery of such colour-change materials was made nearly 300 years ago, but the term 'electrochromism' was only invented in 1961. Electrochromic materials have recently become the subject of intensive research in glass companies and physics departments across the world, made possible by the development of thin film coating techniques, and stimulated by the search for glazing systems which can vary the

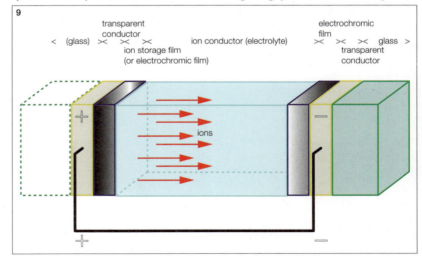

9

transparent conductor
(glass) >< >< ><   ion conductor (electrolyte)
ion storage film
(or electrochromic film)

electrochromic film
>< >< glass >
transparent conductor

ions

amount of light they transmit.

In the early days, from the 1950s onwards, colour changes studied were largely dependent on the materials available which exhibited the phenomenon, and on the eventual use envisaged by the researchers. The commonest of these are tungsten bronzes. A typical system uses two thin layers of electrochromic film separated by a layer of electrolyte which can pass charged ions, and this triple layer is sandwiched between two films of transparent conductor. Switching current back and forth through the outer conducting films causes ions to migrate across the central electrolyte, thus doping up or down the electrochromic material, making one side darker or lighter. By balancing the state of the main electrochromic layer, it can be darkened or lightened. A fuller description of the phenomenon can be found in Appendix One.

The difficulty with such a tungsten bronze system lies in its darkened colouration, which is blue. Blue-clear devices are commonly available, and in use in car mirrors. However, many inorganic and organic compounds are electrochromic, and the search for tailor-made colouration is now on.

The Gentex Company automotive mirror represents an organic electrochromic device, and is one of the most commercially developed products to date. Toyota is developing an automotive roof based on polyaniline, which is one of the current preferred organic electrochromic products. The car industry has become a favourite test-bed for electrochromic products because of the small

10. Applications of electrochromic systems. The diagram shows four different applications. The so-called 'smart window' is only one of these.

11. The colour of electrochromics. The commonly available electrochromics exhibit blue as a characteristic colouration, but mixed oxides enable more favourable, and neutral colouration to be achieved. The graphs show spectral transmittances for mixtures of tungsten bronze with the oxides of molybdenum, vanadium and lithium, at different voltages. Negative voltages produce a low curve, increasing from 400 nm to 800 nm (ie allowing a greater proportion of red light through the material). An increase in voltage to 2 volts increases the total transmittance, and produces a curve which oscillates at a consistent high level. Such materials are much more likely to be acceptable for conventional architectural use.

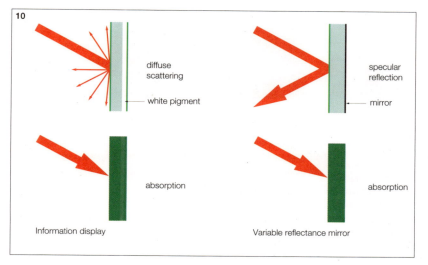

diffuse scattering — white pigment
Information display

specular reflection — mirror

absorption

absorption
Variable reflectance mirror

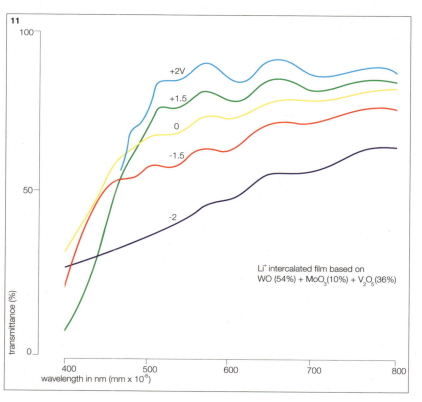

+2V
+1.5
0
-1.5
-2

Li+ intercalated film based on WO (54%) + MoO_3 (10%) + V_2O_5 (36%)

transmittance (%)

wavelength in nm (mm x 10⁻⁶)

sizes required, and because of the low life expectancy which buyers are prepared to accept. Life and size are both significant problems for electrochromic coatings.

The amount of work going on in this field at the time of writing is a measure of the anticipated success that researchers believe electrochromic materials will have. By 1992, over 200 US and international patents had been granted every year since the early 1980s, with four times as many being granted in Japan than in the rest of the world. Now, in the mid-1990s, some success is being seen other than in small-scale automotive applications. Two hundred prototype windows 400 mm by 400 mm have been installed in the Seto Bridge Museum in Kojima, Japan, and fifty in the Daiwa House in Mita City.

Significantly for their development in architecture, the issue of colouration in electrochromic materials is now being seriously addressed. For most of the 300 years of their study, the materials under scrutiny have had colouration properties which have been accepted as an intrinsic quality of their chemistry, with blue dominating the colour changes occurring. To the physicist involved in the work concerned, this has often been a matter of indifference in terms of light transmission. To the architect, however, colouration in transmission and reflection is fundamental. Research has now been carried out into more complex films containing tungsten oxide and molybdenum oxide, which may form the basis of durable multi-component films more neutral in colour. The graphs produced by Sato and Seino working in

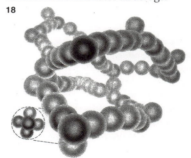

history of silica aerogels, and some of their intrinsic unfavourable characteristics, are described in Appendix Four. The difficulties may be summarized by stating that they are excellent insulators, but made of particles of glass so small that they exhibit Rayleigh scattering, which tends to give them a tinted yellow or blue haze in transmission.

The problem with aerogels for architects, moreover, lies not only in relation to chromatic and optical difficulties, and to the need for low pressures and good seals. They are also extremely fragile, and difficult to make, transport and form into building components. At the time of writing, the Airglass Company of Sweden is marketing tiles 190 mm square, which makes their use very restrictive. They also have a haze value of thirty per cent, which is too high a figure for what is normally perceived as 'clear' glazing.

BASF in Germany produces aerogel grains 2 mm to 10 mm in diameter which are 'fractals', meaning that the structure is the same at whatever level of magnification they are viewed. Although these look solid, they are in fact almost entirely surface within the grain; the grains exhibit Rayleigh scattering. Pilkington have solved the problem of

16. Aerogel block. The translucent aerogel represents a very effective but extremely delicate window component. The photograph demonstrates the colouring implicit in the micro-structure, characteristic of Rayleigh scattering. When seen against a white background a yellow haze is apparent: a black background exhibits an equivalent in blue.

17. The granular form of aerogel. This material accepts the problems of aerogel fragility and is in the form of 1–6 mm diameter pellets poured between panes. A 16 mm granular filling achieves a U-value of under 0.8 W/m² °C.

18. The presumptive structure of silica aerogel. The 'presumptive' structure of an aerogel is made up of small particles (seen enclosed by the circle) with a density the same as ordinary glass, each of which is less than one nanometre across. These are grouped into clusters of secondary particles with a density about half that of glass. These in turn form chains to create the extremely porous aerogel, with a density one twentieth of glass.

the need for a vacuum or gas-tight seal for the cavity by the use of multiple-capillary breather tubes, which also solve the problem of the grains settling when the unit 'breathes'. One German subsidiary of Pilkington is showing interest in exploiting this technology.

It is difficult to imagine a more hostile environment for an aerogel

than a building site. However, when the manufacturing of a composite has been mastered, an entirely new form of window will revolutionize the glass building. U-values of 1.0 W/m² °C have been reported for an aerogel window 20 mm thick, dropping to 0.5 when the aerogel is evacuated to 0.1 atmosphere. This compares with a figure of 1.4 W/m² °C for a well designed low-E unit, and matches the performance of a triple glazed unit. Moreover, thermal performance is not the only area of interest for aerogels; they also attenuate sound considerably. An evacuated aerogel window has already been constructed at the Thermal Insulation Laboratory in Denmark. For all this, aerogels present real and intrinsic physical difficulties, and the day of the aerogel window may remain a long way off.

The fragility of silica aerogels is not experienced with polymeric cellular macrostructures containing closed cells or orientated microstructures. Both polycarbonate and acrylic have been used to make translucent insulation, and the AREL polycarbonate honeycomb is available.

Given that the prime function of the aerogel is to inhibit convection, the evacuated window offers an obvious alternative, and evacuated glazing is now a technology in its own right. As the flood of technical papers shows, work in the USA, Europe and particularly in Australia is now progressing towards a marketable evacuated glazing system, using pillar arrays to keep the panes apart. Claimed thermal transmittance values have continuously increased since the first papers in 1988, from 0.6 W/m² °C up to more like 1.0 W/m² °C. This seems mainly to be the result of introducing solutions to the very real mechanical and manufacturing problems. However, provided good transparency can be achieved, the transparent window with a transmittance of 0.3–0.5 W/m² °C may be just over the horizon.

With the almost perfect insulator as a goal, the glass and polymer industries have a wonderful race to win to achieve the transparent blanket. Winning this will set yet another goal, of course, which is the switching of the transmittance, but with switchable coatings and pumps, such a variable autonomic thermal glazing must be on the agenda.

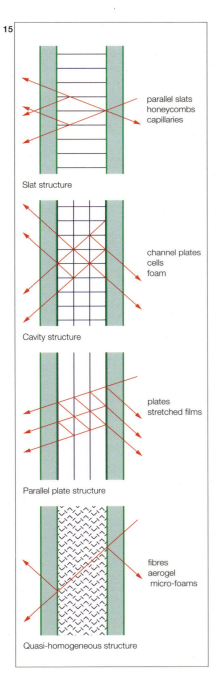

Slat structure

parallel slats
honeycombs
capillaries

Cavity structure

channel plates
cells
foam

Parallel plate structure

plates
stretched films

Quasi-homogeneous structure

fibres
aerogel
micro-foams

14. Pixel control. This image shows a section of a cell sheet which is used to separate lighted pixels in gas discharge displays. The use of hydrofluoric acid etching on photosensitive glasses can enable minute patterns to be created with high precision.

15. Transparent insulation: generic types. Four generic types of translucent insulation have been identified: 1 slat structures, which include honeycombs and capillaries as well as more conventional slats; 2 parallel plate structures, which include stretched films; 3 cavity structure, which can be channel plates, cells and foams; 4 quasi homogeneous structure, which include fibres, aerogels and micro-foams.

heat transmission

If light transmission and radiation are capable of being transformed by newly-developed technology, heat transmission in terms of conduction is also an urgent item on the agenda, and is on the verge of fundamental improvement.

For centuries the window has been the weakest part of the building envelope in thermal terms, with its associations with so-called 'cold radiation', down draughts, condensation and energy loss. The creation of multiple glazing has improved the comfort and condensation characteristics, but this has still left the window being perceived as a thermally defective element. The promoters of low-emissivity glazing quite rightly proclaim the energy efficiency of their products, but these coatings only address radiation transfer, leaving as an important objective the reduction of convective and conductive heat loss. Fill gases, such as krypton, xenon, argon, sulphur dioxide and freons, can diminish radiative loss by up to seventy per cent, but demand extremely reliable sealants. Also, freons can decompose and polymerize into oils under ultraviolet light. Sulphur hexafluoride has been used to improve sound insulation, but has been found to reduce thermal insulation if too much is used. Many claims have been made for gas filling, but it is thought in the industry that they are of little significance without low-E coatings.

However, we are still faced with conventional glazing having insulation qualities three or more times worse than a conventional wall. In the British Building Regulations, until recently, the window was considered such a defective part of the building envelope that maximum window areas were laid down by law not, as in previous centuries, because of a need for taxation revenue, but because they were considered unavoidably wasteful in terms of energy.

The concept of translucent and transparent insulation has changed all this. The idea of translucent insulation is, in a sense, much more imaginable than the complex physics of wavelength control involved in radiation transmission. It has, however, proved remarkably difficult to achieve. Attempts to produce it have typically included plastic spacer structures in multiple glazing made of tiny rods, tubes or beads, sometimes in association with evacuation of the cavity. Australian experiments have been carried out using a vacuum, an obvious idea, with the equally obvious defect that the two bounding glass surfaces are sucked together: hence the use of tiny beads. Recent developments promise better materials which should lead to a revolution in the idea of glazing being intrinsically an embarrassment for those concerned with energy conservation. The Fraunhofer Institute in Germany pioneered this work. Generic types of transparent insulation are parallel plate, slat, cavity or quasi-homogeneous structures, all of them quite different from the foamed polymeric plastics which are essentially opaque. Many of the structures defined are intrinsically translucent: the coarseness of their structure characteristically scatters light.

The creation of genuinely transparent, or nearly transparent insulation materials is one of the Holy Grails of glass architecture, and we need to be clear about what is meant by 'transparent' in this context. Classifying translucent insulation materials in terms of transparency can be done with reference to the path of an incoming light beam. We are not only talking about diffusion, but also of distortion, chromatic aberration and the slicing of images.

Parallel plate structures are essentially either multiple glazing, or glazing with cavity films. They generally suffer from optical reflection at the surfaces with consequent light loss. Slat structures include a potentially great variety of systems, including complex versions such as honeycombs and capillaries. In principle, light loss can be minimized since the slats can be considered as reflecting venetian blinds. Cavity structures include transparent multiple ducts and transparent foams which can have bubbles measured in millimetres; as with parallel plate systems, light loss by reflection prejudices their performance as a window. The closed cells restrict convection loss even more than that experienced with slat structures.

Light transmission and visual transparency are important for all these systems, but cost is also a constraint on their use. The fourth category of transparent insulation, the quasi-homogeneous materials, is perhaps the most promising in that it includes products which can be made as sheets with potentially high transparency. A typical one, still in the early stages of commercial development, is silica aerogel. The

15

16

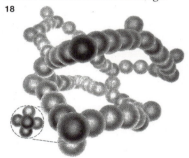

17

history of silica aerogels, and some of their intrinsic unfavourable characteristics, are described in Appendix Four. The difficulties may be summarized by stating that they are excellent insulators, but made of particles of glass so small that they exhibit Rayleigh scattering, which tends to give them a tinted yellow or blue haze in transmission.

The problem with aerogels for architects, moreover, lies not only in relation to chromatic and optical difficulties, and to the need for low pressures and good seals. They are also extremely fragile, and difficult to make, transport and form into building components. At the time of writing, the Airglass Company of Sweden is marketing tiles 190 mm square, which makes their use very restrictive. They also have a haze value of thirty per cent, which is too high a figure for what is normally perceived as 'clear' glazing.

BASF in Germany produces aerogel grains 2 mm to 10 mm in diameter which are 'fractals', meaning that the structure is the same at whatever level of magnification they are viewed. Although these look solid, they are in fact almost entirely surface within the grain; the grains exhibit Rayleigh scattering. Pilkington have solved the problem of

16. Aerogel block. The translucent aerogel represents a very effective but extremely delicate window component. The photograph demonstrates the colouring implicit in the micro-structure, characteristic of Rayleigh scattering. When seen against a white background a yellow haze is apparent: a black background exhibits an equivalent in blue.

17. The granular form of aerogel. This material accepts the problems of aerogel fragility and is in the form of 1–6 mm diameter pellets poured between panes. A 16 mm granular filling achieves a U-value of under 0.8 W/m² °C.

18. The presumptive structure of silica aerogel. The 'presumptive' structure of an aerogel is made up of small particles (seen enclosed by the circle) with a density the same as ordinary glass, each of which is less than one nanometre across. These are grouped into clusters of secondary particles with a density about half that of glass. These in turn form chains to create the extremely porous aerogel, with a density one twentieth of glass.

the need for a vacuum or gas-tight seal for the cavity by the use of multiple-capillary breather tubes, which also solve the problem of the grains settling when the unit 'breathes'. One German subsidiary of Pilkington is showing interest in exploiting this technology.

It is difficult to imagine a more hostile environment for an aerogel

18

than a building site. However, when the manufacturing of a composite has been mastered, an entirely new form of window will revolutionize the glass building. U-values of 1.0 W/m² °C have been reported for an aerogel window 20 mm thick, dropping to 0.5 when the aerogel is evacuated to 0.1 atmosphere. This compares with a figure of 1.4 W/m² °C for a well designed low-E unit, and matches the performance of a triple glazed unit. Moreover, thermal performance is not the only area of interest for aerogels; they also attenuate sound considerably. An evacuated aerogel window has already been constructed at the Thermal Insulation Laboratory in Denmark. For all this, aerogels present real and intrinsic physical difficulties, and the day of the aerogel window may remain a long way off.

The fragility of silica aerogels is not experienced with polymeric cellular macrostructures containing closed cells or orientated microstructures. Both polycarbonate and acrylic have been used to make translucent insulation, and the AREL polycarbonate honeycomb is available.

Given that the prime function of the aerogel is to inhibit convection, the evacuated window offers an obvious alternative, and evacuated glazing is now a technology in its own right. As the flood of technical papers shows, work in the USA, Europe and particularly in Australia is now progressing towards a marketable evacuated glazing system, using pillar arrays to keep the panes apart. Claimed thermal transmittance values have continuously increased since the first papers in 1988, from 0.6 W/m² °C up to more like 1.0 W/m² °C. This seems mainly to be the result of introducing solutions to the very real mechanical and manufacturing problems. However, provided good transparency can be achieved, the transparent window with a transmittance of 0.3–0.5 W/m² °C may be just over the horizon.

With the almost perfect insulator as a goal, the glass and polymer industries have a wonderful race to win to achieve the transparent blanket. Winning this will set yet another goal, of course, which is the switching of the transmittance, but with switchable coatings and pumps, such a variable autonomic thermal glazing must be on the agenda.

electronic controls

While photochromic and thermochromic glazing is essentially passive in its operation (with the proviso on active thermochromics already made), the need for power in electrochromic and liquid crystal devices requires comment on the necessary development of the control systems which turn them on and off, and the potential this offers.

The development of 'intelligent' skins demands that the control of transmission is carried out in response both to the energy needs of the building, and to the needs of the occupants immediately affected (in terms of view or irradiation). Both photoelectric or photovoltaic systems can be used to switch window devices, using so-called 'fuzzy logic' in an artificial neural network, which may 'learn' the needs of the building or its occupants. This is the beginning of the intelligent building.

Much of the technology already referred to relies on a 'servant' technology in the form of a thin electrode film. As was mentioned in the review of liquid crystals, while architects are considering the implications of glass which can be

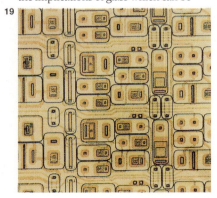

19. Designed nanometric control: silicon urbanism. The detailed city planning on a gated diode switch used in telephone switching takes place on a microchip 3 mm by 4 mm. It comprises components designed to survive electrical overload by lightning. Islands of single crystal silicon are embedded in a polycrystalline silicon substrate: the large islands are the gated diodes. The connection circuit elements showing as gold are aluminium 15 to 30 micrometres wide, and the islands are 4 micrometres thick. The technology needed to make these elegant, beautifully ordered designs, refined and small as it is, is still too large for transparent intelligent coatings, but gives an indication of the scale at which precise manufacture can take place.

20. Silicon architecture. Architecture has a meaning for a computer technologist rather different from that used by an architect of buildings. The smallest feature size of this logic circuit is 500 nm, with forming being achieved with the help of an electron beam.

21. Micromachining. This is a proposed mechanical acoustic filter a few hundred microns wide, using so-called 'comb drives'. Current micromachining projects include rotors 100 microns in diameter for micromotors and silicon chips incorporating millions of moving metal mirrors.

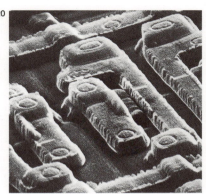

switched between transparent and translucent, the manufacturers themselves are busy working on panels for display. This work is reminiscent of early television technology.

In the aerospace and automotive industries, head-up displays are already in use using holographs, with glass being the combiner surface. The car industry, among others, is also working on the integration of antennae into glazing using metal strips or etched conducting films with transparent electrodes. Fibre optics are under consideration for signalling systems. Liquid crystal displays are increasing in possible size by about 75 mm per year, and panels 450 mm square were available in 1992. The one metre diagonal display (700 mm², or 450 mm by 900 mm) should be available by 1996.

The commonest conductive films in current commercial use are indium-tin-oxide (ITO) or doped tin oxide. This is usually applied by vacuum evaporation or sputtering in the case of ITO, or by chemical vapour deposition for fluorine doped tin oxide.

The new types of electronic

conductors which are now appearing, including the exotic conductive polymer metals, are expected to contribute greatly to the emerging technology of electronic glazing.

The significance of electrically-powered glazing, such as electrochromics, and the incorporation of electronics, lie in the proposition of control systems which can be part of an autonomic network, and which may be sensitive to the ambient environment. We are used to the simple operation of a thermostat in a heating system, or the louvre blade driven by the solar cell. There is a clear progression from this to the implementation of glazing which understands its environment, and is either programmed, or programmes itself to optimize its performance or show a movie. The introduc-

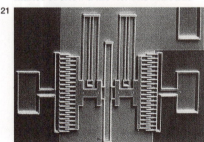

tion of so-called 'smart materials' is already occurring in the aerospace and other industries, and is the subject of regular international conferences. Much of the discussion is related to phenomena such as metal fatigue, where early-warning devices are invaluable. This gives us a hint, however, of the material with a neural network in which both sensors and motors (the active part of the system) play a part.

the transport of light

In considering the potential advances in the filtering and control of light, it is important not to forget the essential and original function of glazing, to provide light to the interior of a building. Ways in which the collection and internal distribution of light can be enhanced have already been referred to above, particularly with reference to the angular control systems.

The prize for light-collection systems is enormous. Bright sunshine is a source producing illumination at ground level of 90,000 lux or more, and

the obscuring of the sun by a cloud only reduces this to about 30,000 lux; even a dull overcast sky has a brightness of about 5,000 lux. A well-lit room, illuminated by its windows, may well have a level of a thousand or more lux beside the window, but this level drops off to a few hundred four or five metres back from the window wall. This rapid reduction in level produces poor lighting conditions as the eye struggles to accommodate the change.

What is perhaps more significant, however, is the loss of light created by

22–25 The Himawari system: The light-catching array, which acts as the collecting terminal for the optical fibre system (22). A wall socket (23). A lamp, supplied by light rather than electricity (24). With Himawari, daylight would be transmitted across the planet from daylit to night zones (25).

the envelope as a whole. Most buildings, conventionally designed, effectively block out daylight, and the idea of light transport is prompting work on more active systems in which light is collected, concentrated and transported to where it is needed.

Such considerations led the author, in a conference paper written in 1990, to propose a collection and transport system based on daylight concentration and optical fibres. The objective was to avoid or reduce the energy involved in lighting buildings electrically, often between 15 and 30 W/m². The idea was simply to use a lens system or some other device to concentrate daylight and produce a bright source at the end of an optical fibre harness, for transport to the interior of the building.

Later the same year, the Asahi 'Himawari' (sunflower) device was being marketed in Japan, after (of course) years of development. The Japanese literature suggested some of the uses, both real and potential. Among the potential uses were underground and underwater lighting and illumination for space vehicles, but installed systems were already capable of illustration, with sunlight being emitted from flexible hoses.

The systems rely on arrays of lens-collectors which track the sun and concentrate the sunlight into one end of an optical fibre cable. The current technology is complex and expensive, but the idea has been turned from speculation into reality. New forms of concentrator are needed to permit the collection of daylight, and parabolic metallized polymer films on a polyester/glass fibre

material are currently in use, and expected to fall in price.

The technology for the transport of light is well known, and is explained in Appendix Four. Small-scale lighting fittings are already very common, and extremely useful in situations where a light source needs to be remote from the place to be illuminated (such as where temperature is critical). Glass fibre light guides are the conventional means of transport, but reflective guides, prism guides, dielectrics and others are under investigation. In the USA, 3M are marketing a total internal reflection film which can be wrapped round the inside of a large tube and contain light projected into one end.

Fluorescent concentrators, which can concentrate either direct or diffuse light, are also potentially useful. Typically such a device comprises either a rare-earth doped glass, or a polymeric transparent plate doped with fluorescent dye molecules. Incident light corresponding to the fluorescent dye absorption is captured and emitted, travelling

by internal reflection within the plate to its edges. Silvering the plate completely, except for the emitting edge, can concentrate the effect. Such concentrators have been used for photovoltaic and photothermal energy conversion, and as wavelength shifters in liquid junction photovoltaics.

Holography is another means by which concentration can be achieved. Imitating the function of a lens or a light bender is an obvious potential use for a hologram, and holographic diffraction is being actively researched for daylighting. Several holographic films stacked over each other produce a performance equivalent to a parabolic concentrating mirror.

The significance of all this lies in the importance of lighting in the overall energy balance of a building. Many engineers say that lighting is the most important single topic to be addressed in the search for a low-energy building. This is because lighting is currently only produced by electricity, and electricity in most Western countries is produced by fossil fuel power stations which are both polluting and inefficient: the efficiency of power conversion is variously quoted between thirty-five and fifty per cent, which implies that 100 W of lighting could require up to 300 W of fuel equivalent. During hours of darkness we all accept that this use is inevitable, but to be using electric lighting during the day must be considered, in the case of many buildings, a crime. Since not all buildings can have their interior space squeezed against the external wall, the use of light transport systems will surely have an interesting future.

power generation

Reference to power generation from solar cells may seem out of place in a book on glass, but recent developments have combined power generation and translucency in a way which promises to be significant in terms of glass architecture. In both conventional photovoltaics and in the new generation of cells, the outer shield of glass is essential, and we are mainly looking at glass (usually low iron and anti-reflection) as the transparent protector to a process occurring in the building skin, sharing silicon as a raw material; this is discussed in Appendix One.

Light is one of the most potent forms of power on earth. It may have taken over 100 million years for the first forests to become the first coal seams, but photosynthesis is a daily occurrence, using the delicate, wind-fluttering mechanism of the leaf to generate structures dozens of metres high and sustain them. We are only now beginning to create photoelectrical systems which produce useful energy, but the building as energy farm is an important concept for the future.

The relationship a photovoltaic panel has to a glazed system is as important as its family relationship with it. Photovoltaics work most effectively from short wavelengths of light, and glass is not very transparent at these wavelengths. This means the panels must be outside a glazing system, and thus shade it, or constitute an opaque part of the building envelope. A significant contributor to the potential for design synergy lies in the opacity of conventional photovoltaics, which means they can act as solar shades as well as solar collectors,

26. Photovoltaic wall, Greenpeace Warehouse, Hamburg, 1993, engineers Windel Thimm & Morgen and Ridder Meyn & Partner. The wall provides 6 kw of electrical energy, traded to the local power company in exchange for night usage, and also acts as a sunscreen to the staircase behind, providing beautiful filtered light through the spaces between the cells. Walls like this can provide about 1 kw for every 10 m² of facade.

27. Digital Equipment Corporation, Petit Lancy, Switzerland, J-F Lecouturier, L Caduff. The pyramid roof to this building has photovoltaic cells on all faces except the north face. The cell arrays follow the course of the sun, and produce nearly 15 kw.

28. Solar panelling at the Odeillo plant in France. The rich ripple of a multi-cell facade.

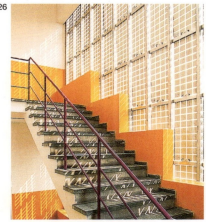

particularly in hot climates.

Of potentially great interest in this regard is the Grätzel cell, which is described as a photoelectrochemical solar cell. This has the potential benefit of transmitting light to a degree. In the device, two tin oxide conduction layers contain an iodine-based electrolyte and a titanium dioxide ceramic conductor. In temperate climates, the value of daylight and sunlight is now realized, particularly in the heating season when the use of natural light provides better quality and energy saving. The arrival of a translucent panel which could generate electricity would be of enormous benefit. The device is still at the stage of laboratory research, but indicates the potential for the translucent solar electrical generator. In principle a partially transparent cell could generate electricity from the near infrared only, where fifty per cent of solar energy is carried.

A sustainable architecture must incorporate energy collection and protection systems which are synergetic and efficient. Biomorphic analogies in build-

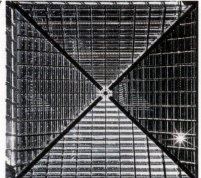

ings can be glib, but it is tempting to speculate that if a tree can collect energy effectively by the process of photosynthesis taking place in its leaves, then buildings might more effectively gather their own energy. The mathematics is encouraging. A building operating at night with 5 W/m² of light for five hours, and needing a further 5 W/m² of power for occupants' activities for twelve hours, will need 85 watt-hours of electricity per square metre per day. The question is whether the solar electrical power systems can deliver this (or a significant part of it), and whether the power collected can be stored without an energy penalty in the making of the battery.

Efficiencies of present photovoltaic and other forms of light-powered panel generators may not improve much, given the intrinsic physics involved, but there is an interesting conclusion to be drawn from the seventeen per cent or so efficiency currently quoted. The remaining eighty-three per cent is absorbed energy, most of which is turned into heat, and this generally means that cells run at 20°C or so above ambient temperature; the cells become warm as they collect the

photons. Given their location behind the protective high transmission glass plate, this means they are potentially active solar collectors. Harnessing this thermal energy, in addition to the electrical power created, would effectively exploit far more of the device. It should also be noted that much higher efficiencies are conceivable in multilayer cells.

The importance of these power generation systems in a glass architecture of the future is fundamental, because of the way they can transform the potential disadvantages of a sunlit surface (overheating and glare) into an advantage, in the collection of the electrical energy needed to light the building when the sun goes down. The skin of glass around such a building changes from location to location, from daylight-welcoming transparency to a hard-working power station. The impact on morphology can also be great. To pursue another biomorphic analogy, in the skin of an animal, its surface area and its detailed performance are interdependently derived through evolution to ensure that the right amount of energy is gained and lost to maintain life. In the architecture of the future the same will be true of the building skin.

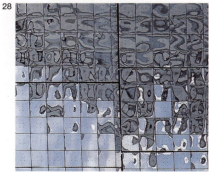

mechanical improvement

Most of this chapter so far has concentrated on developments concerned with the behaviour of light. However, glass is a building material, and as such has to behave in the same way as other building materials, with appropriate properties of strength and robustness, fire resistance and ease of working and fixing. Its weight and the sizes in which it is available are also important.

The problem of size, and in particular the issue of arbitrary size constraints applying to different secondary techniques, is raised here as an issue of manufacture. Large sizes are generally very desirable in building panel materials to

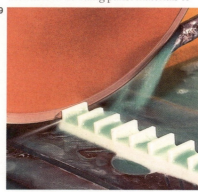

reduce joints and fixings, but also mean large weights, and this is another aspect of physical property which is important, and seems unalterable. However, we have seen how composites have opened the door to fundamental improvements in thermal performance without referring much to the reduction in weight of such a panel. The great advantage of glass as a transparent material is its hardness, and the panels of the future must include composites which use glass for

29. Macor by Corning. The new ceramic glasses have remarkable physical properties, and these include an all-important ability to withstand machining. This capability places them in the same category of the most robust building materials.

30. Glass table by Renzo Piano Building Workshop, 1986–90. This is one item in a collection of glass furniture, which ingeniously overcomes the fragility of soda-lime glass and exploits its strength in compression.Tie rods pass through the legs, terminating in countersunk nuts.

31. The new ceramic glasses exhibit the thermal and mechanical properties which match those of the best high-performance structural materials.

the outer tough protective layers, combined with the intrinsic low specific gravity of plastics and materials such as aerogels as lightweight centres.

Strength is another area in which enormous improvements should be sought. The fragility of flat glass in the normal forms currently available is its greatest weakness, and we must ask whether this is inevitable. The answer is: not entirely. The difference in strength between glasses of different chemistries, and between annealed soda lime and the strengthened varieties has already been referred to in some detail. In practical terms, the differences are not great for currently available glasses. Ideally, in the future we would be looking for floated flat glasses which exploit the inherent robustness under thermal shock of borosilicates, pure silica glasses and the immensely strong and workable ceramic glasses. Materials such as Schott's Zerodur, a transparent ceramic glass, is practically unaffected by temperature changes, pore free, and can be sawed, drilled, milled and polished. It is also very expensive. An important aim would be to turn glass into more of an

'engineering' material, in which analysis of strength can be carried out which securely predicts performance. The molecular bonding strengths of glass support this objective, and it should be vigorously pursued.

Such an objective presents major difficulties, however, in consideration of the differences between reliability and strength. The concept of the Weibull Modulus is explained in Appendix One, and one of the great dreams of the glass designer is the achievement both of a high Weibull Modulus (that is, a high predictability) and of a high strength.

In addition to strength, fire resistance is a vital property in any building panel which is to have the widest applications. To a large extent, the achievement in strength and robustness by changes in chemistry will bring with it the natural consequence of improved resistance to fire, because the melting point of glass is so high, and because the defective structural nature will be substantially corrected by the use of the chemistries themselves. The low thermal expansion co-efficients and arguably stronger surfaces of the borosilicates, for example, provide fire resistance at the same time as they provide strength. Once the problem of breakage in fire is resolved, we are left only with the problem of insulation (to protect the environment on the far side away from the fire), but this is an issue that is not peculiar to glass, and one which has been solved by transparent intumescent interlayers, where improvements in performance and price will surely come.

In respect of working and fixing, we

have seen immense strides in the last twenty years as direct bolt systems have proliferated, and as 'structural sealants' have slowly proved themselves. However, we have still been left with the problem that the strongest conventional flat glass material requires a working and handling regime which would be considered ludicrous in a material which was less essential in architecture. The sequence of design, site measuring, templating, cutting, drilling, edge polishing and toughening contribute significantly to the high cost of toughened glass. What is needed is a glass which can be dealt with like aluminium, steel or plywood, and some of the new strong chemistries offer this potential.

Weathering, too, has received fresh attention, and advances are promised. At the end of 1994, Nippon Soda of Japan, working with the University of Tokyo, developed a self-cleansing glass using titanium oxide which deodorizes and sterilizes material under ultraviolet, either from the sun or from fluorescent room light. A colourless, transparent titanium dioxide film on the glass decomposes bacteria and odorous gases.

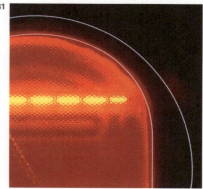

This coating is laid over a silicon film to prevent reaction with the sodium in the glass. Its long-term future in relation to conventional dirtying has yet to be reported.

The improvement of the mechanical properties of glass may not have the glamour of the development of smart coatings for example, but if advanced materials are always to be laid over a fragile substrate, a major piece of the performance profile is missing. Architects must work with manufacturers to establish the potential of more robust materials. A major problem for manufacturers is that a material which is difficult to break and lasts for a century or more will not do much for their annual turnover, but this does not mean the subject should be ignored. The real opportunity for the manufacturers is the all-glass structure, many of which are now being designed, always at the edge of the achievable, and sometimes with anxiety on the part of the designers. There is a wonderful programme of development available here.

manufacture: the technological challenge

The materials and techniques described so far in this chapter represent great challenges for the glass-makers in terms of research and technology. Complex and sometimes intractable as they are, they seem straightforward when seen in the context of manufacturing the multiple composites which need to be produced to achieve the full potential of the envelope of the future.

The first issue to address is the size of

32. The Bystronic cutter. Even the most conventional activities in production rely on very advanced technology, such as this cutter which optimizes and cuts to ensure minimum wastage.

33. Sputtering at Glas Trösch Beratung, Bützberg, Switzerland. Advanced materials rely increasingly on thin film technology. In this view into a sputtering chamber the target material can be seen at the top, and the plate being coated at the bottom. Sputtering creates the plasma which is deposited on to the plate.

34. Chemical modification. Treatment of photosensitive louvres can be used to create tiny integral modifications to the transparency of a material. The louvres here are 3.2 mm wide.

the product available to the designer. The search for large sizes is a common one in architecture, as architects seek generosity and the minimization of joints, regulated by the ability to get materials to a site.

For glass, the maximum size is based generally on the ribbon width in a float plant (just over 3 m), and the length in which annealed glass can easily be transported. This has produced a conventional maximum size of about 3 m by 6 m. Whilst this maximum rectangle has served architecture well for nearly fifty years, it is one of the irritations to architects who love to exploit glass that secondary processors have always been content to deal with smaller sizes. Toughening, laminating and coating plants have consistently been set up which fail to exploit the sizes which can be obtained for the annealed product: toughening ovens and laminating autoclaves are simply too small. Quite apart from the architectural implications of these limitations, such a failure creates a continual worldwide search by the architect trying to find the largest available size for his components. This is not

a trivial matter, for the scale of a component may well be the generator of a concept, as well as the factor which reduces the amount of joint. On the matter of size itself, manufacturers will say that architects always seem to want a larger size than is currently available. There are two reasons for this. Firstly, the usable width of a float ribbon does not achieve common floor-to-floor heights; another half-a-metre would make all the difference. Secondly, economical cutting particularly for thick material, has a critical impact on cost. Secondary processors invest great amounts in cutting machines, such as those made by Bystronic, computer-controlled to ensure maximum usage: the larger the starting size, the greater the opportunities for optimization.

However successful the manufacturers are at creating an integrated production range, without compromise at the secondary processing level, the concerns of manufacturing in the future will concentrate most significantly on advanced secondary technology: coating, multiple-glazing systems, and the development of new translucent and transparent glazing, ever more intelligent.

Multiple coating in thicknesses measured in nanometres is now commonplace, and the next decades will surely see enormous advances in the perfor-

mance of these layers. Switchable systems, electronic films and high performance interlayers, such as aerogels, all require integration into complex skins, and both primary and secondary producers and processors will need to devise technologies to create the composites of the twenty-first century.

The building site is clearly not the right place for this to happen: it is too expensive and too dirty. Automated clear factory plants will be essential to pro-

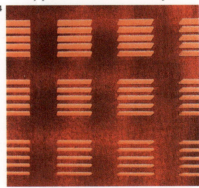

duction, and production methods themselves will need invention, development and improvement.

A typical example of the difficulty to be encountered can be seen in the incorporation of aerogels into glazing. As already noted, the product itself can still only be made in small areas. When areas increase, a way will have to be devised to produce composite sandwich panels, preferably on-line and automatically. A designer-technologist might ask for a material comprising two outer glass layers (perhaps coated with a switchable system), perhaps 4 mm thick each, with an inner 15 mm aerogel layer. If this were to be made by hand, however, it

35

would be extremely expensive, as well as difficult to execute.

The natural objective is an on-line, continuous process, producing the material like a rolled or float glass is produced today. This will not be easy, but only by such technological leaps will mass-production produce the cost benefits necessary for a low price, and only with a low price will the materials contribute properly and effectively to the financial criteria which help drive energy conservation.

With the advances in effectiveness and life of the all-important adhesives and sealants, already achieved and confidently predicted, the new composites will revolutionize glazing in the same way that the plate process did in the seventeenth century, the sheet process in the early twentieth century, and the float process in the 1950s.

Production techniques have always driven the price of products, and price is always a prime determinant of the extent of use. The virtuous circle of production, price and size of market has seen exotic products become commonplace in all fields of human endeavour. We should

35. Foturan is a transparent glass ceramic made by Schott, comprising a silver-doped silicate glass which stores a reproduction of a light mask when exposed to intensive ultraviolet light. It represents a glassy analogy to other silicon microstructures, and offers the opportunity for configurations of surface which are measured in a few microns. 100,000 holes can be formed in a square centimetre in a piece as thin as 0.2 mm.

36, 37. The Audi A8 incorporates a range of integrated high technology devices, including a photovoltaic sun roof, laminated and coated twin pane side windows to reflect infrared and absorb ultraviolet radiation, and an elegant lamp lens with a high pressure cleaning system.

36

not be discouraged by the difficulties, but designers must understand what they are if proper exploitation is to be encouraged. Establishing potential market size is a first task of any research and development programme, and architects are in a key position to help in this task.

In addition to this, it should be a standard objective, when new technologies and processes are developed, that the end product should be made by an automated line designed to suit variable orders.

technology transfer

As we review new and anticipated materials and processes, there is much to be gained by looking at the other industries in which glass and panel technology is required. The car industry, and the aerospace and marine industries have produced significant advances not seen in building; partly because of the intrinsically short life the products are expected to have, partly because of the small scale of the components and devices, and partly because of the economies of scale which are endemic in vehicles.

An early clue to the author about

light-bending was seen in the headlights of automobiles. These are in glass formed to produce directed light, very simply redirected by the adhesion of a triangular paper mask. Heating, wiring and glazing fixed by adhesives to be flush with surrounding metalwork, and fixing details designed for ease of replacement, are all now commonplace, driven by the market-based desire for elegance, performance and economy.

The early use of green-tinted glass in America has already been referred to in Chapter Two. The significant issue here is the critical performance requirements in terms of radiation transmission: it was seen to be essential to cut out heat, but not at the expense of light.

Thin float glass found its first real market in automobiles, where 3 mm and 4 mm toughened sheets soon displaced

37

the previous sheet materials. By the early 1990s, automotive 'double' glazing with a 3 mm interlayer was made in Germany by Sekurit Glass Chemie and built into a production car, the Audi A8.

Strength and safety also occupy much research and development work in the automotive industry, and lamination, toughening and curving technology is all very advanced. Moisture sensors designed to activate windscreen wipers are also under development.

Switchable glazing is in an advanced state of development and application in cars, partly because of the small sizes, comparatively short life expectancy, and perceived consumer tolerance to coloured light. The electrochromic dimming mirror and roof light are now in production, and by 1992 devices by Schott and OCLI were all-inorganic solid-state electrochromic designs which had become products.

The aerospace industry too has shown the way in certain forms of glazing. An article by the author published in 1969 showed the use of bevelled-edge fixing in the Concorde aircraft, later picked up on in early versions of the Advanced Passenger Train in the UK, and now in use in buildings to produce flush glazing. Electrochromic glazing in commercial aircraft is under development, and its use is anticipated for the generations of Boeing aircraft due in the late 1990s. It almost goes without saying that an electrochromic device is being developed for NASA space applications, based on tungsten oxide and iridium oxide systems.

Finally, the idea of the so-called 'smart skin' has quite a different significance in aerospace applications from those current in architecture. Conferences in the smart skin can seem very attractive to architects until the programme is looked at in detail. What is often being discussed is fibre optic applications used to detect metal distortion and fatigue. This application of neural networks only serves to show the idea for future generations of glass architecture and thinking skins.

the thinking skin

This introduction of neural networks, including potentially autonomic systems, into complex building envelopes brings us naturally to the idea of the intelligent building, incorporating skins which could perceive conditions around them, and react through central or local processors to produce lively and (where necessary) instant responses.

The idea of the responsive envelope is threaded through twentieth century architecture, from Scheerbart to Le Corbusier in the 1930s and on to the highly-engineered buildings of the eighties and nineties. With the development of building services, building management systems, computer-controlled environmental systems and the idea of thermostatic and solar cell control, the intelligent building is with us already. It is, however, only in a very rudimentary form.

In the late eighties, much thought revolved around the idea of the automated home, with integrated computer-controlled, programmable, video telecommunication, security and electrical systems. While metal wiring has been the conventional way of carrying signals,

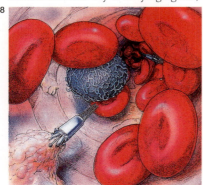

38

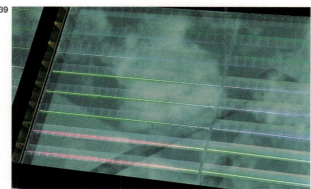

39

38. The hypothesis of the nanometric machine, conceived by Richard P Feynman, K Eric Drexler and others proposes the construction of machines with a size a few atoms across. They have excited scientists working in the field of biology as well as those working in physical technology. The machines shown here are programmed to consume fat and other unwanted material. These are broken down chemically and discharged into the blood stream for removal by the kidneys. Nanomachines would also be able to create the ultimate reduction of the microcomputer, with the components measured in nanometres rather than micrometres as with the present silicon chip.

39. Holographic structures in the Terrace Housing at the IGA '93, Stuttgart, HHS Planners and Architects. The subtle and beautiful playing with light and performance will characterize glass buildings in the future.

40. Experimental solar array. This beautiful gold solar array was part of the Discovery Mission. It is seen folded in figure 2 of this chapter. The unconscious aesthetics of the space scientist demonstrate new rich possibilities in design.

fibre-optic cables are expected to replace this for reasons of avoidance of electrical interference and reliability.

In 1988, a 'smart house' was built at Rosmalen in the Netherlands with extensive building monitoring systems, a photochromic wall paint and a liquid crystal window. In 1990, a Japanese smart house was built at the University of Tokyo. This incorporated exterior and interior sensors for temperature, lighting levels, humidity, airflow, occupancy and carbon

40

dioxide levels. Exterior sensors monitored ambient conditions. The TRON Association, founded in Japan, has 140 member companies, including the major computer manufacturers worldwide. This is producing the basic software systems for the responsive house. An autonomous house has been built at the Fraunhofer Institute for Solar Energy Systems in Freiburg, Germany.

The use of neural fibre optic networks in aircraft has already been mentioned, and these may be expected in structures in due course, to monitor stress and other parameters. Several American companies are working for the US Air Force on research projects concerned with embedded sensors designed to measure wavelength, temperature and other variables including physical strain. The objective in the long term is to create neural networks which monitor all vital parameters, and to include processing at the sensing location. The behaviour of light within the fibres in so-called 'twin mode' fibres measures temperature without the need for a sensor, and the use of multiple wavelengths allows the measurement of temperature and strain at the same time. Guides are being created which can sense dirt, rain and touch.

The important components for the thinking skin are with us: the computer systems and control systems which analyse, predict and respond; the neural systems which feel and communicate, and also think themselves; and the proliferating variable multi-state materials which can perform in accordance with the needs both of the building as a whole, and of localized parts of it.

The key to the achievement of such buildings is glass. Not the glass we are used to in our buildings at the end of the twentieth century, but glass as the key element in a new generation of materials, in which it is combined with different versions of itself, with polymers, and with coatings measured in nanometres producing multi-chroic behaviour. Complex layers of oxides, liquid crystals and aerogels will produce glasses with highly-insulating thermal properties, selective radiation transmission, diffusing or opacity at will, and which can carry messages, all on a substrate as hard and as strong as steel.

The importance of these developments is not simply that they represent technological ingenuity and virtuosity, or that they are the manifestation of performance competition in a world where added value equals profit. We are living at a time when the management of resources is becoming an important issue. In the twenty or so years since the Club of Rome published Limits to Growth, we have seen many of the issues referred to in it roll towards us in an often frightening way. From concerns about energy use and resource depletion, we have seen how pollution may threaten our biosphere, and we are seeing the deadly inter-relationship between energy use, resource conversion and pollution, from the abuse of the internal combustion engine to the emissions of the fossil fuel power station.

We are told that fifty per cent of all energy is used in buildings in most countries in the developed world. Halving this, while at the same time designing buildings which are photovoltaic energy farms, could make a significant impact both on the energy bill (personally and nationally) and on the polluting emissions in countries not blessed with hydroelectric power. A report published by the British government in 1988 pointed out that half the country's energy could be created from renewable resources, thus removing the threat of resource depletion and the enormous problems of carbon dioxide emission at a stroke. The importance of embodied energy is only now being quantified, and this, too, must drive us towards more responsible buildings.

The new glass architecture will have

41. Greenpeace Warehouse, Germany. This wall indicates the richness that can be obtained by the integration of photovoltaics into the architecture they serve.

41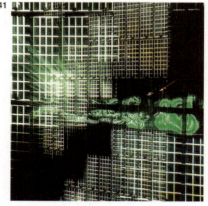

to demonstrate that it does not simply provide an exhibition of technical prowess, but that it contributes to sustainable symbiosis. For all this, we must not miss, as we contemplate the seriousness of ozone layer depletion, air quality and the death of trees, the magic of these new buildings. Michael Davies has put the image of these before us in a beautiful and inspiring way:

'Look up at a spectrum washed envelope whose surface is a map of its instantaneous performance, stealing energy from the air with an iridescent shrug, rippling its photogrids as a cloud runs across the sun; a wall which, as the night chill falls, fluffs up its feathers and turning white on its north face and blue on the south, closes its eyes but not without remembering to pump a little glow down to the night porter, clear a view-patch for the lovers on the south side of level 22 and to turn 12% silver just after dawn.'

This is not a dream, because technology plus poetry equals architecture, whether it be in the Gothic cathedral or the glass buildings of the twenty-first century. All architects and glass-makers have to do is make it happen.

05   appendices

This part of the book is concerned with glass technology and production, structured to provide an understanding of materials and products, and to facilitate access to information. The five appendices cover the following aspects of glass technology: materials and performance; glass manufacture; the manufacturing sectors; other glasses and glass products; and the transparent plastics.

Appendix 1: Glass performs in the way it does because of what it is as a material. Only by understanding its nature can we make it, modify it, exploit it and tailor it to our needs. This understanding is complicated by the proliferation of secondary techniques, particularly coating.

The consideration in this appendix describes the constitution of glass, its physics and chemistry, and proceeds to review the physical properties which derive from its internal structure, including reference to the different glass types. This is followed by a detailed discussion of the nature of light, radiation transmission and transparency, with an evaluation of the transmission characteristics of particular materials, including the impact of coatings to create new generations of radiation transmissions, and the advanced chromogenic materials which can vary their transmissions.

Appendix 1 goes on to review other flat glass products, and the proliferation of materials which are the result of what is called 'secondary manufacture', in which a basic product is taken and amended. Finally, composite systems, in which the future of glass architecture lies, are described, including the area of photovoltaics. The appendix closes with a generic glass cata-

logue, and a table of comparative physical properties.

Appendix 2: How glass is made is fundamental to its eventual nature and performance characteristics. Appendix 2 describes the production methods currently being used to make glass. Primary manufacturing and secondary manufacturing processes are described, as well as the various coating methods which have revolutionized glazing.

Appendix 3: A proper exploitation of the skills and production available demands an understanding of the structure of the industry to enable a designer to source expertise and products. Appendix 3 briefly describes this.

Appendix 4: Glass is made in an enormous range of chemistries and forms. This appendix reviews glasses other than those conventionally considered as architectural glazing materials, among which may be found the architectural products of the future.

Appendix 5: This reviews the other important family of materials in the architecture of transparency, the transparent plastics, and describes their physics and chemistry, manufacturing methods and physical properties.

materials and performance

1. Typical molecular structures. The networks of SiO₄ shown diagrammatically in two dimensions: tetrahedra in crystal form, looser arrangements in fused silica, and comparatively amorphous arrangements in sodium silicate glass.

the constitution, chemistry and physics of glass

Glass, chemically, is an inorganic product of fusion which has cooled to a rigid state without crystallizing; or, less technically but more evocatively, a super-cooled liquid. This latter paradoxical term (given that glass appears solid), relates to the properties of certain materials, known as glass formers, to cool from the fluid, molten state to a solid state, while maintaining the amorphous state characteristic of liquids.

The solidifying of an element or compound is normally accompanied by its becoming micro-crystalline and opaque. It is a characteristic of the oxides of silicon (Si), boron (B), germanium (Ge), phosphorus (P), arsenic (As) and certain other compounds, that when heated to the point of fusion and then cooled in a controlled way, they maintain an amorphous, non-crystalline state, lending the material its transparency.

In the twentieth century, transparency is a property by no means unique to glass among solids. Certain plastics, which are complex molecular strand materials, are also transparent: these include polymethyl-methacrylate (acrylic, Perspex or Plexiglass), polythene, and polycarbonate. These materials are discussed in Appendix Five. Apart from being recent in invention, however, these new materials do not share the durability and resistance to corrosion and high temperature of glass. Glass, as a material which is intrinsically both 'rocky' and transparent, is uniquely placed to serve the purposes of building.

molecular structure

A 'slice', taken on a molecular scale, through a crystalline substance and two typical glasses shows their comparative structures.

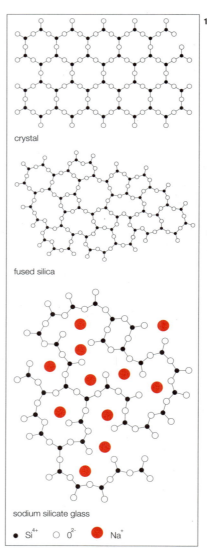

1

crystal

fused silica

sodium silicate glass

● Si⁴⁺   ○ 0²⁻   ● Na⁺

When most materials in a molten state are cooled, crystals usually start to form as the temperature falls below the melting point. In a glass former, however, cooled appropriately, the spatially linking bonds in the molecular structure make it difficult for crystals to form. Cooling the material increases its viscosity,

and the mobility of its molecules decrease. If the cooling is carried out quickly through the critical temperatures, viscosity can be increased at a rate which prevents any crystal growth. This avoidance of what glass-makers call devitrification is the key to the glass-maker's art. The critical temperatures concerned vary, both with the nature of the glass former and with the number of other materials in the glass melt. However, all glasses share the characteristics of the classic volume: temperature curve. As the glass cools, its viscosity increases to such a high value that it effectively becomes a solid. In the temperature range known as the transformation temperature, the material changes from a plastic to a brittle state and becomes glass.

The use of a glass former on its own has historically not been sufficient to produce glasses of the required sort at an acceptable cost. The development of practical, commercial glasses has required the solution to problems of manufacture and of use. The chemical constitution of glass and its physical performance result from the combination of glass formers with other materials: production agents which facilitate manufacture, and performance modifiers which change performance characteristics. The production agents themselves change performance considerably. For example, the high alkali content of soda-lime glass reduces the melting point of the material, but increases the coefficient of thermal expansion by twenty times over that of pure silica, and is a prime cause of its liability to fracture under thermal stress.

The eventual properties of a glass are dependent upon the glass former used, the impurities in it, and the other

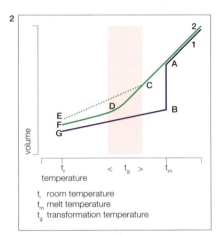

2

volume

t_r   <   t_g   >   t_m

temperature

t_r room temperature
t_m melt temperature
t_g transformation temperature

materials added to aid manufacture and
improve performance.

glass mixtures
trace element impurities

The most common glass former in use is silica (SiO_2), readily available as sand and the most abundant material on the planet. The earth's crust consists of 27% silicon (compared to 47% oxygen, 5% iron and 0.8% aluminium), and silicates and alumina silicates are by far the most plentiful solids. In its natural state, however, sand contains many materials that, to the glass-maker, are impurities, and which may colour it or affect its performance. Iron oxide is a common impurity, and just 0.1% will give glass the slight green tint which becomes very noticeable in thick flat glass. Special glasses, such as optical products, must contain less than one-hundredth of this amount, and require much more selective extraction or purification. Other impurities include the oxides of chromium, nickel and cobalt, all of which colour the eventual glass slightly, and are the cause of the different tints of glass available from different international manufacturers.

2. The glass-making curve. The difference between glass-making and unglassy crystallization is clearly seen in the characteristic cooling curves, in which volume is plotted against temperature. Cooling takes place from right to left. As material '1' cools to its melting point t_m, it crystallizes, and its volume drops from A to B. As material '2' (a glass former such as silica) cools, crystallization can be inhibited. Cooling continues further to point C and, if the cooling is slow enough, condensation continues to point D. This zone, from C to D, is a critical one in glass-making, in which the glass transforms from a plastic to a rigid state. This zone is called the 'transformation temperature', t_g. From C to D the glass-cooling curve flattens out towards E or F (which means the volume changes very little), where the glass reaches room temperature, t_r.

fluxes The melting point of silica is over 1,700°C. The creation of high temperatures for mass production is always an expensive matter, and the introduction of certain materials to glass formers can reduce viscosity in the molten state, and thus lower melting and working temperatures. These materials are called fluxes, and include:

sodium oxide	Na_2O
potassium oxide	K_2O
boric oxide	B_2O_3

Potassium oxide also increases the chemical resistance of the glass.

An important flux is 'cullet', or broken glass, which is an essential ingredient in helping to melt the sand.

melting and refining agents The production of a glass free of defects requires the addition of materials ensuring its consistency and, in particular, the avoidance of tiny gas bubbles. Typical materials include:

sodium sulphate	Na_2SO_4 (Glaubers salts)
sodium nitrate	$NaNO_3$
sodium chloride	$NaCl$ (common salt)
arsenious oxide	As_2O_3
calcium fluoride	CaF_2
carbon	C

crystallization preventers These include:

aluminium oxide	Al_2O_3 (alumina)

which increases the viscosity of the glass melt as it cools.

Performance modifiers include stabilizers, spectral transmission modifiers and opalizers.

stabilizers These improve chemical durability, and include:

calcium oxide	CaO (lime)
aluminium oxide	Al_2O_3 (alumina)
magnesium oxide	MgO
zinc oxide	ZnO
boron trioxide	B_2O_3

Calcium oxide also acts as a flux.

spectral transmission modifiers All non-glassy materials absorb photons (light particles) at some energy levels, and become spectral transmission modifiers, but some materials are specifically used to 'colour' glass. These affect the transmission of the glass within, and outside, the visible spectrum. They are most easily identified by the colour produced in the glass. Typical additives, with the colours each one produces, include:

chromic oxide	green
cobalt oxide	blue
cuprous oxide	red
cupric oxide	light blue
ferrous oxide	blue/green
ferric oxide	brown
selenium	pink
uranium oxide	yellow
nickel oxide	greyish brown, yellow, green, blue/violet

Additives used to decolourize glass include:
selenium
cobalt oxide
neodymium oxide

These are often introduced to correct the green colouration caused by iron impurities in the sand used as the glass former.

opalizers These affect the ability of the glass to transmit undistorted and undiffused light, and when introduced produce an opal translucent glass. They include:

calcium fluoride, which opalizes soda lime glass
calcium phosphate, which opalizes borosilicate glass

Although the number of materials in a glass may be large, the amounts of additives are usually very small (and most glasses comprise significant quantities of only a very few). For example, soda-lime glass used for containers and flat glass typically contains:

silica, as the glass former: 72.7%
sodium oxide and potassium oxide as fluxes: 13.1% and 0.5%
sodium sulphate, as the refining agent
calcium oxide, as a stabilizer: 8.4%
aluminium oxide, as a crystallization preventer and stabilizer: 1.1%

glass types

The basic constituent of soda-lime glass is silica. However, the problems of manufacture have historically led to the introduction of other materials – fluxes, melting and refining agents, crystallization preventers and stabilizers – to ease production and enhance quality. Unfortunately these materials bring with them a worsening of many of the properties which we now look for.

It is an accident of nature, therefore, that the planet's best established glass maker, the

Stiffness is a concept which depends upon the intrinsic qualities of a material to resist a change of shape, and on the shape in which the material is encountered. One of the important measures of strength is strain under stress: this is known as Young's Modulus (E), and is expressed as:

E = stress/strain

Strain is a unitless measure of change of shape in the direction measured. It is defined as C/L, where 'C' is the amount of change (in, say, metres), and 'L' is the original dimension. It can be seen that if C = L, then the amount of change is equal to the original length: the material has doubled in length. In such a case the strain is 1. All this taken together means that the Young's Modulus is effectively the tensile stress necessary to double the length of the material involved, assuming it does not break. A large value of E suggests that a lot of stress (in, say, kg/cm^2) is needed to create a particular strain (for example, lengthening).

To give some practical examples, the Young's Modulus of diamond (a very stiff material) is 1,200,000 MN/m^2, and that of biological tissue around 0.2 MN/m^2. Aluminium alloys are typically 73,000 MN/m^2, steels (which are stiffer) are about 210,000 MN/m^2 and timbers typically 11,000 MN/m^2.

Glass has a Young's Modulus of about 70,000 MN/m^2, so it can be seen that its resistance to shape change under stress is quite good, and it is similar to aluminium, which is quite a common structural material.

While the Young's Modulus is important with regard to understanding the innate properties of a *material*, engineers are more concerned with how an *element of construction* behaves. The concept of stiffness depends on the shape of something as well as the inherent physical properties of the material of which it is made. The stiffness of an element or structural member is a result both of Young's Modulus and of shape, and is expressed by the equation:

Stiffness = E x I

where 'I' is the so-called 'second moment of area'. This second moment of area relates to the cross-sectional shape of the element being considered. The further the area extends away from the Neutral Axis (the 'centre' of the shape), the greater is the second moment of area, which is why 'I' beams are so effective.

Stiffness and Young's Modulus are central to an engineer's consideration of strength in an element of design, but he also needs to know a property more related to failure (or resistance to failure). In addition to the consideration of stiffness, strength is conventionally considered in terms of the amount of compression or tension a material can withstand before failing or losing its properties of elasticity and consistency of shape.

In common with concrete, glass is very strong in compression, and comparatively weak in tension. Typical values of 1000 N/mm^2 for compression compare with 75–200 N/mm^2 for slate, 90–146 N/mm^2 for granite and between 7.5 and 70 N/mm^2 for concrete. Typical values of 100 N/mm^2 for tension compare with 60–100 N/mm^2 for aluminium and around 500 N/mm^2 for mild steel.

Such values would appear to place glass quite favourably in an engineer's vocabulary. However, glass is not a conventional material from the point of view of strength. Stress resistance in glass is dependent upon the length of time load is applied, and very much upon the integrity of the glass surface. Theoretical values for the tensile strengths of glass, based on the known chemical bonding of the glass network and the energies needed to break them, are hundreds of times greater than those which can actually be achieved in the manufactured product, and this is mainly due to defects in the surface. The normal presence of large numbers of random microcracks in the surface results in practical strengths well below theoretical strengths, and surface qualities are thus far more important than composition.

The historical importance of Griffith and his study of surface is referred to in Chapter Two of this book, and it is in the surface that glass appears to present its critical tendency to fail unpredictably. Griffith cracks, and the minute surface damage which seems to affect glass so badly have led to it being continuously doubted as an engineering material. Griffith cracks reduce glass strength from a figure around 20GPa to about 3GPa. Normal float varies in strength up to about 200MPa but the design strength used is at the lower end of the range of 50MPa and below, to take account of general handling and weathering which can introduce imperfections into the surface. This compares with a strength for glass in fibre form of 2.5GPa. There is no apparent direct relationship between the composition of glass and its strength values. At normal temperatures glass is not plastic, and it breaks when its elastic limit is exceeded. Although the molecular bonding of glass is very high, the manufactured product, with its unique chemistry and its complex (and usually 'damaged') surface, makes glass an unreliable material to consider in terms of usual strength parameters.

For this reason, many glass scientists prefer ultimately not to consider glass as having 'strength', but as having survival probabilities, which vary with the stress level. This involves Weibull analysis: a large Weibull Modulus of 20 relates to a material which is very consistent, and probably acceptable to engineers. A Weibull Modulus of 5 would relate to a material which is variable, and glass is such a material. Ironically, experimenters have deliberately abraded their glasses to make them more consistent by bringing their strength down. The obtaining of high strengths *and* a high Weibull Modulus is something which engineers would dearly love to have, although the glass-makers could find themselves selling much less glass.

Glass strengths and surface qualities can be amended by thermal or chemical toughening, which are described in detail on pages 262–3. In thermal toughening the glass is heated, and then rapidly cooled to induce compressive stress in the surface and tensile stress in the interior. This results in strengths five times that of untoughened glass at the expense of reduced maximum working temperature (the glass begins to 'detoughen' at around 300°C), but suffers the major disadvantage that the glass cannot be cut or worked after toughening. Chemical toughening achieves a similar result by replacing sodium ions (Na^+) by the larger potassium ions (K^+) in the surface, thus effectively compressing it.

■ **hardness**
Hardness in materials, their resistance to abrasion, indentation, etc, is difficult to define. The 'scratch' test uses the Moh hardness scale. The other tests are a measure of resistance to indentation. Glass is an intrinsically

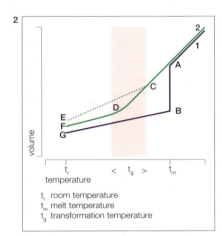

2

- t_r room temperature
- t_m melt temperature
- t_g transformation temperature

2. The glass-making curve. The difference between glass-making and unglassy crystallization is clearly seen in the characteristic cooling curves, in which volume is plotted against temperature. Cooling takes place from right to left. As material '1' cools to its melting point t_m, it crystallizes, and its volume drops from A to B. As material '2' (a glass former such as silica) cools, crystallization can be inhibited. Cooling continues further to point C and, if the cooling is slow enough, condensation continues to point D. This zone, from C to D, is a critical one in glass-making, in which the glass transforms from a plastic to a rigid state. This zone is called the 'transformation temperature', t_g. From C to D the glass-cooling curve flattens out towards E or F (which means the volume changes very little), where the glass reaches room temperature, t_r.

materials added to aid manufacture and improve performance.

glass mixtures
trace element impurities

The most common glass former in use is silica (SiO_2), readily available as sand and the most abundant material on the planet. The earth's crust consists of 27% silicon (compared to 47% oxygen, 5% iron and 0.8% aluminium), and silicates and alumina silicates are by far the most plentiful solids. In its natural state, however, sand contains many materials that, to the glass-maker, are impurities, and which may colour it or affect its performance. Iron oxide is a common impurity, and just 0.1% will give glass the slight green tint which becomes very noticeable in thick flat glass. Special glasses, such as optical products, must contain less than one-hundredth of this amount, and require much more selective extraction or purification. Other impurities include the oxides of chromium, nickel and cobalt, all of which colour the eventual glass slightly, and are the cause of the different tints of glass available from different international manufacturers.

fluxes The melting point of silica is over 1,700°C. The creation of high temperatures for mass production is always an expensive matter, and the introduction of certain materials to glass formers can reduce viscosity in the molten state, and thus lower melting and working temperatures. These materials are called fluxes, and include:

sodium oxide	Na_2O
potassium oxide	K_2O
boric oxide	B_2O_3

Potassium oxide also increases the chemical resistance of the glass.

An important flux is 'cullet', or broken glass, which is an essential ingredient in helping to melt the sand.

melting and refining agents The production of a glass free of defects requires the addition of materials ensuring its consistency and, in particular, the avoidance of tiny gas bubbles. Typical materials include:

sodium sulphate	Na_2SO_4 (Glaubers salts)
sodium nitrate	$NaNO_3$
sodium chloride	NaCl (common salt)
arsenious oxide	As_2O_3
calcium fluoride	CaF_2
carbon	C

crystallization preventers These include:

aluminium oxide	Al_2O_3 (alumina)

which increases the viscosity of the glass melt as it cools.

Performance modifiers include stabilizers, spectral transmission modifiers and opalizers.

stabilizers These improve chemical durability, and include:

calcium oxide	CaO (lime)
aluminium oxide	Al_2O_3 (alumina)
magnesium oxide	MgO
zinc oxide	ZnO
boron trioxide	B_2O_3

Calcium oxide also acts as a flux.

spectral transmission modifiers All non-glassy materials absorb photons (light particles) at some energy levels, and become spectral transmission modifiers, but some materials are specifically used to 'colour' glass. These affect the transmission of the glass within, and outside, the visible spectrum. They are most easily identified by the colour produced in the glass. Typical additives, with the colours each one produces, include:

chromic oxide	green
cobalt oxide	blue
cuprous oxide	red
cupric oxide	light blue
ferrous oxide	blue/green
ferric oxide	brown
selenium	pink
uranium oxide	yellow
nickel oxide	greyish brown, yellow, green, blue/violet

Additives used to decolourize glass include:
selenium
cobalt oxide
neodymium oxide

These are often introduced to correct the green colouration caused by iron impurities in the sand used as the glass former.

opalizers These affect the ability of the glass to transmit undistorted and undiffused light, and when introduced produce an opal translucent glass. They include:

calcium fluoride, which opalizes soda lime glass
calcium phosphate, which opalizes borosilicate glass

Although the number of materials in a glass may be large, the amounts of additives are usually very small (and most glasses comprise significant quantities of only a very few). For example, soda-lime glass used for containers and flat glass typically contains:

silica, as the glass former: 72.7%
sodium oxide and potassium oxide as fluxes: 13.1% and 0.5%
sodium sulphate, as the refining agent
calcium oxide, as a stabilizer: 8.4%
aluminium oxide, as a crystallization preventer and stabilizer: 1.1%

glass types

The basic constituent of soda-lime glass is silica. However, the problems of manufacture have historically led to the introduction of other materials – fluxes, melting and refining agents, crystallization preventers and stabilizers – to ease production and enhance quality. Unfortunately these materials bring with them a worsening of many of the properties which we now look for.

It is an accident of nature, therefore, that the planet's best established glass maker, the oxide of silica, is capable of producing an almost perfect glass on its own.

Fused silica has a thermal expansion coefficient of 0.54×10^{-6}/ °C, compared with a figure of 7.9 for soda lime. Translated to a window size, expansion and contraction of glass is not generally problematic. A 1 m dimension only expands by 0.3 mm over the temperature range of 40°C to which it may normally be subjected. This compares with an expansion of about 1 mm for a 1 m length of aluminium over the same temperature scale. The real advantage occurs when local and rapid heating is applied: in these circumstances the pure silica is a significantly better performer, and much less likely to fracture.

Of greater significance, however, are its temperature/viscosity characteristics, which determine how viscous or stiff it is at different temperatures.

Three temperatures need to be known to describe the glass-making and thermal properties of a glass, corresponding to particular aspects of viscosity as the temperature rises:

— the strain point is the temperature above which stress release and flow become important characteristics in behaviour
— the annealing point is the temperature at which stresses in the glass are quickly relieved
— the softening point is the temperature at which the glass becomes soft enough to flow (and extend) under load

For soda-lime glass these are:

strain point   520°C
annealing point   545°C
softening point   735°C

3

	PbO	BaO	B₂O₃	SiO₂	H₂O	Na₂O	K₂O	Al₂O₃	CaO	MgO	FeO/Fe₂O₃	Co₂O₄	Se	NiO
Fused silica				99.9	0.1									
Borosilicate			13.0	81.0	0.03	4.0	0.4	2.5						
Aluminosilicate		6.0	5.0	62.0/57.0	0.03	1.0	16.0	9.0	7.0					
Fluorescent tube		0.8		71.4	0.03	15.0	1.7	2.2	4.6	3.9				
Container				72.8	0.03	14.5	1.7		10.5					
Lead	29.0/82.0		0.0/11.0	57.0/3.0	0.03	4.0	8.5/9.0	1.0/2.0						
Clear soda lime				73.0	0.03	13.1/17.0	0.0/0.5	1.3	5.0/8.4	4.0/3.0	0.1			
Green				73.0	0.03	15.9	0.3	1.3	6.5	3.0	0.5			
Blue/Green				73.0	0.03	15.9	0.3	1.3	6.5	3.0	0.5	0.0005		
Auto. bronze				73.0	0.03	15.9	0.3	1.3	6.5	3.0	0.39	0.0008	0.0012	
Arch. bronze				73.0	0.03	15.9	0.3	1.3	6.5	3.0	0.3	0.0040	0.0012	
Grey/blue				73.0	0.03	15.9	0.3	1.3	6.5	3.0	0.3	0.0085	0.0020	
Grey/green				73.0	0.03	15.9	0.3	1.3	6.5	3.0	0.32	0.0064		0.041
Dark/grey				73.0	0.03	15.9	0.3	1.3	6.5	3.0	0.09	0.0020		0.010

(MECHANICAL FUNCTION: Fused silica through Lead; TRANSMISSION FUNCTION: Clear soda lime through Dark/grey)

3. Chemical mix of common glasses. The table shows the approximate percentage contents of the glasses in common use in architecture and product design. The most common form of window glass, clear soda-lime glass, occupies the central slot across the table. The dominance of silica is marked by the vertical slot. The chemistry of the materials above the soda lime slot is primarily concerned with changes to mechanical performance. That of the materials below the slot are mainly concerned with altering radiation transmission, and acts to filter the colour of light. The tiny quantities of materials needed to amend the balance of wavelength transmission is evident, and helps to explain the necessary restriction in the ranges made available to ensure colour matching. A table such as this can only be indicative of contents. Precise contents are very much the domain of producers, and should always be obtained from them for any specific product.

For fused silica they are:

strain point   987°C
annealing point   1082°C
softening point   1594°C

It is worth noting that the melting point of pure silica (also known as quartz) is 1726°C, and that the melt temperature in a soda-lime flat glass plant is about 1600°C. The additives in soda lime have a dramatic effect on its softening point, and its ease of manufacture.

With a Young's Modulus similar to that of soda lime, it is these thermal performance characteristics which give fused silica its advantages in the use, for example, in high temperature tungsten halogen light sources.

Although high temperature characteristics give fused silica important and useful properties, its use in large-scale manufacturing is, at present, of limited practicality. The lowering of the melting point was important historically in making the production of glass possible. Today, higher temperatures are much easier to achieve, but only at a cost, both in

manufacturing plant and in terms of energy.

Considering the number of materials available and necessary to make glasses, it can be seen that the number of glasses which can be made is infinite, with very variable compositions and performances. However, the most-used glasses in building fall into five groups, chemically:

soda-lime glasses These are the most common glasses, used for flat glass, light bulbs, containers, etc. Significantly, the soda-lime family is the one used in the development of the float process.

fused silica, or quartz, glasses These include the only important single component glass, and are characterized by high melting and working temperatures, a very low coefficient of thermal expansion (and thus resistance to thermal shock), and high chemical resistance. Its high melting point makes it both expensive and difficult to produce as a primary melt glass. Heating it to a lower temperature still produces a glass, but not one of good transparency. An alternative form can be made from so-called 'phase separable' alkali-borosilicate glasses. Heating these to 600°C produces a phase-separated material: the alkali-borate phase can be leached out with acid, and the remaining 9% silica phase, known as the product Vycor, can be transformed into a porous clear glass suitable for dialysis. Glasses in the fused silica family are used typically for high technology applications such as laboratory ware and light guides, where their strength and very low thermal expansion coefficient are so useful.

borosilicate glasses Boric oxide acts both as a glass former and as a flux; it replaces much of the sodium oxide, and the content of alumina is increased significantly. The resulting glass is very resistant to chemical corrosion, and has a low thermal expansion coefficient, one-third that of soda-lime glasses (although six times that of fused silica). The borosilicate glass family has an enormous range of uses: in laboratories as containers and plumbing, as the glass for lamps, and in domestic cooking utensils. The trade product Pyrex is a typical form. Heat-strengthening borosilicate glasses increases their impact resistance and with their low thermal expansion make fire-resistant glazing.

lead glasses Lead oxide replaces much of the calcium oxide, and acts both as a flux and a stabilizer, producing a glass of low melting and working temperatures, and high refractive index and specific gravity. The quantity of lead oxide can be varied enormously (by a factor of three), and the high lead content glasses (in which lead oxide comprises more than 80%) are used for radiation shielding.

4–6. Refraction. It is a commonly visible phenomenon that light rays bend when they pass from one transparent material to another. Figure 4 shows ray 3 reflected at the critical angle. Figure 5 shows the essential action of the lens. Figure 6 shows the bending of light in water.

alumino silicate glasses While still comprising more than 50% silica, the aluminium content of these glasses is ten times that of a soda-lime glass. Boric oxide is present, and the resultant glass has great chemical durability. A typical glass is known as E-glass, and is used for the manufacture of glass fibres.

There are other important groups of glasses of less immediate current use in the building industry; and these are described elsewhere.

Table 3 shows the chemical composition of various glasses, and table 40 on page 269 shows the physical properties of the main groups compared with other materials.

physical properties

The intrinsic and essential properties of glass are transparency and durability. Other properties become significant in accordance with the use to which the material is put. The various fluxes and modifiers, which are introduced in order to facilitate manufacture, have an effect on these properties, and glass design development has identified a wide range of compositions to permit the achievement of specific physical properties. The principal significant properties of glasses used for buildings are in table 40 and as follows:

— light/radiation
   transmittance/reflectance/absorptance
— refractive index
— thermal properties
— strength
— hardness and abrasion resistance
— chemical durability
— weathering durability
— specific gravity
— fire resistance
— sound attenuation

■ **light/radiation transmittance**

This is important both in terms of total quantity and in terms of spectral distribution, and has been discussed in general terms earlier. The control and tailoring of radiation transmission, reflection and absorption is of fundamental importance in the consideration of glass in architecture, and is discussed as a subject in its own right later in this appendix.

■ **refractive index**

This is a measure of the amount by which light is 'bent' as it passes through a glass and is comparatively constant for all glasses. It is 1.52 for soda-lime glasses, and varies from 1.47 for borosilicate glasses to 1.56 for lead glass. The refractive index for a glass varies according to the wavelength of the radiation considered, and the index of all glasses decreases with increasing wavelength. The refractive index is most important in optical use, as discussed in Appendix Four.

When light passes from an optically dense material to a less dense material it is refracted away from the normal (normal meaning perpendicular to the surface). At the 'critical angle' it is reflected back from

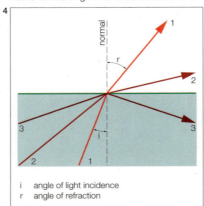

i angle of light incidence
r angle of refraction

the surface, and retained within the optically denser material. This phenomenon of refraction is the key to the straight rod apparently bending in water, and to the principles of lenses and fibre optics. In mathematical terms, this phenomenon is expressed as:

$$n = \frac{\sin i}{\sin r} = \frac{\text{velocity of light in vacuo}}{\text{velocity of light in medium 2}}$$

where n is the refractive index of medium 2 (such as glass), and i and r are the angles of incidence and refraction (see figures 4–6).

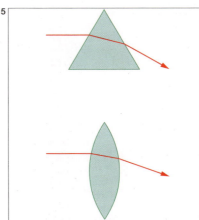

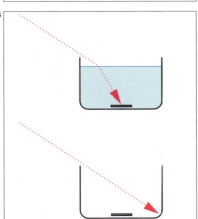

■ thermal properties

Significant thermal properties include:

— maximum working
    temperature
— specific heat
— thermal conductivity
— thermal expansion

The mechanical performance of glass, as a product of fusion and as an intrinsically brittle material, is highly dependent upon its thermal properties.

All glasses are characterized by three temperature points, which relate to the viscosities exhibited:

— The softening point: this is the temperature at which the glass flows readily under load, and is important to the manufacturing process. The viscosity is $\log_{10} n = 7.8$ poises
— The annealing point: this is the point above which stresses in the glass are relieved quickly. The viscosity is $\log_{10} n = 13$ poises
— The strain point: this is the temperature above which stress release and flow begin to have an effect; it is the effective working temperature. The viscosity is $\log_{10} n = 14.5$ poises

The annealing point is usually in the order of 10% above the strain point, and the softening point 50–60% above the strain point. Typical figures are given in table 40.

maximum working temperature

Strain point is usually well above the performance requirements for buildings, but it becomes important when glass is used for

7. Specific heat. The specific heat of glass occupies the same sort of range as other building materials. Water is seen as having a specific heat over five times as large, which explains its value for heat storage in passive solar design.

8. Thermal conductivity. Glass is a fairly good insulator, but metals conduct heat very well: aluminium conducts over 400 times more readily than glass. Porous materials exhibit conductivities which vary widely with their air or water content. With the conductivity of air as low as it is, its value in insulation is obvious.

9. Thermal expansion. The diagram shows the expansion which might be expected in a 5 m length of a material over a temperature difference of 100°C. Soda-lime glass has a low expansion compared to most materials. High performance glasses are among the materials with the smallest expansions, and ceramic glass exhibits virtually no expansion at all.

7

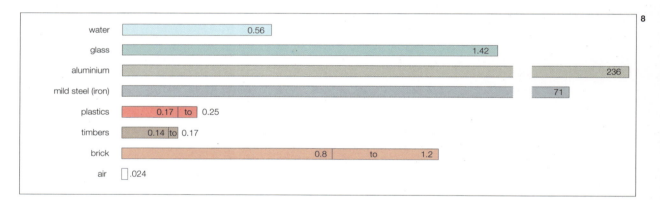

8

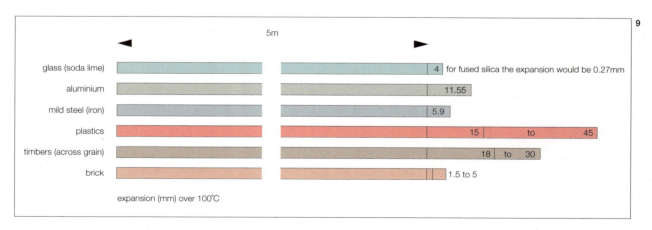

9

cooking or other high temperature applications. Typical strain points are:

soda-lime glass	520°C
borosilicate glass (Pyrex)	515°C
fused silica	987°C

It should be noted that the advantages of borosilicate glass are not concerned so much with the temperatures at which they can work, but with their ability to withstand thermal shock, a rapid change in temperature. This is dependent upon the specific heat of glass (which affects the rate at which heat will raise its temperature), its thermal conductivity (the rate at which heat travels through the glass and is distributed), and the coefficient of thermal expansion.

specific heat is a measure of the amount of heat required to raise the temperature of a material through 1°C for every unit of its weight. It is thus a measure of how much heat can effectively be stored in the material.

The specific heats of glasses are comparatively constant, varying by about 25%. The values of 0.85–1.00 kJ/kg °C for glass compare with 0.92 kJ/kg °C for aluminium, 1.26 kJ/kg °C for polycarbonate and 4.19 kJ/kg °C for water. The value for fused silica is much lower than for soda-lime glass.

thermal conductivity expresses how quickly heat passes through a material, measured here in W/m °C. This property varies very widely in materials. Plastics and timbers conduct heat rather poorly which makes them good insulators. Glass is a fairly good insulator.

10. Strength. Longitudinal elasticity: Young's Modulus. This is a simple property in theory, which can turn out to be complex in reality. The lack of homogeneity, or the presence of faults, in a material can significantly affect its ability to retain its shape when pressure is applied to it. The diagram shows the effect of stiffness: the resistance to a change in length of a material when a stretching force is applied to it. The extension shown is that which would occur in centimetres when a force of 0.1 GPa is applied to a piece of material 10 m long. This is effectively 1,000 x the reciprocal of the Young's Modulus. Glass is seen to be stiff: the problem of strength arises as a result of its brittle nature in the flat state.

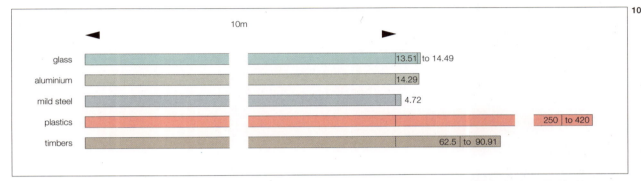

Values vary over a range of about 35%, from 1.02 W/m °C for soda-lime glass to 1.13 for borosilicate and 1.38 for fused silica. These figures are very low compared with 71 for iron and 218.5 for aluminium. The temperature gradients set up by local heating contribute to the thermal shock effects.

thermal expansion is a critical property in design, both because of the resulting need to create space around elements which expand, and because of the problems of differential expansion between materials which are combined to work together in a building element.

Whereas the other thermal properties of glass vary little with composition (± 15–20%), thermal expansion coefficients vary by a factor of 20, from $0.54 \times 10^{-6}/°C$ for fused silica to over $10 \times 10^{-6}/°C$, and borosilicate about $3 \times 10^{-6}/°C$. Soda-lime glass has a coefficient of $7.9 \times 10^{-6}/°C$. These values compare with $12 \times 10^{-6}/°C$ for steel and $24 \times 10^{-6}/°C$ for aluminium.

Glasses with low thermal expansion coefficients have an intrinsically good thermal shock resistance, and conversely those with high coefficients are those most effectively treated by thermal toughening.

Borosilicate will survive quenching from

300°C to the temperature of cold water, but soda-lime will break in quenching from 100°C.

The importance of thermal shock characteristics, and of the range of expansion coefficients resulting from differences in chemical composition, is a measure of the way performance can be amended by composition.

■ strength

The strength of a material is a property which cannot be described in terms of one characteristic. The ability to withstand compression, tension, bending, twist, shear and other stresses, all deriving ultimately from their different molecular structures and their inner super-molecular structure, is not usually uniform in materials. The invention of reinforced concrete is an example of a combination of materials designed to be good in tension and compression, which act together to satisfy specific requirements. With its extraordinary chemistry, and its state as an uncrystallized pseudo-liquid, glass is a brittle material with widely differing strength qualities. While many building materials are employed very much, or even specifically, with regard to their strength, glass is not generally considered as an engineering material, and the uneven and somewhat unpredictable strength of common

glasses is one of their major disadvantages. To understand the nature of this unpredictability, and its importance, it is essential to understand the concepts of strength which are necessary to the engineer. The main concepts under consideration are stiffness and failure.

The stresses commonly referred to in a discussion of materials' strengths are tensile, compression and shear stresses. In elementary terms, the phenomena are straightforward. Substances placed under stress (or 'load') suffer strain (or deformation of dimension). In early stages of stress materials are often elastic, which means that they return to their original shape. However, at higher levels of stress they suddenly refuse to return: such a level is called the elastic limit, and is a measure of the effectiveness of the material as a structural element. A beam which remained deflected after loading when the load was removed would be useless. Beyond the elastic limit further stress eventually causes failure. Materials are characterized by their elastic limit, and by the point at which they fail, but also by their stiffness: the extent to which they resist changes of shape under stress. It will be readily understood that stiffness is a critical criterion in the ability of a material to perform structurally.

Stiffness is a concept which depends upon the intrinsic qualities of a material to resist a change of shape, and on the shape in which the material is encountered. One of the important measures of strength is strain under stress: this is known as Young's Modulus (E), and is expressed as:

E = stress/strain

Strain is a unitless measure of change of shape in the direction measured. It is defined as C/L, where 'C' is the amount of change (in, say, metres), and 'L' is the original dimension. It can be seen that if C = L, then the amount of change is equal to the original length: the material has doubled in length. In such a case the strain is 1. All this taken together means that the Young's Modulus is effectively the tensile stress necessary to double the length of the material involved, assuming it does not break. A large value of E suggests that a lot of stress (in, say, kg/cm²) is needed to create a particular strain (for example, lengthening).

To give some practical examples, the Young's Modulus of diamond (a very stiff material) is 1,200,000 MN/m², and that of biological tissue around 0.2 MN/m². Aluminium alloys are typically 73,000 MN/m², steels (which are stiffer) are about 210,000 MN/m² and timbers typically 11,000 MN/m².

Glass has a Young's Modulus of about 70,000 MN/m², so it can be seen that its resistance to shape change under stress is quite good, and it is similar to aluminium, which is quite a common structural material.

While the Young's Modulus is important with regard to understanding the innate properties of a *material*, engineers are more concerned with how an *element of construction* behaves. The concept

of stiffness depends on the shape of something as well as the inherent physical properties of the material of which it is made. The stiffness of an element or structural member is a result both of Young's Modulus and of shape, and is expressed by the equation:

Stiffness = E x I

where 'I' is the so-called 'second moment of area'. This second moment of area relates to the cross-sectional shape of the element being considered. The further the area extends away from the Neutral Axis (the 'centre' of the shape), the greater is the second moment of area, which is why 'I' beams are so effective.

Stiffness and Young's Modulus are central to an engineer's consideration of strength in an element of design, but he also needs to know a property more related to failure (or resistance to failure). In addition to the consideration of stiffness, strength is conventionally considered in terms of the amount of compression or tension a material can withstand before failing or losing its properties of elasticity and consistency of shape.

In common with concrete, glass is very strong in compression, and comparatively weak in tension. Typical values of 1000 N/mm² for compression compare with 75–200 N/mm² for slate, 90–146 N/mm² for granite and between 7.5 and 70 N/mm² for concrete. Typical values of 100 N/mm² for tension compare with 60–100 N/mm² for aluminium and around 500 N/mm² for mild steel.

Such values would appear to place glass quite favourably in an engineer's vocabulary. However, glass is not a conventional material from the point of view of strength. Stress resistance in glass is dependent upon the

length of time load is applied, and very much upon the integrity of the glass surface. Theoretical values for the tensile strengths of glass, based on the known chemical bonding of the glass network and the energies needed to break them, are hundreds of times greater than those which can actually be achieved in the manufactured product, and this is mainly due to defects in the surface. The normal presence of large numbers of random microcracks in the surface results in practical strengths well below theoretical strengths, and surface qualities are thus far more important than composition.

The historical importance of Griffith and his study of surface is referred to in Chapter Two of this book, and it is in the surface that glass appears to present its critical tendency to fail unpredictably. Griffith cracks, and the minute surface damage which seems to affect glass so badly have led to it being continuously doubted as an engineering material. Griffith cracks reduce glass strength from a figure around 20GPa to about 3GPa. Normal float varies in strength up to about 200MPa but the design strength used is at the lower end of the range of 50MPa and below, to take account of general handling and weathering which can introduce imperfections into the surface. This compares with a strength for glass in fibre form of 2.5GPa. There is no apparent direct relationship between the composition of glass and its strength values. At normal temperatures glass is not plastic, and it breaks when its elastic limit is exceeded. Although the molecular bonding of glass is very high, the manufactured product, with its unique chemistry and its complex (and usually 'damaged') surface, makes glass an unreliable material to consider in terms of usual strength parameters.

For this reason, many glass scientists prefer ultimately not to consider glass as having 'strength', but as having survival probabilities, which vary with the stress level. This involves Weibull analysis: a large Weibull Modulus of 20 relates to a material which is very consistent, and probably acceptable to engineers. A Weibull Modulus of 5 would relate to a material which is variable, and glass is such a material. Ironically, experimenters have deliberately abraded their glasses to make them more consistent by bringing their strength down. The obtaining of high strengths *and* a high Weibull Modulus is something which engineers would dearly love to have, although the glass-makers could find themselves selling much less glass.

Glass strengths and surface qualities can be amended by thermal or chemical toughening, which are described in detail on pages 262–3. In thermal toughening the glass is heated, and then rapidly cooled to induce compressive stress in the surface and tensile stress in the interior. This results in strengths five times that of untoughened glass at the expense of reduced maximum working temperature (the glass begins to 'detoughen' at around 300°C), but suffers the major disadvantage that the glass cannot be cut or worked after toughening. Chemical toughening achieves a similar result by replacing sodium ions (Na⁺) by the larger potassium ions (K⁺) in the surface, thus effectively compressing it.

■ **hardness**

Hardness in materials, their resistance to abrasion, indentation, etc, is difficult to define. The 'scratch' test uses the Moh hardness scale. The other tests are a measure of resistance to indentation. Glass is an intrinsically hard material, comparable with steel; its hardness is one of its most important properties, and the basis of glazes.

The Moh scale from 1 to 10 extends from talc (magnesium silicate) at 1 to diamond at 10. Quartz, a natural form of silica, has a hardness of 7. Soda-lime glass has a hardness of 5.4–5.8.

■ chemical durability

The hardness of glass is matched by its chemical durability. The ability of glass to resist chemical attack is the reason for its widespread use in the making of containers where the absence of contamination is important. Transparency, permitting the inspection of contents is an enormous additional advantage.

Chemical durability is commonly measured on a scale of 1–4, shown in table 40. This relates to resistance to water, acid, and weathering from water and sulphur dioxide. Normal weathering corrosion can be of the order of 8 microns per year. Hard borosilicates are particularly acid resistant, and soda-lime glasses can be made up to resist alkaline attack. Most glasses, however, are susceptible to lime and concentrated solutions of caustic

11. Specific gravity. The cubes show the different volumes of the materials which comprise the same weight.

soda (sodium hydroxide), and are attacked by hydrofluoric and phosphoric acids, which, as a result, are used in etching.

■ weathering durability

This is a result of the combination of hardness and chemical durability, depending as it does on the natural resistance of the material to chemical attack, and its ability to withstand the cleaning necessary to its performance as an undistorting transmitter of light.

■ specific gravity

High specific gravity in a material provides advantages in certain respects (for example in sound insulation), but is generally disadvantageous in contributing to difficulties in handling, fixing and support. Glass is a fairly light material with a specific gravity of 2.47 for soda lime and 2.2 for fused silica. Lead glass has a specific gravity between 3 and 6. The addition of fluxes and modifiers generally has the effect of increasing specific gravity. Comparative specific gravities are 2.7 for aluminium, 7.86 for iron, and 1.1–1.2 for transparent plastics. The low specific gravities of plastics are important in their usefulness as lightweight alternatives to glass.

■ fire resistance

The performance in fire of conventional window glass is very poor. Until recently, the use of embedded wire to obtain structural integrity in glazing subjected to fire, has been the only effective way of providing resistance. Now however, the use of strong, low expansion materials, such as borosilicate glasses, and the invention of sandwich systems incorporating fire-resisting interlayers, has transformed the potential of glazing as a fire barrier.

■ sound attenuation

As a component in a wall, glass must frequently satisfy sound attenuation requirements. Installed as a single sheet its performance is limited, but multiple systems can provide good attenuation, particularly if combinations of glass thicknesses are used to control sympathetic vibration and selectively dampen sound at different frequencies. Adequate spacing (substantially more than conventional double glazing) with sound-absorbing lining is essential if good performance is to be achieved (as is necessary, for example, in airport control towers). Laminated glass also provides an improvement in sound attenuation compared with conventional single glazing.

light transmission
the nature of light and
radiation transmission

While the use of glass as a building material requires designers to consider all its physical properties, it is its ability to transmit radiation in general, and visible light in particular, which gives glass its unique significance.

The prime performance characteristic of glass in relation to architecture is the transmission of light, and light itself is in many ways a mysterious phenomenon. Light transmission has been variously described in terms of wave or particle theory, in ways which have become continuously enriched since James Clerk Maxwell postulated his theory of electromagnetic radiation in 1864.

The idea of wavelength helps to explain the apparent periodic and pulsating nature of radiation, seen in the phenomena of diffraction and interference. Thinking of light as being propagated in waves helps explain these phenomena, in terms of variations in distances between waves, and the frequencies with which they occur.

Considered in terms of particles, we can propose that when atoms are extremely excited and vibrating, they discharge their energy in the form of photons that escape from the atoms at the speed of light and interact with whatever they hit, passing easily through space and bouncing off or being absorbed by various gases and non-transparent solids. As the temperature of a body rises above what is known as absolute zero, -273°C, the temperature at which all matter ceases to 'move', the energy associated with that movement is emitted as electromagnetic radiation which can broadly be considered as heat. The hotter it gets, and the more excited the atoms or molecules become, the higher

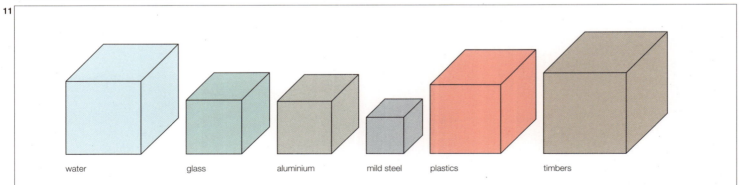

water   glass   aluminium   mild steel   plastics   timbers

12. Solar radiation and room radiation. The two curves demonstrate the different wavelength distributions of solar radiation, and the radiation emitted by a material at 21°C. The vertical scale is not the same for both curves in respect of absolute energy emission.

13. Spectral distribution of sunlight. Sunlight approximates to what is known as black body radiation. Black body radiation is defined as the thermal radiation present in a closed cavity with opaque walls at a uniform temperature. It is characterized by a continuous spectrum. The colour of light sources (such as tungsten filament and fluorescent lamps) is commonly defined in terms of the nearest black body curve. The loss of energy caused by the earth's atmosphere, and the dips occurring at different wavelengths, combine to produce the spectrum of sunlight experienced at sea level.

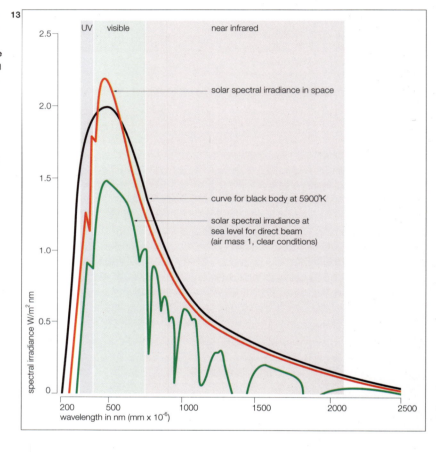

13

solar spectral irradiance in space

curve for black body at 5900°K

solar spectral irradiance at sea level for direct beam (air mass 1, clear conditions)

spectral irradiance W/m² nm

wavelength in nm (mm x 10⁻⁶)

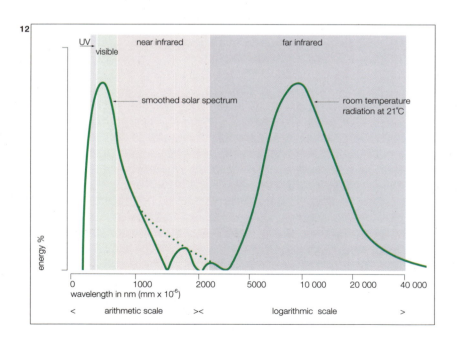

12

smoothed solar spectrum

room temperature radiation at 21°C

energy %

wavelength in nm (mm x 10⁻⁶)

< arithmetic scale >< logarithmic scale >

the frequency of the radiation, and the shorter the wavelength (frequency in radiation is inversely proportional to wavelength).

Thought of in terms of wavelength, radiation commonly encountered in everyday life includes radio-waves, with wavelengths ranging from a few millimetres to a few kilometres, and X-rays and gamma rays, with wavelengths less than 100nm (nm = nanometre, and 1 nm = 10^{-6}mm, or one-millionth of a millimetre).

The energy emitted by a hot body (that is, any body hotter than -273°C), is characterized by a curve which indicates how much energy is being put out at different wavelengths. Physicists can predict mathematically the shape of the curve for a body made of an ideal material, and the term black body radiation is given to the infinite family of theoretical smooth curves which characterize bodies radiating at different temperatures. The emission and absorption characteristics of a material are proportional, and a black body (a perfect radiation absorber) is also a perfect emitter. In fact, bodies are not ideal and homogeneous in terms of materials. They are made of chemicals the atomic structure of which causes them to emit energy in a unique way. This curve is not smooth for any particular material, but has characteristic peaks and troughs, resulting from its molecular structure. Despite this bumpy nature, however, the curve can be identified by its general shape and position, and where its peak energy output occurs.

The sun, the most atomically active body in our planetary system, emits energy with a curve similar in shape and position to a black body with a temperature of 5900°K. It is this temperature which, in other fields,

14. Transparency and the photon. Photons are absorbed when their energy levels correspond with the differences of energy levels of electrons in the transparent material. This is the essence of filter action.

is also called the colour temperature, which we may strive for in a lamp if we wish to simulate sunlight.

The solar spectrum (the band of wavelengths across which the sun emits radiation) extends between wavelengths of about 300 and 2100 nm. Light is that band of radiation with wavelengths between approximately 400 and 780 nm, to which the human eye responds. Between 300 and 400 nm radiation is the ultraviolet zone, and between 780 and 2100 nm is the near infrared. The content of solar radiation is described by the characteristic solar curve, approximating to that of a black body peaking at about 500 nm. The effective content of the solar spectrum actually experienced (for example at sea level) varies in terms of amount and spectral distribution in accordance with the material it passes through. Figure 13 shows the curve in space, and at a typical point at the earth's surface (the UK), compared with the emission curve for a black body.

We have noted that radiation energy is inversely proportional to wavelength: the longer the wavelength, the lower the energy. Moreover, as can be seen from the solar curve, energy emitted by the sun follows a curve indicating that only a small proportion of energy is put out at the ultraviolet end of the spectrum, that most is put out at a wavelength around 500 nm, and that energy emission then gradually falls as the wavelength increases.

The energy content of solar radiation is divided as follows:

ultraviolet	3%
visible	53%
near infrared	44%

All this energy, when absorbed by a material, whether it be glass, a building or a person, is eventually converted into heat. A body thus warmed will itself emit heat, radiating this at wavelengths which correspond to its temperature. Radiation emitted by, for example, a carpet warmed by the sun, occurs at very long wavelengths (3000–50,000 nm). For reasons which are briefly explained below, glass is an almost perfect transmitter of short wave solar energy: the wavelength at which it transmits radiation most readily coincides almost exactly with the peak emission wavelength of the sun. At the longer wavelengths characteristic of the radiation emission of a warm carpet, or warm air, however, it is completely opaque or absorbing. It is easy to see how a knowledge of selective transparency and absorptivity in a glass is essential to the understanding of its performance.

■ transparency and the photon

Although it is convenient to consider the transmission of light as a wave phenomenon, discussed in terms of wavelength and frequency, the concept of transparency demands consideration of it in terms of particles interacting with the atomic structure of materials: this double view is typical of the age of the quantum theory. Knowing how photons travel through glass, and keep or lose their energy in relation to wavelength, is particularly important in the development of new materials with predicted transmission performances.

Most of the building materials we are familiar with, such as timber, concrete and steel, are opaque in the forms in which we normally encounter them. Glass, however, is transparent to the visible part of the solar

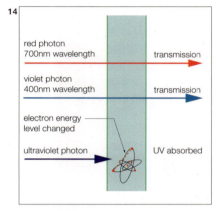

red photon
700nm wavelength — transmission

violet photon
400nm wavelength — transmission

electron energy
level changed

ultraviolet photon — UV absorbed

spectrum, making it a very special product for architecture and a multiplicity of other uses.

The particle theory of electromagnetic radiation proposes that light consists of photons of different energy levels, and that these levels correspond to the colours we see. Photon energy is inversely proportional to wavelength: the higher the energy of a photon, the lower the wavelength; for example, a photon associated with red light having a wavelength of 700 nm will have only about 57% of the energy of a photon associated with violet light at 400 nm. The phenomena of transmission and absorption are related to the action photons have on the electrons in the atoms and molecules of materials they impinge on.

The atomic structure of materials incorporates positively charged nuclei, around which are negatively charged electrons at different energy levels, the differences between which can correspond to the energies of photons responsible for visible light, infrared and ultraviolet radiation. It is a property of matter that photons will interact with these electrons, but only if the energy level of the photon corresponds with the differences of energy levels between the electron states. Photon

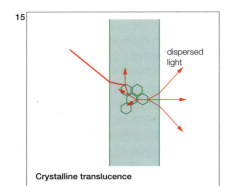

15

Crystalline translucence

interaction leads to electrons being promoted to higher energy levels and photons being absorbed, with a corresponding absorption of the colour of photons concerned. When absorbed by a material, a photon is able to lose its excess energy to the vibrations of the matrix, resulting in an increase in temperature of the material which then emits that heat as long-wave radiation.

To be perfectly transparent, a material must be such that the separations of valency electron energy states do not correspond with the energies of the photon. If this condition is not met, and the material has energy level separations corresponding with the energies of photons of a particular colour, then that colour will be absorbed. We will see later how this knowledge provides the theoretical basis for designed transmission, absorption and reflection performance, and for the consideration of materials as potential colour filters, absorbing or transmitting light of different colours by design.

In a glass or other colourless transparent material, photons in the visible region are not absorbed. In most glasses, the valency electron energy separations are in the ultraviolet part of the spectrum, which is why they usually absorb ultraviolet light. However, if a

15. Translucency typically occurs in crystalline materials, where many interreflections cause light beams to be dispersed.

16. Transmission of soda-lime glass. The spectral transmission of a typical soda-lime glass corresponds broadly with the solar spectral irradiance across the visible spectrum, but also remains fairly high in the near infrared, dropping markedly between 2,000 and 2,500 nm.

transparent material is in a finely divided state, or micro-crystalline, the large number of randomly orientated surfaces serve to scatter the light, producing translucence.

Glass is not micro-crystalline, and its ability to become solid while retaining its liquid-like structure is why it is often called a 'super-cooled liquid'.

Some materials absorb light across the whole visible spectrum and appear black, or absorb some colours and reflect others, thus appearing opaque but coloured. However, if the material concerned is only a few hundred atoms or molecules thick, only a small proportion of the photons will be absorbed, and the thin film of material will be transparent to a greater or lesser degree, the colours it transmits or absorbs varying with the material concerned, provided there are no interference effects.

The wonder of glass transparency is that, as shown in figure 16, the wavelengths of radiation it transmits correspond to those parts of the solar spectrum to which the eye is sensitive, the visible parts.

A perfect transmitter would permit the passage of all energy over the wavelengths considered. Glass, in its various forms, and the coatings which may be applied to it, transmits light at different wavelengths in different proportions. Some of these are intrinsic to the chemical properties of glass, and are virtually unchangeable, but as glass and window science has progressed, we have become more concerned with describing and achieving required performances, whether in single sheet materials, or in more complex layered assemblies.

This may all seem like irrelevant physics in a book on glass in architecture. However, in so far as the future of glass depends upon

selective control of the solar spectrum and the accurate prediction of performance, the workings of glasses and coatings, and how to control what happens to photons, need to be understood at the most basic level, if only to enable architects, designers and glass scientists to communicate with one another.

■ the light transmission of glass

Transparency is a complex phenomenon. The nature of light, and the variation in transmission and absorption experienced by different materials, give different glasses their varying performances and uses.

A typical glass has a transmission coefficient of 60% to over 80%, between about 400 and 2,500 nm. However, it does not transmit at all below 300 nm unless it has a

very low iron content, and transmits very little between 3000 nm to 4000 nm, and above. It is the re-emission of surfaces heated behind glass at wavelengths above 3000 nm which causes the greenhouse effect.

So-called coloured or tinted glasses have an appearance and performance deriving from the differing degrees of absorptivity and transmissivity given by the chemicals in the melt.

The performance of a glass as a transmitter is a result of its selective transmittance across ultraviolet, visible light and near infrared wavebands.

The range of selectivity of transmission between light and heat is limited by the fact that 53% of all the energy in solar radiation is in the visible spectrum. It therefore is not possible to decrease total radiation transmission

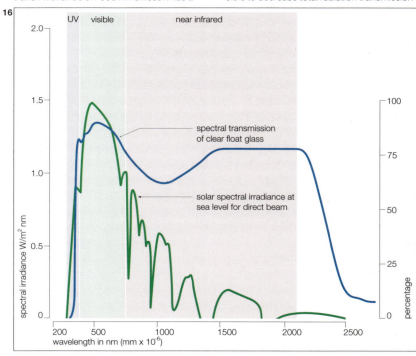

16

spectral transmission
of clear float glass

solar spectral irradiance at
sea level for direct beam

below 50% without affecting light transmission. The best possible theoretical heat performance for a 50% light transmitter is about 26% direct solar heat transmission (giving a total solar heat transmission of about 49% allowing for absorption and re-radiation).

The apparent colour of a glass is a result of the selective absorption of the visible spectral range. Thus a green glass appears so because light reflected from it towards an observer has suffered absorption of light of other spectral wavelengths.

Most architectural high performance body-tinted glasses rely on iron oxide in various quantities to absorb infrared radiation and on cobalt oxide, selenium and other chemicals to affect the glass colour. In adding the colourizers, the light transmission of the glass is reduced. Current commercial glasses usually introduce colourizers at the same time as reducing iron oxide contents, and thus decrease the vision : thermal efficiency ratio of the glass.

The standard mix used for clear float glass makes up 99.5% of the composition of all commercial window glass. The remaining 0.5% is a variable mix consisting primarily of ferric and ferrous oxide, with small amounts of cobalt oxide, selenium and nickel oxide. The very small quantities of colourizers required make fine-tuning difficult. For example, 180 g of cobalt oxide make the difference between bronze and grey glass in a 4,000 kg truck-load of frit.

Mixes of glass which increase colourizers at the expense of iron oxide are characterized by increases in thermal transmissivities at the expense of transmission in the visible spectrum.

The selective transmissivities and absorptivities of different glasses can be

17. Comparative energy transmissions of glasses. The graph shows percentage transmissions of typical glasses. Of particular significance is the reduction of transmission in the visible part of the spectrum, compared with that of infrared. Unless the cutting out of light is an objective, the chemistry of window glass should usually maximize transmission in the visible zone. The favourable distribution of green glass from this point of view is worth noting. Manufacturers should be consulted for the performance of particular glasses.

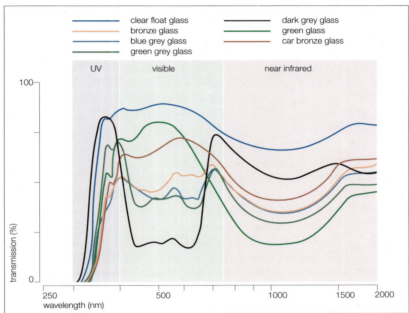

described in terms of the following criteria.
— Dominant wavelength of transmission: The dominant wavelength value is that of the light most dominant in the beam giving the essential colour hue in transmission. Glasses are characterized by two or three peaks of light transmission. For most glasses one of these is around 400 nm at the violet end of the visible spectrum.
— Transmission at 1,050 nm: This wavelength is the centre of the absorption band created by ferrous oxide, which is the principal functioning agent in heat-absorbing glasses.
— Colour purity: This may be described in terms of excitation purities; neutral tones have low purities (10% or less), and purer colours rate 40% or more.
— Light transmission: This is measured over the whole of the visible spectrum.

— Infrared transmission: This is measured for wavelengths of 750 nm upwards.
— Total transmission: This is the total transmission of solar radiant heat, including that re-emitted after absorption.

The curves of figure 17 compare the spectral transmission of six typical tinted glasses with clear glass, bearing in mind that manufacturers vary their specific mixes as they compete and try to avoid patents.

clear glass (6 mm)

dominant wavelength of transmission	~ 500 nm
transmission at 1,050 nm	65%
colour purity	~ 1%
light transmission	~ 85%
infrared transmission	~ 70%
total transmission	~ 84%

17 The curve is characterized by three ferric oxide absorption bands at 380 nm, 420 nm and 440 nm, and a major ferrous oxide band in the infrared region at 1050 nm. This latter band comprises a smooth dip in transmission in the red (to 75% at the red end of the visible spectrum), and in the infrared part of the spectrum, giving the glass its characteristic green tint.

green glass (6 mm)

dominant wavelength of transmission	~ 497 nm
transmission at 1,050 nm	18%
colour purity	4%
light transmission	76%
infrared transmission	~ 25%
total transmission	61%

The curve is similar in form to that of clear glass, as might be expected given that it has the same constituents but with five times as much iron oxide. This produces a transmission at 1050 nm of less than 20%. Thus, while the light transmission is only cut from 85% to 74%, the total transmission is cut from 84% to 61%. Green, iron oxide, glass has an excellent performance in terms of its light : total transmission characteristics.

car bronze glass

dominant wavelength of transmission	574 nm
transmission at 1,050 nm	42%
colour purity	7%
light transmission	71%
infrared transmission	~ 48%
total transmission	69%

The curve moves the peak transmission towards the red end of the visible spectrum, and has much less infrared absorption than green glass at 1050 nm, due to the reduction of iron oxide from 0.5% to 0.39%. The introduction of cobalt oxide and selenium accounts both for the colour and the reduced light transmission.

architectural bronze glass

dominant wavelength	
of transmission	580 nm
transmission at	
1050 nm	36%
colour purity	6–12%
light transmission	50%
infrared transmission	~ 42%
total transmission	61%

This glass has 25% less iron oxide in it than car bronze, but five times as much cobalt oxide and nearly twice as much selenium. Peaks of transmission occur at 580 nm and at 700 nm (right at the red end of the spectrum), and the selenium colouration (red/brown) at 475 nm is moderated by the cobalt oxide (blue) at 590 and 640 nm. The curve is within 20% of the car bronze curve in the infrared wavebands, but considerably less in the visible spectrum. Significantly, vehicle glazing is required, both in the USA and Europe, to have light transmissions higher than 70–75%. The question may be asked why manufacturers considered it worthwhile to introduce so much cobalt oxide and selenium (reducing visible transmission and producing a bumpier visible transmission curve), while at the same time reducing the heat effective iron oxide. The answer is usually that it is a response to customer demand.

architectural grey/green glass (6 mm)

Dominant wavelength	
of transmission	510 nm
Transmission at	
1050 nm	30%
Colour purity	6%
Light transmission	42%
Infrared transmission	~ 40%
Total transmission	58%

This glass has approximately the same iron oxide content as that of architectural bronze, but 60% more cobalt oxide; however, it has no selenium, the brown content of the colouration in this case being given by nickel oxide. As with all grey glasses, the curve is characterized by considerable absorption in the visible spectrum, with the peaks at both ends of the spectrum and a bumpy centre.

architectural grey/blue glass (6 mm)

Dominant wavelength	
of transmission	465 nm
Transmission at	
1050 nm	35%
Colour purity	6%
Light transmission	41%
Infrared transmission	~ 42%
Total transmission	61%

This glass has more or less the same content as architectural bronze glass in terms of both iron oxide and selenium, however, it has just over twice as much cobalt oxide. The curve is very similar to that of grey/green with visible spectrum bumps in different places. Architectural grey/blue glass is characterized by a high violet and ultraviolet transmission of around 70% and a low infrared transmissivity.

dark grey glass (5 mm)

Dominant wavelength	
of transmission	491 nm
Transmission at	
1050 nm	51%
Colour purity	3%
Light transmission	18%
Infrared transmission	~ 58%
Total transmission	57%

This glass, designed to have a low light transmission, has the same iron oxide content as clear glass (and correspondingly high infrared transmission) and achieves absorption in the visible spectrum with cobalt oxide and with the same amount of nickel oxide as iron oxide. There is no selenium. The curve is characterized by a very high violet and ultraviolet transmissivity at the red end of the visible spectrum. The curve is similar to that for clear glass with the visible spectrum transmission from 430 to 630 nm cut back from greater than 85% to less than 20%, typifying how the tailoring of content can produce designed performance.

■ coatings

The performance of glasses in terms of the transmission of radiation has been revolutionized in the last twenty years or so by the emergence of surface modification and coating technologies.

Surface modification techniques are concerned with the changing of the constituents or structure of the glass at the surface, frequently during the primary manufacturing process, and coating is concerned with the laying down of very thin films on to an annealed or toughened glass as a substrate.

Many of the first surface-modified and coated products were ostensibly concerned primarily with increasing the reflectance of a glass to incoming radiation, with a view to reducing solar-derived overheating. The emerging technology had a difficult birth. Early products were formulated for manufacture both 'on-line' in the float plant (either in the float bath or in the lehr-gap) and as secondary coatings, but the coatings were sometimes unstable; it is reported that one major American manufacturer spent ten years on the development of a surface modification process to be incorporated into the float plant. Problems have been overcome in products such as Pilkington's Spectrafloat (now withdrawn) and Reflectafloat. However, given the complexities of manufacture, and the restricted palette of materials which could form a stable product, many of these early products were somewhat expediently derived in appearance and performance. Whichever way the surface layer was formed, the colour and spectral behaviour was as much the result of selecting materials which were known to form a stable product, with a technique which could be made to work, as it was related to a design intention. Moreover, the beguiling nature of the materials created often led to their use for the appearance they had rather than for the way they performed, with the result that their potential was partially obscured by their capacity to produce a particular aesthetic or image.

Although the transmission/reflection performance of early coated products was known and was an important part of their appeal, some manufacturers were concerned about long-term life. In the early 1970s, the products generally available used precious or not-so-precious metals deposited on to clear or body-tinted glasses, but the products were limited, and often had to be double-glazed to protect the coatings.

Since that time, the use of comparatively thick coatings of materials such as gold, silver, copper and chromium, has been replaced substantially by the use of extremely thin films using vapour deposition or sputtering, in which many substances, elements or compounds can be literally vapourized and deposited as a thin film only a few hundred atoms thick.

While some films are still vulnerable to mechanical damage, the ability of the glass industry to provide materials in which multiple films can be laid on top of each other and still be relatively transparent has completely changed the way in which glasses can be made to perform.

Coated glasses are currently normally incorporated into multiple glass assemblies partly because many coatings are soft and partly because of the need to obtain low U-values and the wish to avoid contamination.

The multiplicity of possible permutations of glasses, coating methods and materials, requires that their descriptions and explanations of their performance characteristics are considered in general terms only. With the possibility now in view of the design and manufacture of products tailor-made to transmission performance profiles, it is more useful to describe performance properties in terms of manufacturing process, and of the intrinsic physical behaviour of the materials and configurations available.

■ coating techniques

The technology of coatings, and the performance of the product created, is as much a result of the method of application as of the intrinsic chemistry and physics of the materials laid down. The method of application, which may vary with the materials applied as films, gives characteristic thicknesses; this can be a significant contributor to mechanical properties such as hardness, and also affects colour. The work of coating technologists thus requires a balance between desired performance and available technique.

The methods of thin film application are dealt with more fully in Appendix Two. However, the process used affects performance, and demands that techniques be viewed briefly here.

Surface modification or coating methods are commonly divided into on-line and off-line techniques, to distinguish between those carried out in the float plant whilst the glass is still molten or hot, and those involving the laying down of films on to the annealed or toughened product.

on-line coatings are intrinsically harder than off-line films since they are fired into the surface of the hot glass. They are commonly applied by solution deposition, or chemical vapour deposition, or electrolysis using charged particles. In what is known as pyrolytic decomposition, carried out using a liquid spray, chemical vapour deposition or powder spraying, the reactants are delivered to the hot glass surface at which they decompose.

off-line coatings are applied by various methods, including dipping, solution deposition, chemical vapour deposition and physical vapour deposition. Spraying is used to make conventional silvered mirrors. In immersion or dip coating techniques the film may be hardened by pyrolysis. Organic films can be laid down by this method.

Wet chemical deposition techniques depend essentially on the interaction between solutions of the materials to be deposited and the surface of the glass.

Physical vapour deposition techniques, of which there are several, depend on the vaporization of the material to be laid down. Methods used include simple evaporation (by heating or electron bombardment), sputtering and ion plating. Of these, magnetron sputtering is currently the most widely used method, and can be used to lay down a very large range of elements and compounds as very thin films.

As might be expected, the performance of coated glasses in respect of most physical properties, except radiation transmission and reflection, is effectively that of glass substrate itself.

An important proviso relates to the change of surface characteristics created by the coating itself. In laying down a coating, particularly one not pyrolytically fused into the glass surface, the essentially hard and durable surface of the glass is covered by a softer, more reactive material. Add to this the possible reactions and physical and chemical behaviour taking place between multiple coatings such as those now available, and it will be seen that an intrinsically inert tough material has been replaced by one much more prone to damage and decay.

These are aspects well known to the glass-maker and coatings applier, and explain the cautious development of the products concerned, despite the intensive research and development effort now underway worldwide.

The primary properties of coated products are related to energy transmission, whether considered technically or aesthetically. The intrinsic behaviour of a coating is a result of its chemical constitution, its thickness, and the characteristics of energy transfer at the boundaries between coatings, and between the coatings and the glass. Given the intrinsic importance of a surface in the phenomenon of radiation transmission (in respect of spectrally selective refraction/reflection, for example), and given the multiplicity of surfaces which may abound, it may be seen that an analysis of physical behaviour demands lengthier discussion than is appropriate here.

A thin film behaves in the same way as any other transparent material. Its surfaces refract or reflect, and its internal structure causes it to transmit or absorb in different proportions across the spectrum. Two or more thin films deposited on top of each other can combine the properties of the materials concerned, or even partially cancel each other out, with the added natural consequence of multiple surface refraction/reflection.

Dozens of materials are currently being used in thin films as performance modifiers, and many more are being evaluated and tested. A typical glazing system using coated products would have two panes of glass, and thus four available surfaces for coating. Given the numbers of different glasses and coatings available or possible, the permutations are almost endless. It is impossible to deal with all of these here, but an indication can be given of the sorts of materials used, and the performance characteristics associated with them.

metallic coatings were among the first to be produced, often by evaporative physical vapour deposition, using chromium, chrome oxide, silver and gold. The reflectance of a metal such as gold increases with increasing wavelength. If the gold is on surface number 2 of a double-glazed unit, part of any incoming solar infrared radiation is reflected and part absorbed, and the glass is heated up. However, the long-wave radiation emission of the inner gold coat is less than that of the glass outwards, and heat energy transmission into the building is low. Such coatings have intrinsic disadvantages of low and spectrally distorted light transmission.

multilayer coatings are usually applied by evaporative vapour deposition, or sputtering, which permits the laying down of exceptionally thin films. Problems of adhesion and vulnerability can be substantially solved using the extreme thinness of coatings by laying down several of them, each of which does a specific job.

In a typical sputtered reflective coating, four materials perform the primary functions of the system:

coating 1: tin oxide: provides an adhesive coating and a Na+ ion barrier
coating 2: silver: provides the reflection performance
coating 3: scavenger: prevents the oxidation of the silver as it proceeds to the oxygen environment of the final sputtering chamber
coating 4: tin oxide: provides a hard final coat

The caution of a manufacturer of such a product in divulging what material is used for coating 3 is an example of the technical confidentiality of this technology. The nature of the build-up, like that of a paint system but only 2–60 nm thick, indicates the complexity and subtlety of the technique concerned.

18. Transfer of heat through low-E double glazing systems. The dots signify conduction. The diagram simplifies transmission; in reality the temperature of the glasses changes and affects the rate of heat transfer.
A: radiation inhibited only by the glass
B: radiation inhibited significantly by the low emission of the coating on surface 3
C: radiation reflected by the coating on surface 2, inhibiting outward emission.

19. The reflectance action of low-E systems. The vertical axis shows percentage reflectance. The action of a low-E system is enhanced by its reflectance to long-wave radiation such as is emitted by surfaces at room temperature.

20. Low-E spectral transmission curves. The curves show the overall transmission of two Pilkington low-E glasses compared with a single pane. The K glass was developed to provide much higher transmission of near-infrared solar radiation, and a better 'Effective U-value'.

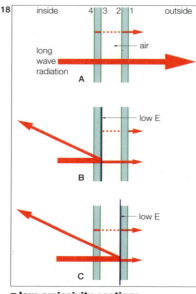

■ low-emissivity coatings

The most important multiple coatings of recent years have been the selective low emissivity (low-E) coatings which have transformed the performance of glazing in the last decade or so. Low-E coatings use materials which have as an intrinsic property a low emission coefficient for thermal radiation. The emissivity of a body or surface is a measure of the rate at which it emits energy as a result of having its temperature raised. In accordance with Kirchoff's Law, good absorbers are also good emitters, so a surface which emits badly will reflect well. Low-E coatings are therefore similar in behaviour to reflective coatings, but are selected for their low emission and reflection of long-wave rather than short-wave heat.

Such coatings are defined as those which are predominantly transparent over the visible wavelength (300 to 700 nm) and reflective in the long-wave infrared. The coating concerned may be on surface number 2 or 3. In a

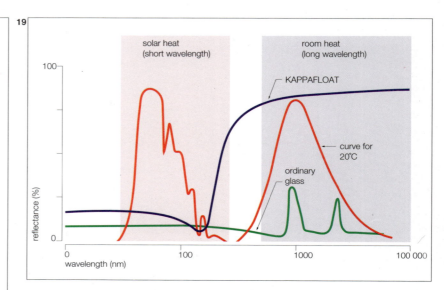

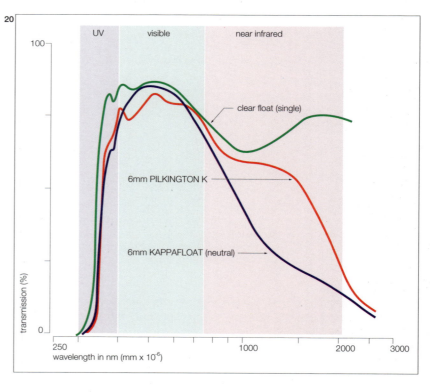

typical system, with the coating on surface number 3, short-wave solar radiation is transmitted to the building interior which it heats up. The interior surfaces themselves then begin to emit long wave radiation back towards the glass. The glass absorbs about 90% of this long-wave energy but with its low-E coating, the amount of heat radiated into the cavity is eight to ten times less than that which would be emitted by a glass surface. When the coating is on surface 2, the heat radiated from surface 3 is reflected back; this is demonstrated in products such as Pilkington's Kappafloat by the reflection of long-wave radiation in the wavebands related to radiation emissions at room temperature. The net result of these low-E systems is that less heat is lost to the external environment: the whole system acts, in effect, to enhance the so-called 'Greenhouse effect'. This is already reducing U-values significantly, and the development of hard coatings has improved the options open to the designer for the position of the coating in the window.

Technically, low-E films are of two types: multilayer dielectric/metal/dielectric, and highly doped semiconductors. The multilayer materials are more 'tunable' and the doped materials tend to be more durable. In the multilayer films, typical dielectric materials are indium oxide, tin oxide and zinc oxide. Silver is the metal most commonly sandwiched between these. It is very reflective to long-wave radiation (infrared and beyond), and being very reflective to the visible spectrum, used alone would be unacceptably reflective (up to 70%). It would also be very prone to damage. It is a good component in a multilayer system, however, combined with barrier films, usually metal oxides, which prevent the chemical attack of the silver during

21. U-values for different glass systems. The table shows typical U-values in W/m² °C for vertical glazing subjected to normal exposure conditions according to BS 6993 Part 1, showing trends due to air space variation and the action of low-E systems.

22. Dichroics and related systems. Dichroics are part of a large family of selective transmitters which use interference in multi-coated glasses. Typical of these are the so-called hot and cold mirrors. The cold mirror (top graph) transmits heat and reflects visible light, whereas the hot mirror (bottom graph) transmits visible light and reflects heat. The dichroic coating on a tungsten halogen lamp reflector is a form of cold mirror.

manufacture. In addition they can be used to prevent silver migration and sodium migration from the glass. The overall thickness of such a system is of the order of 70 nm. The transmission properties of these films are created both by the optical properties of the layers individually, and by the optical interference between them, so it can be seen that their behaviour is quite complicated. The multilayer films are commonly applied by physical vapour deposition, including both vacuum evaporation and sputtering. Chemical vapour deposited 'hard' coats are also available. The doped semiconductor materials are generally applied by chemical vapour deposition either on or off the float line, and doped tin oxide pyrolytic coatings have proved very successful. This technology is the basis for Pilkington's K-Glass.

■ **interference coatings**
These involve the principle of thin layer interference to produce highly reflective neutral films. Solar radiation is separated into component rays by the refractive coatings, and these are superimposed to produce a constructive interference pattern reducing or increasing the intensity of reflection. The advantage of such films over metallic coatings is that they can be completely neutral in colour, since the reflectance is dependent on the thickness of the coating, its composition and refractive indices. The metallic oxides used can be applied by sputtering, and very hard dip-coated products are also available.

The sophisticated physics of low-E and interference coatings gives a hint both of the complexity and of the potential of thin film technology. Although the performance prediction techniques related to

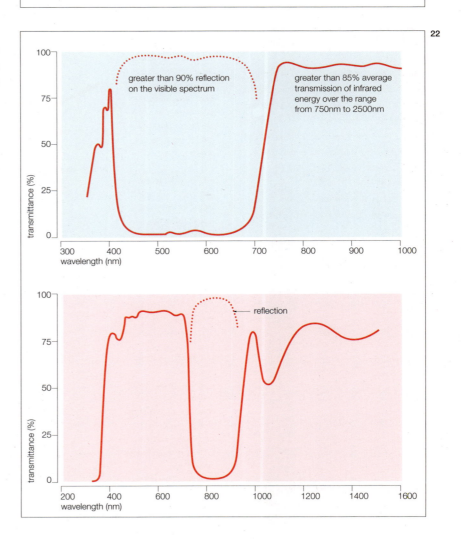

21

Unit make up	Air space mm						
	6	8	10	12	14	16	20
4mm/air/4mm	3.2	3.0	2.9	2.8	2.7	2.7	2.7
4mm/argon/4mm	2.9	2.8	2.7	2.6	2.6	2.6	2.6
4mm/air/4mmK	2.6	2.3	2.1	1.9	1.8	1.7	1.7
4mm/argon/4mmK	2.2	1.9	1.7	1.6	1.5	1.5	1.5
4mm/air/4mm/air/4mm	2.3	2.1	2.0	1.9	1.8	1.8	1.8

22

greater than 90% reflection on the visible spectrum

greater than 85% average transmission of infrared energy over the range from 750nm to 2500nm

reflection

these new materials are gradually improving, the complicated nature of transmission, reflection and inter-reflection, of surface refraction and interference, all varying with thickness and chemical composition, make prediction of all the optical properties a matter for sophisticated simulation. Given that the nature of the film can depend upon the voltages and gas pressures used in the machines and the times they are applied for, the production of an identical product two days running demands very good technology. In addressing the problem of replacement in a building, such plants rely on careful control of the plant, the logging of settings, and the holding of samples for each order. It is not surprising that the technological explosion is being kept under very careful control.

More advanced coatings are, however, already with us. A glass is now on the market and in use in Scandinavia which heats up when a current passes across a coating on its surface. Metallic or conductive coatings, applied before or during the toughening process, enable a sheet resistance of 14 ohms per square to be produced. The application of a voltage provides a heating effect of 100–500 W/m². Used as surface 3 of a double-glazing system, with a low-E coating on surface 2 to conserve the energy emitted by the heating layer, a U-value of 1.4 W/m²K is achieved. The use of such a material turns a transparent membrane into a warm blanket, and there are many installations already operating. The next few decades should see the rapid development of whole new generations of coating designs, complete with the autonomic responsive and predictive systems to go with them.

23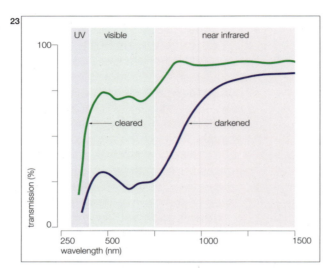

23. Photochromic glass: spectral transmission. Photochromic glass is very transparent to near infrared radiation, but comparatively attenuating to visible light. The visible light transmission of the curve above lies in the zone occupied by 6 mm green heat-absorbing glass. Transmission is reduced by two-thirds in the visible waveband in the example shown.

■ **dichroics**

Dichroics, as the etymology suggests, are filters which transmit one range of wavelengths and reflect the remainder. Typical uses of dichroic filters are for the reflectors in high temperature tungsten halogen lamps, in which light needs to be reflected towards the room or object illuminated, but in which heat (near infrared radiation) needs to be allowed to pass back through the 'reflector' to the heat sink behind, and thence into the surrounding void (see figure 22).

Typical dichroic filters are manufactured in a process which uses between 10 and 40 interference layers, each about 50 nm in thickness, of silicon oxide alternated with tungsten oxide and tantalum oxide. The action is produced by the designed constructive and destructive interference of the alternating low and high refractive indices. The coatings are typically laid down by thermal evaporation or the so-called 'metamode' method, in which the metals are oxidized after being laid down, or by chemical dipping, the sol-gel process.

■ **variable transmission glasses**

The disadvantages of fixed transmission glasses have been evident since they were first invented and the objective to vary the performance of a glass at will has long been held. The realization of a requirement to obtain variable transmission, to respond to climate and the varying needs of occupants, has led to an accelerating search for appropriate materials. This search began with passive systems in which a change in spectral transmission was induced by a change in the incoming radiation itself, or the ambient lighting or temperature conditions. Such passive systems have the apparent advantage that they are autonomic. The hope that such systems would be analogous to the human skin proved ill-founded, since the state of the glass does not always correspond with the transmission requirement. However, photochromic and thermochromic products have provided a useful foundation and adjunct to the more recent electrochromic materials.

■ **photochromism**

Photochromism is one of the best known darkening phenomena in relation to light transmission. The important difference between photochromic and electrochromic filters discussed below is that the darkening phenomenon derives from the chemistry of the glass itself rather than from a coating. The switching mechanism is light itself (mainly ultraviolet light), and this offers an ostensibly extremely attractive device in situations where the limiting of radiation transmission is an objective, such as in sunglasses.

Photochromism is one of the oldest known switching ideas, and reference to it is reported back to the 1880s. It was not until 1937, however, that R H Dalton, a scientist at Corning Glass Works in the USA, noted a phenomenon relating to the already known behaviour of glasses containing copper. Such glasses became red when heated. Dalton discovered that exposure to short-wave ultraviolet radiation prior to re-heating led to this colouration taking place at a lower temperature, more quickly. The process was patented in 1943.

Behind Dalton's discovery is the property of materials called optical sensitizers to become reducing agents when exposed to ultraviolet light. Chemical reduction involves the removal of oxygen or combination with hydrogen, or lessening the positive valency by adding electrons. Included in glasses containing copper or silver, they cause the metal to become colloidal, absorbing certain wavelengths of light.

A similar phenomenon takes place with certain non-metallic materials. By a principle known as heterogeneous nucleation, the metallic materials already mentioned become what are called nucleating agents: under heat they promote the growth of crystals of lithium metasilicate, sodium fluoride or barium disilicate, and the glass becomes opal. It was from such a material that sunglasses were developed in 1971.

The basis for the effects employed in glazing are typically metal halides and polymers, in which transmission is varied by different absorption spectra. In a typical glass, silver halides such as silver bromide (AgBr) or silver chloride (AgCl) are detached. In the solidified glass matrix the halides do not occur, but become silver and chlorine ions evenly distributed through the glass. The glass is made by adding silver salts and halides (metal compounds of flourine, chlorine or bromine) into the glass melt (usually a boron-silicon glass), under extremely closely controlled conditions. Thermal treatment after the melting process created the formation of silver halide.

In the annealing process, the mobility of these ions increases under the effect of heat to form the silver halide crystals. The low linkage forces between the silver and the chlorine, for example, enable the crystals to be broken down by the energy of light wavelengths between 300 and 400 nm. This decomposition creates the darkening. Removal of this near ultraviolet permits molecular recombination, the reaction reverses and the glass lightens

Attractive as the idea of an automatic passive filter may be, several difficulties have haunted manufacturers. Photochromic glasses are not easy to make, and perhaps typify the problems of complex-chemistry glasses. An expensive glass is usually used in the first place, and the costly ingredients are made into the glass by a complicated manufacturing technique. Consistent performance is difficult to achieve, and large, building-size pieces difficult to make with even performance. Moreover, reaction times are rather slow as indicated in figure 24.

Three specific problems have emerged. The first relates to the evenness of distribution of the photochromic constituent in the glass mix, and the proper concern of manufacturers to avoid a patchy material. In the early 1980s, manufacturers were unhappy about making pieces larger than a few centimetres, although now Corning have made areas up to one metre square in thin sheets for lamination to float. In principle, there is no reason why a fully-fledged float photochromic glass should not be produced, although there would very likely be a difficulty in the silver in the glass

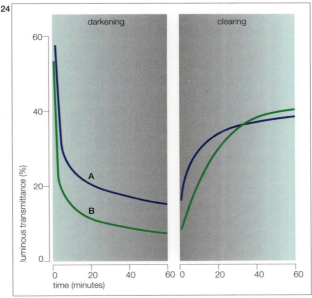

24. Photochromic glass: reaction time. The curves show typical reaction times for photochromic glass (in this case 1.5 mm thick Corning 8102 glass), which depend considerably on glass composition and temperature. Darkening and lightening transmission over time are as indicated by the curves. Curve A shows reaction times for warm temperatures.

Daytime darkening at 25°C (77°F)

Overnight clearing	60%
60 seconds in sunlight	27%
10 minutes in sunlight	22%
60 minutes in sunlight	19%

Overnight clearance at 20°C (68°F)

5 minutes fading in the dark	32%
10 minutes fading in the dark	45%
Overnight fading	60%

Curve B applies to temperatures around 3°C

dissolving in the tin in the float bath

The second problem relates to speed of response. A typical reaction time is three to four minutes at room temperature. This raises a potential problem when the radiation environment is subject to the vagaries of, for example, passing clouds. However, this is a problem which relates to local climatic conditions and the essential performance requirements of the use.

The third problem relates to the lack of control which the materials exhibit. Photochromic glasses tend to darken at fairly low light levels, and if used in a building tend to darken during daylight hours whatever the weather. The environmental designer, interested in using absorption protection, needs a glass which will darken on the east side in the morning and on the west side in the evening, but only if there is an overheating problem. It is difficult to teach a photochromic glass this behaviour.

Despite these difficulties, photochromic materials offer potential in the future, particularly given their apparent long-term durability, and the great variety of compounds exhibiting the effect. Many inorganic and organic compounds are being researched, and the American Optical Corporation has developed a photochromic plastic. PPG have produced plastic photochromic spectacle material. Photochromic aerogels with insulating polymers are also on the agenda.

The newer polychromic glasses, announced in 1975, are based upon similar chemical principles to those used for photochromic glasses. These are light-sensitive glasses in which different colours are absorbed by means of silver particles concentrated in the tips of the pyramid crystals which form. The colour seen and transmitted

depends upon what colour light is absorbed.

It seems likely that light-sensitive variable transmission glasses will not be perfected for buildings before electrochromic glasses come on to the market. However, the ability of the glass-maker to create a glass whose behaviour is light/UV sensitive is not only usable in terms of variable transmission; in Louverre Corning have turned the principle to good effect by enabling opal louvres to be created in the body of the glass.

■ thermochromism

Like photochromism, thermochromism is a century-old area of research, going back to the 1870s. In thermochromic materials, temperature either induces a phase change, or generates a chemical reaction. Like photochromic materials, thermochromics do not need decision-switching. They are essentially passive reacting devices, and are commonly used in household and commercial temperature indicators. Having said this, with the use of clear heating elements (such as indium tin oxide) as thin films, thermochromics could be turned into active systems by heating the glass to different temperatures to obtain different colours. Such a technique would transform their potential.

Many organic and inorganic compounds exhibit thermochromism, and gel polymers are now under development for windows. Thin film technology is being applied for transition metal oxides which change from a semiconducting to a metallic state when certain temperatures are reached. The critical factor for the building designer is the temperature at which this change takes place: this has to correspond with the need to vary transmission, which explains the current research effort into transformation tempera-

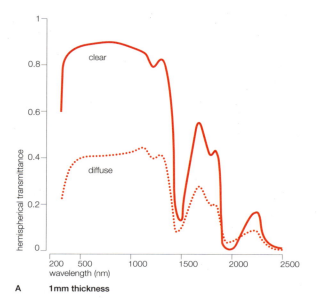

A   1mm thickness

25

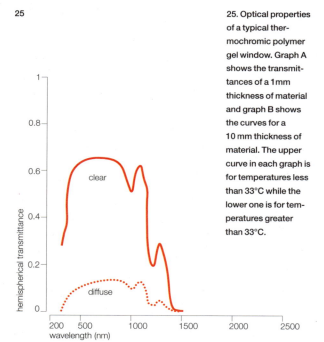

B   10mm thickness

25. Optical properties of a typical thermochromic polymer gel window. Graph A shows the transmittances of a 1mm thickness of material and graph B shows the curves for a 10 mm thickness of material. The upper curve in each graph is for temperatures less than 33°C while the lower one is for temperatures greater than 33°C.

tures, and the percentage transmissions associated with these. Vanadium dioxide-based thermochromic coatings seem to offer the best current basis for success, given the relationship of their transformation temperatures to human comfort temperatures, as shown by Granqvist.

■ chromogenics

The interest in passive variable materials such as photochromics and thermochromics remains, but the use of thin film coating has revolutionized the effort to produce glazing with switchable transmission performance. This work has been progressing for several decades, and chromogenics, the science of colour change in glasses, has in the 1990s become a consolidated worldwide area of research and development. The technology includes electrochromics, liquid crystal and various other systems which can be made to change the transmission of light.

■ electrochromism

Electrochromism is the phenomenon whereby the switching of an electric current across a material causes its chemical structure to change, resulting in a change in the spectral transmission characteristics. The phenomenon is known in many inorganic and organic substances, with most of the currently interesting ones being oxides used in the form of transparent thin films

Colour change and electrochromic materials have a long scientific history. As long ago as 1704, Diesbach discovered Prussian Blue, a hexacyano ferrate dye which can be changed from blue to clear by an increase or decrease of its ion content. By 1815 Berzelius had reported the ability of tungsten trioxide to exhibit colour changes when subjected to

heat treatment, and this was followed in 1824 by Wohler's work with tungsten trioxide and sodium, in which he produced a material with a gold appearance, now commonly referred to as sodium tungsten bronze. The phenomenon of colour change using electric current was well described by Kraus in Liechtenstein in 1953, and in 1969 S K Deb published a seminal paper on the subject. The term 'electrochromism' was invented by Platt in 1961, ironically as it turned out, because he was actually describing the colour change of organic dye molecules rather than the now much more commonly used inorganic materials.

Historically, the study and development of electrochromic materials has depended partly on the intrinsic properties of the particular materials discovered and studied, and partly on the perception of the researchers and makers of their eventual use. This latter consideration has led to four main types of device being identified. Information display devices have been the subject of considerable study, but without yet delivering a product to the market place. Variable reflectance mirrors, on the other hand, are already with us. The potential use for variable emittance devices is only now becoming clear. The fourth type of device, the electrochromic window, has proved elusive, but is close to successful application, and is discussed below. Significantly for the development of the so-called 'smart window', the actual darkened colour of devices in the other three categories has not been considered of great importance. Perhaps for this reason, work on tailor-made colouration is comparatively recent.

Although the possibility of neutral and tailor-made electrochromics is now within sight, tungsten oxide is by far the most exten-

sively studied electrochromic material to date, and a description of the nature of an electrochromic device, and its action, is discussed in terms of this most common of materials.

A typical tungsten oxide bronze system is shown in figures 26 and 27. The electrode film carries current; the electrolyte is a substance having the characteristic that it loses ions when in contact with an electric current. In such an open device, one of the electrodes has to be in contact with the air, so that a supply of moisture (H_2O) is available for the process: the H_2O is broken down into hydrogen, oxygen and electrons.

This particular form of electrochromism depends on the behaviour of a form of tungsten, given the chemical abbreviation 'W'. A film of tungsten oxide, WO_3, is pale yellow. When reduced (the removal of oxygen or the addition of hydrogen) to a tungsten bronze it becomes intense blue. Tungsten bronzes have been known for about 150 years. They are formed when some of the tungsten ions in WO_3 are reduced by the chemical reaction:

$$xM^+ + xe^- + WO_3 = M_xWO_3$$

where M is an alkali metal or hydrogen atom.

A typical alkali metal is lithium or sodium. Sodium-containing bronzes have been studied most in bulk form, and their colour in reflection (ie their appearance) varies from dark grey through blue, purple, red and orange to golden yellow, as the proportion of sodium increases. Transmission through such films is always blue, increasing in intensity as the amount of M increases. A deep intense blue appears when the oxide layer is electrolytically reduced.

In an electrochromic device, the tungsten bronze is a few hundred nanometres thick,

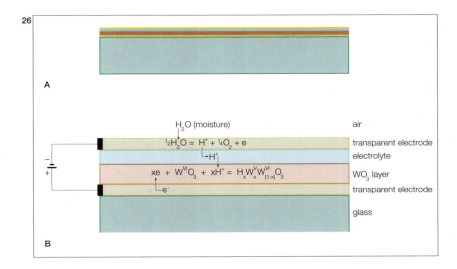

26

A

B

H_2O (moisture)   air

$\frac{1}{2}H_2O = H^+ + \frac{1}{4}O_2 + e$ transparent electrode

H^+ electrolyte

$xe + W^{VI}O_3 + xH^+ = H_x W^V_x W^{VI}_{(1-x)}O_3$ WO_3 layer

e^- transparent electrode

glass

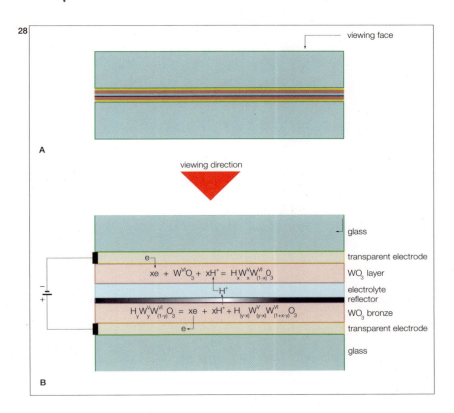

28

viewing face

A

viewing direction

B

glass

transparent electrode

$xe + W^{VI}O_3 + xH^+ = H_x W^V_x W^{VI}_{(1-x)}O_3$ WO_3 layer

H^+ electrolyte
reflector

$H_y W^V_y W^{VI}_{(1-y)}O_3 = xe + xH^+ + H_{(y-x)} W^V_{(y-x)} W^{VI}_{(1+x-y)}O_3$ WO_3 bronze

e^- transparent electrode

glass

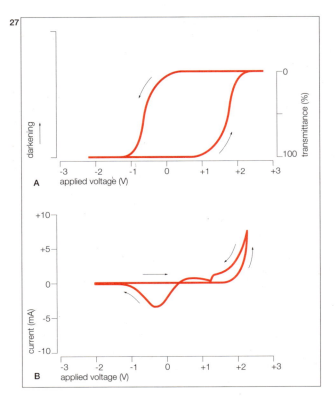

27

A

darkening ↑   transmittance (%)

0 ... 100

-3 -2 -1 0 +1 +2 +3
applied voltage (V)

B

+10
+5
0
-5
-10
current (mA)

-3 -2 -1 0 +1 +2 +3
applied voltage (V)

26, 27. Electro-
chromism: an open
system. The diagrams
show a system which
is open to the air,
comprising a sand-
wich whose outer
films are transparent
electrodes, enclosing
an electrolyte film and
film of the tungsten
bronze electro-
chromic layer. The
graphs show the
darkening and light-
ing behaviour. 26B
shows the top zone
of 26A in detail. 27A is
the darkening-voltage
cycle, 27B is the cur-
rent-voltage cycle.

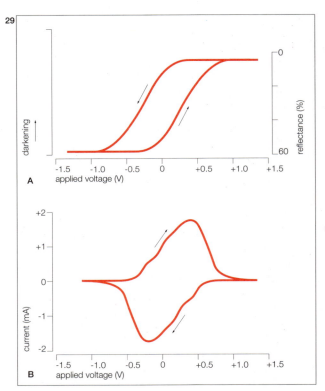

29

A

darkening ↑   reflectance (%)

0 ... 60

-1.5 -1.0 -0.5 0 +0.5 +1.0 +1.5
applied voltage (V)

B

+2
+1
0
-1
-2
current (mA)

-1.5 -1.0 -0.5 0 +0.5 +1.0 +1.5
applied voltage (V)

28, 29. Electro-
chromism: a closed
system in the form
of a dimming mirror.
The diagram shows
a system which is
enclosed by glass on
both sides, enclosing
outer films of trans-
parent electrodes,
which in turn enclose
an electrolyte film and
two films of the tung-
sten bronze elec-
trochromic material.
The graphs show the
darkening and light-
ing behaviour. 28B
shows the top zone
of 28A in detail. 29A is
the darkening-voltage
cycle, 29B is the cur-
rent-voltage cycle.

and protons, which are highly mobile, are used as the ions entering the tungsten oxide. When the exposed electrode film is made positive, protons migrate via the electrolyte towards the inner negatively-charged electrode film. At the same time, electrons from the negatively-charged inner electrode reduce some of the tungsten ions in the WO_3 layer from what is known as a "6' to a "5' state. The oxygen ions remain in the '-2' state, and electroneutrality is maintained in the WO_3 film by protons migrating from the positive electrode. A reaction takes place; WO_3 is converted by the addition of hydrogen into a tungsten bronze, and thus turns blue.

Reversing the current, making the open electrode negative, reverses the colouration back to the colourless state. The minimum voltage required for colouration is only 1.2 volts, and dissipation of colour starts at 0.2 volts. The performance of such an open electrochromic system is shown in figures 26, 27.

The problem with such open systems is that they rely on contact with the air, and that the electrode films are very vulnerable to chemical and mechanical damage.

A closed electrochromic system has both faces protected by sandwiching it between two sheets of glass. The hydrogen ions are obtained from a second WO_3 layer in a reduced (ie 'hydrogen rich'), and therefore darkened, form. Switching the current backwards and forwards alternately darkens and lightens the two layers, as they receive and lose the hydrogen ions through the electrolyte. This process has already been turned into a product by the insertion of a centrally reflecting layer which permits the migration of the hydrogen atoms. The result is a dimming mirror, the degree of reflectance of which can be held at any level by switching off the cur-

30. The twisted nematic liquid crystal. The diagram shows the action of a twisted nematic crystal. The discs represent the liquid crystals. The liquid crystal polymers have a tendency to form chains which rotate across the gap. The exit side polarizer, the analyser, is positioned to allow through light rotated through 90°, producing clear light. An electric field can cause the polymers to untwist, leading to the passage of light being blocked by the polarizer.

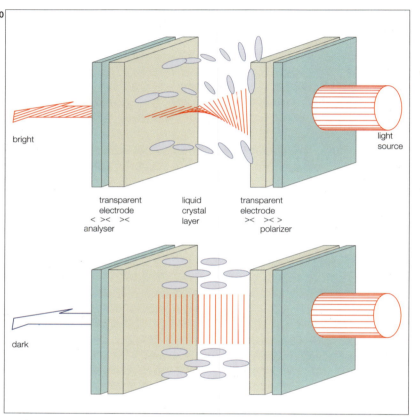

rent. The reflectance changes from 60% down to 15% or 20% in less than five seconds using 1.5 volts. The performance of a closed system is shown in figures 28, 29.

Both inorganic and organic compounds exhibit the required properties for electrochromism, including a variety of mixed valency, highly coloured semi-conductors. Over one third of the elements in the Periodic Table form mixed-valency compounds, including molybdenum and cobalt. Typical inorganic materials work by injection or ejection of ions and electrons in tungsten bronzes, which switch from clear to blue or bronze, as in the system described above.

The organic compounds used for electrochromic devices also use oxidation-reduction reactions. However, these can be prey to problems such as decomposition in sunlight. Many important steps have to be taken, and problems overcome, before such devices are marketable in the building industry. Stability (the moving parts problem operating at a molecular level) has already been mentioned. The problem of colour also has to be solved, to satisfy the usual architectural requirements for neutral or controlled colour transmission and reflection.

Electrochromism is the subject of intensive study, with tungsten bronzes by no

means the only materials under investigation. This study has already led to marketable products. The closed system dimming mirror device described above, using a tungsten bronze system, was developed by Schott in Germany (and similar devices are now being marketed by others), but even as this work was going on researchers elsewhere, including at Chalmers University of Technology, were studying nickel oxide coatings in the belief that they were much more stable over much longer periods of time, and more suitable than tungsten or iridium oxide coatings for large-scale window applications.

With the recognition of the importance of colouration, particularly neutral colouration, by the researchers, work is now proceeding into mixed electrochromic oxide systems which can be uncoloured. Progress is described in Chapter Four.

■ liquid crystals

Liquid crystals are based on the use of materials with a rod-like molecular structure, which alters the way light is transmitted depending on the alignment of the rods. Typical materials are only a few nanometres long, which can be aligned for distances measured in thousands of nanometres.

These materials became the basis for practical applications when stable versions were discovered by George Gray in England in the early 1970s. In a typical device, between five and fifteen types of cyanobiphenyl molecules are combined in cells thousands of layers thick. Simple nematic crystals are aligned but can slide up and down each other; smectic crystals are arranged in layers. Most crystal types are smectic at low temperatures, nematic when warmed, and eventually become ordinary fluids when warm enough.

In 1992 there were two forms of smectic crystals available commercially compared with five nematics.

When built into devices, liquid crystals are again divided into two types: those which use polarizers, and those which do not. The versions with polarizers tend to be optically inefficient, with a practical limit in light transmission of 35%. Liquid crystals which do not use polarizers can transmit light much more effectively, and a typical device is called a polymer dispersed liquid crystal (or PDLC), or nematic curvilinear aligned phase (NCAP) crystal. These can be switched from light to dark, and from clear to translucent, and are the types in use for windows and large area display. The commonest liquid crystal type is the twisted nematic, in which the polymers form chains that rotate between polarizing plates. The degree of rotation is controlled during manufacture.

The current state of liquid crystal applications are simply enumerated. They come in four basic types: twisted nematics, guest–host, surface stabilized ferroelectric

31. Schematic of an active matrix display. The thin film transistor array shows the indium tin oxide pixels separated by the thin film transistors, the drain buses and the gate lines.

32. The supertwisted nematic liquid crystal. More advanced and sophisticated super-twisted nematics (STNs) form twist angles of 270°. The construction of a passive display is shown above, and is easier to make but more difficult to operate. The active matrix display is more difficult to make, and uses thin film transistors (TFTs) made by photolithography.

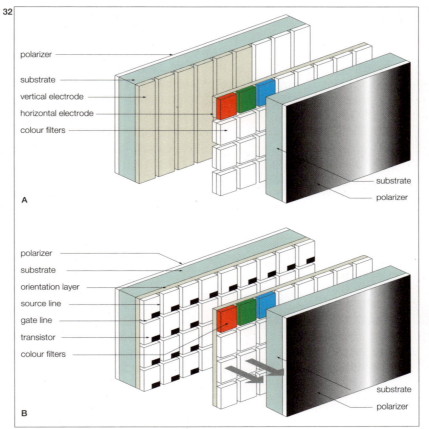

32

polarizer
substrate
vertical electrode
horizontal electrode
colour filters

substrate
polarizer

A

polarizer
substrate
orientation layer
source line
gate line
transistor
colour filters

substrate
polarizer

B

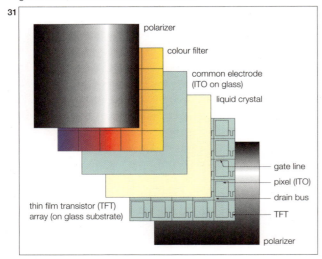

31

polarizer
colour filter
common electrode (ITO on glass)
liquid crystal

gate line
pixel (ITO)
drain bus
TFT

thin film transistor (TFT) array (on glass substrate)

polarizer

and polymer dispersed liquid crystals. In window applications they rely, as do electrochromics, on thin film technology to carry current across a transparent coating. Twisted nematic systems are used for electronic displays, but these need polarizers, which reduce transmission, and they are difficult to make in large areas. Stabilized ferroelectric systems are to be seen in electro-optic switches, but are also difficult to make.

The preferred materials for windows are guest–host and polymer dispersed liquid crystals.

Guest–host systems use dichroic dye molecules mixed with liquid crystals, and are being developed for displays and optical shutters. Cholesteric-nematic phase change guest–host liquid crystals switch by a field induced phase change. They are fast-acting (15 and 360 ms for on and off) and in development for spectacles and car mirrors.

The final group of liquid crystal materials are the PDLC (polymer dispersed liquid crystals) and NCAP (nematic curvilinear aligned phase) systems, both relying on nematic liquid crystals distributed in micro-cavities. Both types display the same characteristics, but they are prepared differently. PDLC

systems are being developed by companies such as General Motors.

The NCAP systems are used by companies more involved in current switchable windows, like the Taliq Corporation of California, and the Nippon Sheet Glass Company. In these devices, the liquid crystals are within an index-matched polymer matrix, in turn encapsulated between two sheets of indium-tin-oxide electrode film. When switched off, the window is translucent opal white. When switched on the liquid crystal droplets align with the electric field and the window is transparent. They need continuous power to remain clear at a load of less than 20 W/m². They are already made in areas up to 1 m by 2.5 m, and the use of pleochroic dyes can darken the off state.

■ suspended particles

Similar in character to liquid crystals, suspended particle devices consist of between three and five layers, with the active layer consisting of needle-shaped particles of polyiodides or parphathite, suspended in an organic fluid or gel. This forms the centre of a sandwich, between outer conducting layers. Applying an electric field causes alignment and an increase in radiation transmission. Light scattering in the on condition needs to be improved if such devices are to have value.

■ electronic glazing

The key to the new generations of active and controllable glazing systems is the ability of technologists to lay down thin transparent films which can carry current. This provides the essential prerequisite to provide systems from simple powered glazing through to the electronic systems of the future. Many of the chromogenic systems described above need servant systems such as those described below.

The commonest conductive films in current commercial use are indium tin oxide (ITO) or doped tin oxide. This is usually applied by vacuum evaporation or sputtering in the case of ITO, or by chemical vapour deposition for fluorine doped tin oxide. The application temperatures of doped tin oxide limits use as top electrical contacts for photovoltaics, integrated circuits, electrochromics and electrooptics, since high temperatures can damage the films over which they are laid.

New classes of electronic conductors are emerging, including conductive organic polymer metals. These are unusual materials, and their electric conductivity can be increased by doping. The most well-known is polyacetylene. Unfortunately, the doping can decrease transparency unacceptably in many of the polymers, and polyacetylene is itself not transparent, and is unstable in air. However materials such as the polythiophenes and polyanilines are potential transparent conductors.

These new polymer metals are expected to make an enormous contribution to the developing technology of electronic devices.

other flat glass products

The five glass types most used in buildings have already been briefly described at the beginning of this appendix. Most architects and designers in the building industry are principally concerned with varying forms of soda-lime glass, occasionally having cause to use the significantly more expensive borosilicate or other glasses. However, the world of glass is a very wide one, and any review of the full range of materials must refer also to the other glasses available, as well as to the products made possible by secondary processes and combination.

■ rolled glasses

Rolled glasses are distinguished from flat glasses by virtue of their manufacturing method, rather than the materials in them. Nevertheless they are an important family to consider in that, by involving the modification of one or both surfaces during the rolling process, they comprise a group of glasses in which the nature of transparency is altered: distortions to the surface alter the path of radiation transmission by refraction, and visual obscuration results. The traditional use for such materials has been for this very purpose, but a knowledge of, and wish to, exploit optics, permits much more inventive applications, such as the so-called 'sparkle glass' developed for the Lloyd's Building in London by the Richard Rogers Partnership. This precise repetitive pattern shows how the rolling technique could be put to great use in the bending and manipulation of light, incorporating, for example, prismatic profiles on the surface. Recent developments in the design and manufacture of the die patterns on the rolling drums have opened up new ranges of products, which could have a major impact when combined with coating techniques.

Conventional rolled glasses include the following products:

raw glass This is a rolled product with or without a figured pattern, produced by the rolling process simply because optically flat, parallel surfaces are not required. The pattern, if there is one, appears on one surface only.

ornamental glass This category covers the multitude of obscuring glasses designed either for decorative effect, or for high dispersion and reduction of glare.

greenhouse glass This is a more precise form, with a surface specially designed to scatter solar radiation evenly.

wire-reinforced glass This uses rolling methods to embed wire mesh into glass to hold it together in the event of breakage, whether through fire or mechanical damage. It may be raw or polished. Traditionally wired glasses (such as 'Georgian wired' in the UK) have had an important place in building design, being an early product considered suitable for certain hazardous locations. As technology develops and costs drop, however, more advanced products are increasingly replacing it.

profile glass In its commonest form this is produced in 'U' shaped profiles, which have the advantage of being self-supporting. Such glasses are generally translucent rather than transparent, given the dispersing nature of the surface created during manufacture.

All these glasses can be clear or body tinted.

■ antique glass

This family, which comprises glass made by blowing, drawing, or any other method, keeps alive old production methods in the making of 'art' glasses.

■ flashed glass

This involves the combining in a fused form of two glasses, usually a clear and a coloured or opal glass. Glasses between 1.5 mm and 7 mm in thickness can be made. Such glasses are much used in table and other domestic glassware, but materials such as flashed opal provide excellently dispersed light transmission, perfect for X-ray viewers and similar devices.

■ anti-reflection glasses

The reflection back from light striking perpendicularly (normally) to a surface of glass is about four per cent, and this increases as the angle becomes oblique.

The need for good vision through a glass uninterrupted by reflection at the surface is commonly required in picture glasses. There are however many applications where such undisturbed viewing is an advantage, or essential such as in optics and lenses.

The conventional way of achieving anti-reflection is by fine etching the surface with hydrofluoric acid to a silk matt, but interference coatings provide more sophisticated products. These may be applied by the methods described earlier (usually physical vapour deposition), or by leaching. Such coatings can reduce reflection to 10% of that produced in a fired surface, and have the added advantage that most of the light which has not been reflected passes straight through the coating without absorption, and thus increases the amount of transmitted light. It is this property which makes the coatings so effective in applications for camera and scientific lenses.

■ heat-treated glasses

Toughening, or tempering, is one of the two ways generally used to improve the strength of glass, at the same time altering its breaking characteristics. Terms differ in different parts of the world, but a distinction is generally made between full tempering (or full toughening) and

33

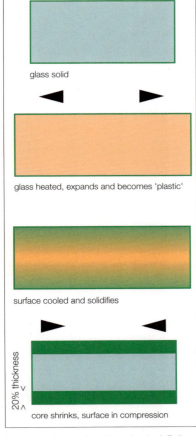

glass solid

glass heated, expands and becomes 'plastic'

surface cooled and solidifies

20% thickness

core shrinks, surface in compression

33. The process of toughening. The diagram shows the four main stages: from above: the annealed glass in its cool state; heating which expands the glass and puts in a plastic state; rapid cooling, which hardens the outer zones; and subsequent slow cooling, pulling the outer zones into compression.

heat strengthening (semi-toughening). Full toughening is needed to give a genuinely stronger product; semi-toughening is used to increase the resistance to thermal stress.

Toughening involves the heating and rapid quenching of an annealed glass. The temperature reached is about 150°C above the transformation temperature, and the glass is thus plastic. The cooling of the surface solidifies it, while the interior of the glass is still cooling and contracting. As the interior continues to contract, it pulls the surface zone into compression, and is itself stretched

into tension. In a typical material, the inner 60% or so of the thickness is in tension, and the outer 20% each side is in compression.

A glass produced in this state exhibits the characteristic when broken of fragmenting into small, comparatively safe, pieces, with no sharp edges. The degree of prestressing can be changed by varying the speed of quenching, and the size of fragments created during breaking can be varied by altering the parameters used in production. Different British and American standards, for example, require different qualities of heat treatment, and can be assessed in different ways. Some standards are based upon the strength of glass (for example, using a ball drop test), and others require a fragmentation analysis.

Toughened glasses can be produced up to four to five times stronger in bending than untempered products, and judgement in specifying must balance the need for a strong product with the wish to create a safety product. The term safety glass needs to be used with caution. The property of fully toughened glass which causes it to be termed 'safe' is the lack of sharp glass fragments caused in breakage. However, 5 m² of 10 mm flat glass weighs 125 kg, and this quantity of fragmented rocky material falling from a storey or more of height can cause damage, even if the particles are small and rounded. Moreover imperfections and impurities in the form of 'stones' occurring in the body of the glass appear to be capable of causing apparently spontaneous failure; nickel sulphide was suspected in a well-reported failure in Australia in the early 1960s. This problem has now been virtually solved by the diminishing of nickel sulphide impurities, and the secondary process of heat soaking which identifies suspect material.

All flat glasses, including borosilicate glasses, can be heat-strengthened. Thin glass can be difficult to toughen, but this presents no difficulties in the 3 mm and 4 mm thick glasses used in the automobile industry, where weight is an important issue. The process undoubtedly turns glass into a much superior product in terms of strength which has, however, the significant disadvantage that it cannot be worked (cut, edge polished, drilled, etc) after processing, and must be carefully worked before processing. The stresses built up in the toughened material are so great that, once released, shattering is inevitable, but heat-strengthened glass will crack in a similar pattern to annealed glass.

■ chemically-strengthened glasses

These glasses are made by replacing small ions in the surface zone of the glass with larger ions, thus putting the surface into compression as with heat-treated glasses. In a typical manufacturing process a sodium-containing glass is heated to just below the transformation temperature in a solution of molten potassium salt. Sodium ions transfer into the salt, and are replaced by potassium ions with a thirty per cent larger radius. If a depth of about 1 mm is affected in this way the glass is strengthened by a factor of five or six. Provided the compression is sufficient to be maintained when the glass is loaded, surface blemishes within the skin depth are inhibited from developing as cracks. This enables the glass to be used to higher levels of tensile stress, with strengths comparable to aluminium alloys. The process is very slow and more suitable for thin glass which is difficult to toughen thermally. Current uses include toughened ophthalmic lenses and electric lamps.

■ laminated glasses

These products extend from simple safety glasses to complex multilayer systems and, in their combination of glasses and plastics, constitute an extremely important group of glass products. The products have been around for some time. In his *Glasarchitektur* of 1914, Paul Scheerbart mentions an 'unsplinterable glass', in which a celluloid sheet is placed between two sheets of glass.

The basic principle behind the use of laminated glass is the combination of the hard and durable but brittle glass, with the elastic properties of plastics. The key to success is adhesion, and the conventional manufacturing technique involves the use of polyvinyl butyral (PVB) sheet. This is laid sandwiched between two sheets of glass, compressed, and then autoclaved for about four hours at 140°C with a pressure of 120 lb/sq in. The treatment turns the PVB into a clear tough adhesive layer. A great range of products is available, and the technique provides scope for invention, but the simplest product is the standard 6.4 mm sheet, comprising two 3 mm glass sheets and a 0.4 mm PVB interlayer.

Such glasses have four prime advantages over the use of flat glass on its own:

— safety: the glass in a broken pane will remain adhered to the pvb, minimizing the risk of injury
— security: laminated glasses, particularly multilaminate products, can provide resistance to severe armed attack or explosion. Multilaminates up to 100 mm or more can be produced
— sound reduction: the resilient PVB layer provides a dampening effect on sound pressure waves. The advantage of the typical 6.4 mm laminated glass over an

equivalent sheet of 6 mm float is shown in
the graph, figure 34
— workability: laminated glasses can be cut
to size after manufacture, which makes
them very suitable for use as simple
security glazing, where the frame sizes
may vary

A further, secondary range of performance
characteristics can be introduced by the use
of tinted interlayers which make the laminated
product heat-absorbing.

Thicker laminates to produce fire
resistance are referred to below.

While PVB laminating is that most conventionally used, the successful manufacture of
combination layered products extends to the
use of other techniques and materials.

■ wire-embedded glasses
Steel meshes or filaments in the inner layer
can add security to the glass.

■ alarm glasses
Wiring may be incorporated into the inner
layer, connected to an electrical alarm circuit
which will set off the alarm if broken. Alternatively, conductive coatings may be used.

■ heated glasses
The technique for producing heated coatings
has already been described, but an alternative method uses very thin element wires
embedded in the interlayer.

■ surface-sealed glasses
Analogous to chemical toughening, but
entirely different in purpose and materials, is
a new process which modifies the surface
chemistry of glass and increases its
weathering durability.

34. Laminated glass:
sound transmission.
The benefit of
laminated glazing
between 160 and
600 Hz is shown.

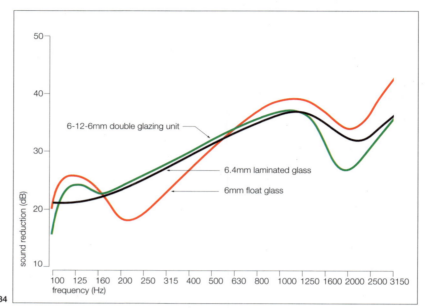

34

Glass is generally, and reasonably,
considered to be a durable and weather-
resistant material. Given regular cleaning,
this is true of a vertical flat glass surface in a
normal environment.

However, at a molecular level the surface
of glass is not a sealed, closed system, and
water in the atmosphere reacts with it.
Typically water is absorbed on the glass surface, diffuses into the glass, and hydrolyses
and decomposes soluble silicates and other
materials in the glass surface, notably sodium
hydroxide and silicic acid in a soda-lime
glass. This causes greater absorption of
water and progressive chemical reaction dissolving more materials in the glass surface,
and forming a thin silica-rich layer which
inhibits further attack. This gives glass a
slightly weathered characteristic. Other
materials in the atmosphere may attack the
glass; carbon dioxide dissolved in rainwater
can cause the creation of white crystals of

sodium carbonate, and alkaline substances
generally attack glass readily.

The degradation of surface is not normally
a problem. With regular washing, the silica
layer protection, while dulling the glass, gives
a surface which is considered satisfactory.
However, in certain conditions such as those
experienced in maritime or industrial environments, the deterioration can become unacceptable.

Water attack can also cause difficulties in
warehousing, where adjacent stacked sheets
may harbour rainwater or condensation
which can ruin the surface.

A process such as that developed by
Ritec in the UK modifies the surface and
effectively seals it. In the process, the cleaned
and dried glass is spray-coated with a
proprietary and currently undisclosed polymer catalyst mixture dissolved in a solvent
system. A chemical reaction takes place in
which the polymer chains link up, both with

the free ends of the non-crystalline molecular
structure of the silanol groups in the glass surface, and with each other. This gives a sealed,
hydrophobic surface, one micron or so thick,
chemically bonded to the glass. It also has a
low coefficient of friction, and thus easily
sheds water and other contaminants. The
application is put on at normal temperature
and pressure, curing in a time between a few
seconds and ten minutes depending on
humidity and temperature.

Although the application technology has
yet to be developed for large scale automated
use, this simple process effectively removes
problems of surface degradation in harsh
environments, such as those experienced on
ships and railway vehicles, and can also halve
surface maintenance and window-washing
periods in buildings, particularly where large
areas of glazed roof are involved. Periodic
reapplication is necessary, which can be a
cause for concern given cost and requirements for access.

composite glass systems
Lamination is based on the principle of the
combination of thin layers of material bonded
together to provide a product which has the
properties and advantages of more than one
material, to suit a particular purpose.
However, the combining of properties is even
more obtainable in composite glass systems,
in which the glass provides the outer durable
protective shield for an interior designed for a
specific function.

■ multiple glazing
The simplest, and most widely used, form of
assembly is the multiple-glazing unit, usually
at present a double or triple system. From its
early uses in buildings such as Aalto's Paimio

Sanatorium in Finland, in 1930, multiple glazing has developed since 1945 to be a major industry in its own right. It has been the glazing industry's first, and simplest, response to the need for energy conservation.

By the simple expedient of trapping a thin slice of dry air, with a thermal conductivity of 0.025 W/m °C, (compared with a value of about 1.0 for glass, itself a poor conductor) between two sheets of glass, the thermal transmittance (U-value) of a window can be reduced from 5 W/m²K to 3 W/m²K or less. The use of body-tinted glasses, coatings, and of cavity gases which perform even better than air, has enabled double-glazed systems to be made which have U-values as low as 1.4 W/m²K, about the same as a plastered cavity brick wall. As research and development proceed, it is likely that even these values will be bettered.

The manufacturing techniques for multiple glazing have been considerably improved over the last twenty or thirty years. The major problems of performance are physical, related to the maintenance of a dry, properly sealed cavity. Early attempts to produce this by means of a glass-to-glass seal proved unpopular for buildings, due to the commercial difficulty of matching sizes and ordering to the market, and the cavities were, in any case, rather small.

More recently, techniques have been invented which use a drying agent in perforated aluminium extrusions (the molecular sieve system), and single-sealing systems using epoxy, polysulphide or butyl sealants, or double systems using polyisobutylene and a secondary seal of polysulphide, polyurethane or silicone.

Cavities can vary from 4 mm to 20 mm or more, to suit the requirements of performance.

35. Multiple glass systems.
Typical multiple-glazing configurations:
A: simple double-glazing showing a conventional spacer containing molecular sieve, and outer edge sealant.
B: acrylic capillaries introduced to inhibit convection; a typical transparent insulation device.
C/D: a typical fire-resisting glazing, in which a clear gel converts into a fire-resisting crust at high temperatures.
E: a coated film introduced into the cavity to amend the radiation transmission and thermal transmittance.
F: a cavity insert which redirects light, as in the Siemens system.
G: formed louvres within the cavity to provide solar control, as in Okasolar.

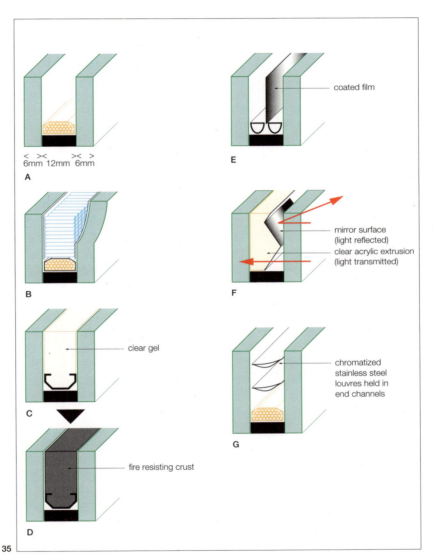

35

The mixing of clear and body-tinted glasses, toughened or otherwise and often coated, in multiple-glazing systems most typifies the state of the art of glazing at present, but it is by no means the only technique using composite glasses.

Products are now appearing on the market which, in response to a functional requirement, combine the transparent weathering properties of glass with other materials, in a sealed product. These tend to be expensive, but they represent solutions to some of the most intractable problems of glazing, and they are coming into use.

■ **cavity-diffusing glazing**

Diffusion can be provided in a glass by a variety of means: opalizing the glass, etching or otherwise modifying its surface, or introducing a diffusing layer into a laminated glass. More effective devices use a cavity in a multiple system to provide a light-diffusing, heat-insulating, and sound-absorbing system. A typical design incorporates a primary cavity composition of clear acrylic tubes with varying diameters of a few millimetres acting as a spacer slab between two glass sheets, with a white or coloured diffusing glass fibre mat on one internal surface. U-values of between 3.4 W/m²K for an 8 mm slab, to 2.6 W/m²K for a 12 mm slab, to 1.0 W/m²K for a 48 mm slab are achieved. The insulation values are thus about 15% better than double glazing of the same cavity depth, although not, it should be noted, as good as low emissivity double glazing. However, with the better sound insulation qualities shown in figure 34 such an assembly is valuable where diffusion or obscuration is required.

■ **fire-resistant glazing**

Prestressed, heat-strengthened, borosilicate glasses can maintain their integrity for up to two hours or more, but they have the disadvantage, as single sheets, of becoming extremely hot themselves in a fire, possibly even causing ignition on the non-fire side. They may thus contain a fire in terms of its gases and flame action, but they present a surface, the other side of which, at 800°C, is both hot and deformed. This makes such a glass unusable if, for example, a means of escape route exists on the other side of the glass.

By creating a multiple system, typically using heat-strengthened glass, with the cavities filled with a polymeric gel, a product is formed which resists fire spread, and provides thermal insulation protection at the same time.

The strengthened glass and perimeter seal assembly is usually the same as for a conventional double-glazing assembly, with extra provision around the edge. In the cavity is a clear polymer gel consisting of a high percentage (about 75%) of water and inorganic salts. In a fire, the gel converts to a crust, which is highly insulating, and the latent heat of the evaporation of the water absorbs much of the heat energy. The glass on the fire side eventually shatters at a temperature of about 500°C, but by the time it does so the crust is sufficiently strong to maintain panel integrity. By the time the temperature on the fire side has reached about 700°C, that on the other side will be about 20°C. Tests show that even after thirty minutes, with a fire side temperature of over 800°C, the other side is only 60°C, and the panel withstands an impact test; 60°C is hot to the touch, but does not radiate dangerously. Such a performance is achieved with an 18 mm cavity to give a thirty minute resistance. Sixty minute fire resistance is achieved with a 28 mm filled cavity, and ninety minutes with triple glazing and two cavities.

The weight of an 18 mm cavity double-glazed unit with gel is about 50 kg/m², as against about 30 kg/m² for a double-glazed unit without the gel, so the weight penalty is not excessive.

Materials such as these, with the borosilicate glasses which withstand temperature while getting very hot, have revolutionized the architecture of transparency in an age increasingly, and properly, concerned with safety.

■ cavity membranes

The potential for use of a well-sealed, clean, dry cavity is enormous. The installation of a thin membrane within such a cavity presents problems of manufacture, but these have been overcome in an ingenious product developed by an American manufacturer, based on work carried out at the Massachusetts Institute of Technology, and funded by the US Department of Energy.

A thin, clear polyester film has a multiple coating sputtered on to it. The polyester film is then factory installed in the cavity, to produce a triple-glazed unit of the same order of weight as a conventional double-glazed unit, but with a U-value of about 1.25 W/m² °C.

The film itself can be coated to produce various transmission performances, and it can be installed within any double glass system with normally available glasses to produce a large range of overall transmission characteristics. It is difficult to manufacture without wrinkles, however. The stretch in the materials is achieved by installing the film in an air space and then heat shrinking it, both of which processes are time consuming and far from easy.

■ cavity-refraction glazing

An obvious, but until recently unachieved, objective in a glazing system is to use the cavity of a multiple-glazing system as the place where solar protection or light modification takes place. Problems of heat build-up, seal and cost have conspired to prevent their appearance. The Siemens Lightsystem typifies what such systems can and should do. An injection moulded polymethylmethacrylate (acrylic) plate, 10 mm or more thick, formed to be flat on one side and comprise parallel linear prisms on the other, is located in the cavity of a double-glazing system. One set of prism faces is coated with a thin film of aluminium, to give a material which transmits the light striking it from one set of directions, but reflects light striking it from a more or less perpendicular direction. Given different angles and depths of prism, this gives rise to a range of products known as sun-shielding or light guidance.

The total system is not transparent in the normal sense; it has the effect of cutting a transmitted image into slices. However, it is very effective in redirecting light as well as being an illuminating example of the use of the properties of glass, durable and strong, and acrylic, very clear and light. Thin film coating technology is used in this product on a plastic rather than a glass component. It is an interesting and important example of the way in which different technologies can be combined to create a product.

The light-bending systems on test at the British Building Research Establishment in the early 1990s demonstrated their inadequacy in providing uninterrupted vision, and associated optical problems such as the appearance of unexpected views of the ground or sky, and effects such as chromatic aberration. It may be expected that new light-bending systems such as Serraglaze referred to in Chapter Four, will supersede these systems.

■ evacuated glazing

The need to improve the thermal resistivity of glazing is of evident great importance, and low emissivity has assisted greatly in its achievement. However, the idea of evacuating a cavity is an obvious adjunct to any low transmittance system, since it inhibits or prevents conduction and convection of heat across the cavity. The idea is a hundred years old: the Dewar flask was invented at the end of the nineteenth century, and Zoller's German patent for evacuated glazing dates back to 1913. However, since then there have been many patents, but little real literature demonstrating progress to technical accomplishment. There are very good reasons for this, related to the maintaining of a vacuum and the difficulty of resisting the inevitable deflection of the panes towards each other resulting from the pressure difference between the atmospheric pressure outside and the partial or total vacuum in the cavity. Only glass can be used for such glazing since the plastics are too permeable to air, and the high vacuum needed of less than 0.1 Pa is difficult to create, maintain and seal. Also, since radiation becomes the greatest resulting cause for heat transfer, compatible low-emissivity coatings are needed in the cavity. Spacers such as transparent honeycombs, foams and aerogels can achieve 0.5 W/m² K, but these tend to reduce transparency partially or totally (aerogels are discussed in Appendix Four).

Recent devices have used pillars of one sort or another. Falbel's American patent of 1976 proposed mica spacers producing a 0.75 mm cavity, and Assarsson's European patent of 1981 involved a profusion of hourglass shaped supports and a very thin cavity of 0.3 mm.

Work in the Physics Department at Sydney University in Australia, as well as in the USA and Europe, is now showing signs of success. Work in Australia in 1992 demonstrated that pillar arrays could be produced which were quite difficult to see and created mid-plane thermal transmittances of 0.6 W/m² K or better, depending on the efficiency of the low-emissivity coatings used.

The overcoming of problems of manufacture and life are still being addressed, and extensive technical literature is describing progress. Prototype devices of one metre square have achieved transmittances of 1.0 W/m² K, of which two thirds derives from radiation, and one third from the separating pillars. The competition, which is price sensitive, is with low-emissivity systems themselves, given that these can produce transmittances of 1.3 W/m² K .

■ photovoltaics

It is a simple scientific reversal to step from the technology of electronic glazing, to the creation of electronic power from a panel. While photovoltaics and the similar generation systems are not glazing systems, they have a family relationship with other glazed cladding systems and thus deserve to be dealt with in a book such as this.

The use of light to create electricity is known to us in the form of the photoelectric cell. Discussion of photoelectricity takes us back to one of the greatest events in man's relationship with, and study of, light. It was Einstein's 1905 paper on the photoelectric effect which earned him his only Nobel Prize. The phenomenon involved is essentially the same as was discussed above on page 249, when light and transparency was described. The importance of the interaction between the photon and the electron was described as a critical factor in how light passed through, or was absorbed by, a material.

In this interaction lies the cause of spontaneous emission, the reason why a fluorescent lamp works, and the principle of stimulated emission discovered by Einstein in 1917, and one of the bases for the laser. If a photon with the right amount of energy strikes an electron,

36. Typical solar cell construction. The top thin layer of n-type silicon about 1 micron thick, carrying a conducting grid arranged as fingers to allow light through. A bottom layer of p-type silicon about 400 microns thick, on the back of which is a metal electrode.

37. Multi-layer solar cell construction. Materials other than silicon are being researched, including gallium arsenide, cadmium telluride, and calcium sulphide. The use of several thin films can be used to allow the absorption of solar energy at different wavelengths.

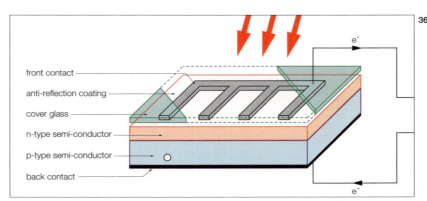

front contact
anti-reflection coating
cover glass
n-type semi-conductor
p-type semi-conductor
back contact

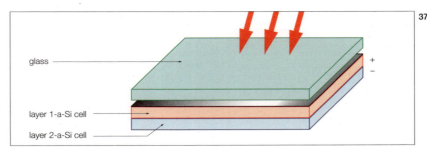

glass
layer 1-a-Si cell
layer 2-a-Si cell

the electron is liberated and flies away from its parent atom.

The central action of a photoelectric cell is the giving of enough energy by a photon to an electron to cause it to escape from a parent metal. This is what Einstein explained in 1905, making the necessary assumption that light can behave as particles. The collection of enough electrons on another metal surface, and their passage through an external circuit back to the originally emitting surface, is the basis for photoelectricity.

Silicon, the basis for glass, has been central to the development of the photovoltaic cell. Silicon is a good electrical insulator (which explains the value of glass in electrical engineering), and this is a result of the lack of so-called 'free electrons', or electrons which can easily be made to leave the surface.

Doping silicon gives it useful semiconductor properties (semiconductor as a term being applied to materials which are not normally conductive, but which can conduct electricity in changed states, such as temperature or doping). Adding a small amount of phosphorus to silicon produces electrically-negative or n-type silicon, providing extra electrons. Electrically-positive or p-type silicon is obtained by the addition of boron (another glass former) which has fewer electrons than silicon, effectively forming empty electron 'holes', which act like positive charges.

An appropriate configuration of n-type and p-type silicon, in the form of thin films under glass, creates the device in which photons create electricity. The construction of such a device is typical of the nanometric technology we are familiar with in the silicon

36 chip. A conducting grid, typically of silver, is laid on a film of n-type silicon 1 micron (1,000 nanometres) thick; the grid is designed to maximize the openness of the silicon to light. Beneath this is a substrate of a much heavier layer of p-type silicon 400 microns thick, formed as a wafer, to the back of which a metal electrode is attached.

Light falling on the n-type side causes electrons to flow out of the n-type material through a load, to combine with a hole. The potential barrier (potential in the electrical sense) is the interface between the two types of silicon, and produces a voltage of about half a volt of direct current.

37 The output of such a cell is proportional to the amount of light falling on it. Unfortunately, there is a natural maximum delivery of electricity available from a photovoltaic system, related to the photon energy required to release the electrons: only short wavelength light will do the job, and even with careful materials selection (such as that which settled on silicon) a maximum use of 17% of the radiation energy in the solar spectrum may be expected in practice. The photovoltaic effect in a conventional cell generates about 0.5 volts across its layers, however large it is, but the amount of current is proportional to the area. A typical panel of about 1.2 m by 500 mm can produce about 75 W under sunlight, or 85 W using enhanced materials, when the full 1,000 W/m² is reaching the cell from sunlight at 100,000 lux. Under an overcast sky of 10,000 lux this power drops by a factor of ten.

Cost and efficiency are the factors which have been addressed in the recent development of photovoltaic cells. Manufacturing involves the growth of silicon crystals, and polycrystalline and amorphous silicon are both cheap to produce. Amorphous silicon is used for devices such as watches and calculators, but because it degrades, it cannot be used in cells for dedicated power loads.

Current manufacturing techniques for wafer cells, such as those described above, uses silicon recovered from silicon chip manufacturing. The recycled material, which is expensive, is produced as long drawn cylinders of silicon which is pure, but not pure enough for use in computer chip manufacture: hence its availability for the manufacture of photovoltaic cells. The cylinder is commonly six inches in diameter, and is trimmed to near squares by the cell makers to enable the cells to be arranged on a five inch grid: this explains the common appearance of the plates: assemblies of five inch square 'tiles' with the corners cut off. The inherent difficulty with such a device is the price and efficiency of the high quality silicon, which shows no sign of dropping to an acceptable level until large-scale manufacture is started, to replace the small-scale recycling now employed. Since large-scale manufacture depends on greater optimism about the market, the cell price is currently trapped at a higher level than need be.

Other materials are used to make photovoltaic systems, and most of them are available as thin films. Thin film technology enables different materials to be laid over each other, each of which is good at absorbing and using photons at different energy levels (or wavelengths). Demonstration cells have been made up to 40% efficient.

A current device considered as a potential successor to the silicon wafers uses two semi-conducting layers, of cadmium sulphide and cadmium telluride, deposited as films on to a substrate of low iron glass coated in tin oxide. The glass acts as the outer layer of the

38. The Grätzel cell.

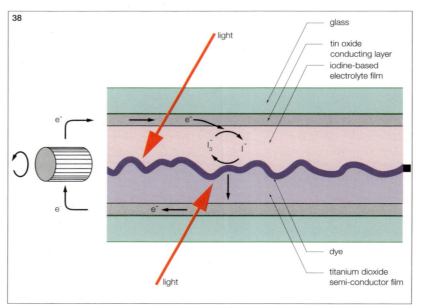

device, protecting the layers beneath, and must be low iron to maximize the photon penetration. The tin oxide coating acts as the front conductor and a metal composite acts as the rear conductor. The price of the semiconductor component tends to generate the price of all photovoltaic cells, and the advantages of such a coated system over the thicker wafer system described earlier is that much smaller quantities of semi-conductor are used (the combined cadmium layers total a thickness of one micron), and the coating does not have to cover the whole of the glass substrate.

Partial covering offers another advantage: the plates have the potential to be partially transparent. It is important to recognize that photovoltaics rely on the absorption of photons, and that a transparent photovoltaic cell is a contradiction in terms. In these circumstances, a device which could comprise a fifty per cent covering of an otherwise transparent

glazing offers obvious benefits. The efficiencies of these coated systems is only half that of the silicon wafers at the moment, but could soon be much greater.

The early 1990s saw photovoltaic arrays producing significant amounts of power. The conventional method of pricing these indicates that a peak-watt (the maximum output at 25°C under sunlight at 1,000 W/m²) can be obtained at a manufacturing cost of about four to five dollars. The problem, of course, particularly in areas such as northern Europe or northern America, is how often this level of sunlight is provided. Nevertheless, despite the intrinsic inability of photovoltaics to farm energy at all photon energies (ie at all wavelengths of light), their cost is continually dropping as their efficiency increases, and large installations are now being seen, even in latitudes north of 50 degrees.

In addition to the photovoltaic cell discussed above, a different type of device

has been developed claimed to be much cheaper, but just as efficient, known as the photoelectrochemical solar cell. These cells were developed by Michael Grätzel and colleagues in the Department of Chemistry at the Swiss Federal Institute of Technology. Layers are built up as a sandwich within two protective sheets of glass, comprising two doped tin oxide conduction layers, between which are two films, one an iodine-based electrolyte, the other a titanium dioxide ceramic semiconductor layer 10 micrometres, or 10,000 nm thick. The device is not fully transparent but it does exhibit light transmission of between 10% and 50% with reasonable layer thicknesses, which gives it a great advantage over conventional opaque photovoltaic cells. A dye is located between the two inner layers. The energy from photons in the light passing through the iodine electrolyte is captured by the dye, and knocks electrons into the titanium dioxide, which then transfers the charge into the tin oxide conducting film to work as electric current. The key to the system is the roughness of the titanium oxide layer. The microscopic undulations and crevices create an effective surface 1000 times greater than the nominal superficial area, making it a much more efficient gatherer of the electrical charge coming into it. Grätzel claims that the percentages of sunlight impinging on the glass surfaces which are converted into useful energy can produce about 150 W/m², at a cost of between £40 and £80 per square metre, as low as ten per cent of that of silicon panels.

Work on these panels is now also going on in Uppsala, where one of the aims is to produce better techniques for the creation of the porous titanium oxide-based films.

39

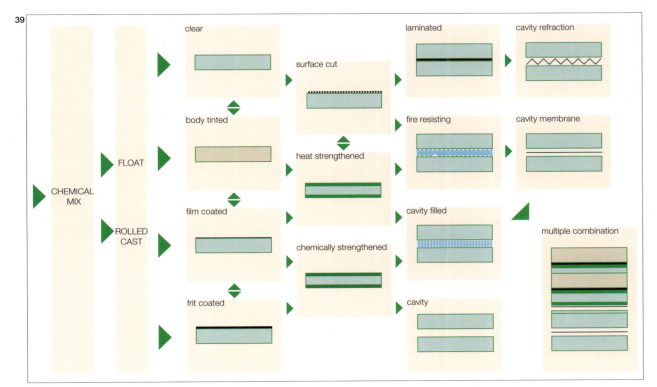

39. The generic glass catalogue. This diagram shows the way in which variety in performance and configuration can be created from the simplest forms of primary glass across to the complexities of multiple glazing. The first two columns represent the primary manufactured product, formed by the primary process and characterized principally by chemistry and the mode of forming. The simple surface applications are included in the second column. The third column shows typical treatments to the glass (as opposed to the applications of layers). The fourth and fifth columns show typical multiple glazing techniques. The progression from left to right is not always the way in which successive treatments are applied. The techniques can be applied in a variety of sequences, subject only to the limitations of physics, to produce an enormous range of products. The bottom right-hand corner represents the richness of current technology.

40. Table of physical properties. It is a characteristic of physical properties that they are stated slightly differently in different sources, and some properties of a material are often not stated at all because they are considered irrelevant to its purpose in the source concerned. It should also be noted that they are often dependent upon the environment or state of the material, such as its temperature or water content. (See note on page 304 for sources and for definitions of properties.)

40

	Density	Strain	Annealing	Softening	Refractive	Thermal conduc-	Thermal expansion	Specific heat	Young's modulus	Chemical durability		
	g/cm³	point °C	point °C	point °C	Index	tivity W/m °C	x10⁻⁶/°C (linear)	J/g °C	G Pa	weather	water	acid
Fused silica glass	2.2	987	1082	1594	1.46-1.48	1.38	0.54	0.77–0.8	73	1	1	1
Borosilicate glass	2.23–2.42	515	565	820	1.47–1.49	1.13	2.8–3.3	0.7–0.8	63–71	1	1	1
Aluminosilicate glass	2.52–2.64				1.53–1.55		4.2–4.6		86	1	1	3
Fluorescent tube glass	2.49	495	524	705	1.51	1.04	8.5	0.83				
Container glass	2.46	490	540	720		1.02	8.7	0.82				
Lead glass	3.03–6.22		437	631	1.56–1.97	0.84	8.4–10.4	0.84	51–59	1/3	1/2	4/2
Soda-lime glass	2.47	520	545	735	1.52	1.42	7.9	0.67–0.8	69–74	3	2	2
Water	1.0				1.333	0.56	non-linear	4.2				
Aluminium	2.7					236	23.1	0.8–0.88	70			
Mild steel	7.8					71 (iron)	11.8 (iron)	0.49	212			
Timbers	0.7–0.8					0.14–0.17	3–6*/36–60**	11–16				
Plastics (clear)	1.1–1.2				1.49–1.59	0.17–0.25	30–90	1.1–1.5	2.4–4.0			
Diamond	3.5				2.42	1000–2600	3.1	0.42				
Zerodur/ceramic							<0.1					

* along grain ** across grain

problems and expertise.

All early processes used casting, blowing or spinning. The Romans made cast plate up to one metre square, but true window-glass production using blown cylinders developed in northern Europe around 1000 AD in response to climatic and stylistic demands. The technique involved the blowing of a large cylinder which was cut, opened out and then flattened. A parallel medieval development was the extension of the technique of making glass as a spun disc.

Both cylinder and disc methods resulted in thin, weak and uneven glass, making it unsuitable for applications requiring optical flatness and strength, such as mirrors and vehicles. Carriage plate was thus traditionally made by casting, grinding and polishing. The use of such glass in buildings was prohibitively expensive except for projects such as Wren's work at Hampton Court at the end of the seventeenth century, already mentioned in Chapter One. The enormous reductions in

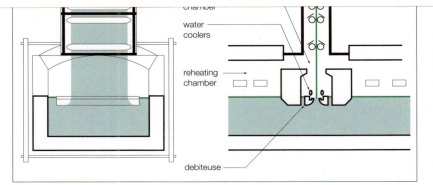

cost, and improvements in quality, experienced during the eighteenth and nineteenth centuries have already been referred to. At the end of the eighteenth century a square metre of carriage plate cost the equivalent of about £10,000, the price of a present-day automobile. By the middle of the nineteenth century the cost of good quality sheet had dropped to 11p per square metre. The glazing of the Crystal Palace indicated that blown sheet from Chances and James Hartleys thin rolled plate were very similar in price.

The making of thin good quality sheet was revolutionized at the beginning of the twentieth century by the simultaneous development of drawn sheet glass in Belgium and the USA. The production of flat glass by cylinder blowing, spinning or casting is intrinsically difficult to mechanize in each case, and manufacturers sought ways of obtaining continuous production. In 1904 Fourcault patented a vertical drawing process. In this process a formed fireclay slot is lowered into the molten glass, which wells up within it. The glass is

This defect does not occur, however, with a production method known as the Colburn or Libbey Owens process, patented in the USA in 1905. In this process the molten glass is drawn up by an iron bait through knurled rollers. It is then reheated and softened to be bent over a roller into a horizontal position. The glass is then drawn through tractors into the annealing lehr.

While avoiding devitrification, the American process shared with the Fourcault method the intrinsic problem of roller contact, in that it was very difficult to avoid damage or degradation to the surface of the glass. This was overcome in the process developed by the Pittsburgh Plate Glass Company, which is basically a vertical version of the Colburn/Libbey Owens process, avoiding the need for rollers or any other form of surface contact. The major problem to be overcome was the tendency of a drawn treacly substance to 'waist'. This is prevented by the use of air-cooled knurled rollers at the edge of the draw.

glass manufacture

glass in architecture

1, 2. A table of extraction energies makes interesting reading against a table of product costs. Typical 1980s costs per metric tonne for materials are shown in table 2. Given annual variations of cost, such figures can only be indicative of range, but the differences between ordinary building materials, glass, the main glass substitutes and two typical metals used for coatings, are striking.

The extent of application of all technologies results from the balancing of cost of provision with the value to the user. In accordance with this principle, the application of glass in buildings over 4,000 years or so of its development and use has depended substantially upon the costs and complexity associated with the various methods of manufacture available.

Glass is remarkable among common products as being unique in its characteristics, while at the same time being manufactured from the two most common elements on the planet.

All glass manufacture is essentially concerned with taking cheap basic materials, together with small quantities of additives,

raw material	extraction energy (GJ/ton)
aluminium	300
plastics	100
copper	100–500
zinc	70
steel	50
glass	20
cement	8
brick	4
timber	2
gravel	0.1
oil	44
coal	29

The prime objective of a flat-glass manufacturer is to act as a successful supplier to stockists by producing, typically, twenty ton lorry loads of glass in ranges of standard sizes: week-to-week production decisions are related to this end and measured against stock in the manufacturer's warehouse. It is significant in this regard that a very large proportion of the research budget of a manufacturer is likely to be concerned with improving and making more efficient the basic primary process, compared with that part related to extensions of technology and new products.

Only by understanding the nature and cost of manufacture is it possible to exploit the potential of the technology.

The drawing process was the principal method of manufacture of cheap flat glass of window quality worldwide until comparatively recently, and remains so in many parts of the world. However, the process suffers from intrinsic production defects which it has proved very difficult to avoid. The action of gravity on the cooling liquid creates variations in thickness which, in a transparent material, have a fundamental effect on its primary property. Until the 1950s, the industry's need for a method of producing glass in different but constant thicknesses, with a good surface, could only be met by the plate process in which the cast or rolled glass is ground and polished.

Advanced techniques for rolled plate glass manufacture took place in parallel with those for sheet glass in the early years of the twentieth century.

The process of manufacture of plate glass remained the same from its invention in 1688 until the 1920s: typically a ton of molten glass was poured on to a bed, rolled to a thickness of about twice that ultimately required, annealed, and then ground and polished, one side at a time.

The Bicheroux process, introduced in the early 1920s, poured the glass between two rollers. This technique permitted the original thickness of glass produced to be to much better tolerances and much closer to that eventually wanted, resulting in less waste of material and less grinding. The reduced original rolled thickness enabled larger sizes to be produced per melting pot.

The lack of continuity in the production, both of rolling and grinding/polishing, remained a difficulty until the Ford Motor Company developed their system in the 1920s, to supply glass for automobiles.

4. The Colburn process.

5. The Bicheroux process. Introduced in the early 1920s, this was the first new way of making plate glass since the invention of the material in the late seventeenth century.

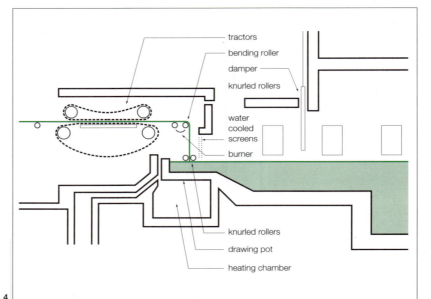

4

tractors
bending roller
damper
knurled rollers
water cooled screens
burner
knurled rollers
drawing pot
heating chamber

Ford invented a system in which molten glass was fed continuously between rollers, and then ground and polished continuously. The sizes of glass produced were suitable for cars only, and Pilkington in the UK developed a similar system from 1923 onwards for larger panes.

Completely continuous moving production (including across the boundary between annealing and grinding/polishing) was achieved on a commercial basis in 1938, when Pilkington's plant, 320 m long, was installed, linking rolling, annealing and twin grinding and polishing of both sides at once.

Rolling, whether for plate manufacture, or for patterned glass, has been in continuous

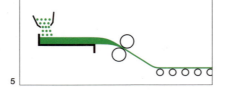

5

use as a technique since this time, and many of the plants still operating were installed that long ago. The rolling process is described in a more detailed way later in this appendix.

Until the 1950s, all flat window glass was made by one of the two techniques so far described. Rolling was used to make patterned glass, large sizes of glass, or the basic product for polished plate, requiring a high degree of optical flatness (such as for mirrors); this glass was intrinsically thick, and expensive when required to have a good surface quality. The other technique, sheet manufacture, satisfied the requirement for cheap window glass, and had an excellent fired finish, but had intrinsic limitations on size and was impossible to make optically flat.

The industry was hunting for a continuous method of production which could provide glass in different, but optically constant thicknesses, with a good surface.

■ the float process

The float process invented and developed by Pilkington represents one of the great pieces of lateral thinking in manufacturing. It takes one of the major characteristics of the rolled plate process (the setting of the material horizontally), and integrates it with the continuous flow principle in one radical step.

The float process operates on the principle that glass at 1100°C helps keep molten the tin on which it floats: tin has a melting point of 232°C, one of the lowest of any metals, and a boiling point of 2720°C. Molten glass poured over tin will therefore, having a lower specific gravity, float on it, with a ponding depth of about 6 mm. In these three properties, melting points, specific gravity and surface tension (which controls the depth of ponding) lie the remarkable characteristics of the float process.

All float plants are designed on the same basic principles, shown in figure 5, the following description relates to a typical fully automated UK plant.

A typical float plant comprises two main functional parts:

— the batch plant
— the float line

the batch plant This is where the basic raw materials are stored, and mixed into the various frits necessary to make the different composition glasses produced on the float line. It is a separate multistorey building 30 m or so high.

The materials for standard clear float are:

— sand
— soda ash (Na_2CO_3, for conversion to Na_2O)

— lime stone (CaCO₃, for conversion to CaO)
— dolomite (Ca/MgCO₃, for conversion to MgO)
— salt cake (crude sodium sulphate)
— cullet (re-cycled broken glass)

After mixing, batches of frit are transported by dumper truck in four tonne truck loads or on conveyor belts, to the filling end of the tank.

the float line This requires the following manufacturing capabilities:

— the production of a continuous flow of molten glass of the required mix at 1,100°C.
— the drawing of this across molten tin to give varying glass thicknesses. The 'natural' thickness of the glass on tin (given surface tension) is between 6 mm and 7 mm. Obtaining thinner glass demands stretching the glass ribbon by pulling it faster by means of rollers in the annealing lehr whilst restraining its tendency to waist in. Obtaining thicker glass demands restraining the natural lateral flow by means of fenders. The thickness range 2.5 mm to 25 mm is regularly produced. It is theoretically possible to produce thicknesses up to 35 mm.

The line comprises the following principal components:

— melting tank
— float bath
— annealing lehr
— automatic cutting
— automatic warehousing

6. The float process.

6

The process is such that it cannot be stopped without major disruption, and the plants may be run for several years without major refurbishment or repairs.

the melting tank This is 60 m long by 12 m wide by 1.5 m deep, and holds 2,100 tons of glass. Large modern tanks hold up to 5,000 tons. The tank sits over a ventilating undercroft 15 m deep, constructed from ventilated brickwork. The undercroft is the source of the air used to supply oxygen to the regenerative furnace in which the tank sits. Burning takes place over the tank. The furnace is commonly fired by oil (with facilities for change over to gas), and operates from both sides with a twenty minute changeover. As one side is firing, the gases generated are disposed of from the other side through the undercroft flues. The undercroft acts as a flue, and heat regenerator.

The frit is supplied from the temporary holding receiver into a tipping trough running on an overhead rail in the front of the furnace. Once filled, the trough runs across the furnace front, and the frit is tipped via a water cooled roller into the furnace, together with the cullet transported from the other end of the line.

The furnace heats the frit up to between 1,500°C and 1,600°C, and the glass flows down the tank and cools to about 1,100°C, final cooling being by cold air blown over the molten glass. The level of molten glass is automatically controlled to ± 5 mm.

The whole process is monitored using closed circuit television (monitors connected to cameras view the tank interior) and computers, from an adjacent glazed control room.

At the end of the tank the 1,100°C melt passes through a refiner in which dissolved gases are disposed of, and is poured through a canal over the tin.

float bath This operates on the principle that the molten glass at 1,100°C melts tin in a shallow bath. The bath is 55 m long by 600 mm deep, and has an internal width of 7.6 m, containing about 1,800 metric tonnes of molten tin. The high density of the tin ensures that the glass floats upon it.

The tank is sealed, and the atmosphere in it fed with hydrogen and nitrogen to prevent the tin oxidizing. The continuity of the process keeps a ribbon of glass flowing down the bath, leaving it for the annealing lehr at 600°C.

The natural ponding depth of 6–7 mm makes the production of 6 mm glass fairly easy. Speeding up the rollers at the head of the annealing lehr stretches the flow to produce thinner glass: waisting is prevented by edge rollers above the bath. Thicker glass is created by damming.

The maximum width of glass possible is commonly 3,500 mm, which yields a useful ribbon of 3,210 mm. A rate of flow of 1,150 m/hr gives 4 mm thick glass. Wider baths, up to 4 m, are being considered for new lines.

Changing the thickness is comparatively quick: changing from 4 mm to 5 mm takes 45 minutes (implying a loss for cullet of about 900 m)

At the end of the bath, glass at 600°C has a surface hardness sufficient to prevent it being marked on the steel annealing lehr rollers.

The float process is monitored by CCTV and computers in the same sort of control facility as for the melting tank.

annealing lehr This process cools the glass under very controlled conditions to produce a material with the correct properties, particularly suitable for cutting. The annealing lehr mainly consists of an enclosed box within which the glass passes over rollers, and the temperature of any width of glass is controlled: this involves heating the edges at certain points while the centre is being cooled. By the time the glass appears, its temperature has dropped to 100°C, cooled under ventilating tubes with holes at 75–100 mm centres, using room air.

automatic checking and cutting As the glass emerges from the lehr it passes through a checking point in which it is illuminated from above by a mercury vapour lamp reflected in a mirror. The mirror reflects an even light down through the glass on to a perfect white surface below the rollers. A CCTV camera positioned above the glass transmits a continuous record of blemishes in the glass. Any blemishes recorded are noted in the computer and the section concerned is cut out and discarded during the subsequent cutting process.

Not all manufacturers provide this. The production processes are as follows:

— washing
— tin oxide sensitizing
— silver coating
— copper coating
— drying
— painting
— drying
— baking
— cooling and washing

washing The glass is dropped by free-fall, and then taken on rollers through a cleaning process. Five oscillating panels with circular disc brushes underneath clean the top surface using a very weak solution of jewellers' rouge (hydrated ferric oxide). The glass is then passed under three washers to remove all excess powder.

tin sensitizing The glass is then passed under a spray of stannous solution, and again washed. The tin sensitizes the surface of the glass, and enhances the formation of the silver in the next process.

silver coating This is carried out within a glass enclosure. The glass is passed under oscillating tubes with nozzles beneath them, spraying out silver nitrate and an activator (ammonia). The chemicals mix above the glass, and silver precipitates out in a chemical reaction, to be deposited on the tin oxide activated glass surface. The excess material is washed off under washers.

copper coating This is necessary to prevent the silver tarnishing on contact with the air, and turning black. Oscillating sprays mix copper sulphate and ammonia, which precipitates copper on to the silver.

drying The coated glass is then air-dried.

painting The next processes involve the application of a stoved paint coating to protect the coatings beneath. A lead naphtha paint is curtain-coated on to the copper coated surface of the glass. This involves the passing of the glass beneath a continuously revolving cylinder dropping a curtain of paint over the production line into a recycling reservoir beneath. As the glass approaches the curtain, the line accelerates the glass beneath the curtain, giving an even coat.

drying The painted glass is again air-dried.

baking The glass is then passed through stoving ovens, raising the temperature to 120ºC.

cooling and washing The glass is finally cooled and washed prior to cutting or warehousing.

products
Mirrors are perhaps used more extensively in furniture than architecture. The production objectives of the plant are to make large sheets of mirror, for warehousing and distribution in large sheets, or for cutting to order in the factory. Thicknesses may vary from 2 mm to 10 mm, with 4 mm and 6 mm being the commonest. The maximum width of glass which can be silvered depends on the plant, but is typically 2600 mm. The maximum length is limited only by the need to turn the sheets at the end of the process, typically about 4 m.

edge working and bevelling
Much mirror production is characterized by edge working and bevelling, which are generally carried out in a silvering plant.

Edges can be worked in a variety of different surfaces, from a whitish, ground glass appearance, to a brilliant polish. The finish is a result of the grinder or polisher used, and the solution of jewellers' rouge employed.

Complex edge work is done by a specialist craftsman who moves the edge against spinning wheels by hand.

straight edge grinding and polishing
For small pieces this is done one edge at a time, with the sheet being carried back to the front of the polishing machine four times, once for each edge. Ordinary edge work is normally carried out on double edgers, with two machines working on opposite edges.

bevelling This is carried out using a bevelling machine. The long machine can deliver many different degrees of ground or polished surface on the bevel.

■ **dip coating**
Immersion, or dip coating, is based on the principle of immersing the glass in a solution of the material to be deposited, draining it out to leave a film, and then heating it to produce a pyrolytic coating. Production of thin even films demands great sophistication of technique.

In the dip coating method, the thoroughly cleaned glass is lowered into the tank containing the coating solution, and then carefully pulled out at constant speed. The rate of withdrawal is smooth and slow, being related to the speed of evaporation of the solvent, to ensure that the flow down the glass from the lifted surface is minimized. The solution is in a volatile liquid which evaporates quickly and undergoes hydrolysis and condensation. The glass is then baked to 650ºC, to produce the hard transparent oxide coating about 70 nm thick.

Large substrate sizes can be used, up to 3 m by 4 m. Products include reflective solar control glasses, such as Irox by Schott, and multiple-dip coatings to form interference layers.

Organic films can also be applied by dipping, which coats both sides of the glass at the same time. The material concerned is dissolved in a volatile solvent, and added to a tank of purified water. The solvent evaporates and the material is left as a layer on the surface which is made 'monomolecular' by a slider. Repeatedly dipping the glass into the tanks coats it, mono-layer by mono-layer. This is a very new technology, but is potentially very interesting.

■ **chemical vapour deposition**
This technique depends upon the production of a solid film by chemical reaction between vapours just above, or actually on, the glass. A typical on-line technique to deposit tin oxide was described earlier.

Chemical vapour deposition can be carried out at atmospheric pressure, and this method is used in the manufacture of Pilkington's Reflectafloat. Low-pressure processes are also used.

Spray coating is a variant of chemical vapour deposition in which the materials are in the form of droplets rather than vapours. Typically, a solution of metal chlorides in water or another solvent is converted with a carrier gas (air, nitrogen or argon) into an aerosol, and deposited on to the moving glass by multiple nozzles.

secondary manufacture

Primary manufacture, the production of flat glass in a series of integrated steps from melting through forming to annealing, creates a wide range of products which, historically, have both satisfied and created the market.

However, architects, designers and consumers in general, have increasingly demanded products which perform better than a simple annealed sheet. Demands for strength, safety and thermal performance have required the industry to develop new materials made to higher standards, and it is not now unusual in a national market for more glass to be used for secondary manufacture than is used for single glazing in its primary floated or rolled form.

To the glass industry as a whole these products are not merely a way of selling more glass to meet higher demands; they are added value products which satisfy a sophisticated and increasing market with materials of much higher intrinsic cost, making greater profit out of a square metre of glass.

The manufacturing techniques used by the secondary industry vary from the simple and comparatively traditional, to the extremely high technology methods resulting from a use of advanced physics. In these techniques lie many of the products of the future, and knowledge of them gives an indication of the directions possible.

■ heat toughening

The production of a safe glass has been an objective of glass-makers for over a thousand years, but it was not until the 1870s that the basic technique was mastered. This involved heating the glass to red heat and quenching it in oil. In 1928, the French devel-

7. Heat toughening.

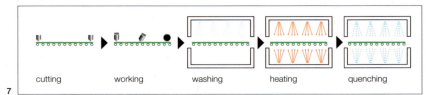

cutting   working   washing   heating   quenching

7

oped Securit; the production method involved the suspension of the glass in an electric furnace, followed by rapid cooling effected by blowing cold air on both sides. This method is still used, but has the disadvantage that it leaves tong marks indented into the surface of the glass where it was held, vertically suspended, during the process.

Over the last ten years or so, the vertical process has been replaced by the horizontal process wherever demands of the market have justified the higher capital investment. It produces a better quality product, free of tong marks, tong distortion, and stretching, and is flat enough for double glazing or laminating. The horizontal process is described in the following paragraphs.

Toughening, by whatever process, demands five stages:

— forming and working
— washing
— heating
— quenching
— heat soaking

forming and working The stresses built up in the heat-toughening process, as described in Appendix One, page 263, make the working of the glass after the process impossible. For this reason, edge grinding and polishing, hole formation, and cutting of any sort must be carried out prior to toughening. The most significant impact this has in normal practice is that all toughened

glass has to be cut and processed to order, to fit the assembly for which it is intended. This places particular demands on procurement time and availability.

washing Careful washing is essential to ensure that the glass entering the furnace is perfectly clean.

heating The essence of heat toughening is carefully controlled heating being carried out prior to quenching. The furnace is a chamber up to 80 m long heated to about 625ºC. The glass is moved through the furnace over rollers about 50 mm in diameter about 150 mm apart, and reaches the temperature of the furnace in a gradual and controlled way. The major difficulty is that of achieving an evenly spread temperature. In modern furnaces the glass plates are oscillated thus enabling the plant to be made shorter.

quenching The glass leaves the furnace and moves into the quenching plant, which typically comprises jets above and below the glass, blowing air at ambient temperature on to the glass surface. The higher the degree of toughening required, the faster the air flow.

heat soaking After toughening, the glass is usually heat soaked at 290ºC for several hours, to check the homogeneous quality of the material, and particularly to check for the presence of nickel sulphide particles which cause the glass to shatter.

products

The use of 'roller hearth' furnaces enables thick and body-tinted glasses to be heated without tong marks. The widths available are dependent on the designed width of the plant, and the current typical hearth in Europe can produce glass 4 m long by 2100 mm wide. The safety standards required are usually defined by the number of particles produced by shattering a sample struck in a standard way and counting the dice in a 100 mm square. The largest size of toughened glass available varies from manufacturer to manufacturer, with maximum dimensions available up to 2.4 m and 5 m.

■ bending

Bending is one of the oldest secondary techniques, and is characteristic, for example, of English Regency architecture early in the nineteenth century.

Bending relies on the controlled heating of glass up to the point where it softens and relaxes into a mould, followed by cooling and hardening. Three methods are currently in use: moulding (or sag bending), tong-held bending and roller-hearth bending.

In a typical moulding process, mild steel moulds 3 mm or so thick are panel-beaten into the required curvature, this being checked with timber templates or sweeps. The mould is dusted with dry powdered plaster to a thickness of 1–1.5 mm to protect the glass from the metal surface. The mould is then set on a bed of bricks on a trolley, and the flat glass, cut to exactly the right girth, is laid across it. The bed is then moved into a kiln, which is heated up to a temperature of between 600 and 700ºC. The heating, bending and cooling process takes about four hours.

Not all manufacturers provide this. The production processes are as follows:

— washing
— tin oxide sensitizing
— silver coating
— copper coating
— drying
— painting
— drying
— baking
— cooling and washing

washing The glass is dropped by free-fall, and then taken on rollers through a cleaning process. Five oscillating panels with circular disc brushes underneath clean the top surface using a very weak solution of jewellers' rouge (hydrated ferric oxide). The glass is then passed under three washers to remove all excess powder.

tin sensitizing The glass is then passed under a spray of stannous solution, and again washed. The tin sensitizes the surface of the glass, and enhances the formation of the silver in the next process.

silver coating This is carried out within a glass enclosure. The glass is passed under oscillating tubes with nozzles beneath them, spraying out silver nitrate and an activator (ammonia). The chemicals mix above the glass, and silver precipitates out in a chemical reaction, to be deposited on the tin oxide activated glass surface. The excess material is washed off under washers.

copper coating This is necessary to prevent the silver tarnishing on contact with the air, and turning black. Oscillating sprays mix copper sulphate and ammonia, which precipitates copper on to the silver.

drying The coated glass is then air-dried.

painting The next processes involve the application of a stoved paint coating to protect the coatings beneath. A lead naphtha paint is curtain-coated on to the copper coated surface of the glass. This involves the passing of the glass beneath a continuously revolving cylinder dropping a curtain of paint over the production line into a recycling reservoir beneath. As the glass approaches the curtain, the line accelerates the glass beneath the curtain, giving an even coat.

drying The painted glass is again air-dried.

baking The glass is then passed through stoving ovens, raising the temperature to 120ºC.

cooling and washing The glass is finally cooled and washed prior to cutting or warehousing.

products
Mirrors are perhaps used more extensively in furniture than architecture. The production objectives of the plant are to make large sheets of mirror, for warehousing and distribution in large sheets, or for cutting to order in the factory. Thicknesses may vary from 2 mm to 10 mm, with 4 mm and 6 mm being the commonest. The maximum width of glass which can be silvered depends on the plant, but is typically 2600 mm. The maximum length is limited only by the need to turn the sheets at the end of the process, typically about 4 m.

edge working and bevelling
Much mirror production is characterized by edge working and bevelling, which are generally carried out in a silvering plant.

Edges can be worked in a variety of different surfaces, from a whitish, ground glass appearance, to a brilliant polish. The finish is a result of the grinder or polisher used, and the solution of jewellers' rouge employed.

Complex edge work is done by a specialist craftsman who moves the edge against spinning wheels by hand.

straight edge grinding and polishing
For small pieces this is done one edge at a time, with the sheet being carried back to the front of the polishing machine four times, once for each edge. Ordinary edge work is normally carried out on double edgers, with two machines working on opposite edges.

bevelling This is carried out using a bevelling machine. The long machine can deliver many different degrees of ground or polished surface on the bevel.

■ dip coating
Immersion, or dip coating, is based on the principle of immersing the glass in a solution of the material to be deposited, draining it out to leave a film, and then heating it to produce a pyrolytic coating. Production of thin even films demands great sophistication of technique.

In the dip coating method, the thoroughly cleaned glass is lowered into the tank containing the coating solution, and then carefully pulled out at constant speed. The rate of withdrawal is smooth and slow, being related to the speed of evaporation of the solvent, to ensure that the flow down the glass from the lifted surface is minimized. The solution is in a volatile liquid which evaporates quickly and undergoes hydrolysis and condensation. The glass is then baked to 650ºC, to produce the hard transparent oxide coating about 70 nm thick.

Large substrate sizes can be used, up to 3 m by 4 m. Products include reflective solar control glasses, such as Irox by Schott, and multiple-dip coatings to form interference layers.

Organic films can also be applied by dipping, which coats both sides of the glass at the same time. The material concerned is dissolved in a volatile solvent, and added to a tank of purified water. The solvent evaporates and the material is left as a layer on the surface which is made 'monomolecular' by a slider. Repeatedly dipping the glass into the tanks coats it, mono-layer by mono-layer. This is a very new technology, but is potentially very interesting.

■ chemical vapour deposition
This technique depends upon the production of a solid film by chemical reaction between vapours just above, or actually on, the glass. A typical on-line technique to deposit tin oxide was described earlier.

Chemical vapour deposition can be carried out at atmospheric pressure, and this method is used in the manufacture of Pilkington's Reflectafloat. Low-pressure processes are also used.

Spray coating is a variant of chemical vapour deposition in which the materials are in the form of droplets rather than vapours. Typically, a solution of metal chlorides in water or another solvent is converted with a carrier gas (air, nitrogen or argon) into an aerosol, and deposited on to the moving glass by multiple nozzles.

Solution deposition and chemical vapour deposition both depend, to a degree, on the chemical characteristics of materials: the ability of substances to dissolve in other substances, and their behaviour as they move into and out of chemical combination or the various states or phases they can occur in. What materials can be used depends on these accidents.

However the flexibility of physical vapour deposition techniques, particularly in its most recent developments, has opened up a new future for glass, and they are dealt with here in correspondingly greater detail.

■ physical vapour deposition

Physical vapour deposition depends on a much more straightforward technique: the vaporizing of a substance, and its subsequent very even delivery in very small amounts, to a substrate. The techniques are characterized by their ability to deposit almost any material as a coating.

There are three basic techniques:

— evaporation
— sputtering
— ion plating

evaporation

The common forms of evaporation deposition are by using an electron beam or direct heat. A stream of electrons is focused on a metal contained in a crucible, which is maintained as an anode, its positive charge accelerating the electrons. The energy of the stream causes the metal to melt and then evaporate. The gaseous material is contained within a very high vacuum environment, to increase the flow of vaporized material to the substrate.

12. Sputtering.

Evaporation techniques suffer from the disadvantage that the source of the evaporant is a point source, and many sources are necessary to ensure uniform coatings. Nevertheless, the high rate of evaporation and purity of the coating have made it an important technology used, for example, in the Libbey-Owens-Ford Varitran plant installed in 1967.

Another disadvantage of the electron beam vaporization process is its high temperature, high energy and high voltage nature; the technique is increasingly being replaced by magnetically-enhanced sputtering.

sputtering

This is a surprisingly old technology, using positively-charged ions rather than negatively-charged electrons. It was discovered in 1852, sometimes used for the manufacture of mirrors from 1877 onwards, and in the 1920s and 1930s was used to apply gold films on to fabrics and the wax masters of phonographs.

The principle of sputtering is a remarkable one: a target is bombarded by ions which physically dislodge atoms from it, causing them to leave the surface and strike the substrate, adhering to it. A film is thus slowly built up. The slowness of the build-up was a cause for sputtering to be overtaken as a technique until the 1960s. Since that time the development of magnetically-enhanced sputtering, notably by Airco Temescal in the USA and others, has placed the technique in the forefront of thin film technology.

Sputtering, unlike electron beam techniques, can operate not only on pure elements, but on alloys and compounds. It can also be carried out in high vacuum gas environments using oxygen or nitrogen to create oxides and nitrides with new performances,

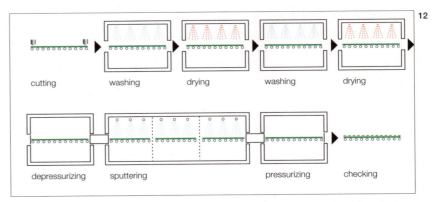

cutting   washing   drying   washing   drying

depressurizing   sputtering   pressurizing   checking

and is an ideal process to be used in the creation of extremely thin, well-controlled films ideally suited to the new generation of tailor-made multiple coatings now being designed.

Magnetically-enhanced sputtering is now being used as a technique worldwide, with economical plants costing only between £5 million and £10 million installed by many secondary manufacturers.

In planar-magnetron sputtering, a sheet of glass is placed in a vacuum chamber which contains a specifically designed cathode target and the sputter gas. A negative charge is applied to the cathode, and a glow discharge (or plasma) ignites within the chamber at the appropriate gas pressure. Positively-charged atoms of the gas are attracted to the target, and strike it with such force that they eject atoms from it, for deposition on to the target.

A typical sputtering plant comprises:

— reception and storage
— cutting
— coating
— testing
— stacking

reception The plant typically receives two sets of products for processing:

— ready cut sizes or toughened product to order
— large stock-size annealed product 6 m by 3 m, for cutting, coating and then storage for stock

cutting This stage in the process is usually carried out with the shape-optimizing cutter described earlier.

coating The coating process comprises the following steps:

— surface polishing
— first washing
— drying
— second washing
— drying
— air-lock pressure reduction
— 3–chamber sputtering
— air-lock pressure normalization
— checking

The glass is passed under three sets of rotating brush scrubbers, lubricated with water and ceri-rouge, to purge and polish the top surface. The rouge is then washed off by brushes rotating parallel to the surface, and warm-air dried.

to respond to individual needs, often on a building by building basis, its strengths and capabilities are dispersed. It can be very difficult to know where to go for a product, and where to find responsiveness rather than an apparently disinterested reference to a catalogue.

An understanding of the industry and its structure is important to designers wishing to get the most out of it.

cylinder manufacture in 1832, and without this knowledge the contract for the Crystal Palace and, perhaps, even the direction of technology might have gone elsewhere.

The design-and-build competition for the Crystal Palace in 1850 had Chance tendering with Paxton using blown sheet, Horeau tendering with a French supplier, and James Hartley of Sunderland tendering with cast plate at a price only slightly in excess of Chance's sheet. Despite the size of the con-

cal improvement on that invented by Fourcault. The Pittsburgh Plate Glass Company then derived an even better drawing process, and became yet another major producer. In the early 1920s, the demand of the automobile industry drove the Ford Motor Company to create a process which put mass production on to a new footing with an improved rolled product, and further expanded the American industry.

The industry in the UK was consolidated

Following this the glass is washed more thoroughly in a big washer, and dried under positive pressure (to keep external air out) within a glazed chamber, after which it is ready to enter the first vacuum chamber.

— the speed with which the substrate moves
— the voltage of the cathode
— the variety of glasses used
— the variety of target materials used

gives directly, percentage transmissions or reflections.

Colour is tested on a Spectrogard or similar machine; colour is checked in reflection and transmission, on the coated and

combines the subtlety of sputtering with the high speed of electron beam vaporization, giving a faster and more adhesive coating, even on complex surfaces.

In these technologies, the glasses of the

when Pilkington Brothers, who had been founded in 1826 as the St Helens Crown Glass Company, started experiments in 1923 concerned with using the Ford process to make larger sheets, and by 1938 Pilkington had a continuous rolling, grinding and polishing machine in commercial operation.

By 1940, the structure of the primary glass industry in the western world was established, with four nations each dominated by a small number of major manufacturers, all related and separated by a network of patents and interdependencies.

the float process

In 1952, an invention was made known which changed everything. By floating molten glass on molten tin, Pilkington managed to create glass almost as flat as their rolled and polished plate, to economic thicknesses, and in large quantities, by a continuous process. By 1955, they had a full-scale production unit at St Helens making glass about 2.5 m wide.

This single invention both revolutionized and ossified the industry. Up to its arrival, most manufacturers were making a range of rolled or sheet products based on their own technical origins and history, with products borrowed from their competitors, subject to the demands of their own markets.

The invention of a process which, as it was developed, could produce thin sheet without surface irregularities, and thicker plate with surfaces almost as parallel as, and with a better finish than those of the ground and polished product, put Pilkington Brothers in a position of technical pre-eminence which they were quick to capitalize on. Through patenting and licensing, they were able to dictate terms to the industry, which became an international 'club' of primary manufacturers dominated by twelve or so producers, four in the USA, one in the UK, two in France, one in Italy, one in Belgium, one in Luxembourg and one in Japan. As with all such groups, a surface of agreement covered an underworld of infighting and challenge, at a technical and commercial level, characterized by cross-ownership.

With the adoption of float techniques, the pattern of development of primary manufacture was set. Characterized by a requirement for extremely high capital investment (a float plant costs between £70 million and £100 million) for a single nature product, the chemical content and performance of which was very difficult to vary, the manufacturers' resistance to change and diversity is understandable.

competition and integration

As company reports and news bulletins make clear, commercial interbreeding is intense. In the 1980s, Pilkington bought Libbey-Owens-Ford (LOF) in the USA, and also bought the German operation of the French BSN Gervais-Danone company Flachglas. BSN abandoned flat glass manufacture in 1979, but their plants were quickly picked up, not only by Pilkington but by the Japanese Asahi in Belgium and Holland, and by PPG in France itself. Asahi, who have 50% of the Japanese market, also bought Glaverbel in Belgium. Guardian Industries in the USA challenged the others by setting up a float plant in 1971, and grew to become one of the largest US manufacturers, setting up Luxguard in Luxembourg, and assisting in setting up a plant in Eastern Europe.

Commercial moves at the end of the 1980s further complicated the interpenetration of the primary manufacturers in the USA, Europe and Japan, and, at the time of writing, Pilkington Glass in the UK, PPG in the USA, St Gobain in France and Asahi in Japan are in a super-league of world producers, with large, complex, and often not particularly publicized intercontinental holdings.

Although figures were not available for the specific building market, they were available for the automotive industry, and market breakdown reflects the power of the Japanese automobile industry, and the solid base of supply in that country concentrated in the hands of two major suppliers.

Any simple representation of size or market share is very misleading as a guide to commercial dominance. 1989 saw the selling of twenty per cent of LOF in the USA by Pilkington to Nippon. This put the 'American' company (jointly owned by the UK and Japanese companies) in an important position in the automotive market, able to make glass with comparatively cheap US production costs for sale to the traditionally chauvinistic Japanese market. Such a move gave enormous potential benefit to Pilkington as the 80% shareholder, and is merely an example of a typical change in the industry at the end of the 1980s, so important in the spreading of technology.

In 1995, Pilkington and PPG settled their differences and dropped all litigation, giving a new calm in the international industry worldwide.

Notwithstanding the increasing internationalizing of the industry the effect of the one-process nature of float glass production has been to concentrate many of the manufacturing, marketing and research objectives of primary manufacturers to the end of making 4 mm and 6 mm float marginally cheaper and/or better than competitors. Competition is very severe, and a look at the trucks parked in the yards of secondary processors is an indication of the spread of the market, and the willingness of consumers to play it.

The high capital cost of float plants, and technical criteria, create a need to operate them every hour of every day, and provide a unique constraint for manufacturers. Their production needs are comparatively inflexible, subject to the development of short-run plants, but they still benefit from an invention, now nearly forty years old, which has revolutionized glass-making, and given us an almost perfect product.

The potential for variety, even in primary glass manufacture, is very great. Large differences in performance and appearance result from minute variations in chemistry and treatment and, given the technical developments of the last twenty years, it might be expected that designers and the market would be presented with a rich palette of materials, as the industry sets out to exploit its inventiveness. Manufacturers' literature gives the impression that this is the case, and producers are producing useful ranges. However, in such a process-dominated industry the incentive to expand the primary product range is small.

secondary manufacturing

While consideration of the glass industry may be dominated by the primary manufacturers, the industry also contains other essential and important sectors which together are providing a spur to change; secondary manufacturing and installation.

market division

Glass is sold by the primary manufacturers to a variety of markets. Such is the complexity of the market that many primary manufacturers claim that they do not know where their glass goes. Even allowing for their caution of confidentiality, this is not entirely surprising. The secondary processors, merchants and installers, set the production demand of the primary manufacturers through their own order books and stock requirements. Historically, this distanced the primaries from the market, but the commercial structure is now changing.

product range

Secondary processing is rich in variety, as a list of products shows:

— proprietary double and multiple glazing
— heat treatment and toughening
— chemical strengthening
— curving
— laminating
— coating
— enamelling
— etching and sand-blasting
— mirrors

Secondary processing has, by its nature, developed from fragmentary, locally-based production units. Laminating, toughening and the making of multiple glazing, can all be carried out with plant costing from less than £1 million up to £10 million for a coating plant, and this enables production and markets to be matched in much smaller units than primary manufacture. However, with the always-present commercial urge for combination and rationalization, secondary processing has now become much more unified, and the subject of increasingly multinational effort. A typical large secondary processing company will have been formed out of perhaps hundreds of small companies, leading to easy takeover by the primary companies. The activities of such a company spread across the whole range of secondary production, including coatings and installation.

The comparative closeness to the market of the secondary processors, merchants and installers, and their increasing cohesion and strength, has provided a new dimension to the industry, and a spur to the primary manufacturers to create secondary product ranges, and to buy into 'downstream' operations. In Europe a high percentage of secondary processors are now owned by the primary manufacturers, providing a tied outlet for their continuous glass production.

The new technologies identified in Chapter Four indicate the sort of developments we may see in secondary processing in the future. Significantly, the nature and complexity of many of these means that we will not see them in the market at an acceptable cost until they are made in large quantities by automated processes. This is the major challenge for the industry in the decades to come, if these marvellous new materials are not to languish in the prototype stage.

specialist manufacturing

Alongside the main primary and secondary industries are the specialist manufacturers, the third group. Special glasses, such as optical and laser glasses, are often product lines in the giant companies, but the giants are complemented by companies such as Schott in West Germany and Corning in the United States. Although specialist manufacturers may concentrate mainly on industries other than the building industry, their contribution to architectural glass is fundamental for two main reasons. Firstly, they make the high value, high technology products which provide the exploration territory for building designers, and secondly, the building products they make often provide new applications for glass.

Borosilicate glasses, so domestically conventional in products such as cookware, have become fire-resisting glasses. Schott is a major manufacturer of both. Corning, where ceramic glass was first created, has invented an integral 'louvre blind' glass named Louverre, as a development of its early photochromic and ceramic glass work. The major primary glass manufacturers themselves are also deeply involved in high technology products.

It is in the catalogues of these specialists and special divisions of the large primary producers that one can often find clues for the future in high performance materials.

the installers

The fourth sector in the industry comprises the installers. This present book is concerned with glass rather than glazing and cladding, but glass in architecture is so much a matter of its incorporation into systems, that reference needs to be made.

Glass is only one of many materials used in the cladding industry, but as the primary source of transparency its importance is obvious. Major glass manufacturers such as PPG, have long published framing systems catalogues. Developments in the last twenty years have seen glazing develop from being a matter of installing glass in a frame, to suspended assemblies and frameless support. This has had an interesting impact on the industry. The method by which glass is fixed had been revolutionized by bolt systems such as Pilkington's Planar, and important collaborations have developed between secondary manufacturers and trade contractors such that between Eckelt and GIG (Grill and Grossmann) in Austria.

In Pilkington's 'Fenestration 2000' Stage 1 Report, one of the more interesting demands for the future is for integrated glazing and framing. The construction industry is seeking to avoid the complications of multiple handling of materials and systems.

We may expect increasing backward and forward integration in response to this demand, as well as in the demand for added value glass products themselves.

from the normal, and that of reflection at the critical angle. These may seem to have little relation to each other, but are in fact related and brilliantly exploited in the design of the optical fibre.

The term 'optically dense' is related to the speed of light through a material. The velocity of light through a vacuum is a little more than 186,000 miles per second, but its speed through glass is only about 124,000 miles per second, about two-thirds as fast. The velocity of light through a material is inversely proportional to its refractive index: the lower the refractive index, the faster light travels through it. With the refractive index of air at 1.000292, and the indices for glasses varying from about 1.5 up to about 1.9, we can see that the variation, and therefore the design potential, are very great. Given the characteristic of glass that light passes through it more slowly than it does through air, consideration of light in terms of the wave theory can be used to show that the attenuation of a light beam, as it passes across the boundary of media of different refractive indices, will cause it to bend. Moreover, different wavelengths will be bent to different degrees. This much was known to Isaac Newton. Remarkably, however, once a light beam is projected to strike a glass surface at a particular oblique angle, the beam is not bent, it is reflected. No transmission takes place at all. This phenomenon can be seen as the sky is reflected off a still lake, or a street scene is visible in reflection of a shop window. The angle at which this takes place is unique to all bounding surfaces (air to water, air to glass, or one glass to another glass), and is known as the critical angle.

At the critical angle the light is reflected back from the surface, and remains within the denser medium. Given this phenomenon of

3. The passage of light down an optical fibre. The core of the fibre is a glass of a high refractive index, and the sheath glass has a low refractive index. All light impinging on the boundary at less than the critical angle is internally reflected, and passes with little loss down the core.

4. The manufacture of optical fibres. In the rod-tube process above a rod of high refractive index is placed inside a tube of the lower index glass, and the two are heated together and drawn to a fibre. In the two crucible process below the melting takes place separately prior to drawing.

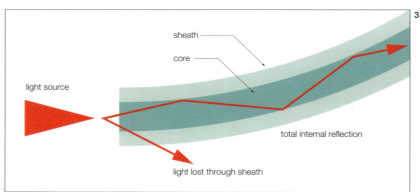

3

the critical angle, light travelling down a rod or fibre of transparent material with a refractive index greater than the material around it will be internally reflected continuously within the rod as long as the angle of incidence is higher than the critical angle. The higher the critical angle for the particular material's configuration, the greater the chance that a proportion of the light signal sent down the fibre will be refracted out of the transmitting material: low critical angles are therefore very important in the avoidance of loss of energy.

The two phenomena together, of light-attenuating refraction and the critical angle, combine together to permit the action of one of the most important inventions in the twentieth century, the fibre optic cable.

The history of fibre optics is fascinating. It started with the discovery by John Tyndall, a British physicist working around 1870, that an arc of water pouring out of a spout would 'contain' a light beam shone down it as it curved and splashed into a container. The high optical density of the water compared with that of the surrounding air produced an internal reflection critical angle which caused the light to be continually reflected inside the stream of water: in short, the air-water boundary was a mirror.

Ten years later the potential of mirror reflection for transmission was demonstrated with Alexander Graham Bell's 'photophone' of 1879–80, which used reflected sunlight from a vibrating mirror activated by the voice to a receiver based on a selenium rod, whose electrical resistance changed with the intensity of light. Connecting the rod to a 'telephone' receiver and a battery produced a reproduction of the transmitted speech. In the same year of 1880 William Wheeler of Massachusetts applied for a patent for a 'light pipe'. Wheeler's way of obtaining internal reflection of the sort seen by Tyndall was to silver surfaces within the pipe. Unfortunately the silver absorbed so much light that it did not get very far: the phenomenon of the critical angle had not impinged on the thinking. At the same time as these two American inventions, the English physicist Charles Vernon Boys produced glass fibres by attaching molten quartz to an arrow and firing it from a bow. The resultant fibres were as fine as hair, but strong enough to suspend physics apparatus.

The three inventions of 1880, distinct and independent as they were, formed the basis for fibre optics, but it was not until 1934 that AT&T obtained their patent for an 'optical

telephone system' which, although clever, was not supported by an adequate technology. Then, in the 1950s, development work proceeded more assiduously, both in the American Optical Company, and by Navinder Kapany in Britain. By the mid-1960s the British Post Office began to review the potential for the British telephone system, and Charles Kao and George Hockman working for Standard Communications Laboratories,

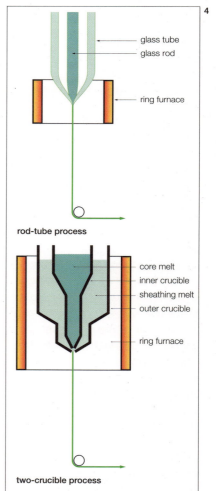

4

glass tube
glass rod
ring furnace

rod-tube process

core melt
inner crucible
sheathing melt
outer crucible
ring furnace

two-crucible process

secondary manufacturing

While consideration of the glass industry may be dominated by the primary manufacturers, the industry also contains other essential and important sectors which together are providing a spur to change; secondary manufacturing and installation.

market division

Glass is sold by the primary manufacturers to a variety of markets. Such is the complexity of the market that many primary manufacturers claim that they do not know where their glass goes. Even allowing for their caution of confidentiality, this is not entirely surprising. The secondary processors, merchants and installers, set the production demand of the primary manufacturers through their own order books and stock requirements. Historically, this distanced the primaries from the market, but the commercial structure is now changing.

product range

Secondary processing is rich in variety, as a list of products shows:

— proprietary double and multiple glazing
— heat treatment and toughening
— chemical strengthening
— curving
— laminating
— coating
— enamelling
— etching and sand-blasting
— mirrors

Secondary processing has, by its nature, developed from fragmentary, locally-based production units. Laminating, toughening and the making of multiple glazing, can all be carried out with plant costing from less than £1 million up to £10 million for a coating plant, and this enables production and markets to be matched in much smaller units than primary manufacture. However, with the always-present commercial urge for combination and rationalization, secondary processing has now become much more unified, and the subject of increasingly multinational effort. A typical large secondary processing company will have been formed out of perhaps hundreds of small companies, leading to easy takeover by the primary companies. The activities of such a company spread across the whole range of secondary production, including coatings and installation.

The comparative closeness to the market of the secondary processors, merchants and installers, and their increasing cohesion and strength, has provided a new dimension to the industry, and a spur to the primary manufacturers to create secondary product ranges, and to buy into 'downstream' operations. In Europe a high percentage of secondary processors are now owned by the primary manufacturers, providing a tied outlet for their continuous glass production.

The new technologies identified in Chapter Four indicate the sort of developments we may see in secondary processing in the future. Significantly, the nature and complexity of many of these means that we will not see them in the market at an acceptable cost until they are made in large quantities by automated processes. This is the major challenge for the industry in the decades to come, if these marvellous new materials are not to languish in the prototype stage.

specialist manufacturing

Alongside the main primary and secondary industries are the specialist manufacturers, the third group. Special glasses, such as optical and laser glasses, are often product lines in the giant companies, but the giants are complemented by companies such as Schott in West Germany and Corning in the United States. Although specialist manufacturers may concentrate mainly on industries other than the building industry, their contribution to architectural glass is fundamental for two main reasons. Firstly, they make the high value, high technology products which provide the exploration territory for building designers, and secondly, the building products they make often provide new applications for glass.

Borosilicate glasses, so domestically conventional in products such as cookware, have become fire-resisting glasses. Schott is a major manufacturer of both. Corning, where ceramic glass was first created, has invented an integral 'louvre blind' glass named Louverre, as a development of its early photochromic and ceramic glass work. The major primary glass manufacturers themselves are also deeply involved in high technology products.

It is in the catalogues of these specialists and special divisions of the large primary producers that one can often find clues for the future in high performance materials.

the installers

The fourth sector in the industry comprises the installers. This present book is concerned with glass rather than glazing and cladding, but glass in architecture is so much a matter of its incorporation into systems, that reference needs to be made.

Glass is only one of many materials used in the cladding industry, but as the primary source of transparency its importance is obvious. Major glass manufacturers such as PPG, have long published framing systems catalogues. Developments in the last twenty years have seen glazing develop from being a matter of installing glass in a frame, to suspended assemblies and frameless support. This has had an interesting impact on the industry. The method by which glass is fixed had been revolutionized by bolt systems such as Pilkington's Planar, and important collaborations have developed between secondary manufacturers and trade contractors such that between Eckelt and GIG (Grill and Grossmann) in Austria.

In Pilkington's 'Fenestration 2000' Stage 1 Report, one of the more interesting demands for the future is for integrated glazing and framing. The construction industry is seeking to avoid the complications of multiple handling of materials and systems.

We may expect increasing backward and forward integration in response to this demand, as well as in the demand for added value glass products themselves.

from the normal, and that of reflection at the critical angle. These may seem to have little relation to each other, but are in fact related and brilliantly exploited in the design of the optical fibre.

The term 'optically dense' is related to the speed of light through a material. The velocity of light through a vacuum is a little more than 186,000 miles per second, but its speed through glass is only about 124,000 miles per second, about two-thirds as fast. The velocity of light through a material is inversely proportional to its refractive index: the lower the refractive index, the faster light travels through it. With the refractive index of air at 1.000292, and the indices for glasses varying from about 1.5 up to about 1.9, we can see that the variation, and therefore the design potential, are very great. Given the characteristic of glass that light passes through it more slowly than it does through air, consideration of light in terms of the wave theory can be used to show that the attenuation of a light beam, as it passes across the boundary of media of different refractive indices, will cause it to bend. Moreover, different wavelengths will be bent to different degrees. This much was known to Isaac Newton. Remarkably, however, once a light beam is projected to strike a glass surface at a particular oblique angle, the beam is not bent, it is reflected. No transmission takes place at all. This phenomenon can be seen as the sky is reflected off a still lake, or a street scene is visible in reflection of a shop window. The angle at which this takes place is unique to all bounding surfaces (air to water, air to glass, or one glass to another glass), and is known as the critical angle.

At the critical angle the light is reflected back from the surface, and remains within the denser medium. Given this phenomenon of

3. The passage of light down an optical fibre. The core of the fibre is a glass of a high refractive index, and the sheath glass has a low refractive index. All light impinging on the boundary at less than the critical angle is internally reflected, and passes with little loss down the core.

4. The manufacture of optical fibres. In the rod-tube process above a rod of high refractive index is placed inside a tube of the lower index glass, and the two are heated together and drawn to a fibre. In the two crucible process below the melting takes place separately prior to drawing.

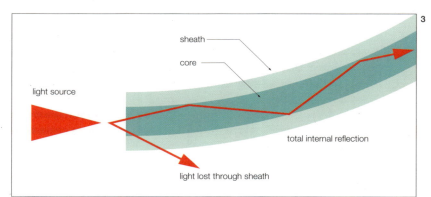

the critical angle, light travelling down a rod or fibre of transparent material with a refractive index greater than the material around it will be internally reflected continuously within the rod as long as the angle of incidence is higher than the critical angle. The higher the critical angle for the particular material's configuration, the greater the chance that a proportion of the light signal sent down the fibre will be refracted out of the transmitting material: low critical angles are therefore very important in the avoidance of loss of energy.

The two phenomena together, of light-attenuating refraction and the critical angle, combine together to permit the action of one of the most important inventions in the twentieth century, the fibre optic cable.

The history of fibre optics is fascinating. It started with the discovery by John Tyndall, a British physicist working around 1870, that an arc of water pouring out of a spout would 'contain' a light beam shone down it as it curved and splashed into a container. The high optical density of the water compared with that of the surrounding air produced an internal reflection critical angle which caused the light to be continually reflected inside the stream of water: in short, the air-water boundary was a mirror.

Ten years later the potential of mirror reflection for transmission was demonstrated with Alexander Graham Bell's 'photophone' of 1879–80, which used reflected sunlight from a vibrating mirror activated by the voice to a receiver based on a selenium rod, whose electrical resistance changed with the intensity of light. Connecting the rod to a 'telephone' receiver and a battery produced a reproduction of the transmitted speech. In the same year of 1880 William Wheeler of Massachusetts applied for a patent for a 'light pipe'. Wheeler's way of obtaining internal reflection of the sort seen by Tyndall was to silver surfaces within the pipe. Unfortunately the silver absorbed so much light that it did not get very far: the phenomenon of the critical angle had not impinged on the thinking. At the same time as these two American inventions, the English physicist Charles Vernon Boys produced glass fibres by attaching molten quartz to an arrow and firing it from a bow. The resultant fibres were as fine as hair, but strong enough to suspend physics apparatus.

The three inventions of 1880, distinct and independent as they were, formed the basis for fibre optics, but it was not until 1934 that AT&T obtained their patent for an 'optical

telephone system' which, although clever, was not supported by an adequate technology. Then, in the 1950s, development work proceeded more assiduously, both in the American Optical Company, and by Navinder Kapany in Britain. By the mid-1960s the British Post Office began to review the potential for the British telephone system, and Charles Kao and George Hockman working for Standard Communications Laboratories,

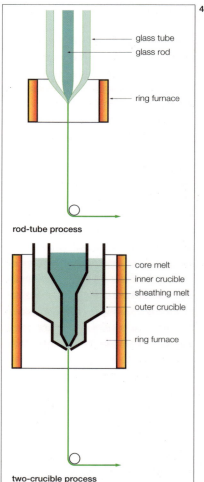

glass tube
glass rod
ring furnace

rod-tube process

core melt
inner crucible
sheathing melt
outer crucible
ring furnace

two-crucible process

secondary manufacturing

While consideration of the glass industry may be dominated by the primary manufacturers, the industry also contains other essential and important sectors which together are providing a spur to change; secondary manufacturing and installation.

market division

Glass is sold by the primary manufacturers to a variety of markets. Such is the complexity of the market that many primary manufacturers claim that they do not know where their glass goes. Even allowing for their caution of confidentiality, this is not entirely surprising. The secondary processors, merchants and installers, set the production demand of the primary manufacturers through their own order books and stock requirements. Historically, this distanced the primaries from the market, but the commercial structure is now changing.

product range

Secondary processing is rich in variety, as a list of products shows:

— proprietary double and multiple glazing
— heat treatment and toughening
— chemical strengthening
— curving
— laminating
— coating
— enamelling
— etching and sand-blasting
— mirrors

Secondary processing has, by its nature, developed from fragmentary, locally-based production units. Laminating, toughening and the making of multiple glazing, can all be carried out with plant costing from less than £1 million up to £10 million for a coating plant, and this enables production and markets to be matched in much smaller units than primary manufacture. However, with the always-present commercial urge for combination and rationalization, secondary processing has now become much more unified, and the subject of increasingly multinational effort. A typical large secondary processing company will have been formed out of perhaps hundreds of small companies, leading to easy takeover by the primary companies. The activities of such a company spread across the whole range of secondary production, including coatings and installation.

The comparative closeness to the market of the secondary processors, merchants and installers, and their increasing cohesion and strength, has provided a new dimension to the industry, and a spur to the primary manufacturers to create secondary product ranges, and to buy into 'downstream' operations. In Europe a high percentage of secondary processors are now owned by the primary manufacturers, providing a tied outlet for their continuous glass production.

The new technologies identified in Chapter Four indicate the sort of developments we may see in secondary processing in the future. Significantly, the nature and complexity of many of these means that we will not see them in the market at an acceptable cost until they are made in large quantities by automated processes. This is the major challenge for the industry in the decades to come, if these marvellous new materials are not to languish in the prototype stage.

specialist manufacturing

Alongside the main primary and secondary industries are the specialist manufacturers, the third group. Special glasses, such as optical and laser glasses, are often product lines in the giant companies, but the giants are complemented by companies such as Schott in West Germany and Corning in the United States. Although specialist manufacturers may concentrate mainly on industries other than the building industry, their contribution to architectural glass is fundamental for two main reasons. Firstly, they make the high value, high technology products which provide the exploration territory for building designers, and secondly, the building products they make often provide new applications for glass.

Borosilicate glasses, so domestically conventional in products such as cookware, have become fire-resisting glasses. Schott is a major manufacturer of both. Corning, where ceramic glass was first created, has invented an integral 'louvre blind' glass named Louverre, as a development of its early photochromic and ceramic glass work. The major primary glass manufacturers themselves are also deeply involved in high technology products.

It is in the catalogues of these specialists and special divisions of the large primary producers that one can often find clues for the future in high performance materials.

the installers

The fourth sector in the industry comprises the installers. This present book is concerned with glass rather than glazing and cladding, but glass in architecture is so much a matter of its incorporation into systems, that reference needs to be made.

Glass is only one of many materials used in the cladding industry, but as the primary source of transparency its importance is obvious. Major glass manufacturers such as PPG, have long published framing systems catalogues. Developments in the last twenty years have seen glazing develop from being a matter of installing glass in a frame, to suspended assemblies and frameless support. This has had an interesting impact on the industry. The method by which glass is fixed had been revolutionized by bolt systems such as Pilkington's Planar, and important collaborations have developed between secondary manufacturers and trade contractors such that between Eckelt and GIG (Grill and Grossmann) in Austria.

In Pilkington's 'Fenestration 2000' Stage 1 Report, one of the more interesting demands for the future is for integrated glazing and framing. The construction industry is seeking to avoid the complications of multiple handling of materials and systems.

We may expect increasing backward and forward integration in response to this demand, as well as in the demand for added value glass products themselves.

from the normal, and that of reflection at the critical angle. These may seem to have little relation to each other, but are in fact related and brilliantly exploited in the design of the optical fibre.

The term 'optically dense' is related to the speed of light through a material. The velocity of light through a vacuum is a little more than 186,000 miles per second, but its speed through glass is only about 124,000 miles per second, about two-thirds as fast. The velocity of light through a material is inversely proportional to its refractive index: the lower the refractive index, the faster light travels through it. With the refractive index of air at 1.000292, and the indices for glasses varying from about 1.5 up to about 1.9, we can see that the variation, and therefore the design potential, are very great. Given the characteristic of glass that light passes through it more slowly than it does through air, consideration of light in terms of the wave theory can be used to show that the attenuation of a light beam, as it passes across the boundary of media of different refractive indices, will cause it to bend. Moreover, different wavelengths will be bent to different degrees. This much was known to Isaac Newton. Remarkably, however, once a light beam is projected to strike a glass surface at a particular oblique angle, the beam is not bent, it is reflected. No transmission takes place at all. This phenomenon can be seen as the sky is reflected off a still lake, or a street scene is visible in reflection of a shop window. The angle at which this takes place is unique to all bounding surfaces (air to water, air to glass, or one glass to another glass), and is known as the critical angle.

At the critical angle the light is reflected back from the surface, and remains within the denser medium. Given this phenomenon of

3. The passage of light down an optical fibre. The core of the fibre is a glass of a high refractive index, and the sheath glass has a low refractive index. All light impinging on the boundary at less than the critical angle is internally reflected, and passes with little loss down the core.

4. The manufacture of optical fibres. In the rod-tube process above a rod of high refractive index is placed inside a tube of the lower index glass, and the two are heated together and drawn to a fibre. In the two crucible process below the melting takes place separately prior to drawing.

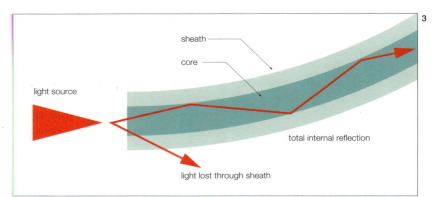

sheath
core
light source
total internal reflection
light lost through sheath

the critical angle, light travelling down a rod or fibre of transparent material with a refractive index greater than the material around it will be internally reflected continuously within the rod as long as the angle of incidence is higher than the critical angle. The higher the critical angle for the particular material's configuration, the greater the chance that a proportion of the light signal sent down the fibre will be refracted out of the transmitting material: low critical angles are therefore very important in the avoidance of loss of energy.

The two phenomena together, of light-attenuating refraction and the critical angle, combine together to permit the action of one of the most important inventions in the twentieth century, the fibre optic cable.

The history of fibre optics is fascinating. It started with the discovery by John Tyndall, a British physicist working around 1870, that an arc of water pouring out of a spout would 'contain' a light beam shone down it as it curved and splashed into a container. The high optical density of the water compared with that of the surrounding air produced an internal reflection critical angle which caused the light to be continually reflected inside the stream of water: in short, the air-water boundary was a mirror.

Ten years later the potential of mirror reflection for transmission was demonstrated with Alexander Graham Bell's 'photophone' of 1879–80, which used reflected sunlight from a vibrating mirror activated by the voice to a receiver based on a selenium rod, whose electrical resistance changed with the intensity of light. Connecting the rod to a 'telephone' receiver and a battery produced a reproduction of the transmitted speech. In the same year of 1880 William Wheeler of Massachusetts applied for a patent for a 'light pipe'. Wheeler's way of obtaining internal reflection of the sort seen by Tyndall was to silver surfaces within the pipe. Unfortunately the silver absorbed so much light that it did not get very far: the phenomenon of the critical angle had not impinged on the thinking. At the same time as these two American inventions, the English physicist Charles Vernon Boys produced glass fibres by attaching molten quartz to an arrow and firing it from a bow. The resultant fibres were as fine as hair, but strong enough to suspend physics apparatus.

The three inventions of 1880, distinct and independent as they were, formed the basis for fibre optics, but it was not until 1934 that AT&T obtained their patent for an 'optical

telephone system' which, although clever, was not supported by an adequate technology. Then, in the 1950s, development work proceeded more assiduously, both in the American Optical Company, and by Navinder Kapany in Britain. By the mid-1960s the British Post Office began to review the potential for the British telephone system, and Charles Kao and George Hockman working for Standard Communications Laboratories,

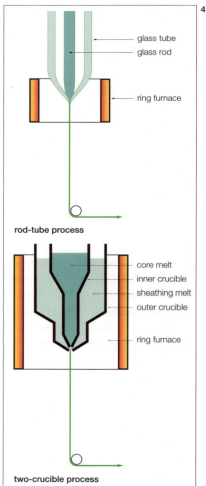

glass tube
glass rod
ring furnace

rod-tube process

core melt
inner crucible
sheathing melt
outer crucible
ring furnace

two-crucible process

other glasses and glass products

the British Subsidiary of ITT, became sure that glasses could be produced of the required transparency. They proposed the principle of transmission via a transparent fibre, and laid the foundations for fibre optic communications. The obvious advantages over conventional wires were low transmission loss, high data capacity, light weight, high security (the fibres being difficult to 'tap'), and immunity to electrical 'noise' in areas of high electrical activity.

Robert Maurer of the Corning Glass Company in the USA visited Britain in the late 1960s to see what was being done. By 1970 he had produced the first real optical fibre, using fused silica, which could transmit light over 600 m. Tyndall's discovery with water of a hundred years earlier had finally been turned into a usable product in the supercooled liquid. Ten years later development in sheathed glass assemblies (using a core of high optical density and a glass sheath of low optical density), enabled light to be transmitted over twenty miles. By 1983 this grew to a hundred miles. Now optical fibres are becoming the basis for the complete telephone networks of nations, where their durability, and non-metallic resistance to interference is satisfying the demands of the increasingly sophisticated market place.

In communications use, transmitted electrical signal impulses are converted into light or infrared impulses, and transmitted down an optical fibre system. The light used for these cables is 'laser' light (laser is the acronym for light amplification for stimulated emission of radiation), and lasers are invariably one colour, sometimes one wavelength. Fibre optics designed to carry lasers are specified in glass terms to accord with the wavelength concerned. This addresses the

cross section
of a
light guide fibre

lightpath through
fibre

variation of the
refractive index
through the fibre

dimensions (μm)

A stepped index fibre   B   gradient index fibre

5. The refractive index profiles of stepped and gradient index fibres. The stepped index fibre on the left relies on the simple use of two glasses. The gradient index fibre comprises glasses of gradually decreasing refractive index from the centre to the outside of the core, enabling the light which has to travel furthest to travel fastest.

issue of different colours behaving differently in terms of refraction.

The design of conventional optical fibres comprises a core of highly refractive optical glass within a sheath of glass with a lower refractive index, with the ultimate aim of obtaining as low a critical angle as possible in order to transmit as much light as possible. A fibre of this design relies on total internal reflection, between two essentially different glasses, of all light striking the glass interface below the critical angle. It is a matter of simple physics that light travelling such a path in a 'pipe' will emerge at the end, however many bends it has to travel through, and this is the beauty of optical fibres. The simplest forms are called stepped index fibres.

The problem of travel distance with the repeated internal reflections becomes important in this technology, since a light impulse emitted at the same time, but at different angles, down the fibre will emerge as a dispersed signal. Since the velocity of light increases with decreasing refractive index, it is possible to consider grading the change of refractive index outwards from the centre of the fibre to ensure that a longer path is compensated for by a higher light velocity, and a signal emerges coherently at the other end. This has driven fibre-optic designers to create gradient index fibres, in which the refractive index of the glass reduces gradually outwards from the centre. Given that this whole subtle gradation must take place in one-tenth of a millimetre, it can be seen that a very high technology manufacturing process is needed.

Stepped index fibres are commonly made by two methods. In the 'rod-tube' process a rod of high refractive index is placed inside a tube made of low refractive index. These are heated to softening point, and at the same time drawn to the eventual fibre diameter whilst being wound round on to a drum. In the 'two-crucible' pot process, the rod and tube are melted separately before being drawn and wound. Gradient index fibres are made by passing a heated fused silica glass tube through a graded environment of vaporized glass formers of intrinsically different refractive indices which condense on the tube in a designed sequence. Silicon, boron, germanium and phosphorus are all used in their oxide form. The 'assembled' multiple tubular sandwich is then heated to collapse, and drawn into the fine thread with the original tubular refractive index gradient proportionally shrunk.

As with thin films, this is a sophisticated, nanometric, technology, where the relationship between electromagnetic radiation and the transparency of glass is critical. It is about as far from flat glass as it is possible to imagine, but one with far-reaching implications for the industry, containing lessons concerning light transmission which architects would do well to note.

Fibre optics are notable not least because they are manifestations of how strong and flexible glass is in fibre form, and how high its light transmission can be if this becomes a priority.

Light-transmitting fibres of glass are simple in operation, but remarkable in that within a flexible glass filament of less than one millimetre diameter, they can transmit light round corners with little loss of intensity. Combined in bundles they are light transmitters which are in common use in photography, spectroscopy and image processing. They can even be used to search and photograph internal human organs in endoscopy, where fibres of diameter 0.02 mm are needed to ensure as short a light path as possible, to obtain good resolution.

Strength, length and flexibility are not the only remarkable properties of the glass used, however. It is significant that the requirement for efficient light transmission over long distances has led the industry to develop glasses with optical losses a thousand times less than normal quality optical glass: light can travel for miles within them. The transparency is sufficient, if the sea were made of such a glass, for us to be able to see to the bottom of the ocean floor.

Fibre optics as discussed above relate to the particular sophisticated forms devised for telecommunications use,

that undergone by building glass. However, despite claimed performance, even the

process, the Vello process, and the Downdraw and Updraw processes. The

Glass 'tubes' vary in diameter from fractions of a millimetre up to one metre

glass in
architecture

4

Test	Test Method	Uncoated PC % Haze*	Lexan Margard % Haze	Glass % Haze
Taber abrasion CS10F wheels 500gm weight	ASTM D-1044 ANSI Z26.1,1983			
100 cycles	Plastic safety glazing test	30	2.1	0.5
500 cycles	Extended test	46	4.5	1.0
1000 cycles	Glass safety glazing test	> 50	12	2.0
Sandriesel test	DIN 52348	37	2.0	1.0
* according to ASTM D1003				

5

	percentage haze produced by 12 psi loading				stated revolutions 24 psi loading			
material/treatment	0 rev	1 rev	50 rev	100 rev	0 rev	1 rev	50 rev	100 rev
Acrylic, untreated	0.4	4.6	22.1	20.8	0.4	8.5	25.8	23.9
Acrylic, Vueguard 901 WC	0.4	0.4*	0.9	0.9	0.4	0.4*	1.0	1.0
Acrylic, Vueguard 901 AG	1.9**	1.9*	1.8	1.7	1.9	1.9*	1.5	1.4
Polycarbonate, untreated	0.4	8.1	17.6	23.3	0.4	11.3	20.8	24.0
Polycarbonate, Vueguard 901 WC	0.4	0.4*	0.8	0.9	0.4	0.4*	1.3	1.5
Polycarbonate, Vueguard 901 AG	7.6**	7.6*	3.8	3.1	7.6	7.6*	3.7	3.6
* an interpolated figure ** an antiglare finish: abrasion actually reduces the percentage haze								

4, 5. Toughness and resistance to abrasion. The susceptibility of transparent plastics to abrasion is a fundamental property, given the need for clarity of light transmission. The properties of transparent plastics are being improved constantly, and manufacturers should always be requested for up-to-date information on any product. These tables only give an indication of the general comparative toughness of materials, in relation to standard tests.

Figure 4 shows the effect of treating a polycarbonate with a proprietary ultraviolet and abrasion resistant surface, which improves the abrasion resistance significantly. The product referred to here is 'Margard' by GE Plastics.

Figure 5 shows the effect of treating acrylic and polycarbonate with 'Vueguard'. The test used for this second table is the steel wool test (Du Pont Method), a severe test in which a weighted steel wool pad is rotated over the material at two different pressures (expressed here in pounds per square inch), with haze readings taken after different numbers of revolutions. The dramatic effect of these treatments is very evident.

The typical 5 or 6 mm product has a transmission of 85%. These figures are reduced to 50% for bronze tinted sheet. Polycarbonate transmits fairly evenly between 385 nm and 2,000 nm, with a local trough at about 1,600 nm. It is effectively opaque to radiation below 385 nm, and so does not transmit ultraviolet light. The spectral distribution is shown on figure 2.

Refractive index: The refractive index of clear polycarbonate is 1.586, much higher than soda-lime glass at 1.52, and higher even than high index lead glasses.

Maximum working temperature: The highest temperature at which polycarbonate retains its properties is around 135ºC, but a maximum service temperature of 120ºC is considered more prudent.

Specific heat: The specific heat of polycarbonate varies between 1.195 and 1.26 kJ/kg ºC, compared to a figure of 0.85–1.00 kJ/kg ºC for glass.

Thermal conductivity: This is 0.19–0.21 W/m² ºC, or about one-fifth that of glass. For single sheets the importance of surface resistivities results in the related thermal transmittance, the U-value, being only 10–20% better than glass, between 4.35 and 5.49 W/m² ºC for typical thicknesses. However a double skin material 6 mm thick has a U-value of 3.5 W/m² ºC, a triple skin product 32 mm thick a value of 1.9 W/m² ºC, and a five wall product 20 mm thick a value of 1.85 W/m² ºC.

Expansion coefficient: This is about 66–67 x 10^{-6}/ºC, or about 20% more than glass, and correspondingly greater clearances should be allowed in glazing. On summer days sheets

the British Subsidiary of ITT, became sure that glasses could be produced of the required transparency. They proposed the principle of transmission via a transparent fibre, and laid the foundations for fibre optic communications. The obvious advantages over conventional wires were low transmission loss, high data capacity, light weight, high security (the fibres being difficult to 'tap'), and immunity to electrical 'noise' in areas of high electrical activity.

Robert Maurer of the Corning Glass Company in the USA visited Britain in the late 1960s to see what was being done. By 1970 he had produced the first real optical fibre, using fused silica, which could transmit light over 600 m. Tyndall's discovery with water of a hundred years earlier had finally been turned into a usable product in the supercooled liquid. Ten years later development in sheathed glass assemblies (using a core of high optical density and a glass sheath of low optical density), enabled light to be transmitted over twenty miles. By 1983 this grew to a hundred miles. Now optical fibres are becoming the basis for the complete telephone networks of nations, where their durability, and non-metallic resistance to interference is satisfying the demands of the increasingly sophisticated market place.

In communications use, transmitted electrical signal impulses are converted into light or infrared impulses, and transmitted down an optical fibre system. The light used for these cables is 'laser' light (laser is the acronym for light amplification for stimulated emission of radiation), and lasers are invariably one colour, sometimes one wavelength. Fibre optics designed to carry lasers are specified in glass terms to accord with the wavelength concerned. This addresses the

cross section
of a
light guide fibre

lightpath through
fibre

variation of the
refractive index
through the fibre

A stepped index fibre   B gradient index fibre

5. The refractive index profiles of stepped and gradient index fibres. The stepped index fibre on the left relies on the simple use of two glasses. The gradient index fibre comprises glasses of gradually decreasing refractive index from the centre to the outside of the core, enabling the light which has to travel furthest to travel fastest.

issue of different colours behaving differently in terms of refraction.

The design of conventional optical fibres comprises a core of highly refractive optical glass within a sheath of glass with a lower refractive index, with the ultimate aim of obtaining as low a critical angle as possible in order to transmit as much light as possible. A fibre of this design relies on total internal reflection, between two essentially different glasses, of all light striking the glass interface below the critical angle. It is a matter of simple physics that light travelling such a path in a 'pipe' will emerge at the end, however many bends it has to travel through, and this is the beauty of optical fibres. The simplest forms are called stepped index fibres.

The problem of travel distance with the repeated internal reflections becomes important in this technology, since a light impulse emitted at the same time, but at different angles, down the fibre will emerge as a dispersed signal. Since the velocity of light increases with decreasing refractive index, it is possible to consider grading the change of refractive index outwards from the centre of the fibre to ensure that a longer path is compensated for by a higher light velocity, and a signal emerges coherently at the other end. This has driven fibre-optic designers to create gradient index fibres, in which the refractive index of the glass reduces gradually outwards from the centre. Given that this whole subtle gradation must take place in one-tenth of a millimetre, it can be seen that a very high technology manufacturing process is needed.

Stepped index fibres are commonly made by two methods. In the 'rod-tube' process a rod of high refractive index is placed inside a tube made of low refractive index. These are heated to softening point, and at the same time drawn to the eventual fibre diameter whilst being wound round on to a drum. In the 'two-crucible' pot process, the rod and tube are melted separately before being drawn and wound. Gradient index fibres are made by passing a heated fused silica glass tube through a graded environment of vaporized glass formers of intrinsically different refractive indices which condense on the tube in a designed sequence. Silicon, boron, germanium and phosphorus are all used in their oxide form. The 'assembled' multiple tubular sandwich is then heated to collapse, and drawn into the fine thread with the original tubular refractive index gradient proportionally shrunk.

As with thin films, this is a sophisticated, nanometric, technology, where the relationship between electromagnetic radiation and the transparency of glass is critical. It is about as far from flat glass as it is possible to imagine, but one with far-reaching implications for the industry, containing lessons concerning light transmission which architects would do well to note.

Fibre optics are notable not least because they are manifestations of how strong and flexible glass is in fibre form, and how high its light transmission can be if this becomes a priority.

Light-transmitting fibres of glass are simple in operation, but remarkable in that within a flexible glass filament of less than one millimetre diameter, they can transmit light round corners with little loss of intensity. Combined in bundles they are light transmitters which are in common use in photography, spectroscopy and image processing. They can even be used to search and photograph internal human organs in endoscopy, where fibres of diameter 0.02 mm are needed to ensure as short a light path as possible, to obtain good resolution.

Strength, length and flexibility are not the only remarkable properties of the glass used, however. It is significant that the requirement for efficient light transmission over long distances has led the industry to develop glasses with optical losses a thousand times less than normal quality optical glass: light can travel for miles within them. The transparency is sufficient, if the sea were made of such a glass, for us to be able to see to the bottom of the ocean floor.

Fibre optics as discussed above relate to the particular sophisticated forms devised for telecommunications use,

Domestic borosilicate glasses have been with us for much longer than those used for buildings, and of course the rapid changes of temperature which kitchenware undergoes is normally much greater than that undergone by building glass. However, despite claimed performance, even the

tubes

The creation of small diameter parallel sided tubes demands an intrinsically different approach to that of blowing. Mass production manufacturing techniques include the Danner process, the Vello process, and the Downdraw and Updraw processes. The

through a ring; in the similar Downdraw process the glass is drawn in a vacuum chamber. Updraw process glass is used to make thickwall tubing, and uses an air jet to form the hollow in the tube.

Glass 'tubes' vary in diameter from fractions of a millimetre up to one metre

how long his research programme would

about 50 nm in size. When an aerogel is

hollowware

made possible the first effective automated

glass in
architecture

4

Test	Test Method	Uncoated PC % Haze*	Lexan Margard % Haze	Glass % Haze
Taber abrasion CS10F wheels 500gm weight	ASTM D-1044 ANSI Z26.1,1983			
100 cycles	Plastic safety glazing test	30	2.1	0.5
500 cycles	Extended test	46	4.5	1.0
1000 cycles	Glass safety glazing test	> 50	12	2.0
Sandriesel test	DIN 52348	37	2.0	1.0
* according to ASTM D1003				

5

	percentage haze produced by 12 psi loading				stated revolutions 24 psi loading			
material/treatment	0 rev	1 rev	50 rev	100 rev	0 rev	1 rev	50 rev	100 rev
Acrylic, untreated	0.4	4.6	22.1	20.8	0.4	8.5	25.8	23.9
Acrylic, Vueguard 901 WC	0.4	0.4*	0.9	0.9	0.4	0.4*	1.0	1.0
Acrylic, Vueguard 901 AG	1.9**	1.9*	1.8	1.7	1.9	1.9*	1.5	1.4
Polycarbonate, untreated	0.4	8.1	17.6	23.3	0.4	11.3	20.8	24.0
Polycarbonate, Vueguard 901 WC	0.4	0.4*	0.8	0.9	0.4	0.4*	1.3	1.5
Polycarbonate, Vueguard 901 AG	7.6**	7.6*	3.8	3.1	7.6	7.6*	3.7	3.6
* an interpolated figure ** an antiglare finish: abrasion actually reduces the percentage haze								

4, 5. Toughness and resistance to abrasion. The susceptibility of transparent plastics to abrasion is a fundamental property, given the need for clarity of light transmission. The properties of transparent plastics are being improved constantly, and manufacturers should always be requested for up-to-date information on any product. These tables only give an indication of the general comparative toughness of materials, in relation to standard tests.

Figure 4 shows the effect of treating a polycarbonate with a proprietary ultraviolet and abrasion resistant surface, which improves the abrasion resistance significantly. The product referred to here is 'Margard' by GE Plastics.

Figure 5 shows the effect of treating acrylic and polycarbonate with 'Vueguard'. The test used for this second table is the steel wool test (Du Pont Method), a severe test in which a weighted steel wool pad is rotated over the material at two different pressures (expressed here in pounds per square inch), with haze readings taken after different numbers of revolutions. The dramatic effect of these treatments is very evident.

The typical 5 or 6 mm product has a transmission of 85%. These figures are reduced to 50% for bronze tinted sheet. Polycarbonate transmits fairly evenly between 385 nm and 2,000 nm, with a local trough at about 1,600 nm. It is effectively opaque to radiation below 385 nm, and so does not transmit ultraviolet light. The spectral distribution is shown on figure 2.

Refractive index: The refractive index of clear polycarbonate is 1.586, much higher than soda-lime glass at 1.52, and higher even than high index lead glasses.

Maximum working temperature: The highest temperature at which polycarbonate retains its properties is around 135°C, but a maximum service temperature of 120°C is considered more prudent.

Specific heat: The specific heat of polycarbonate varies between 1.195 and 1.26 kJ/kg °C, compared to a figure of 0.85–1.00 kJ/kg °C for glass.

Thermal conductivity: This is 0.19–0.21 W/m² °C, or about one-fifth that of glass. For single sheets the importance of surface resistivities results in the related thermal transmittance, the U-value, being only 10–20% better than glass, between 4.35 and 5.49 W/m² °C for typical thicknesses. However a double skin material 6 mm thick has a U-value of 3.5 W/m² °C, a triple skin product 32 mm thick a value of 1.9 W/m² °C, and a five wall product 20 mm thick a value of 1.85 W/m² °C.

Expansion coefficient: This is about 66–67 x 10⁻⁶/°C, or about 20% more than glass, and correspondingly greater clearances should be allowed in glazing. On summer days sheets can easily reach 50°C, implying expansion of 3 mm over a 1.5 m length, assuming an original 20°C installation temperature.

Strength: Polycarbonate is a generally strong glazing material, with a yield point at 62.5 N/mm^2 (the same order as that of glass), and a compressive strength of 85 N/mm^2. It also has a high 'falling dart' impact strength. Its Charpy notched impact strength is over 40 kJ/m^2, about three times that of acrylic. Its toughness is a major reason for its use.

Hardness: Polycarbonate has a reasonably hard surface (although soft when compared to glass) which is enhanced by a silicone polymeric dipped coating or flow coating. It is frequently used for spectacles and safety visors for this reason. In so far as hardness results in abrasion resistance, the Taber abrasion test establishes percentage haze after abrasion with a wheel of specified roughness, at different speeds of rotation and with different pressures. Table 5 shows how the intrinsic softness of polycarbonate compared with glass or acrylic can be improved by coating it. The haze created by light abrasion almost approaches that of glass.

Chemical and weathering durability: Polycarbonate is fairly resistant to the materials and conditions likely to be encountered in buildings. It is resistant to attack by dilute acids, inorganic salts and alcohol, and is not affected by cement or plaster. It has a tendency to yellow under ultraviolet light, and most reputable architectural products are coated with acrylic, which acts as a filter, or co-extruded with a high concentration of UV absorbing product typically 40 microns thick on both sides of the sheet

to enhance its weathering properties.

Flammability: The performance of polycarbonate in fire is good for a plastic material, being self-extinguishing when tested to BS2782 Method 508A. Depending upon its thickness it can reach Class 1 Surface Spread of Flame under BS476 Part 7, and is classed as a Class 0 material under the UK Building Regulations. The gases produced in combustion are not unusually toxic, and similar to the products of burning wood. The material burns with difficulty and requires a continuous application of external flame source to sustain combustion. The main products of combustion are carbon dioxide and carbon monoxide.

Specific gravity: The specific gravity is 1.2, about one-half that of glass and about the same as PMMA. This means that one square metre of the material 6 mm thick weighs 7.2 kg rather than the 15 kg of an equivalent glass sheet, making a significant handling difference where this is considered important.

working and installing Working polycarbonate is generally easy using ordinary workshop equipment. It can be sawn, cut and drilled with standard techniques. Up to 3 mm thicknesses can be punched, and the material can be turned and milled.

Polishing polycarbonate, particularly after working it, can be carried out using a very fine abrasive followed by a cloth wheel with an alkaline-free polish paste such as chromium oxide. Alternatively methylene chloride vapour polishing can be carried out. Great care is needed with long-life UV-coated materials.

The material can be beaded using normal

glazing techniques, or bonded or mechanically fastened. Consideration has to be paid to the thermal expansion coefficient of the material when glazing into rebates or screw fixing. It can be curved cold during installation to a radius at least 100 times the thickness (ie a 6 mm thickness can be cold curved to a radius of 600 mm), or 175 times the thickness for multiwall materials. Cleaning requires the use of a soft cloth and water with a soap or detergent, or alcohol.

Recent developments have included the laminating of polycarbonate to glass using a px adhesive to permit the differential expansion to take place without stress build-up.

05.303

**author's
acknowledgements**

This book is the result of many years' work following its original commissioning by Maritz Vandenburg, who must thus share some of the responsibility for it, and who has always been encouraging as it has evolved. The original commission set off a trail of research and investigation which reinforced the view I had formed many years before, that glass was the most important material available to an architect.

I owe a debt of gratitude to a very large number of people who have contributed to the research carried out, and to the subsequent writing of the book, by means of advice, information, and support at critical times in its creation and production.

I must start by thanking Jill Kerr at English Heritage, whose help at the completion of the main text was critical and whose advice on the, to me, unfamiliar field of historical survey was invaluable. She was as encouraging in her support for what I had written as she was gentle in her correction of it and I am immensely in her debt. I must also thank David Goodall, my friend and colleague of many years, whose conversations about glass technology whilst he was at Pilkington continuously enlightened me, and whose subsequent role as tech-

nical editor was both essential and a joint voyage of exploration. Similar thanks go to Claes Goran Granqvist, the Professor of Solid State Physics at Uppsala University, whose work into advanced materials remains an inspiration and who was assiduous in reading my attempts to explain physics. Dr John Duffy, of the Chemistry Department at Aberdeen University provided a great deal of help as I was working on the issues of transparency.

Friends at Pilkington Glass have been invariably helpful and open over the years and I must particularly thank Dr Mike Jenkins whose knowledge of coatings I have been most grateful for, and Brian Norman, who provided insights into the issue of strength as well as offering advice on parts of the technical texts. Mark Bristow at Solaglas was very helpful and Solaglas were also very patient in their opening of doors as I explored the realms of secondary processing. In relation to technology, both Schott and Corning were very generous in the provision both of data and of illustrative material.

The Case Studies demand a specific litany of gratitude. Fine architects and architectural firms have to suffer the mixed blessing of attention resulting from their talent and creation,

variously called marketing and the provision of information. For this book, my requests were more onerous than usual in the inclusion of original full size details which often meant a lot of work for the architects involved. I am therefore naturally grateful to Katy Harris, Stefan Belhling and the others at Sir Norman Foster and Partners, to Mike Davies and John Young at Richard Rogers Partnership, to Gunnar Birkerts, to Michael Flynn and his colleagues at Pei Cobb Freed, to the office of Philip Johnson, to Arthur Erickson and his colleagues, to the office of Renzo Piano and all at the Building Workshop, to Mark Mendell at Cannon Design, to Jan Dvorak and his colleagues at Ingenhoven, Overdiek und Partner, to Hugh Dutton, Martin Francis and their colleagues at RFR, to Nicholas Grimshaw, Jan Bentham, Rick Mather and Eva Jiricna.

Professor Jeffrey Cook was very helpful in relation to the subject of early solar architecture, providing invaluable material from the archives at Arizona State University. I must also thank Dr Rod Scott at BP Solar, to whom I owe much of the discussion of photovoltaics, on which Meike Hülsmann of Greenpeace Germany also provided useful information. Much of the material on space appli-

cations could not have been obtained without the aid of George Sexton and Diana Pabon in Washington, and my colleague Andrea Compagno provided great help in relation to the intelligent facade. Chris Parry and latterly Elizabeth Jay of GE Plastics and Dr Mike Lombard of ICI Acrylics offered invaluable information in relation to the clear plastics. In the collection of images, I must thank Jeff Cook, Russell Jones, Dennis Sharp, Henry Freeland, A D Jack, Martin Francis and Peter Milner, all of whom went out of their way to procure or supply illustrations which were proving very difficult to get.

Christine Ebner produced the first set of excellent Case Study drawings, and John Hewitt completed the task beautifully. I must thank both of them for their care and for the expert draughtsmanship. I must thank John Hewitt particularly for the creative way he approached the diagrams in the Appendix and elsewhere. At Phaidon, I am extremely grateful to David Jenkins, for surgery as well as construction, to my editor Vivian Constantinopoulos for her immense patience and untiring efforts to get the content right, to Christine King for her all-important sub-editing and to Sophia Gibb and Luisa Nitrato-Izzo for their painstaking

picture research. My thanks are also due to Mark Vernon-Jones for his work on the design of the book and for creating cohesion out of a content which was very diverse, but which presented some significant graphic challenges.

Finally, I must thank my long-suffering family, who have had to put up with source material and texts cluttering up the car on summer holidays, who hope I will never write another book, but who will probably be disappointed.